HISTORICAL RE
FOR HIGHER DEGREES IN
THE UNITED KINGDOM AND THE
REPUBLIC OF IRELAND

LIST No. 78

PART II
THESES IN PROGRESS 2017

COMPILED BY
LAUREN DE'ATH AND EMILY MORRELL

UNIVERSITY OF LONDON
SCHOOL OF ADVANCED STUDY
INSTITUTE OF HISTORICAL RESEARCH

JULY 2017

HISTORICAL RESEARCH FOR HIGHER DEGREES IN THE UNITED KINGDOM AND THE REPUBLIC OF IRELAND

The annual lists recording *Historical Research for Higher Degrees in the United Kingdom and the Republic of Ireland* appear in two separate parts, one of which notes *Theses Completed*, the other *Theses in Progress*. Both parts have, as usual, been prepared from information supplied by university registrars, secretaries of faculty boards and heads of departments, to all of whom grateful acknowledgements are made. Theses in progress in universities in the Republic of Ireland are also included. We are very grateful to the Royal Irish Academy, and in particular Professor Peter Gray, for their support and assistance in obtaining this information.

In order to comply with data protection requirements, titles of theses have only been included where students have given express permission (either directly or through their head of department or other representative). We would encourage postgraduate students who would like to have their details included in future editions (and in the online version of the *Theses Lists*) to contact the IHR directly via email: ihrpub@sas.ac.uk.

The present list records theses in progress on 1 January 2016. For each thesis the provisional title, the author, the name of the supervisor (in brackets), the university and the degree in view are given. Theses in process of examination when the information was collected are listed as still in progress. Theses in other than history departments are included, but only if they are primarily of historical interest. Like the one recording *Theses Completed 2015*, the list of *Theses in Progress* is arranged under broad chronological headings. In general it should be noted that in cases where the subject extends over several centuries the thesis is normally placed under the earliest date. Besides consulting the period which specially concerns them, readers are, therefore, advised to look at sections earlier than those relating to their particular interests.

Copies of *Theses Completed 2016* are available, at a cost of £10 plus £2.50 (£5 overseas) postage, from the School of Advanced Study Bookshop, University of London, Room 248, Senate House, London WC1E 7HU. Copies of *Theses Completed* for each of the years 1991–2015 (Lists 53–77) are available for £6 each from the same address. Two cumulative volumes, *History Theses, 1901–70*, compiled by Phyllis M. Jacobs (1976), price £10, and *History Theses, 1981–90*, compiled by Joyce M. Horn (1994), price £15, may also be obtained. No stocks are available of earlier issues of *Theses in Progress* as the present list supersedes all earlier issues.

Theses Completed 2016 and *Theses in Progress 2017* are published on the IHR's website (www.history.ac.uk) within two to three months of publication in print. This is the last year in which the hard copy books will be published; the series will be relaunched as a digital resource.

ISBN 978 1 909646 60 5

Contents

Contents

Contents

Contents

Contents

PHILOSOPHY OF HISTORY

1 The imagined past: the fictionalisation of historic landscapes. Christopher Green. (Dr. James Pardoe.) Chester Ph.D. (Hist. & Archaeol.)

2 Mind, action and politics: thinking through Hobbes. Alexandra Chadwick. (Professor Quentin Skinner.) London Ph.D. (Q.M. Hist.)

3 Application of Bourdieu's theory of cultural capital to the 19th-century working class. Heba Gilbert. (Professor Malcolm S. Chase.) Leeds M.A. (Hist.)

4 A study of the popularity and dissemination of non-academic history. Megan Stahl. (Professor Gerard J. De Groot.) St. Andrews Ph.D. (Hist.)

5 Derrida, Christianity and the end of history. Mark Mason. (Professors Keith W. Jenkins and Alun Munslow.) Chichester M.Phil./Ph.D. (Hist.)

HISTORICAL METHODS

6 Exploring the limits of the archaeological study of identity. Daniel Van Helden. (Dr. Penelope Allison and Professor Sarah Tarlow.) Leicester Ph.D. (Archaeol. & Anc. Hist.)

7 Stories in stone: memorialisation, the creation of history and the role of preservation. Emily Williams. (Professor Sarah Tarlow and Dr. Ruth Young.) Leicester Ph.D. (Archaeol. & Anc. Hist.)

8 Deconstructing Anglo-Saxon archaeology: a critical study of approaches to ethnic identity in English-language scholarship of the *adventus saxonum*. James Harland. (Professor Guy Halsall.) York Ph.D. (Hist.)

9 A place for worship? Heritage and religiosity in England. Robert Piggott. (Professor Barry Doyle.) Huddersfield Ph.D. (Music, Hum. & Media)

10 Sharing human origins: from Palaeolithic collections to community involvement at the British Museum. Joanne Hall. (Professors Clive Gamble and Katie Willis.) London M.Phil./Ph.D. (R.H.U.L. Geog.)

11 Attitudes to migration in the 19th century: using very large historical corpora for socio-historical research. Ruth Byrne. (Professor Ian Gregory and Dr. Andrew Hardie.) Lancaster Ph.D. (Hist.)

12 Heritage and memory. Martyn Richardson. (Professor Keith Laybourn.) Huddersfield M.Phil. (Music, Hum. & Media)

13 Testing the assumptions of financial models in certain historical instances. Hallam Dixon. (Dr. Brian A'Hearn.) Oxford M.Sc. (Mod. Hist.)

14 *Archaiologos fictio* – archaeological fantasies. Alistair Sims. (Professor Raimund Karl.) Bangor Ph.D. (Hist., Welsh Hist. & Archaeol.)

15 Re-creating and curating H.M.S. *Victory*: the afterlife of a battleship. Sarah Westbury. (Dr. Christer Petley.) Southampton M.Phil. (Hist.)

16 Holocaust and genocide museums. Aaran Rees. (Dr. Tim Cole and Dr. Grace Brockington.) Bristol M.Litt. (Hist. Stud.)

17 Historical and cultural politics in national museum making in England. Tom Carter. (Dr. Iain J.M. Robertson, Dr. Vicky Morrisroe and Mr. Harry Cohen.) Gloucestershire Ph.D. (Hum.)

18 Public history, oral history and regeneration: a co-production approach. Elizabeth Pente. (Professor Paul Ward.) Huddersfield Ph.D. (Music, Hum. & Media)

19 Contemporary visual art, the archive and collective memory. Rachel Bracha. Dundee Ph.D. (Hist.)

20 Securing a future: a heritage management comparative case study of interpretation at private and publicly owned historic houses. Catherine Goddard. (Professor Alison Oram and Dr. Briony McDonagh.) Leeds Beckett Ph.D. (Cultural Stud.)

21 World heritage and international collaboration: U.K. world heritage sites and the value of international partnerships. Brandi Hall. (Dr. Alison Hems and Dr. Rebecca Schaaf.) Bath Spa Ph.D. (Hist. & Cultural Stud.)

22 The S.S. *Great Britain*: heritage history. James Muirhead. (Dr. Tim Cole and Dr. Peter Coates.) Bristol M.Litt. (Hist. Stud.)

23 Beyond the family tree: with particular reference to Jewish genealogy, how does family history research help to change and define personal identity? Adrienne Wallman. (Dr. Corinna Peniston-Bird.) Lancaster Ph.D. (Hist.)

24 Representing the Troubles: contested histories, critical museology and conflict exhibitions. Matthew Jackson. (Dr. Fearghal McGarry.) Belfast M.Phil./Ph.D. (Hist. & Anthr.)

25 The ageing population and participation in museums and heritage sites: policy and emerging practice in the U.K. Caro Skyrme. (Dr. Alison Hems and Professor Michael Tooby.) Bath Spa Ph.D. (Hist. & Cultural Stud.)

26 The history and heritage of Swansea's copper industry and the development of interpretation of the Hafod-Morfa copperworks through the application of mobile digital technology. Matthew Small. (Professor Huw V. Bowen.) Swansea Ph.D. (Hist.)

27 Church heritage trails in north Wales. Polly Wilton. (Professor Raimund Karl.) Bangor Ph.D. (Hist., Welsh Hist. & Archaeol.)

28 A critical examination of the claims that the digitisation of archived materials leads to an increase in access. Isphur Bhandal. (Professor Edward Higgs and Dr. Paul Gooding.) Essex Ph.D. (Hist.)

29 An ancestor in crime: digitisation and the discovery of family deviance. Aoife O'Connor. (Professor Robert B. Shoemaker.) Sheffield Ph.D. (Hist.)

30 Heritage studies (archives, cultural history). Eve Hartley. (Professor Barry Doyle.) Huddersfield M.Phil. (Music, Hum. & Media)

31 An archaeology of the voice: how can oral history be located meaningfully within the environment as augmented reality? Simon Bradley. (Professor Paul J. Ward and Dr. Rupert Till.) Huddersfield Ph.D. (Music, Hum. & Media)

32 Child substitution – new approaches to the changeling motif in medieval European culture. Rose Sawyer. (Dr. Alaric Hall and Dr. Iona M. McCleery.) Leeds Ph.D. (Med. Stud.)

33 The use of digital and participatory history resources by academic, family and local historians. Mia Ridge. (Dr. Elton Barker and Dr. Deborah Brunton.) Open University Ph.D. (Hist.)

34 Performance, gender and identity in oral history. Joanne E. Dyrlaga. (Professor Paul Ward.) Huddersfield Ph.D. (Music, Hum. & Media)

35 The creation of a planning policy framework for the sustainable conservation of the historic built environment that contributes towards a carbon neutral future in Wales. Philip Williams. (Professor Raimund Karl.) Bangor Ph.D. (Hist., Welsh Hist. & Archaeol.)

36 The impact of the 2007 British Army restructure on the role of British regimental museums. Ian McKay. (Dr. James Pardoe.) Chester M.Phil. (Hist. & Archaeol.)

37 Wiki on the rocks – a study of the western globalisation progress of knowledge within archaeology. Jeanette Gimmerstam. (Dr. Sarah Scott and Dr. Terence Hopkinson.) Leicester Ph.D. (Archaeol. & Anc. Hist.)

HISTORIOGRAPHY

38 Narratives of the past: Scottish historiography in the age of Ossian. Xandra Bello. (Professor Ralph O'Connor and Dr. Michael Brown.) Aberdeen Ph.D. (Hist.)

39 The historiography of Roman-Sasanian relations from A.D. 224–630: a comparative study between English and Arabic/Kurdish scholarship. Botan Maghdid. (Professor Simon James and Dr. Naoise Mac Sweeney.) Leicester Ph.D. (Archaeol. & Anc. Hist.)

40 Challenging the historical and historiographical models of saintly intercession. Jordan Flanders. (Dr. John Nightingale.) Oxford D.Phil. (Mod. Hist.)

41 *Brut y Brenhinedd, Brut y Tywysogyon* a hanesyddiaeth Gymreig yr oesoedd canol. [*Brut y Brenhinedd, Brut y Tywysogyon* and medieval Welsh historiography.] (*In Welsh medium.*) Owain Wyn Jones. (Professor A. Huw Pryce and Dr. Katharine Olson.) Bangor Ph.D. (Hist., Welsh Hist. & Archaeol.)

42 The historians and historiography of St. Albans in manuscript and print, c.1200–c.1686. Jessica Coatesworth. (Dr. Stephen Mossman and Dr. Charles Insley.) Manchester Ph.D. (Hist.)

43 Magna Carta: public commemoration, celebration and meaning, 1215–2015. Steven Franklin. (Professor Justin A.I. Champion.) London M.Phil./Ph.D. (R.H.U.L. Hist.)

44 Languages and political identity: Visconti historiography and the making of the territorial state. William Kolkey. (Professor Christopher J. Wickham.) Oxford D.Phil. (Mod. Hist.)

45 The reception history of Martianus Capella from the 14th to the 16th century. Katie Reid. (Professors Peter Mack and Charles S.F. Burnett and Dr. Alessandro Scafi.) London Ph.D. (Warburg)

46 'Wrong but wromantic': remembering royals and royalists of the English Civil War, 1650–present. Sarah K. Betts. (Dr. Geoffrey T. Cubitt.) York Ph.D. (Hist.)

47 English-language military history and historiography, c.1650–1794. Gary Evans. (Dr. Raingard Esser.) West of England Ph.D. (Hist.)

48 Material representations of the British empire. Naomi Gardner. (Dr. Zoe Laidlaw.) London M.Phil./Ph.D. (R.H.U.L. Hist.)

49 The changing face of Robin Hood, c.1700–1900. Stephen Basdeo. (Professor Paul Hardwick and Dr. Rosemary Mitchell.) Leeds Trinity Ph.D. (Hist.)

50 1798 in 1998. Aaron Armstrong. (Dr. James P. Loughlin and Dr. Allan Blackstock.) Ulster Ph.D. (Hist.)

51 Mapping African historiography in web 3.0. Nathan Richards. (Professors Tim Hitchcock and Caroline Bassett.) Sussex D.Phil. (Hist.)

52 'The illusion of finality': time and community in the writings of E.A. Freeman, J.B. Bury and the English-Teutonic circle of historians. Oded Y. Steinberg. (Dr. Oliver Zimmer.) Oxford D.Phil. (Mod. Hist.)

53 Nineteenth-century historiography – specifically the work of Frederick York Powell and late Victorian uses of history. Rory Allan. (Dr. E. Jane Garnett.) Oxford D.Phil. (Mod. Hist.)

54 The medieval period in 19th-century Irish historiography. Ruairi Cullen. (Professor Peter Gray.) Belfast Ph.D. (Hist. & Anthr.)

55 Perceptions of crusading from 1830–2001: crusader medievalism in the English-speaking West. Michael Horswell. (Professor Jonathan P. Phillips.) London M.Phil./Ph.D. (R.H.U.L. Hist.)

56 Roman finds in the Victorian press: how newspaper articles reflected their understanding of the urban archaeology of the Roman world and views of their own past. Heather Keeble. (Dr. Jeremy Taylor and Dr. Sarah Scott.) Leicester Ph.D. (Archaeol. & Anc. Hist.)

57 British military historians and the writing of military history, c.1854–1914. Adam Dighton. Salford Ph.D. (Cen. Eur. Sec.)

58 Representing and memorialising war in the north-east, 1855–1910. Guy Hinton. (Dr. Joan Allen and Professor Jeremy Boulton.) Newcastle Ph.D. (Hist.)

59 How the period 1890–1945 is portrayed in contemporary Russia, and its influence on the media and education. James Pearce. (Dr. Jonathan Davis.) Anglia Ruskin D.Phil. (Hist.)

60 How memorialisation can be used in coming to terms with the past, using Germany and Great Britain as a comparison. Adam West. (Dr. Alex Von Lunen.) Huddersfield M.Phil. (Music, Hum. & Media)

61 Markets, economics, imperialism and social theory: a theoretical and historical analysis of the market in modern political economy. Matthijs Krul. (Professor Gareth Dale and Dr. John Roberts.) Brunel Ph.D. (Pol. & Hist.)

62 Our history, our streets, our voice, our future: reclaiming the historiography of the Whitechapel murders. Charlotte Mallinson. (Professor Paul Ward.) Huddersfield Ph.D. (Music, Hum. & Media)

63 Liberty, property and materiality: an historical archaeology of later 18th-century protest in England. Tom Whitfield. (Dr. Jane Webster and Dr. Rachel Hammersley.) Newcastle Ph.D. (Archaeol.)

64 W.W.I heritage project. Ann-Marie Foster. (Dr. James McConnel.) Northumbria Ph.D. (Hist.)

65 Finding one nation: Disraeli in Conservative political memory, 1920–90. Adam Garrie. (Professor Richard C. Vinen and Dr. Paul Readman.) King's College London M.Phil./Ph.D. (Hist.)

66 Photographic historiography of Soviet architecture. Marie Collier. (Professor John Milner.) London Ph.D. (Courtauld Inst.)

67 Holocaust-related trials and historiography. Lynne Humphrey. (Professor Dan Stone.) London Ph.D. (R.H.U.L. Hist.)

68 Theatres of memory: formation of identity in the historic city. Taras Nakonecznyj. (Dr. Shane Ewen and Dr. Natasha Vall.) Leeds Beckett Ph.D. (Cultural Stud.)

69 Through the eye of the needle: reconfiguring British Isles history as narrative embroidery. Anna Henderson. (Dr. Julie-Marie Strange and Dr. David Matthews.) Manchester Ph.D. (Hist.)

70 H.J. Dyos and the origins of urban history. Gary Davies. (Professor Simon Gunn.) Leicester Ph.D. (Urban Hist.)

71 Critique of ideologies of political violence, Colombia, 1957–91: a dialectical historiography of thoughts in defence of society. Juan M. Diaz. (Dr. Carrie Hamilton and Dr. Eric Jacobsen.) Roehampton Ph.D. (Hist.)

ANCIENT HISTORY

General

72 The Thor and Jormungandr conflict myth: the ancient Near Eastern origins of the storm-god's battle with the sea serpent. Cattlyn Obel. (Professor Stefan Brink and Dr. Lena-Sofia Tiemeyer.) Aberdeen Ph.D. (Hist.)

73 Transformations in culture, society and politics in early to middle iron age central and western Anatolia. Damjan Krsmanovic. (Dr. Naoise Mac Sweeney and Dr. Ian Whitbread.) Leicester Ph.D. (Archaeol. & Anc. Hist.)

74 Ethnic identity in the ancient Greek colonies in Sicily and Asia Minor, 8th–6th century B.C.: interpretation and heritage. Panagiotis Georgopoulos. (Dr. Naoise Mac Sweeney and Professor Lin Foxhall.) Leicester Ph.D. (Archaeol. & Anc. Hist.)

75 Slavery in ancient Greece and the Near East: a comparative study. David Lewis. (Professor Edward M. Harris and Dr. J.H. Haubold.) Durham Ph.D. (Classics)

76 The image of the king: can the royal hunts of Alexander the Great be seen as engaging with Aristotle's theory of *pambasileia* in order to legitimise his rule as king of Asia? James Mullen. (Dr. Joseph Skinner and Dr. Rowland Smith.) Newcastle Ph.D. (Anc. Hist.)

77 The fulfilment of all righteousness: Matthew's unique perspective on Jesus' baptism. Pedro Antonius. (Dr. Mark T. Finney.) Sheffield Ph.D. (Hist.)

78 The gender pairs: focusing on an overlooked aspect of Luke-Acts. Marie Flanagan. (Dr. Mark T. Finney.) Sheffield Ph.D. (Hist.)

79 Luke's understanding of the Oikoumene in Luke and Acts. Deok Hee Jung. (Dr. Mark T. Finney.) Sheffield Ph.D. (Hist.)

80 The interface between demonology and second temple purity systems in the Markan exorcism stories. Bryan Stanton. (Dr. Mark T. Finney.) Sheffield Ph.D. (Hist.)

81 The veil in biblical and classical antiquity: a sociocultural and exegetical study of 1 Corinthians 11:2–16. Rongxi Wu. (Dr. Mark T. Finney.) Sheffield Ph.D. (Hist.)

82 How did the rise of Christianity affect the social and political spheres of Rome, Italy and the western provinces and gender relations in those regions? Jeannie M. Sellick. (Dr. Philip Booth.) Oxford M.Phil. (Mod. Hist.)

83 'The gods of the peoples are idols' (Psalms 96:5): paganism and idolatry in Near Eastern Christianity. Sebastian Nichols. (Dr. Ted Kaizer.) Durham Ph.D. (Classics)

84 Mathematics for history's sake: a new approach to Ptolemy's geography. Daniel Mintz. (Dr. John O'Connor and Dr. Adrian Gratwick.) St. Andrews Ph.D. (Classics)

85 The culture and political world of the 4th century A.D.: Julian, *paideia* and education. Victoria Hughes. (Dr. R.B.E. Smith and Professor John Moles.) Newcastle Ph.D. (Anc. Hist.)

86 The progress of the divine-human aporia as the blossoming of axiality. David N. Gyllenhaal. (Dr. Philip Booth.) Oxford M.Phil. (Mod. Hist.)

Egypt

87 Egyptian cultural identity in the architectural forms of Egyptian cities in the Roman period. Youssri Abdelwahed. (Dr. Edmund V. Thomas and Dr. Ted Kaizer.) Durham Ph.D. (Classics)

88 Debt in late antique Egypt, 400–700 C.E.: approaches to a time in transition. Elizabeth F. Buchanan. (Professor Boudewijn Sirks and Dr. Mark Whittow.) Oxford D.Phil. (Mod. Hist.)

Greece and Mediterranean

89 Dynamic social changes and identity: a petrological study of bronze age ceramics from selected Sardinian nuraghi. Maria Gradoli. (Dr. Ian Whitbread and Dr. Mark Gillings.) Leicester Ph.D. (Archaeol. & Anc. Hist.)

90 Substances in Greek rituals. Luke Evans. (Dr. Paola Ceccarelli and Dr. Andrej Petrovic.) Durham Ph.D. (Classics)

91 The gardens of ancient Greece: rhetoric and reality. Margaret Hilditch. (Professor Lin Foxhall and Dr. Naoise Mac Sweeney.) Leicester Ph.D. (Archaeol. & Anc. Hist.)

92 Traumatising the Greeks: the modern diagnosis of P.T.S.D. and its applicability to the Ancient Greeks. Owen Rees. (Dr. Tony Adams, Dr. Jason Crowley and Dr. April Pudsey.) Manchester Metropolitan Ph.D. (Hist.)

93 Travelling objects: commercial relationships and cross-cultural interaction in the western Mediterranean in the archaic age. Marcella Raiconi. (Professors Lin Foxhall and Colin Haselgrove.) Leicester Ph.D. (Archaeol. & Anc. Hist.)

94 The impact of exploration on Greek geographical knowledge. William Bhandari. (Dr. Paola Ceccarelli and Dr. Johannes H. Haubold.) Durham Ph.D. (Classics)

95 At capacity: a statistical analysis of Greek vessel sizes. Victoria Adams Keitel. (Professor Amy Smith and Dr. Hella Eckardt.) Reading Ph.D. (Archaeol.)

96 Greek warfare by land and by sea. Vincent Fourcade. (Professor Hans van Wees.) London Ph.D. (U.C. Hist.)

97 Examining social and political developments in archaic and classical Athens through an analysis of changes in the iconography of warrior departure scenes on Attic pottery between 600 B.C. and 400 B.C. Nigel Porter. (Dr. Mark Jackson and Dr. Sally Waite.) Newcastle Ph.D. (Anc. Hist.)

98 Ritual in old comedy: representation and context. Elena Chepel. (Professors Ian Rutherford and Timothy Duff.) Reading Ph.D. (Classics)

99 Healing in archaic classical Greece. Michaela Senkova. (Professor Lin Foxhall and Dr. Daniel Stewart.) Leicester Ph.D. (Archaeol. & Anc. Hist.)

100 Criminalisation and stigmatisation in classical Athens. Amy Stanley. (Professor Stephen Todd.) Manchester Ph.D. (Classics & Anc. Hist.)

101 Ancient sources related to Greek forensic rhetoric. Miklos Könczöl. (Professors Edward M. Harris and George R. Boys-Stones.) Durham Ph.D. (Classics)

102 The iconography of arms and armour in Greek coinage of the classical and Hellenistic periods: military, historical, socio-political, symbolic and administrative aspects. Elphida Kosmidou. London Ph.D. (Inst. Archaeol.)

103 Treatment and perception of the war dead in archaic and classical Greece. Cezary Kucewicz. (Professor Hans van Wees.) London Ph.D. (U.C. Hist.)

104 Documents included in the text of the Attic orators. Mirko Canevaro. (Dr. Paola Ceccarelli and Professor Edward M. Harris.) Durham Ph.D. (Classics)

105 Remember the Athenians: an examination of the Greek tragic chorus as a mechanism for exploring the continuation of memory in 5th-century B.C. Athens. Liz Fitzgerald. (Dr. Louis Rawlings and Professor Lorna Hardwick.) Cardiff Ph.D. (Hist. & Archaeol.)

106 Ideology and pragmatism in Greek military thought, 490–338 B.C. Roel Konijnendijk. (Professor Hans van Wees.) London Ph.D. (U.C. Hist.)

107 Leadership in Herodotus. Stephen Fitzsimons. (Dr. Peter Liddel.) Manchester Ph.D. (Classics & Anc. Hist.)

108 Analysis of selected works of Aristophanes. Effrosyni Zagari. (Professor Peter Kruschwitz.) Reading Ph.D. (Classics)

109 Fighting for a living: the impact of professional soldiers on the late classical and early Hellenistic Greek world (4th to mid 2nd centuries B.C.). Charlotte Van Regenmortel. (Professor Graham Shipley and Dr. Daniel Stewart.) Leicester Ph.D. (Archaeol. & Anc. Hist.)

110 Painter of Boetian red figure vases from the 4th century B.C. Glen Newell. (Professor Amy Smith.) Reading Ph.D. (Classics)

111 The gendering of the child on Slab V of the Parthenon Frieze. Hilary Guise. (Professor Amy Smith.) Reading Ph.D. (Classics)

112 Praise, blame and identity construction in Greek tragedy. Katherine Cook. (Professor Barbara Goff.) Reading Ph.D. (Classics)

113 Defining a 'Mediterranean bridge': Sparta, Crete and the maintained connectivity. Andrea Scarpato. (Dr. Daniel Stewart and Professor Graham Shipley.) Leicester Ph.D. (Archaeol. & Anc. Hist.)

114 Perceiving the past in early Hellenistic Greece: investigating the narratives of the past and its use in remodelling the Hellenistic reality. Manolis Pagkalos. (Professor Graham Shipley and Dr. Naoise Mac Sweeney.) Leicester Ph.D. (Archaeol. & Anc. Hist.)

115 The idea of Stoicheion in grammar and cosmology from Plato to Agrippa. Juan Acevedo. (Professor Charles Burnett.) London Ph.D. (Warburg)

116 Myth and music: lead figurines of Artemis Orthia. James Lloyd. (Professor Ian Rutherford.) Reading Ph.D. (Classics)

117 Muses of Tanagra. Natalie Motevasselani-Choubineh. (Professor Amy Smith.) Reading Ph.D. (Classics)

118 The history of theurgy from Iamblichus to the Golden Dawn. Sam Webster. (Professor Ronald Hutton.) Bristol Ph.D. (Hist. Stud.)

Ancient Rome and the empire

119 Propagandist town planning between the republic and principate: Caesar, Pompey and the attainment of consent. Eleanora Zampieri. (Dr. Sarah Scott and Dr. Neil Christie.) Leicester Ph.D. (Archaeol. & Anc. Hist.)

120 The many images of the Achaemenoids at Rome. Mauro Serena. (Professor Annalisa Marzano.) Reading Ph.D. (Classics)

121 Unrest in the Roman Republic and the early Principate: discordia and discordiae between repression, accommodation and consensus-building. Emilio Zucchetti. (Dr. Federico Santangelo, Professor Jakob Wisse and Dr. Amy Russell.) Newcastle Ph.D. (Anc. Hist.)

122 Cultural interaction, artistic progress and leisure culture: an object biographical approach to decorated gaming counters from Roman and medieval Spain, Gaul and Italy. Elisabeth Janovsky. (Dr. Sarah Scott and Ms. Deirdre O'Sullivan.) Leicester Ph.D. (Archaeol. & Anc. Hist.)

123 An architectural and social archaeology of Roman baths and bathing in eastern Sicily: the public and private thermae of Catania in context. Roberta Ferrante. (Dr. Neil Christie and Professor Simon James.) Leicester Ph.D. (Archaeol. & Anc. Hist.)

124 The Roman maritime villas of southern Latium. Roberta Ferritto. (Professor Annalisa Marzano and Dr. Matthew Nicholls.) Reading Ph.D. (Classics)

125 The social and economic impact of artificial light in the Roman world. David Griffiths. (Dr. Penelope Allison and Professor David J. Mattingly.) Leicester Ph.D. (Archaeol. & Anc. Hist.)

126 The social and economic significance of Indo-Roman trade to the Roman empire. Sushma S. Jansari. (Dr. R.W. Benet Salway.) London Ph.D. (U.C. Hist.)

127 Retirement in the Roman world. Samuel Jones. (Professor Tim Parkin.) Manchester Ph.D. (Classics & Anc. Hist.)

128 The growth of Rome: impacts and implications of (sub)urban expansion. Matthew Mandich. (Dr. Neil Christie and Dr. Daniel Stewart.) Leicester Ph.D. (Archaeol. & Anc. Hist.)

129 Shaping the empire: agrimensores, emperors, and the creation of the Roman provincial identity. Jason Morris. (Dr. Andrew Merrills and Dr. Jeremy Taylor.) Leicester Ph.D. (Archaeol. & Anc. Hist.)

130 An interdisciplinary approach to the study of the Roman fishing industry. Lee Graña Nicolaou. (Professor Annalisa Marzano.) Reading Ph.D. (Classics)

131 Obstetrical care in the Roman world. Rachel Plummer. (Professor Tim Parkin.) Manchester Ph.D. (Classics & Anc. Hist.)

132 Economic rationalism in ancient Rome. Mick Stringer. (Professor Annalisa Marzano and Dr. Matthew Nicholls.) Reading Ph.D. (Classics)

133 Brand theory and the Roman economy. Roderick White. (Dr. R.W. Benet Salway.) London M.Phil. (U.C. Hist.)

134 The formation of Christianity: martyrdom as means of resistance to Roman power and proselytism tool. Linda Wimmer. (Professors Jakob Wisse and Dr. Ashley Scott.) Newcastle Ph.D. (Classics)

135 Dogs and gods: a study of the significance of dogs in Roman religion. Valerie Wolfkamp. (Dr. Mark Horton and Professor Ronald Hutton.) Bristol M.Litt. (Hist. Stud.)

136 Multiple identities in pre-Roman and early Roman northern Italy: the integration of the Lomellina into the Roman empire during the late iron age. Sarah Schleffer. (Professors David Mattingly and Colin Haselgrove.) Leicester Ph.D. (Archaeol. & Anc. Hist.)

137 The morality of killing a republican Roman citizen. Janet Kroll. (Dr. Valentina Arena.) London M.Phil. (U.C. Hist.)

138 The development of the administration of the Roman republican army. Elizabeth Pearson. (Professor Tim Cornell and Dr. Andrew Fear.) Manchester Ph.D. (Classics & Anc. Hist.)

139 Children in politics: Gentilician strategies during the Roman Republic (3rd–1st centuries B.C.E.). Sara Borrello. (Dr. Federico Santangelo, Dr. Micaela Langellotti and Dr. Amy Russell.) Newcastle Ph.D. (Anc. Hist.)

140 The political and legislative role of the Tribunes of the plebs in the mid-Republican period (218–180 B.C.). Roberto Ciucciovè. (Dr. Federico Santangelo and Dr. Rowland Smith.) Newcastle Ph.D. (Anc. Hist.)

141 Constructing memories of Roman-Barbarian interaction in north-western Europe: 'myths' and national traditions in Dutch archaeological interpretation. Sergio Gonzalez Sanchez. (Professor Simon T. James and Dr. Andrew Merills.) Leicester Ph.D. (Archaeol. & Anc. Hist.)

142 Roman funerary reliefs and North African identity: a contextual and comparative investigation of iconography from Tripolitania and beyond. Julia Nikolaus. (Professor David J. Mattingly and Dr. David Edwards.) Leicester Ph.D. (Archaeol. & Anc. Hist.)

143 The place and role of deities in Pompeian households: a case study of Venus. Carla Brain. (Professor Penelope Allison and Dr. David Edwards.) Leicester Ph.D. (Archaeol. & Anc. Hist.)

144 Sallust on the Roman past: chronologically digressive material in the *Bella* and *Historiae*. Edwin Shaw. (Dr. Valentina Arena.) London Ph.D. (U.C. Hist.)

145 The facilitators of 'Caesar Octavianus'. Louise Hodgson. (Dr. Ingo Gildenhard and Dr. Ted Kaizer.) Durham Ph.D. (Classics)

146 The gods and the intellectuals: theological discussions of the late Roman Republic in Cicero's *De Natura Deorum*. Lauren Emslie. (Professor Jakob Wisse and Dr. Federico Santangelo.) Newcastle Ph.D. (Classics)

147 Foreign powers and the Roman empire in periods of civil war, 44 B.C.–A.D. 284. Hendrikus Van Wijlick. (Dr. Ted Kaizer and Dr. Andrej Petrovic.) Durham Ph.D. (Classics)

148 The periphery of Leptis Magna: suburban topography and land use of a Roman city. Andrea Zocchi. (Professor David Mattingly and Dr. Gareth Sears.) Leicester Ph.D. (Archaeol. & Anc. Hist.)

149 Herakles on the edge: how do objects depicting the figure of Herakles inform our understanding of artistic choices during the expansion of the Roman Empire? Jane Ainsworth. (Dr. Sarah Scott and Professor Graham Shipley.) Leicester Ph.D. (Archaeol. & Anc. Hist.)

150 Early imperial Roman military bases as social spaces. Anna Walas. (Professor Simon James and Dr. Jeremy Taylor.) Leicester Ph.D. (Archaeol. & Anc. Hist.)

151 Plutarch. Caitlin Prouatt. (Professor Tim Duff.) Reading Ph.D. (Classics)

152 The legal basis of the so-called persecutions of Christians from the reign of Nero to before Decius. Stephen Royston Davies. (Dr. R.W. Benet Salway.) London Ph.D. (U.C. Hist.)

153 Intellectual narratives and elite Roman learning in the *Noctes Atticae* of Aulus Gellius. Joe Howley. (Dr. Jason Koenig.) St. Andrews Ph.D. (Classics)

154 Septimius Severus' 'messages' at Leptis Magna. Maria Lloyd. (Dr. Matthew Nicholls and Professor Annalisa Marzano.) Reading Ph.D. (Classics)

155 Towards a visual history of late antique Roman art. David Rini. (Professor Peter Kruschwitz.) Reading Ph.D. (Classics)

156 Dress and identity in the Roman and late antique world: the case of North Africa (*c.*A.D. 200–700). Amy Wale. (Dr. Mary Harlow and Dr. Andrew Merrills.) Leicester Ph.D. (Archaeol. & Anc. Hist.)

157 The nature of the Roman economy from the 3rd-century crises to beyond the fall of the Roman west. James M. Wakeley. (Dr. Bryan Ward-Perkins.) Oxford M.Phil. (Mod. Hist.)

158 *Terrae Amissae*: a comparative study of south-west Germany and Transylvania in the mid 3rd century A.D. Evan Scherer. (Professor Ian Haynes and Dr. James Gerrard.) Newcastle Ph.D. (Archaeol.)

159 Late antique female segregation: gendered spaces in Rome and Constantinople. Robert Heffrom. (Dr. Julia Hillner.) Sheffield Ph.D. (Hist.)

160 Emperor and the army in the later Roman empire, 284–565. Michael Stawpert. (Professor Peter Heather and Dr. Dionysios Stathakopoulos.) King's College London M.Phil./Ph.D. (Hist.)

161 Engendering the future: divination and the construction of gender in the late Roman republic. Christopher Mowat. (Dr. Federico Santangelo, Dr. David Creese and Dr. Jorg Rupke.) Newcastle Ph.D. (Anc. Hist.)

162 Colonial mimesis: a comparative approach to sculpture and imagery from the Roman provinces. Stephanie Moat. (Dr. Jane Webster and Dr. Chris Fowler.) Newcastle Ph.D. (Archaeol.)

163 Ravenna as a viewed city: display, power and public space in the late Roman to early Byzantine capital, *c.*A.D. 400–600. Brittany Thomas. (Dr. Neil Christie and Dr. Andrew Merrills.) Leicester Ph.D. (Archaeol. & Anc. Hist.)

164 The fall of the house of Constantine (324–66). George Woudhuysen. (Dr. Bryan Ward-Perkins.) Oxford D.Phil. (Mod. Hist.)

165 A transforming landscape: land, society and culture in the Val di Chiana, 350–850. Antonia Clark. (Dr. Neil Christie and Dr. Jeremy Taylor.) Leicester Ph.D. (Archaeol. & Anc. Hist.)

166 The Catechumenate in late Roman North Africa: Augustine of Hippo, his contemporaries and early reception (*c.*360–530 A.D.). Matthieu Pignot. (Dr. Conrad Leyser and Dr. Neil McLynn.) Oxford D.Phil. (Mod. Hist.)

167 Senators, bishops, decuriones and barbarians, 4th–5th centuries. Aleksander K. Paradzinski. (Dr. Bryan Ward-Perkins.) Oxford D.Phil. (Mod. Hist.)

168 Legislation and administration in the reign of Valentinian III. Geoffrey Lambert. (Dr. R.W. Benet Salway.) London Ph.D. (U.C. Hist.)

169 What happened to the Roman army in the *Notitia Dignitarum*? Stephen Pearce. (Dr. David M. Gwynn.) London M.Phil./Ph.D. (R.H.U.L. Hist.)

170 Religious elites and the late Roman state, in the diocese of 'Oriens', A.D. 451–638. Simon S. Ford. (Dr. Neil McLynn and Dr. D. Taylor.) Oxford D.Phil. (Mod. Hist.)

171 Procopius' framing of Justinian's late antique military and economic strategies in the western Mediterranean. Christopher Lillington-Martin. (Dr. Arietta Papaconstantiou.) Reading Ph.D. (Classics)

Early and Roman Britain

172 Insular identities on Neolithic Anglesey. Neil McGuinness. (Dr. Gary Robinson.) Bangor Ph.D. (Hist., Welsh Hist. & Archaeol.)

173 The social context of prehistoric extraction sites in the U.K. Peter Topping. (Dr. Chris Fowler and Dr. Jan Harding.) Newcastle Ph.D. (Archaeol.)

174 A study of the use of natural places as a focus for burial during the Neolithic and bronze ages in north-west Wales. Rosemary A. Roberts. (Dr. Gary Robinson.) Bangor Ph.D. (Hist., Welsh Hist. & Archaeol.)

175 Fields, farms and megaliths: unravelling the unique Neolithic: early bronze age landscapes of Exmoor, south-west Britain. Douglas Mitcham. (Dr. Mark Gillings.) Leicester Ph.D. (Archaeol. & Anc. Hist.)

176 Growing up and starting work in later British prehistory. Meredith Laing. (Professor Colin Haselgrove and Dr. Joanna Appleby.) Leicester Ph.D. (Archaeol. & Anc. Hist.)

177 Hillforts of north-east Wales. Erin Robinson. (Professor Raimund Karl.) Bangor Ph.D. (Hist., Welsh Hist. & Archaeol.)

178 The role of ordinary women in British iron age societies. Hazel Butler. (Professor Raimund Karl.) Bangor Ph.D. (Hist., Welsh Hist. & Archaeol.)

179 Iron age open shrines in context. Frank Hargrave. (Professor Colin Haselgrove and Dr. Penelope Allison.) Leicester Ph.D. (Archaeol. & Anc. Hist.)

180 In search of the spear people: the archaeology of iron age weapons and warfare in east Yorkshire in their European context. Yvonne L. Inall. (Dr. Peter Halkon and Dr. Malcolm Lillie.) Hull Ph.D. (Hist.)

181 Reconstructing the Arras culture: a mortuary study of the Yorkshire region. Tammy Macenka. (Professor Colin Haselgrove and Dr. Joanna Appleby.) Leicester Ph.D. (Archaeol. & Anc. Hist.)

182 The manufacture, use and disposal of pottery in iron age Norfolk and Suffolk. Sarah Percival. (Professor Colin Haselgrove and Dr. Ian Whitbread.) Leicester Ph.D. (Archaeol. & Anc. Hist.)

183 The goddess in Celtic paganism: historical fact over romantic fiction. Lilia Khousnoutdinova. (Professor Ronald Hutton.) Bristol M.Phil. (Hist. Stud.)

184 Later iron age coinage in Britain: reconstructing insular social structures and endogenous aspects. Marta Fanello. (Professor Colin Haselgrove and Dr. Oliver Harris.) Leicester Ph.D. (Archaeol. & Anc. Hist.)

185 Mortuary practices in later iron age southern Britain and northern Gaul. Andy Lamb. (Professors Colin Haselgrove and Simon James.) Leicester Ph.D. (Archaeol. & Anc. Hist.)

186 The stamped wheel-turned pottery of Roman Britain and its relationship to the stamped hand-made pottery of the post-Roman period in Britain/London. Diana Briscoe. (Professors Clive Orton and Andrew Reynolds.) London Ph.D. (Inst. Archaeol.)

187 A dog's life: an interdisciplinary study of changing human-animal relationships in Roman Britain. Lauren Bellis. (Dr. Richard Thomas and Dr. Naomi Sykes.) Leicester Ph.D. (Archaeol. & Anc. Hist.)

188 Animals at Ashton: diet, identity and human-animal dynamics in a Romano-British small town. Meghann Mahoney. (Dr. Richard Thomas and Dr. Jeremy Taylor.) Leicester Ph.D. (Archaeol. & Anc. Hist.)

189 Making your mark in Britannia: the use of intaglios and their role in the production and presentation of identity under the Roman empire. Ian Marshman. (Dr. Penelope Allison and Professor David J. Mattingly.) Leicester Ph.D. (Archaeol. & Anc. Hist.)

190 The evolution and the role of private baths in Roman Britain: an elite becoming and being Roman. Giacomo Savani. (Dr. Sarah Scott and Professor Marijke van der Veen.) Leicester Ph.D. (Archaeol. & Anc. Hist.)

191 Roman metalwork hoards in Britain. Rachael Sycamore. (Professors David Mattingly and Colin Haselgrove.) Leicester Ph.D. (Archaeol. & Anc. Hist.)

192 The Clayton collection: artefacts from the central sector of Hadrian's Wall. Frances McIntosh. (Ms. Lindsay Allason-Jones, Professor Ian Haynes and Dr. James Gerrard.) Newcastle Ph.D. (Archaeol.)

193 More than a Roman monument: a place-centred approach to the long-term history and archaeology of the Antonine Wall. Darrell J. Rohl. (Professor Richard Hingley and Dr. Robert Witcher.) Durham Ph.D. (Archaeol.)

MEDIEVAL EUROPE

Subjects covering long periods

194 Past endemic malaria and adaptive responses in the fens and marshlands of eastern England. Ross Kendall. (Dr. Rebecca Gowland.) Durham Ph.D. (Archaeol.)

195 Mountains, steppes and empires: a historical geography of the north Caucasus in late antiquity and the middle ages. Nicholas J.B. Evans. (Dr. Mark Whittow and Dr. Jonathan Shepard.) Oxford D.Phil. (Mod. Hist.)

196 'Si Adam et Eva peccaverunt, quid nos miseri fecimus?' The reception of Augustine's ontological discourse on the soul in late antiquity and the early middle ages. Symke Haverkamp. (Professor Karla Pollmann and Dr. Simon Maclean.) St. Andrews Ph.D. (Classics)

197 Fatherhood in Gaul between late antiquity and the early middle ages. Hannah Probert. (Dr. Julia Hillner.) Sheffield Ph.D. (Hist.)

198 Rebels, riots and retainers: lower class violence in the late antique West. Michael Burrows. (Professors Julia S. Barrow and Ian N. Wood.) Leeds Ph.D. (Med. Stud.)

199   The Paris Basin during late antiquity. Ioannis Choupas. (Professors Helena Hamerow and Christopher J. Wickham.) Oxford D.Phil. (Mod. Hist.)

200   Religious transition in the late antique countryside: agency, identity and change in a Gallic province. Claudia Eicher. (Dr. Neil Christie and Dr. Deidre O'Sullivan.) Leicester Ph.D. (Archaeol. & Anc. Hist.)

201   The purpose of bureaucratic inventories in late antiquity. Simon Hosie. (Dr. Julia Hillner.) Sheffield M.Phil. (Hist.)

202   The idea of Rome in late antiquity. Ioannis Papadopoulos. (Professor Ian N. Wood.) Leeds Ph.D. (Med. Stud.)

203   Powerful youth in late antiquity. Jennifer A. Thompson. (Dr. Neil McLynn.) Oxford D.Phil. (Mod. Hist.)

204   Visigothic period buckles: portable wealth in late antique Spain and western Europe. Javier Williams. (Dr. Neil Christie and Dr. Sarah Scott.) Leicester Ph.D. (Archaeol. & Anc. Hist.)

205   Cult of St. Margaret of Antioch. Frances Cook. (Dr. Anne Lawrence.) Reading Ph.D. (Hist.)

206   Historical musicology in the Nordic countries from the earliest times in Scandinavia until the conversion, c.A.D. 1000. Hilde Nielsen. (Professor Stefan Brink and Dr. Tarrin Wills.) Aberdeen Ph.D. (Hist.)

207   Liquid culture: alcohol and drunkenness in early Scandinavia, from a geographical and historical perspective. Lisa Turberfield. (Dr. Tarrin Wills and Professor Stefan Brink.) Aberdeen Ph.D. (Hist.)

208   Space, monuments and religion: Christianisation of urban space in the late antique Levant (A.D. 325–628). Morgan Dirodi. (Dr. Bryan Ward-Perkins.) Oxford D.Phil. (Mod. Hist.)

209   Byzantium and Armenia: a new perspective. Toby Bromige. (Dr. Jonathan P. Harris.) London Ph.D. (R.H.U.L. Hist.)

210   The Britons: power, identity and ethnicity, 350–1000. Edwin Hustwit. (Professor A. Huw Pryce.) Bangor Ph.D. (Hist., Welsh Hist. & Archaeol.)

211   Inheritance law and the Visigothic woman. Adrienne Showering. (Professor Peter Heather.) King's College London M.Phil./Ph.D. (Hist.)

212   Landscape and memory at Thirlmere. Rod Grimshaw. (Dr. Sam Turner and Professor Diana Whaley.) Newcastle Ph.D. (Archaeol.)

213   Baptismal art in the late antique and early medieval western Mediterranean (A.D. 400–800). Stefanie Lenk. (Dr. Gervase Rosser and Dr. Jas Elsner.) Oxford D.Phil. (Mod. Hist.)

214   Byzantine regional development c.400–800: settlement, ideology, social relations, wealth and power. Kristina Terpoy. (Dr. Mark Whittow and Professor Ine Jacobs.) Oxford D.Phil. (Mod. Hist.)

215   Image and performance, agency and ideology: human figurative representation in Anglo-Saxon funerary art, A.D. 400–750. Lisa Brundle. (Dr. Sarah Semple.) Durham Ph.D. (Archaeol.)

216 Embroidery and its context in the British Isles during the early medieval period (A.D. 450–1100). Alexandra Makin. (Professor Gale Owen-Crocker, Dr. Elizabeth Coatsworth & Dr. Ina Berg.) Manchester Ph.D. (English, Amer. Stud. & Creative Writing)

217 Legislative innovation: barbarian and canon law in Merovingian Gaul. Patrick Griffith. (Professor Peter Heather and Dr. Alice Rio.) King's College London M.Phil./Ph.D. (Hist.)

218 The reception of mountains since antiquity. Matthew Adams. (Dr. Mary Garrison and Dr. Jon Finch.) York Ph.D. (Med. Stud.)

229 Moats in the landscape: new perspectives on moated sites. Natasha Coveney. (Dr. Richard Jones.) Leicester Ph.D. (Hist.)

220 Adolescent deviance in Welsh and Irish monasteries: a meme-based analysis of early and high medieval hagiographical literature. Christian-Michael Zottl. (Dr. Susan Johns and Professor A. Huw Pryce.) Bangor Ph.D. (Hist., Welsh Hist. & Archaeol.)

221 The Christian laws of medieval Norway: ecclesiastical tradition and legal innovation on the periphery of the Christian West. Alexander Busigyn. (Dr. Haki Antonsson and Dr. David L. d'Avray.) London Ph.D. (U.C. Scand. Stud.)

222 The early Irish law of pledging. Jaqueline Bemmer. (Professor Thomas Charles-Edwards.) Oxford D.Phil. (Mod. Hist.)

223 Selected early Irish population groups: origins, status and history. Eoghan J. Moore. (Professors Thomas Charles-Edwards and Christopher J. Wickham.) Oxford D.Phil. (Mod. Hist.)

224 Against the laws of gods and men: an interdisciplinary study of deviance in early medieval Scandinavia. Keith Ruiter. (Dr. Hannah Burrows and Professor Stefan Brink.) Aberdeen Ph.D. (Hist.)

225 The archaeology, topography and continuing context of the medieval leather industry in London, c.600–1600. Margaret Broomfield. London Ph.D. (Inst. Archaeol.)

226 Slave raiding and the slave trade in Britain and Ireland and the Slavic lands, 7th–11th centuries. Janel M. Fontaine. (Dr. Alice Rio.) King's College London M.Phil./Ph.D. (Hist.)

227 Gender dynamics in the double monasteries of Castile-Léon (7th–11th centuries). Lorene Guerre. (Mrs. Henrietta Leyser and Dr. Juan-Carlos Conde.) Oxford M.St. (Mod. Hist.)

228 Carving the cross into the changing landscapes of early Irish society: the early medieval cross sculpture of south-east Ireland in context. Kimberley Thounhurst. (Professors Nancy Edwards and A. Huw Pryce.) Bangor Ph.D. (Hist., Welsh Hist. & Archaeol.)

229 Jousting in a literary context. Eleanor Wilkinson-Keys. (Dr. Catherine Batt and Dr. Karen Watts.) Leeds Ph.D. (Hist.)

230 Sickness, disability, and miracle cures: narratives in Anglo-Latin hagiography, c.700–c.1200. Veronique J. Thouroude. (Professor Sarah Foot.) Oxford D.Phil. (Mod. Hist.)

231 The North Sea world in the 8th–11th centuries. Benjamin M. Feltham. (Dr. Mark Whittow.) Oxford D.Phil. (Mod. Hist.)

232 The coming of paper: the transformative effect of paper diffusion in medieval England. Jesse Lynch. Exeter Ph.D. (Hist.)

233 Anglo-Saxon minster burial practice in England, 700–1050: belief and community. Alexandra A. Sheldon. (Professors Sarah Foot and John Blair.) Oxford D.Phil. (Mod. Hist.)

234 The written and the world in early medieval Iberia. Graham D. Barrett. (Professor Christopher J. Wickham.) Oxford D.Phil. (Mod. Hist.)

235 Custom, Christianity, and physiology: the social learning of violence among the warrior classes of Gaul, c.500–700 . Patrick Morris O'Connor. (Professor Peter Heather and Dr. Alice Rio.) King's College London M.Phil./Ph.D. (Hist.)

236 The Vikings in Wales: a reappraisal of the evidence. Rose S. Hedley. (Professor Daniel J. Power.) Swansea Ph.D. (Hist.)

237 Religious roles of Norse women throughout the Viking age. Rachel Backa. (Professor Stefan Brink.) Aberdeen Ph.D. (Hist.)

238 Methods of commemorating the dead in Norse during the Viking age, 9th–14th centuries. Douglas Dutton. (Dr. Hannah Burrows and Professor Stefan Brink.) Aberdeen Ph.D. (Hist.)

239 The narrative functions of madness and altered states of consciousness in Old Norse sources. Katarzyna Maczynska. (Dr. Alaric Hall and Dr. Iona M. McCleery.) Leeds Ph.D. (Med. Stud.)

240 Insult in early medieval society, 800–1200. Dale Copley. (Dr. Thomas Pickles.) Chester Ph.D. (Hist. & Archaeol.)

241 The transmission of medieval chant between England and Scandinavia. Sean Dunnahoe. (Dr. Helen Deeming.) London Ph.D. (R.H.U.L. Music)

242 Supernatural vengeance in the literature of the medieval North Atlantic periphery. Max Bienkowski. (Dr. Alaric Hall and Dr. Alan V. Murray.) Leeds Ph.D. (Med. Stud.)

243 Topography of urban and rural burials and ecclesiastical regulations between the 9th and 11th centuries: a comparative study of England and north Italy. Monica Cortelletti. London Ph.D. (Inst. Archaeol.)

244 King and emperor: the development of the ideology of sacred kingship in England and Ottonian Germany from the 9th–11th centuries. Sami Kalliosaari. (Dr. Alaric Hall and Professor Julia S. Barrow.) Leeds M.Phil. (Med. Stud.)

245 Keeping up the go(o)d spirit – interpretations and parallels of Norse and Celtic mythology and religious practice in Orcadian folklore. Sandra Lantz. (Professor Stefan Brink.) Aberdeen Ph.D. (Hist.)

246 An examination of the development of the Norse giants from their myths to the sagas, þættir and Skaldic poetry in which they appear. Blake Middleton. (Professor Stefan Brink and Dr. Lisa Collinson.) Aberdeen Ph.D. (Hist.)

247 The archetype of the liminal wise man, his encounters with and employment of the supernatural, and his embodiment of the Norse ideas of authorship and belief in the sagas. Barrett Sink. (Dr. Hannah Burrows and Professor Ralph O'Connor.) Aberdeen Ph.D. (Hist.)

248 Tom, Dick and Leofric: the transformation of English personal naming, 850–1350. James Chetwood. (Dr. Charles M. West.) Sheffield Ph.D. (Hist.)

249 What does the variability of depictions of children and childhood in Old Norse literature signify? Pam Corray. (Dr. Hannah Burrows and Professor Stefan Brink.) Aberdeen Ph.D. (Hist.)

250 How does the treatment of women by gods, heroes and historical men in Old Norse literature reflect on both sexes, morally and socially? Claire Organ. (Dr. Hannah Burrows and Professor Stefan Brink.) Aberdeen Ph.D. (Hist.)

251 The limits of communion in the Byzantine church (861–1300). Andrei Psarev. (Dr. Eric Morier-Genoud.) Belfast M.Phil./Ph.D. (Hist. & Anthr.)

252 The queen and the book: Arthurian literature as queenly *speculum*. Rebecca Lyons. (Dr. Helen Fulton and Dr. Sarah Rees Jones.) York Ph.D. (Med. Stud.)

253 The origin, function and status of -thorpe and -by settlements in Norfolk. Simon Wilson. (Dr. Andy Seaman.) Canterbury Christ Church M.Phil. (Hist.)

254 Territories over time? Tenure, landholding and settlement: the Anglo-Norman landscape along the Hampshire/Wiltshire border c.900–1200. Ross Dunworth. (Dr. Ryan Lavelle and Dr. Simon Roffey.) Winchester M.Phil./Ph.D. (Hist.)

255 The reception of Cyprian of Carthage in early medieval Europe. Eleni Leontidou. (Professor Rosamond McKitterick.) Cambridge Ph.D. (Hist.)

256 The representation of Norse women in medieval textual sources and modern visual media. Lillian Cespedes Gonzalez. (Dr. Elena C. Woodacre and Dr. Ryan L. Lavelle.) Winchester M.Phil./Ph.D. (Hist.)

257 The influence of the reigns of Cnut in England and Denmark upon the social, economic, religious and political culture of Scandinavia from the 11th century onwards. Deniz Cem Gulem. (Professors Stefan Brink and Michael Gelting.) Aberdeen Ph.D. (Hist.)

258 Land ownership and landscape history in northern Cumbria. Peter Messenger. (Dr. Angus J.L. Winchester.) Lancaster Ph.D. (Hist.)

259 Broads and deeps: the environmental and economic impact of peat extraction in Norfolk and Lincolnshire. Andrew E. Woodhead. East Anglia Ph.D. (Hist.)

260 Travel and travellers in medieval and early modern Scotland. Sara A. Robinson. (Professor Richard D. Oram and Dr. Michael A. Penman.) Stirling Ph.D. (Hist.)

261 Wyre Forest hamlets: society, environment, economy and family in medieval and early modern Shropshire and Worcestershire. Daniel Smith. (Dr. Kate Olson.) Bangor Ph.D. (Hist., Welsh Hist. & Archaeol.)

262 The fold course in East Anglia. John C. Belcher. East Anglia Ph.D. (Hist.)

263 The French chronicles of London. Beresford Bell. (Professor Caroline M. Barron.) London M.Phil./Ph.D. (R.H.U.L. Hist.)

264 The horse trade and the economy in medieval East Anglia. Jordan Claridge. East Anglia Ph.D. (Hist.)

265 Chantries in medieval London. Anne Clarke. (Dr. Clive R. Burgess.) London M.Phil./Ph.D. (R.H.U.L. Hist.)

266 The illustrated Apocalypse and the cult of saints. Emma Croker. (Dr. Anke Holdenried and Dr. Beth Williamson.) Bristol M.Litt. (Hist. Stud.)

267 Elite female identity as expressed through garden creation in medieval England. Rachel M. Delman. (Dr. Steven Mileson and Dr. Ian Forrest.) Oxford D.Phil. (Mod. Hist.)

268 Past and present in medieval Spain. Amanda Dotseth. (Professor John H. Lowden.) London Ph.D. (Courtauld Inst.)

269 Medieval women's status and authority in the middling classes through study of wax seals. Laura Evans. (Professor Phillipp Schofield and Dr. Elizabeth New.) Aberystwyth Ph.D. (Hist. & Welsh Hist.)

270 Ordering the invisible: the construction of scientific and theological diagrams in the middle ages. Sarah M. Griffin. (Dr. Gervase Rosser.) Oxford D.Phil. (Mod. Hist.)

271 Medieval necromancers. Alison Harthill. (Professor Helen Nicholson.) Cardiff Ph.D. (Hist. & Archaeol.)

272 Rational explanations for the walking dead in medieval Britain. Polina Ignatova. (Dr. Paul Hayward.) Lancaster Ph.D. (Hist.)

273 Hospitality in medieval Wales. Lowri Jones. (Professor Phillipp Schofield and Dr. Karen Stöber.) Aberystwyth Ph.D. (Hist. & Welsh Hist.)

274 Judaeo-Christian relations in medieval England. Tomoko Kikuchi. (Dr. Kenneth Austin and Professor Ronald Hutton.) Bristol M.Litt. (Hist. Stud.)

275 Medieval ecclesiastical gatehouses in England. Harriet Mahood. (Professor Lindy Grant.) Reading Ph.D. (Hist.)

276 The military orders slave system: diverse, profitable, accepted. Nicholas McDermott. (Professor Helen Nicholson.) Cardiff Ph.D. (Hist. & Archaeol.)

277 Routeways in the landscape: movement and direction in the landscape of Cranborne Chase. Royston Nicholls. (Dr. Richard L.C. Jones.) Leicester Ph.D. (Hist.)

278 Landscape history. Stephen Nunn. East Anglia Ph.D. (Hist.)

279 Encounter, worship and ritual at sea in the medieval Mediterranean. Jessica Tearney-Pearce. (Professor David Abulafia.) Cambridge Ph.D. (Hist.)

280 The movement of saints' corporeal relics in western Europe, c.800–1200. Elizabeth Wiedenheft. (Dr. Claire Taylor and Dr. Rob Lutton.) Nottingham Ph.D. (Hist.)

281 The cultural implications of English medieval graffiti. Rebecca Williams. (Professor Brigitte Resl.) Liverpool Ph.D. (Hist.)

282 Interfaith relations in medieval Algarve. Jonathan Wilson. (Dr. Damien Kempf.) Liverpool Ph.D. (Hist.)

283 The archaeology of conflict in Wales, *c.*1000–1450: the weapons. Samantha Colclough. (Professors Nancy Edwards and A. Huw Pryce.) Bangor Ph.D. (Hist., Welsh Hist. & Archaeol.)

284 Papal overlordship and *protectio* of the king, *c.*1000–1373 . Benedict Wiedemann. (Professor David d'Avray.) London Ph.D. (U.C. Hist.)

285 The text and reception of *de medicina equorum* by Jordanus Ruffus: animal-care practitioners and the horse as non-human patient. Sunny Harrison. (Dr. Iona M. McCleery and Dr. William T. Flynn.) Leeds Ph.D. (Med. Stud.)

286 Urban communities, networks and the development of English towns in the central middle ages. Susan Nightingale. (Dr. Ryan L. Lavelle and Professor Michael A. Hicks.) Winchester M.Phil./Ph.D. (Hist.)

287 Norman castles built on Anglo-Saxon cemeteries: power, prestige or practicality? Therron Welstead. (Professor Janet E. Burton.) Wales Ph.D. (Trinity Saint David Hist.)

288 Deception and trickery in medieval warfare, 1050–1450. James Titterton. (Dr. Alan V. Murray and Dr. Karen Watts.) Leeds Ph.D. (Med. Stud.)

289 Using post-conquest charters to establish a mappable aspect of wastelands in the medieval/post-medieval periods in Norfolk, Suffolk, Hertfordshire and Essex. Adam Stone. East Anglia Ph.D. (Hist.)

290 Pilgrimage in medieval East Anglia. Michael Schmoelz. East Anglia Ph.D. (Hist.)

291 Power and society in the frontier space of medieval Anatolia, *c.*1070–*c.*1390. Wiktor G. Ostasz. (Dr. Mark Whittow and Dr. Judith Pfeiffer.) Oxford D.Phil. (Mod. Hist.)

292 Law and order in medieval Chester, 1086–1505: evidence from the Domesday Book and the Chester city courts. Vanessa Greatorex-Roskilly. (Professor Peter G.I. Gaunt.) Chester Ph.D. (Hist. & Archaeol.)

293 A history of Barnwell priory, Cambridge. Jacqueline Harmon. (Professor Nicholas C. Vincent.) East Anglia Ph.D. (Hist.)

294 Stabilising monetary systems: London's currency and credit markets from the 12th–21st centuries. Anthony Hotson. (Mr. Nicholas H. Dimsdale.) Oxford D.Phil. (Mod. Hist.)

295 'The work of giants': hypertrophy and abnormal size in late medieval England, *c.*1100–1600. Timothy Brinded. Chichester M.Phil./Ph.D. (Hist.)

296 Spitting on an angel, trampling on a saint: reading the medieval English pavement. Karen Brett. (Professor Christopher Norton.) York Ph.D. (Hist. of Art)

297 The lost dimension: medieval window lead – a study of sources, craft and conservation. Joanne Dillon. (Ms. Sarah Brown.) York Ph.D. (Hist. of Art)

298 Relationship between pre-modern natural philosophy and theology with particular reference to the perceptions of God. Linda Friday. (Professor Helen Parish.) Reading Ph.D. (Hist.)

299 Illicit sexual activity in medieval English provincial towns. Helen Kavanagh. (Professor J.N. Peregrine B. Horden and Dr. Clive R. Burgess.) London M.Phil./ Ph.D. (R.H.U.L. Hist.)

300 The function of hospitaller houses in England, Ireland, Scotland and Wales. Christie Majoros. (Professor Helen Nicholson.) Cardiff Ph.D. (Hist. & Archaeol.)

301 Drawing upon the gods: medieval depictions of the pagan deities and their relationship to contemporary Ovidian commentaries. Anne McLaughlin. (Professor Charles S.F. Burnett and Dr. Rembrandt Duits.) London Ph.D. (Warburg)

302 Horrific treatment in medieval texts. Jessica Monteith. (Professor Helen Parish.) Reading Ph.D. (Hist.)

303 Images of self and others in medieval Serb, Ragusan (Dubrovnik) and Bosnian sources. Marko Pijovic. (Dr. Catherine Holmes.) Oxford M.St. (Mod. Hist.)

304 The Augustinian canons in medieval Scotland. Garrett B. Ratcliff. (Dr. Kirsten Fenton and Professor Judith A. Green.) Edinburgh Ph.D. (Hist.)

305 Benedictine abbeys and their social impact: a case study in a Reading abbey manuscript. Fredrica Teale. (Dr. Nicholas Karn and Dr. Lena Wahlgren-Smith.) Southampton M.Phil. (Hist.)

306 Exile and return: political prophecy and England's borders, c.1136–1450. Victoria Flood. (Professors Helen Fulton and W. Mark Ormrod.) York Ph.D. (Med. Stud.)

307 The Book of Sentences and its influence on later medieval texts concerning magic and witchcraft. Victoria Page. (Dr. Anne Lawrence.) Reading Ph.D. (Hist.)

308 The history of St. Radegund's abbey, Bradsole, Dover. Christine Havelock. (Dr. Alan T. Thacker.) London M.Phil./Ph.D. (Inst. Hist. Res.)

309 Connecting Charnwood: a medieval woodland landscape, its external and internal links. Ann Stones. (Dr. Richard L.C. Jones.) Leicester Ph.D. (Eng. Loc. Hist.)

310 Factors influencing settlement development in Norfolk. Arthur Groves. East Anglia Ph.D. (Hist.)

311 The Ironmongers Company of London. Leah Rhys. (Professor Caroline M. Barron.) London M.Phil./Ph.D. (R.H.U.L. Hist.)

312 Rural piety: medieval religious houses and the *cura animarum* in parochial Somerset. Hannah West. Exeter M.Phil. (Med. Stud.)

313 Medieval London carpenters, c.1240–c.1540. Doreen Leach. (Professor Caroline M. Barron.) London M.Phil./Ph.D. (R.H.U.L. Hist.)

314 Rural society and the environment: the impacts of the medieval drainage of the Fens, c.1250–1550. Michael Gilbert. (Professor Christopher C. Dyer and Dr. Richard Jones.) Leicester Ph.D. (Eng. Loc. Hist.)

315 The experience of converted prostitutes in the Monastero di Sant'Elisabetta delle Convertite in Florence. Gillian Jack. (Dr. Emily Michelson and Professor Frances Andrews.) St. Andrews Ph.D. (Hist.)

316 The site of memory: the phenomenology of holy pilgrimage and devotional relics from the Santa Casa di Loreto. Jillian A. Wertheim. (Dr. Hanneke Grootenboer.) Oxford M.St. (Mod. Hist.)

317 A crowded urban space: conflict and identity in an English town, 1300–1800. Derek Crosby. (Dr. James Davis.) Belfast Ph.D. (Hist. & Anthr.)

318 A prosopographical study of bishops' careers in northern Europe. Michael Frost. (Professor Stefan Brink.) Aberdeen Ph.D. (Hist.)

319 The lordship of the bishop of Durham in the East Riding of Yorkshire, 1300–1700. Christopher Bywell. (Professors David Crouch and John Marriot.) Hull Ph.D. (Hist.)

320 The changing perception of leprosy in medieval and early modern England. Victoria Louise Carrington. (Dr. David Appleby and Dr. Rob Lutton.) Nottingham Ph.D. (Hist.)

321 Unveiling Cologne's *Holy Virgins*: the curiosities of medieval and early modern textile skull reliquaries. Cherissa Casey. (Dr. Emanuele Lugli & Dr. Jane Hawkes.) York Ph.D. (Hist. of Art)

322 Food in late medieval and early modern Spanish religious identities. Jillian Williams. (Dr. Kenneth Austin and Dr. Fernando Cervantes.) Bristol M.Litt. (Hist. Stud.)

323 The permissibility of graffiti from the 14th century onwards. Rebecca Hiscott. (Dr. John Walker and Dr. Helen Fenwick.) Hull Ph.D. (Hist.)

324 A cultural, scientific and technical study of the Durham lead cloth seal collection, 1450–1820. Gary Bankhead. (Dr. Christopher Caple, Dr. Pam Graves, Dr. Mary Brooks and Dr. Michael Lewis.) Durham M.Phil. (Archaeol.)

325 The iron and steel industries of the Derwent Valley: a historical archaeology. John Bowman. (Dr. Jane Webster and Professor Sam Turner.) Newcastle Ph.D. (Archaeol.)

326 The history and development of the stained and painted glass of York Minster from the late 15th century to 1829. Louise Hampson. (Ms. Sarah Brown and Dr. Kate Giles.) York Ph.D. (Hist. of Art)

327 Faith, warfare and power: Protestant noble identity during the French wars of religion. David Nicoll. (Professor Penny Roberts.) Warwick M.Phil./Ph.D. (Hist.)

Early medieval to *c*.1000: general and continental

328 Exile in the Western successor-states, *c*.435–650. Harold Mawdsley. (Dr. Julia Hillner and Dr. Simon T. Loseby.) Sheffield Ph.D. (Hist.)

329 Integrating *Magna Dacia*: a narrative reappraisal of Jordanes. Octavio Vieira Pinto. (Professors Julia S. Barrow and Ian N. Wood.) Leeds Ph.D. (Med. Stud.)

330 The making of poetic history in Anglo-Saxon England and Carolingian Francia. Catalin Taranu. (Dr. Alaric Hall and Professor Catherine E. Karkov.) Leeds Ph.D. (Med. Stud.)

331 A study of three medieval abbreviations of patristic commentaries. Margaret Silvers. (Dr. Mary Garrison and Professor Linne Mooney.) York Ph.D. (Med. Stud.)

332 Food asceticism and the virtue of humility in Merovingian monks. Jennifer D. Chaloner. (Dr. Conrad Leyser.) Oxford D.Phil. (Mod. Hist.)

333 The art of northern Europe, *c*.500–700 A.D.: Christian or pagan? Matthias Friedrich. (Dr. Jane Hawkes.) York M.A. by Research (Hist. of Art)

334 Symeon Stylites the Younger and his cult in context: hagiography and society in 6th- to 7th-century Byzantium. Lucy A.R. Parker. (Dr. Philip Booth.) Oxford D.Phil. (Mod. Hist.)

335 The 6th and early 7th centuries: preconditions of the rise of the emporia. Irene Bavuso. (Professor Christopher J. Wickham.) Oxford D.Phil. (Mod. Hist.)

336 Byzantine approaches to 6th-century liturgical vessels from Lycia and Isauria. Ahmet Ari. (Dr. Flora Dennis and Professor Elizabeth A. James.) Sussex D.Phil. (Hist. of Art)

337 The African policy of Justinian I and Justin II. Miranda Williams. (Dr. James D. Howard-Johnston.) Oxford D.Phil. (Mod. Hist.)

338 Ecclesiastical networks and the papacy at the end of late antiquity, A.D. 550–700. Sihong Lin. (Professor Paul Fouracre and Dr. Charles Insley.) Manchester Ph.D. (Hist.)

339 Friendship in the works of Venantius Fortunatus. Hope Williard. (Dr. William T. Flynn and Professor Ian N. Wood.) Leeds Ph.D. (Med. Stud.)

340 Contextualising the Scandinavian *specula principum*. Heidi Djuve. (Dr. Hannah Burrows and Professor Stefan Brink.) Aberdeen Ph.D. (Hist.)

341 The chosen people of St. Cuthbert – defining the Haliwerfolc. Richard Vert Jnr. (Dr. Giles Gasper and Dr. Leonard Scales.) Durham Ph.D. (Hist.)

342 Islamic coins in Europe in the 8th and 9th centuries. Asma Alshaiban. (Dr. Stacey Hynd.) Exeter M.Phil. (Hist.)

343 Theology and the history of the recent past in the Carolingian world. Robert Evans. (Professor Rosamond McKitterick and Dr. Richard Sowerby.) Cambridge Ph.D. (Hist.)

344 Canonical rules in the Carolingian world (Francia and Anglo-Saxon England *c.*750–987). Stephen Ling. (Professor Joanna E. Story.) Leicester Ph.D. (Hist.)

345 Carolingian diplomacy with the Islamic world, 751–888. Samuel Ottewell-Soulsby. (Professor Rosamond McKitterick.) Cambridge Ph.D. (Hist.)

346 The *leges gentium* under the Carolingians. Anna Turnbull. (Dr. Marios Costambeys.) Liverpool Ph.D. (Hist.)

347 Augustine of Hippo and the art of ruling in the Carolingian imperial period. Sophie Mösch. (Professor Peter Heather and Dr. Alice Rio.) King's College London M.Phil./ Ph.D. (Hist.)

348 The heirs of Alcuin: educational standards and career advancement in 9th-century Carolingian Europe. Darren Barbar. (Professor Julia S. Barrow and Dr. William T. Flynn.) Leeds Ph.D. (Med. Stud.)

349 The *Liber Vaccae* and the practical applications of cosmology. Sarah Ortega. (Dr. Iona M. McCleery and Dr. William T. Flynn.) Leeds Ph.D. (Med. Stud)

350 *De libris quos legere solebam*: multi-text manuscripts and the accumulation and transfer of knowledge at Reichenau and St. Gall in the 9th century. Mary Young. (Dr. Charles M. West.) Sheffield Ph.D. (Hist.)

351 The Paulicians and the Byzantine empire. Carl Dixon. (Dr. Claire Taylor and Dr. M. Cunningham.) Nottingham Ph.D. (Hist.)

352 Pope John VIII and contemporary papal history. David P.W. Barritt. (Dr. Conrad Leyser and Professor Christopher Wickham.) Oxford D.Phil. (Mod. Hist.)

353 Politics and pastoral care: the bishops of north-western Lombardy during the post-Carolingian period (888–962). Michele Baitieri. (Dr. Ross Balzaretti and Dr. Claire Taylor.) Nottingham Ph.D. (Hist.)

354 Lords of the North Sea world. Anthony Mansfield. (Dr. Philip Morgan and Dr. Kathleen Cushing.) Keele Ph.D. (Hist.)

355 Mercia and England in the 10th and 11th centuries: a re-assessment. Rebecca Griffiths. (Dr. Charles Insley and Dr. Paul Oldfield.) Manchester Ph.D. (Hist.)

356 Imperial history and Italian history in the 10th and 11th centuries: authorship, audience and reception. Simon Williams. (Dr. Marios Costambeys.) Liverpool Ph.D. (Hist.)

357 Made to order: discourses of power in the Byzantine Compilation Movement, *c*.900–1000. Thomas Adamson-Green. (Dr. Catherine Holmes.) Oxford M.St. (Mod. Hist.)

358 The influence of Byzantium in Italy beyond its territorial holdings in the 10th century. Andrew M. Small. (Dr. Mark Whittow.) Oxford M.Phil. (Mod. Hist.)

359 Liturgical manuscripts in the 10th century. Lenneke Van Raaiji. Exeter Ph.D. (Hist.)

360 Byzantine foreign policy in diplomacy in the personal reign of Constantine VII Porphyrogennetos (A.D. 945–59). Prerona Prasad. (Dr. James D. Howard-Johnston.) Oxford D.Phil. (Mod. Hist.)

361 Religious identity and transition in settlement era (C.E. 950–1050) Norse Greenland. Jess McCullough. (Deidre O'Sullivan and Dr. Neil Christie.) Leicester Ph.D. (Archaeol. & Anc. Hist.)

362 Marriage and gender: the role of Duchess Dobrava in the Christianisation of Poland and/or gender aspects in early Polish Christianity. Kaja Met. (Dr. Lesley Abrams and Dr. Natalia Nowakowska.) Oxford M.St. (Mod. Hist.)

363 Journeys to holiness: lay sanctity in the central middle ages, *c*.970–1120. Adrian Cornell du Houx. (Dr. Paul Hayward.) Lancaster Ph.D. (Hist.)

364 Fulbert of Chartres: the authority of a pre-Gregorian bishop. Julia Watson. (Professor Lindy Grant.) Reading Ph.D. (Hist.)

365 Property, power and religious change in the diocese of Milan, *c*.990–1150. James R.A. Norrie. (Professor Christopher J. Wickham and Dr. Conrad Leyser.) Oxford D.Phil. (Mod. Hist.)

Early medieval: Britain and Ireland

366 Power and identity in early medieval Britain: how significant was Rome in the development of power and identity in Britain beyond A.D. 410? Paul Gorton. (Dr. Alaric Hall and Dr. Richard F. Jones.) Leeds Ph.D. (Med. Stud.)

367   Worth their place? A multi-disciplinary study of the social and political significance of particular places in Anglo-Saxon Mercia.   Graham Aldred.   (Dr. Neil Christie and Dr. Mark Gillings.)   Leicester Ph.D.   (Archaeol. & Anc. Hist.)

368   Visualising the Old Testament in Anglo-Saxon England.   Elizabeth Alexander.   (Dr. Jane Hawkes.)   York Ph.D.   (Hist. of Art)

369   Layered kingship in Anglo-Saxon England.   Daniel Cutts.   (Professors David Dumville and Stefan Brink.)   Aberdeen Ph.D.   (Hist.)

370   For the love of God: male cross-dressing and religion in pagan Anglo-Saxon England.   Katherine Fliegel.   (Dr. Charles Insley and Professor Paul Fouracre.)   Manchester Ph.D.   (Hist.)

371   Anglo-Saxon medical recipes in non-medical manuscripts: matters of culture, context and community.   Sarah Gilbert.   (Dr. Helen Foxhall Forbes and Professor Richard Gameson.)   Durham Ph.D.   (Hist.)

372   Papal privileges in Anglo-Saxon England.   Benjamin Savill.   (Dr. Sarah Foot.)   Oxford D.Phil.   (Theol.)

373   Waterways and white gold: the ivories of Anglo-Saxon England, *c*.500–1066.   Lyndsey Smith.   (Dr. Jane Hawkes.)   York Ph.D.   (Hist. of Art)

374   Representing power and majesty in Anglo-Saxon England.   Heidi Stoner.   (Dr. Jane Hawkes.)   York Ph.D.   (Hist. of Art)

375   Perceptions of a mutable landscape: dwelling on the edge, early medieval north-west Staffordshire.   Matthew Blake.   (Dr. Richard L.C. Jones.)   Leicester Ph.D.   (Eng. Loc. Hist.)

376   Reforming the early English church: Bede and Archbishop Theodore.   Emma Vesper.   (Dr. P. Darby and Professor J. Story.)   Nottingham Ph.D.   (Hist.)

377   Change in Northumbria: was Aldfrith of Northumbria's reign a period of innovation or did it merely reflect the development of processes already underway in the late 7th century?   William Watson.   (Dr. Alexander Woolf.)   St. Andrews Ph.D.   (Hist.)

378   Bede and Latin orthography.   Richard Exley.   (Dr. Mary D. Garrison.)   York Ph.D.   (Hist.)

379   Pastoral care in early medieval England.   Gerald Dyson.   (Professor Catherine R.E. Cubitt.)   York Ph.D.   (Hist.)

380   Power and identity in early medieval Scotland.   Arkady J.N. Hodge.   (Professor Thomas Charles-Edwards.)   Oxford D.Phil.   (Mod. Hist.)

381   The symbolic value of the image of the snake in Anglo-Saxon culture, 700–900.   Charlotte Ball.   (Professor Joanna E. Story.)   Leicester Ph.D.   (Hist.)

382   Atoning for killing: the practice of penance and the perception of bloodshed among early medieval Irish, 5th to 9th century.   David Burke.   (Dr. Clare Stancliffe and Professor Richard Gameson.)   Durham Ph.D.   (Hist.)

383   The political patronage of religious institutions by elite women, *c*.750–1000.   Sarah Greer.   (Professor Simon J. MacLean.)   St. Andrews Ph.D.   (Hist.)

384   The art of the so-called pocket gospel books of the insular world.   Eleanor Jackson.   (Dr. Jane Hawkes and Dr. Hanna Vorholt.)   York Ph.D.   (Hist. of Art)

385 Alcuin's rhetoric: theological, philosophical and rhetorical tradition – a new edition. Artur Costino. (Dr. Mary Garrison and Dr. Michele Campopiano.) York Ph.D. (Med. Stud.)

386 Royal agents in late Anglo-Saxon England: earls, bishops and abbots. Mary E. Blanchard. (Professor Sarah Foot.) Oxford D.Phil. (Mod. Hist.)

387 Differing patterns of Viking migration and settlement in Suffolk: an analysis of Scandinavian place names in their landscape context. David Boulton. East Anglia Ph.D. (Hist.)

388 The status of the Ætheling: aspects of succession and kingship in late Anglo-Saxon England, with specific reference to Edmund II Ironside. David McDermott. (Dr. Ryan L. Lavelle and Professor Barbara A.E. Yorke.) Winchester M.Phil./Ph.D. (Hist.)

389 The reeve in late Anglo-Saxon England. Chelsea Shields-Mas. (Professor Catherine R.E. Cubitt.) York Ph.D. (Hist.)

390 Royal lordship and regional government: East Anglia, *c*.869–1086. Richard Purkiss. (Professor Sarah Foot.) Oxford D.Phil. (Mod. Hist.)

391 Kingship, morality and masculinity: the creation of royal identities in later Anglo-Saxon England, *c*.871–1016. Ryan Goodman. (Dr. Charles Insley and Professor Paul Fouracre.) Manchester Ph.D. (Hist.)

392 The cult of St. Æthelwold. Rebecca Browett. (Dr. Alan Thacker.) London Ph.D. (Inst. Hist. Res.)

393 Suburban development in later Saxon and Norman England. Andrew Agate. London Ph.D. (Inst. Archaeol.)

394 The ideology of vengeance: theology, literature and practice in England, *c*.900–*c*.1150. Abigail Steed. (Dr. Helen Foxhall Forbes and Dr. Giles Gasper.) Durham Ph.D. (Hist.)

395 Exile and return of Anglo-Saxon kings. William White. (Dr. Mary Garrison and Dr. Matthew Townend.) York Ph.D. (Med. Stud.)

396 *Sylloge tacticorum*: English translation and historical commentary. Georgios Chatzelis. (Dr. Jonathan P. Harris.) London Ph.D. (R.H.U.L. Hist.)

397 Changing the tradition: case studies of how insular scribes adopted Caroline Minuscule in *c*.10th-century Britain. Colleen Curran. (Professor Julia Crick and Dr. Peter Stokes.) King's College London M.Phil./Ph.D. (Hist.)

398 'Lost' coins from minting towns in England between 924 and 1158 A.D. – trade, geld or religion. Roger Hills. (Dr. Katherine Weikert and Dr. Ryan Lavelle.) Winchester M.Phil./Ph.D. (Hist.)

399 The patristic sources of Archbishop Wulfstan. Anthony Smart. (Professor Catherine R.E. Cubitt.) York Ph.D. (Hist.)

400 Climbing ladders: children and monastic formation in England, *c*.950–1200. Steven G. Hodgson. (Professor Sarah Foot.) Oxford D.Phil. (Mod. Hist.)

401 Æthelwold's circle, saints' cults and monastic reform, 956–1006. Alison V. Hudson. (Dr. Lesley Abrams and Dr. Conrad Leyser.) Oxford D.Phil. (Mod. Hist.)

402   A history of taxation in England, *c.*991–1232. Robert P. Cohen. (Dr. Stephen Baxter.) Oxford D.Phil. (Mod. Hist.)

Eleventh century

403   Monasticism without frontiers: the extended monastic community of the Abbot of Cluny in England and Wales. Christopher Pearce. (Professor Janet E. Burton.) Wales Ph.D. (Trinity Saint David Hist.)

404   The historic landscape of the Cistercian Abbey of St. Mary de Voto, Tintern, County Wexford. Bill Marshall. (Professor Janet E. Burton.) Wales M.Phil. (Trinity Saint David Hist.)

405   How military currents diverged in the Norse countries during the 11th and 12th centuries, showing both the evolution of materiel and warfare over time and space. Benat Elortza. (Professors Stefan Brink and Michael Gelting.) Aberdeen Ph.D. (Hist.)

406   Curing the common soul: rethinking Byzantine heresy, with particular focus on literary motifs (11th–12th centuries). Elisabeth Mincin. (Dr. Tim Greenwood.) St. Andrews Ph.D. (Hist.)

407   To investigate to what extent the development of astrological techniques in England prior to 1200 was influenced by ideas outside Christendom. Christopher Mitchell. (Dr. Richard L.C. Jones.) Leicester Ph.D. (Eng. Loc. Hist.)

408   Royal/ducal demesne in England and Normandy in the 11th century (Exon. Domesday Project). Alexander P. Dymond. (Dr. Stephen Baxter.) Oxford D.Phil. (Mod. Hist.)

409   Henry II of Germany (1002–24): power, kingship and the reshaping of the Ottonian past. Ashley Plum. (Dr. Kathleen Cushing and Dr. Marios Costambeys.) Keele Ph.D. (Hist.)

410   Walter Giffard I, II and III, Lords of Longueville sur Scie and Earls of Buckingham, 1010–1164. Sarah Fry. (Dr. Katherine Weikert and Dr. Ryan Lavelle.) Winchester M.Phil./Ph.D. (Hist.)

411   Adelaide and dispute settlement. Alison Creber. (Dr. Serena Ferente and Professor Janet L. Nelson.) King's College London M.Phil./Ph.D. (Hist.)

412   The Godwinsons and brotherhood. Mohammed Zain Ahmed. (Professor Francoise Le Saux.) Reading Ph.D. (Med. Stud.)

413   Pope Leo IX: a study of his life. Andrew Smith. (Dr. Steve Marritt and Dr. Stuart Airlie.) Glasgow Ph.D. (Soc. Sc.)

414   Aristocracy, politics and power in Byzantium, 1025–81. Jonas A. Nilsson. (Dr. Catherine Holmes.) Oxford D.Phil. (Mod. Hist.)

415   Scotland's early stone castles, *c.*1050–1350. William Wyeth. (Professor Richard D. Oram and Dr. P. Dixon.) Stirling Ph.D. (Hist.)

416   Child kingship in England, Scotland, France and Germany, *c.*1050–*c.*1250. Emily Joan Ward. (Professor Elisabeth van Houts.) Cambridge Ph.D. (Hist.)

418 Questions of ideology and patronage: the Romanesque in north Wales. Aimee Pritchard. (Professors Nancy Edwards and A. Huw Pryce.) Bangor Ph.D. (Hist., Welsh Hist. & Archaeol.)

419 The conqueror's wife: Matilda of Flanders as countess of Normandy and queen of England. Charlotte Cartwright. (Professor Pauline A. Stafford.) Liverpool Ph.D. (Hist.)

420 Lordship and community: the honorial baronage of the North Midlands in the long 12th century. Hannah Boston. (Dr. George S. Garnett.) Oxford D.Phil. (Mod. Hist.)

421 The transmission, reception and use of royal histories in England and the empire during the long 12th century. Johanna M. Dale. East Anglia Ph.D. (Hist.)

422 Miracles for the mad: the representation of insanity in English miracles collections from the long 12th century. Claire Trenery. (Professor J.N. Peregrine B. Horden.) London M.Phil./Ph.D. (R.H.U.L. Hist.)

423 Rewriting saints: Anglo-Norman revisions of Anglo-Saxon hagiography. Kimberley A. Cosgrove. (Professors Björn K.U. Weiler and Phillipp Schofield.) Aberystwyth Ph.D. (Hist. & Welsh Hist.)

424 Anglo-Norman monasticism. Jennie England. (Dr. Sethina Watson.) York Ph.D. (Hist.)

425 The re-use of Roman material culture in Anglo-Norman England. Jane-Heloise Nancarrow. (Dr. Aleks McClain and Professor Helen Fulton.) York Ph.D. (Med. Stud.)

426 From Jew to Gentile: Jewish converts and conversion to Christianity in medieval England, 1066–1290. Joshua Curk. (Dr. Paul A. Brand.) Oxford D.Phil. (Mod. Hist.)

427 Royal legislation and conciliar consent in Anglo-Norman and Angevin England, c.1066–1216. Daniel P. Helen. (Dr. Thomas B. Lambert.) Oxford M.St. (Mod. Hist.)

428 Frontiers in context: the varied impact of the Norman-Breton border on the development of post-conquest England and Normandy. Kerrith C. Davies. (Dr. George S. Garnett.) Oxford D.Phil. (Mod. Hist.)

429 The impact of the Norman conquest on the conquerers: social networks and experiences of the cross-channel Empire after 1066. James D. Moore. (Professor Stephen D. Baxter.) Oxford D.Phil. (Mod. Hist.)

430 The life stories of Anglo-Saxon women of the land-holding classes, 1066–1135. Berenice Wilson. (Professors Julia S. Barrow and Pauline Stafford.) Leeds Ph.D. (Med. Stud.)

431 Representation of the Danes in chronicles written in England during the Anglo-Norman period prior to 1154. Paul Store. (Dr. Ryan Lavelle.) Winchester M.Phil./ Ph.D. (Hist.)

432 Géraud de Sales in medieval Monasticism. Janet Burn. (Dr. Claire Taylor and Dr. Rob Lutton.) Nottingham Ph.D. (Hist.)

433 The role of Venice in the political relations between the Byzantines and Southern Italy, 1081–1197. Daniele Morossi. (Professor Graham A. Loud.) Leeds Ph.D. (Med. Stud.)

434 'Band of brothers' – kin group dynamics among the Hautevilles and other Norman noble families in the Mezzogiorno and Syria, c.1030–c.1140. Francesca Petrizzo. (Professor Graham A. Loud.) Leeds Ph.D. (Med. Stud.)

435 Unrequited desire: Peter Abelard and his contemporaries: psychoanalytic explorations of late 11th- and early 12th-century writers and the role of fathers and fatherhood in the high middle ages. Christopher Heginbotham. (Professor Andrew Jotischky.) Lancaster Ph.D. (Hist.)

436 Identity on crusade. Alexander Larkinson. (Dr. Christopher Tyerman.) Oxford M.St. (Mod. Hist.)

437 'Laws of war' in the crusading era. Ian Wilson. (Professor Jonathan P. Phillips.) London M.Phil./Ph.D. (R.H.U.L. Hist.)

438 The experience of sickness and health during Crusader campaigns to the eastern Mediterranean, 1095–1274. Joanna Phillips. (Dr. Iona M. McCleery and Dr. Alan V. Murray.) Leeds Ph.D. (Med. Stud.)

439 Paid service in crusading armies, 1095–1241. David Benjamin. (Professor Norman J. Housley.) Leicester Ph.D. (Hist.)

440 Antioch and Byzantium in the era of the crusades up to 1204. Thomas Sayers. (Dr. Conor Kostick and Dr. Claire Taylor.) Nottingham Ph.D. (Hist.)

441 The representation and function of emotion in the sources for the crusades, 1095–1291. Stephen Spencer. (Dr. Thomas Asbridge.) London Ph.D. (Q.M. Hist.)

442 Jewish chronicles of the first crusade in comparative context. Conner M. Noteboom. (Dr. Lesley Smith and Dr. Simon John.) Oxford M.St. (Mod. Hist.)

Twelfth century

443 Monastic relations: vernacular literary production in 12th- and 13th-century Barking and St. Albans. Katharine Bilous. (Dr. Sethina Watson and Dr. Elizabeth Tyler.) York Ph.D. (Med. Stud.)

444 Observation, diagnosis, triage and treatment: punishing English heresy as a medicinal process in the 12th and 13th centuries. Suzanne Coley. (Dr. Nicholas Karn.) Southampton M.Phil. (Hist.)

445 The ethics of sincerity in the 12th and 13th centuries. Emily Corran. (Professor David d'Avray.) London Ph.D. (U.C. Hist.)

446 Harold II's posthumous reputation in the 12th and 13th centuries. Kelsey S. Haver. (Dr. Benjamin Thompson.) Oxford M.St. (Mod. Hist.)

447 Rights of marriage: uxorial agency in Wales in the 12th and 13th centuries. Danna Messer. (Professor A. Huw Pryce.) Bangor Ph.D. (Hist., Welsh Hist. & Archaeol.)

448 Scandinavian kningship in a European context. Thomas Tollefsen. (Dr. John Hines.) Cardiff Ph.D. (Hist. & Archaeol.)

449   The legacy of the Anglo-Norman legal treatise in the *Leges Anglorum Londoniis collectae*. Katherine J. Har. (Dr. George S. Garnett.) Oxford D.Phil. (Mod. Hist.)

450   National categories in 12th-century England. Ilya Afanasyev. (Dr. Benjamin J. Thompson.) Oxford D.Phil. (Mod. Hist.)

451   From knights to nobles: the critical 12th century. Jack Beaman. (Dr. Conor Kostick and Dr. Claire Taylor.) Nottingham Ph.D. (Hist.)

452   St. Edmund's cult and community in the 12th century. Liam Draycott. East Anglia Ph.D. (Hist.)

453   Gender and 12th-century insular hagiography. Eilidh Harris. (Professor John G.H. Hudson.) St. Andrews Ph.D. (Hist.)

454   Images of kingship in English and German chronicles in the 12th century. Ryan Kemp. (Professors Björn K.U. Weiler and Sarah Hamilton.) Aberystwyth Ph.D. (Hist. & Welsh Hist.)

455   The role of lesser aristocratic women in 12th-century England. Hanna I. Kilpi. (Dr. Stephen Marritt and Professor Julia Smith.) Glasgow Ph.D. (Arts)

456   Edifice and education: architectural representation in 12th-century monastic texts. Karl P. Kinsella. (Dr. Lesley Smith.) Oxford D.Phil. (Mod. Hist.)

457   12th century decoration of St. Mary's church, Gloucestershire. Daniel Lyons. (Professor Julia S. Barrow and Dr. Eva Frojmovic.) Leeds Ph.D. (Med. Stud)

458   The cartularies of Scone Abbey: a critical analysis. Michael Penman. (Professor Richard Oram and Dr. Michael Penman.) Stirling Ph.D. (Hist.)

459   The kinetic structure of the mosaics at San Marco in Venice. Thomas G. Ryley. (Dr. Gervase Rosser.) Oxford M.St. (Mod. Hist.)

460   Nature of purgatory in 12th-century monastic literature. Graham Simpson. (Professor Andrew Jotischky.) Lancaster Ph.D. (Hist.)

461   'To be adorned with morals': Urbanus Magnus and 'courtesy literature' in 12th-century England. Fiona Whelan. (Dr. Lesley Smith.) Oxford D.Phil. (Mod. Hist.)

462   To live is to have glory, to die entails gain: battle rhetoric in 12th-century crusade narratives. Connor Wilson. London M.Phil./Ph.D. (R.H.U.L. Hist.)

463   Stephen of Rouen's *Draco Normannicus*. Jennifer Korst. (Dr. Mark Hagger and Professor A. Huw Pryce.) Bangor Ph.D. (Hist., Welsh Hist. & Archaeol.)

464   Legacy of St. Anselm of Canterbury in the early 12th century. Judith R. Dunthorne. (Dr. Giles M. Gasper and Professor Richard Gameson.) Durham Ph.D. (Hist.)

465   Challenges to authority and responses to them in the reign of Theresa of Portugal, 1112–28. Lorena Fierro Diaz. (Dr. Conrad Leyser and Dr. Robert Portass.) Oxford M.St. (Mod. Hist.)

466   The reign of Emperor John II Komnenos: the transformation of the old order, 1118–43. Maximilian C.G. Lau. (Dr. Mark Whittow.) Oxford D.Phil. (Mod. Hist.)

467   Stave churches and their predecessors: a comparison of Norwegian stave churches, their ecclesiastic precursors and contemporaneous Norse pagan temples. Lyle Tompsen. (Dr. David Petts and Dr. Sarah Semple.) Durham Ph.D. (Archaeol.)

468   Miracles and medicine in the Norman kingdom of Sicily. Amy Devenney. (Professor Graham A. Loud and Dr. Iona M. McCleery.) Leeds Ph.D. (Med. Stud.)

469   The crusader principality of Antioch as a frontier society, 1130–93. Andrew Buck. (Dr. Thomas S. Asbridge.) London Ph.D. (Q.M. Hist.)

470   *Leges Edwardi Confessoris* as a representation of English law. Thomas R. Hemming. (Dr. Thomas B. Lambert.) Oxford M.St. (Mod. Hist.)

471   Co-operation and competition: queenship in the emerging Angevin empire, 1135– 1216. Gabrielle Storey. (Dr. Elena C. Woodacre and Dr. Katherine Weikert.) Winchester M.Phil./Ph.D. (Hist.)

472   John of Salisbury and law. Maxine Esser. (Professor John G.H. Hudson.) St. Andrews Ph.D. (Hist.)

473   The Romanesque bronze doors and portal sculpture of San Zeno, Verona. Christopher Heginbotham. (Dr. Michele Vescovi and Dr. Cordula van Wyhe.) York M.A. (Hist. of Art)

474   Law and monasticism in Gratian's 'Decretum'. Travis R. Baker. (Dr. Paul A. Brand.) Oxford D.Phil. (Mod. Hist.)

475   The laws of war during the crusades to the East, c.1140–1204. Nicholas Palmer. (Professor Norman J. Housley.) Leicester Ph.D. (Hist.)

476   Nobility and royal functionaries in the kingdom of Sicily: social control and organisation of the aristocracy in the Norman mezzogiorno (1140–89). Hervin Fernández-Aceves. (Professor Graham A. Loud.) Leeds Ph.D. (Med. Stud.)

477   The *denari provisini* and the economy of Rome in the communal period, 1143–1398. Mariele Valci. (Dr. Richard Goddard and Dr. Christie Neil.) Nottingham Ph.D. (Hist.)

478   The Plantagenet administration of Normandy, 1144–1204. John H. Stevenson. (Professor Daniel J. Power.) Swansea Ph.D. (Hist.)

479   The Augustinian Canons in England and their writings on pastoral care, c.1150–1300. Rebecca S. Springer. (Dr. Ian Forrest.) Oxford D.Phil. (Mod. Hist.)

480   A time of great necessity: images of crisis and reform in the 12th century. Daniel Murphy. (Professor Martial J.M. Staub.) Sheffield Ph.D. (Hist.)

481   Women and warfare in the *Romans d'antiquité*. Sophie Harwood. (Professor Rosalind Brown-Grant and Dr. Alan V. Murray.) Leeds Ph.D. (Med. Stud.)

482   Gender identities in William of Tyre's chronicles: *History of deeds beyond the sea*. Ashley Firth. (Dr. Katherine Lewis.) Huddersfield Ph.D. (Music, Hum. & Media)

483   Benjamin of Tudela's *Book of Travels*: transmission and reception. Marci Freedman. (Dr. Stephen Mossman, Dr. Paul Oldfield and Dr. Renate Smithuis.) Manchester Ph.D. (Hist.)

484   Lives of episcopal saints in England and Wales, c.1170–1300. Cory W.G. Richards. (Professors Björn K.U. Weiler and Phillipp Schofield.) Aberystwyth Ph.D. (Hist. & Welsh Hist.)

485   Theological aspects of the bishop's role in England and Wales, 1174–1228. David Runciman. (Dr. Julie Barrau.) Cambridge Ph.D. (Hist.)

486 The relationship between the medieval English laity and the evolution of the Carthusian order in England, c.1178–1500. Kaan Gorman. (Professor Emilia M. Jamroziak and Dr. Melanie Brunner.) Leeds Ph.D. (Med. Hist.)

487 *Perfectissimus*: the Carthusians in England, c.1178–c.1220. Rosalind Green. (Dr. Giles Gasper and Dr. Christian Liddy.) Durham Ph.D. (Hist.)

488 The assize of mort d'ancestor in the late 12th and early 13th centuries. William Eves. (Professor John G.H. Hudson.) St. Andrews Ph.D. (Hist.)

489 Eschatology, crusade and reform in English historical writing, c.1180–c.1220. Hugh Reid. (Professor Richard Sharpe.) Oxford D.Phil. (Mod. Hist.)

490 Lordly power and lordships: Earls Ranulf III and John le Scot of Chester, c.1181–1237. Gavin R. Moore. (Dr. Kathryn Hurlock, Dr. Jason Roche and Dr. Anthony J. Adams.) Manchester Metropolitan Ph.D. (Hist.)

491 Kingship and gender in the reigns of King Richard I and King John. Daniel Greenwood. (Dr. Katherine Lewis.) Huddersfield M.Phil. (Music, Hum. & Media)

492 Noble networks: elite participation in the third crusade. Stephen Bennett. (Dr. Thomas S. Asbridge.) London M.Phil./Ph.D. (Q.M. Hist.)

493 The de Lacy constables of Chester and earls of Lincoln: the transformation of an honour, 1190–1311. Andrew Connell. (Professor Louise J. Wilkinson.) Canterbury Christ Church M.Phil. (Hist.)

494 The Leiden psalter. Emma Luker. (Professor John Lowden.) London Ph.D. (Courtauld Inst.)

495 *Terra matris*: the castles of the military orders and the sacred geography of the Baltic crusades. Gregory Leighton. (Professor Helen Nicholson.) Cardiff Ph.D. (Hist. & Archaeol.)

496 Simon V of Montfort: the exercise and aims of independent baronial power at home and on crusade, 1195–1218. Gregory Lippiatt. (Dr. Christopher J. Tyerman.) Oxford D.Phil. (Mod. Hist.)

Thirteenth century

497 The function of the cross-dresser in French and English literature from 1200 to 1500. Vanessa Wright. (Dr. Melanie Brunner, Professor Rosalind Brown-Grant and Dr. Catherine Batt.) Leeds Ph.D. (Med. Stud.)

498 Anchorites in Shropshire: an archaeological and literary analysis of the anchoritic vacation. Victoria Yuskaitis. (Professor Emilia M. Jamroziak and Dr. Catherine Batt.) Leeds Ph.D. (Med. Stud.)

499 What's in a name? Inscribing Christ with epithets in later Byzantine art. George Bartlett. (Professor Elizabeth A James and Dr. Flora Dennis.) Sussex D.Phil. (Hist. of Art)

500 The inclusion of women in the elitist male religious networks of the high middle ages. Hollie Devaney. (Dr. Julian Haseldine and Professor David Crouch.) Hull Ph.D. (Hist.)

501 Monastic wellbeing and healthcare in 13th- and 14th-century England: analysis of patients, spaces used and care available. Tamsin Gardner. Exeter M.Phil. (Med. Stud.)

502 Attitudes towards place and space in Byzantine hagiography in the 13th and 14th centuries. Lilly E. Stammler. (Dr. C.M. MacRobert and Dr. James D. Howard-Johnston.) Oxford D.Phil. (Mod. Hist.)

503 An investigation into the punishment of heresy in Languedoc during the 13th century. Harry Barmby. (Dr. Claire Taylor and Dr. Rob Lutton.) Nottingham Ph.D. (Hist.)

504 *Tot erant reges vel reguli*: political interactions, noble networks and the formation of factions in 13th-century Scotland. Alexander Crawford. (Dr. Alastair Macdonald and Dr. Jackson Armstrong.) Aberdeen Ph.D. (Hist.)

505 The Courtenay heiresses' aristocratic prestige, female agency and royal control in 13th-century France . Charlotte Crouch. (Professor Lindy Grant.) Reading Ph.D. (Med. Stud.)

506 Communal justice in 13th-century England. Kenneth Duggan. (Professor David Carpenter and Dr. Alice Taylor.) King's College London M.Phil./Ph.D. (Hist.)

507 Excommunication and politics in 13th-century England. Felicity Hill. East Anglia Ph.D. (Hist.)

508 Thirteenth-century Byzantine polities: persistence and success. Matthew Kinloch. (Dr. Catherine Holmes.) Oxford D.Phil. (Mod. Hist.)

509 Blessed are those who weep: the gift of tears in the 13th century. Kimberly-Joy Knight. (Professor Frances Andrews.) St. Andrews Ph.D. (Hist.)

510 Women in court: the legal status and property rights of heiresses and widows in 13th-century England. Shengyen Lu. (Professors Jane Winters and Paul Brand.) London M.Phil./Ph.D. (Inst. Hist. Res.)

511 Royal and aristocratic perception and patronage of lepers in the 13th century. Kate Phillips. (Professor Lindy Grant.) Reading Ph.D. (Med. Stud.)

512 Burgundy in the age of crusading, 1095–1361. Hilary Rhodes. (Dr. Alan V. Murray and Dr. Jonathan Jarrett.) Leeds Ph.D. (Med. Stud.)

513 Preaching in procession: Dominican churches, Italian lay piety, and the processionarium of the friars preachers. John H. Schnakenberg. (Dr. Lesley Smith and Professor Richard Conrad.) Oxford M.St. (Mod. Hist.)

514 The development of spatial and spiritual practice in 13th-century Latin hagiography. Hannah Shepherd. (Dr. Bill Aird and Dr. Cordelia Beattie.) Edinburgh Ph.D. (Hist.)

515 Images of *scientia* and the end of the world in 13th-century drawings at Vercelli. Jennifer Shurville. (Dr. Gervase Rosser and Dr. Martin Kauffmann.) Oxford D.Phil. (Mod. Hist.)

516 The cultural shift of Occitany during the 13th century. Olivier Sirjacq. (Dr. Rebecca Rist.) Reading Ph.D. (Hist.)

517 Dominicans and emotion in the 13th century. Nicholas Townson. (Professor Peter P.A. Biller.) York Ph.D. (Hist.)

518 The origins and development of professional legal attorneys by reference to 13th-century eyre proceedings. Andrew D. Whiting. (Professor Paul Brand.) Oxford D.Phil. (Mod. Hist.)

519 Architectural visions: an analysis of the architectural plans of the Temple of Solomon in Richard of St. Victor's *In Visionem Ezekielis*. Honor R. Wilkinson. (Dr. Gervase Rosser.) Oxford M.St. (Mod. Hist.)

520 A critical analysis and edition of Ralph of Coggeshall's *Chronicon Anglicanum*. Harriett Webster. (Dr. Brendan Smith and Dr. James Clark.) Bristol Ph.D. (Hist. Stud.)

521 Paulus Hungarus and Damasus: two Hungarian canonists in early 13th-century Bologna. Gergely Gallai. (Dr. Peter Clarke.) Southampton M.Phil. (Hist.)

522 'Three imposters?' Forms of unbelief in the early 13th century. Thomas Gruber. (Dr. Matthew Kempshall.) Oxford D.Phil. (Mod. Hist.)

523 The mendicant presence in Latin Greece: the Franciscan and Dominican orders in the Peloponnese, 1204–1500. Lori A.F. Ribeiro. (Professor E.M. Jeffreys.) Oxford D.Phil. (Mod. Hist.)

524 The transmission of Latin philosophical and theological writings in late Byzantium. Rizos M. Konstantinou. (Dr. Charalambos Dendrinos.) London M.Phil./Ph.D. (R.H.U.L. Hist.)

525 National identity and cross-Channel land tenure, 1204–59. Jessica Rosenthal Mcgrath. (Dr. Benjamin Thompson.) Oxford M.St. (Mod. Hist.)

526 The construction of individual religious criminality in southern France: heresy, the Albigensian Crusade (1209–29) and beyond. Timothy McManus. (Dr. Claire Taylor and Dr. Rossano Balzaretti.) Nottingham Ph.D. (Hist.)

527 The political functions of the translation ceremonies of saints' relics in England, 1215–83. Kalil J. Copley. (Dr. Ian Forrest.) Oxford M.St. (Mod. Hist.)

528 England in Europe during the reign of Henry III, 1216–72. Lucy Hennings. (Dr. John L. Watts.) Oxford D.Phil. (Mod. Hist.)

529 The Holy Land pilgrimage of Thietmar (*c*.1217–18). Philip Booth. (Professor Andrew Jotischky.) Lancaster Ph.D. (Hist.)

530 Matthew Paris's networks of information. Nathan Greasley. (Professor Björn K.U. Weiler and Dr. Rhun Emlyn.) Aberystwyth Ph.D. (Hist. & Welsh Hist.)

531 Matthew Paris and his collaborators: scribes at St. Albans' scriptorium (1230–59). Manuel Munoz Garcia. (Professor Julia Crick and Dr. Peter Stokes.) King's College London M.Phil./Ph.D. (Hist.)

532 Constructing dynastic Franciscan identities in Bohemia and the Polish duchies. Kirsty Day. (Professor Emilia M. Jamroziak and Dr. Melanie Brunner.) Leeds Ph.D. (Med. Stud.)

533 Heresy and the military organisation of the crusades against the Hohenstaufen (1239–68) and Stedinger (1232–34). Michelle T. Hufschmid. (Dr. Christopher Tyerman.) Oxford D.Phil. (Mod. Hist.)

534 *Articuli reprobati contra theologicam veritatem*: the propositions condemned at the University of Paris in 1241. Deborah M. Grice. (Dr. Matthew Kempshall.) Oxford D.Phil. (Mod. Hist.)

535 Copying activity in Thessalonike in the Palaeologan period, 1246–1430. Panayiotis Tofis. (Dr. Charalambos Dendrinos.) London Ph.D. (R.H.U.L. Hist.)

536 Noble families, power, family and identity: the Bohuns, 1249–1399. Lucia Pascual. (Dr. Nigel E. Saul.) London M.Phil./Ph.D. (R.H.U.L. Hist.)

537 A spark of synderesis: Bonaventure's development of the concept of synderesis and its late medieval reception, 1250–1400. Gustav Zamore. (Dr. Annie Sutherland and Dr. Lesley Smith.) Oxford D.Phil. (Mod. Hist.)

538 The Italian cities and the fall of the Latin East: trade, diplomacy and conflict, 1250–91. Oliver Berrou. (Professor Jonathan P. Phillips.) London M.Phil./Ph.D. (R.H.U.L. Hist.)

539 The historical, biographical and intellectual context of John of Garland's *De Triumphis Ecclesiae*: a new critical edition. Martin Hall. (Professor Jonathan P. Phillips.) London M.Phil./Ph.D. (R.H.U.L. Hist.)

540 The early history of the florin. Stefano Locatelli. (Dr. Georg Christ and Dr. Paul Oldfield.) Manchester Ph.D. (Hist.)

541 The Lord Edward and the earldom of Chester: lordship and community, 1254–72. Rodolphe Billaud. (Professor Louise J. Wilkinson.) Canterbury Christ Church M.Phil. (Hist.)

542 The narrative and heraldic painted glass in the chapter house of York Minster. Hilary Moxon. (Dr. Jane Hawkes and Dr. Jeanne Nuechterlein.) York Ph.D. (Hist. of Art)

543 The diocese of Sarai: ideological transmission between the city and the steppe. Neil O'Docherty. (Dr. Jonathan Shepard and Dr. Mark Whittow.) Oxford M.Phil. (Mod. Hist.)

544 The representation of nature in Palaiologan literature. Kirsty L. Stewart. (Professor Marc Lauxtermann.) Oxford D.Phil. (Mod. Hist.)

545 The conduct of the Barons' War of 1264–7 between King Henry III and the baronial opposition. Fergus P.W. Oakes. (Professor Matthew J. Strickland and Dr. Stephen Marritt.) Glasgow Ph.D. (Arts)

546 'My well-beloved companion': men, women, marriage and power in the earldom and duchy of Lancaster, 1265–1399. Rebecca Holdorph. (Professor Anne Curry.) Southampton Ph.D. (Hist.)

547 Italian mosaic art, 1270–1529. Carol Ann Hydes. (Professors Elizabeth A. James and Michelle O'Malley.) Sussex D.Phil. (Hist. of Art)

548 The bishop and his diocese: rethinking diocesan policy and administration with evidence from the episcopal registers, 1272–1327. James Richardson. (Dr. Sethina Watson.) York Ph.D. (Hist.)

549 Vows and freedom in Dante Alighieri. Evelina Piscione. (Dr. Serena Ferente and Dr. Alice Taylor.) King's College London M.Phil./Ph.D. (Hist.)

550 Insular saints' cults in late medieval Scotland, *c.*1286–1542. Tom Turpie. (Dr. Stephen I. Boardman.) Edinburgh Ph.D. (Hist.)

551 The papacy and the eastern Mediterranean, 1291–1362. James Hill. (Professor Graham A. Loud and Dr. Melanie Brunner.) Leeds Ph.D. (Med. Stud.)

Fourteenth century

552 A repository of knowledge and a cultural artefact: the place of the guild book of the Barber Surgeons of York in the history of vernacular English medical manuscripts. Richard D. Wragg. (Professor Michelle P. Brown and Mr. Peter Murray Jones.) London Ph.D. (Inst. Eng. Stud.)

553 The spiritual privileges of the late medieval English laity, c.1300–1540. Angela Clark. (Professor Michael A. Hicks and Dr. Elena C. Woodacre.) Winchester M.Phil./Ph.D. (Hist.)

554 Glittering beasts: the patronage and craft culture of heraldic stained glass in England, c.1300–1540. Oliver Fearon. (Ms. Sarah Brown.) York Ph.D. (Hist. of Art)

555 The role of the English honorary officers of state in the late medieval ages. Kristina Afford. (Professor Michael A. Hicks and Dr. James Ross.) Winchester M.Phil./Ph.D. (Hist.)

556 Reading and visual processing in late medieval England. Lucy Allen. York Ph.D. (Med. Stud.)

557 Anglo-Scottish-Flemish macroeconomic history: prices, wages and money supply, 1300–1500. Katherine L. Ball. (Dr. Nick Mayhew.) Oxford D.Phil. (Mod. Hist.)

558 Monuments and marriage in late medieval England: origins, function and reception of double tombs. Jessica Barker. (Professor John Lowden.) London Ph.D. (Courtauld Inst.)

559 Man in a red hat, St. Mary's Church, Fairford: the creation of a remarkable late medieval glazing scheme. Keith Barley. (Dr. Jeanne Nuechterlein.) York M.A. by Research. (Hist. of Art)

560 The Stanley family and its reputation in the later middle ages. Kate Bicknell. (Professors Anne Curry and George Bernard.) Southampton M.Phil. (Hist.)

561 Lay women's religion in late medieval England. Katie Clark. (Professor Michael A. Hicks and Dr. Carolin Esser-Miles.) Winchester Ph.D. (Hist.)

562 Pregnancy and childbirth in late medieval England. Claire Collins. (Dr. Anne Lawrence.) Reading Ph.D. (Hist.)

563 The 'Christ-knight' and military culture in late medieval sermons. Jennifer R. Depold. (Dr. Ian Forrest.) Oxford D.Phil. (Mod. Hist.)

564 Visionary literature for devotional instruction: its function and transmission in late medieval observant female religious communities in north-western Europe. Clarck Drieshen. (Professor Emilia M. Jamroziak and Dr. Catherine Batt.) Leeds Ph.D. (Med. Stud.)

565 English seafarer communities in the later middle ages: a study in socio-economics and geographical mobility of a multi-faceted occupational group. Brenna Gibson. (Dr. Craig Lambert and Professor Chris Woolgar.) Southampton Ph.D. (Hist.)

566 Negotiating the later medieval life-cycle through image and text in western Europe. Sara Gordon. (Dr. Martin Kauffmann and Dr. Benjamin Thompson.) Oxford D.Phil. (Mod. Hist.)

567 Aspects of cultural interaction in the late medieval Adriatic world: art and devotion. Milena Grabacic. (Dr. Gervase Rosser and Dr. Catherine J. Holmes.) Oxford D.Phil. (Mod. Hist.)

568 The use of late medieval edged weapons. James Hester. (Professor Anne Curry.) Southampton M.Phil. (Hist.)

569 Commerce or status: the emergence of the late medieval middle class. Hannah Ingram. (Dr. Richard Goddard and Dr. Rob Lutton.) Nottingham Ph.D. (Hist.)

570 No two alike: the representation of space in English local maps in the late middle ages. Beth Kaneko. (Dr. Sethina Watson and Dr. Tom Nickson.) York Ph.D. (Med. Stud.)

571 The symbiotic relationship between parish elites and less privileged parishioners. Jessica Lee. (Dr. Tim Ayers and Dr. Sethina Watson.) York Ph.D. (Med. Stud.)

572 Wounded bodies and performed masculinities in late medieval knighthood. Jack Litchfield. (Dr. Iona M. McCleery and Dr. Catherine Batt.) Leeds Ph.D. (Med. Hist)

573 Painted architecture and pictorial place: the representation of architecture in Italy in the 14th and 15th centuries. Livia Lupi. (Dr. Amanda Lillie.) York Ph.D. (Hist. of Art)

574 'Lewed pepul loven tales olde': preaching, populism and the useful past in later medieval England. David Mason. (Dr. Ian Forrest.) Oxford M.St. (Mod. Hist.)

575 Between the sheets: reading beds and chambers in late medieval England. Hollie Morgan. (Dr. P. Jeremy P. Goldberg and Dr. Nicola F. McDonald.) York Ph.D. (Med. Stud.)

576 Conceptions of purgatory and sleep imagery in *The Lanterne of Light* and other late medieval English writings. Patrick J. Outhwaite. (Dr. Kantik Ghosh and Dr. Ian Forrest.) Oxford M.St. (Mod. Hist.)

577 Symbols and ceremonies: the influence of the classical past on public ritual in late medieval Rome. Dhwani Patel. (Dr. Serena Ferente and Professor Peter Heather.) King's College London M.Phil./Ph.D. (Hist.)

578 Disability in the later middle ages. Alison Purnell. (Dr. P. Jeremy P. Goldberg and Dr. Nicola F. McDonald.) York M.Phil. (Med. Stud.)

579 In the image of the Holy Family: ideals and obligations of Christian parenthood and their transmission to parents in late medieval England. Mary E. Russell. (Dr. Benjamin J. Thompson.) Oxford D.Phil. (Mod. Hist.)

580 Parks, gardens and designed landscapes of medieval north Wales and north-west Shropshire. Spencer Smith. (Dr. Kathryn Hurlock, Dr. Anthony J. Adams and Dr. Ben Edwards.) Manchester Metropolitan Ph.D. (Hist.)

581 The development of firearms in late medieval England. Daniel Spencer. (Professor Anne Curry.) Southampton Ph.D. (Hist.)

582 Late medieval London society. Adele Sykes. (Dr. Clive R. Burgess.) London Ph.D. (R.H.U.L. Hist.)

583 Hospitality in a Cistercian abbey: the case of Kirkstall in the later middle ages. Richard Thomason. (Professor Emilia M. Jamroziak and Mrs. Katherine Baxter.) Leeds Ph.D. (Med. Stud.)

584 Sir Gawain, St. Winefride and the Virgin Mary: cult and chivalry in the late middle ages. Charles R. Turner. (Dr. Deborah Youngs.) Swansea Ph.D. (Hist.)

585 Chaucer, Lydgate and Gower and the influence of medieval Latin literature and classical philosophy in the construction and representation of gender in the late middle ages. Marie Walmsley. (Professor Pat Cullum.) Huddersfield M.A. (Music, Hum. & Media)

586 Determining the distinctiveness of rich and poor areas in late medieval towns and cities. Mark Webb. (Deirdre O'Sullivan and Dr. Ruth Young.) Leicester Ph.D. (Archaeol. & Anc. Hist.)

587 Tapestry and gender: the Neuf Preux and the Neuf Preuses tapestries' potential for identity formation at the Burgundian and French courts of the 14th and 15th centuries. Romina Westphal. (Professors Rosalind Brown-Grant and Brigitt Borkopp-Restle and Dr. Eva Frojmovic.) Leeds Ph.D. (Med. Stud.)

588 Anglo-French tournaments during the 14th and 15th centuries. Rachel E. Whitbread. (Dr. Craig Taylor.) York Ph.D. (Hist.)

589 Seeing 'through a glass darkly': kinetic and temporal semantics in the dramatic and visual culture of late medieval England. Sian C.V. Witherden. (Dr. Gervase Rosser and Dr. Jane Griffiths.) Oxford M.St. (Mod. Hist.)

590 Late medieval mural paintings in Poor Clares' convents. Michaela Zoschg. (Dr. Joanna L. Cannon.) London Ph.D. (Courtauld Inst.)

591 Cornwall and the kingdom: connectivity, mobility and integration, 1300–1420. Samuel Drake. (Professor Nigel E. Saul.) London Ph.D. (R.H.U.L. Hist.)

592 The rise of the Nevilles and Percies: aristocratic identities in 14th-century art and architecture. Isobel Armstrong-Frost. (Dr. Tim Ayers.) York Ph.D. (Hist. of Art)

593 The influence of digital media on the study of medieval music manuscripts: monophonic secular song in 14th-century France. Samantha Blickham. (Dr. Helen Deeming.) London Ph.D. (R.H.U.L. Music)

594 Chivalry in 14th-century England and Wales. Laura Callingham. (Dr. Brendan Smith and Dr. Marianne Ailes.) Bristol M.Litt. (Hist. Stud.)

595 Wills and the negotiation of Jewish identity in 14th-century Crete. Erin Claiborne. (Dr. Catherine Holmes.) Oxford M.St. (Mod. Hist.)

596 Marino Sanudo: the geographical knowledge of an Italian merchant in the 14th century. Jacqueline Derrick. (Dr. Sophie Page.) London Ph.D. (U.C. Hist.)

597 The role and identity of household knights in 14th-century England. Pierre Gaite. (Professor Helen Nicholson.) Cardiff Ph.D. (Hist. & Archaeol.)

598 Fourteenth-century history of the London Armourers' Company and their involvement in the war in France. Brad Kirkland. (Professor Linne Mooney and Dr. Sarah R. Rees Jones.) York Ph.D. (Med. Stud.)

599   Sussex and the sea: the economic and cultural links in the 14th century.   Helen Mbye.   (Dr. Nicholas Karn and Dr. Craig Lambert.)   Southampton M.Phil.   (Hist.)

600   Gentry perceptions of violence in the 14th century.   Rhian McLaughlin.   (Professor W. Mark Ormrod.)   York Ph.D.   (Hist.)

601   Cistercian patronage and artistic practice in trecento Tuscany.   John Renner.   (Dr. Joanna L. Cannon.)   London Ph.D.   (Courtauld Inst.)

602   Mendicant poverty in poetry and reality in 14th-century England.   Bridget Riley.   (Dr. Rebecca Rist.)   Reading Ph.D.   (Med. Stud.)

603   The church in 14th-century Ireland.   Paul Seage.   (Dr. Brendan Smith and Dr. James Clark.)   Bristol M.Litt.   (Hist. Stud.)

604   The abbey at St. Albans and its civic control over the town in the 14th century. Rebecca Toefper.   (Dr. Nicholas Karn and Professor Peter Clarke.)   Southampton M.Phil.   (Hist.)

605   The queen's lands: examining the role of queens as female lords in 14th-century England.   Katia Wright.   (Dr. Elena C. Wooadacre and Dr. James Ross.) Winchester M.Phil./Ph.D.   (Hist.)

606   The templar lands in Lincolnshire in the early 14th century.   Mike Jefferson.   (Dr. Gwilym Dodd and Dr. Richard Goddard.)   Nottingham Ph.D.   (Hist.)

607   Providence and excerption of the Lancelot-Grail Cycle in early 14th-century England. Charles H. Roe.   (Dr. Sophie Marnette and Dr. Laura Ashe.)   Oxford M.St.   (Mod. Hist.)

608   The life and career of Richard Fitzalan, earl of Arundel and Surrey (*c*.1307–76): a study in 14th-century aristocratic power.   Michael Burtscher.   (Dr. Malcolm G.A. Vale and Dr. Rowena E. Archer.)   Oxford D.Phil.   (Mod. Hist.)

609   Dante's christology: finding Christ in the *Commedia*.   Rory Sellgren.   (Dr. Matthew Treherne and Dr. Mark R. Wynn.)   Leeds Ph.D.   (Med. Stud.)

610   The illuminated manuscripts of Helgafell.   Stefan Drechsler.   (Dr. Hannah Burrows and Professor Jane Geddes.)   Aberdeen Ph.D.   (Hist.)

611   An annotated translation of Emperor John VI Kantakouzenos' *History*, Book III.   Brian McLaughlin.   (Dr. Charalambos Dendrinos.)   London M.Phil./Ph.D.   (R.H.U.L. Hist.)

612   The Gascoigne family of Yorkshire, from Edward III to Henry VIII.   Christopher Bovis.   (Dr. Jonathan Finch and Professor Mark W. Ormrod.)   York Ph.D.   (Med. Stud.)

613   The late medieval reception of the *Polychronicon*.   Edwina Thorn.   (Dr. James Clark and Dr. Anke Holdenried.)   Bristol Ph.D.   (Hist. Stud.)

614   The significance of local patrons in the nave windows of York Minster.   Anastassia J. Dimmek.   (Dr. Gervase Rosser.)   Oxford M.St.   (Mod. Hist.)

615   The devotional ivory booklet, Cologne (V&A).   Georgina Lee.   (Dr. Gervase Rosser.) Oxford M.St.   (Mod. Hist.)

616   Edward III's affinity in war and peace, 1337–69.   Matthew Hefferan.   (Dr. Gwilym Dodd and Dr. James Bothwell.)   Nottingham Ph.D.   (Hist.)

617 Negotiating authority in 14th-century France: Jeanne de Penthièvre, duchess of Brittany. Erika M. Graham. (Dr. Craig D. Taylor.) York Ph.D. (Hist.)

618 Women in business in Genoese Chios (1346–1566). Chiara Ravera. (Dr. Ross Balzaretti and Dr. Richard Goddard.) Nottingham Ph.D. (Hist.)

619 All the king's men: chivalry and the military aristocracy of England from Crécy to the death of Edward III. Matthew Thompson. (Dr. Andrew Ayton.) Hull Ph.D. (Hist.)

620 The Caroline myth? Reassessing the role of Charles IV's patronage in bringing the Gothic to Bohemia. Thomas R. Price. (Dr. Gervase Rosser.) Oxford M.St. (Mod. Hist.)

621 Ladies of the garter, c.1348–1461: royal patronage and female political agency in late medieval England. Chloe McKenzie. (Professors Anne Curry and Maria Hayward.) Southampton M.Phil. (Hist.)

622 The impact of the Black Death (1348–9): comparison of life courses of the clergy and the rural community of Winchester diocese. John Merrimen. (Dr. Rebecca Oakes and Dr. Christina Welch.) Winchester M.Phil./Ph.D. (Hist.)

623 Humoral theory circulating in religious literature in England c.1350–1540. Rebecca Maryan. (Dr. Rob Lutton and Dr. Ross Balzaretti.) Nottingham Ph.D. (Hist.)

624 Women, wives, widows and wards in the Inquisitions Post Mortem, 1350–1509. Joanna Arman. (Professor Michael A. Hicks and Dr. James Ross.) Winchester M.Phil./Ph.D. (Hist.)

625 Associative political culture in the Holy Roman Empire: the Upper Rhine, c.1350–1500. Duncan Hardy. (Dr. John L. Watts.) Oxford D.Phil. (Mod. Hist.)

626 Preaching and penitence in the age of observance: the *summa confessorum* of the Franciscan Nicholas of Osimo and the economic ethics of Observant Franciscans in the late middle ages (c.1350–c.1453). Andrea Mancini. (Dr. Melanie Brunner and Professor Emilia M. Jamroziak.) Leeds Ph.D. (Med. Stud)

627 Dance and visual culture in Tuscany, c.1350–1450. Jasmine M. Chiu. (Dr. Gervase Rosser.) Oxford D.Phil. (Mod. Hist.)

628 Royal women in late 14th-century England. Louise Tingle. (Dr. Bronah Kane.) Cardiff Ph.D. (Hist. & Archaeol.)

629 An annotated edition of the unpublished metaphrasis of St. John of Sinai's *Ladder of Divine Ascent* by Matthaios Blastares. Elliot Mason. (Dr. Charalambos Dendrinos.) London M.Phil./Ph.D. (R.H.U.L. Hist.)

630 The politics of the Gascon wine trade, c.1360–1453. Robert Blackmore. (Professor Anne Curry.) Southampton M.Phil. (Hist.)

631 Margins and marginality in 15th-century London, 1370–1520. Charlotte Berry. (Professor Matthew Davies.) London M.Phil./Ph.D. (Inst. Hist. Res.)

632 Relationships between urban and aristocratic power structures in England, 1377–1500. Tom Graham. (Dr. John L. Watts.) Oxford D.Phil. (Mod. Hist.)

633 Political propaganda in England, c.1377–1485. Sarah Gaunt. (Professor Timothy J. Thornton.) Huddersfield Ph.D. (Music, Hum. & Media)

634 Diplomatic encounters between England and the Baltic/Central European powers, 1377–1461. Lauren Bowers. (Dr. Craig D. Taylor.) York Ph.D. (Hist.)

635 Conceiving individuality and emotions: English rhetorical approaches to war and peace, 1377–1422. Trevor Smith. (Dr. Alan V. Murray and Dr. Catherine Batt.) Leeds Ph.D. (Med. Stud.)

636 Mirrors for princes and Charles VI. Kristin L.E. Bourassa. (Dr. Craig Taylor.) York Ph.D. (Hist.)

637 Military ordinances: the development of the English army, 1385–1585. Andrew Martinez. (Professor Anne Curry.) Southampton M.Phil. (Hist.)

638 The guild returns of 1388–9: a comparative examination of English guilds on a national level at the end of the 14th century. Claire Kennan. (Professor Nigel E. Saul.) London M.Phil./Ph.D. (R.H.U.L. Hist.)

639 Church, state, and Reformation: the use and interpretation of *praemunire* from its creation to the English break with Rome. Daniel Gosling. (Professor Stephen Alford.) Leeds Ph.D. (Hist.)

640 The burgesses and abbey of Cirencester, 1399–1539. Natasha Catling. (Dr. James Clark.) Bristol M.Phil. (Hist. Stud.)

Fifteenth century

641 Communities on the move: the transformation of communities of women religious in late medieval and early modern England. Elizabeth Goodwin. (Professor Martial J.M. Staub.) Sheffield Ph.D. (Hist.)

642 A consideration of painted wooden tympana, *c.*1400–*c.*1700, in English churches. Terence Nixon. (Professor Tim Ayers.) York Ph.D. (Hist. of Art)

643 Investigating the battlefield burial practices and the wider social attitudes of the English to battlefield casualties from the 15th to the 17th century. Sarah Taylor. (Dr. Glenn Foard.) Huddersfield M.Phil. (Music, Hum. & Media)

644 Gendering desecrated bodies: female martyrs, criminals and other sinners in pictures of punishment during the Florentine Renaissance. Yoojeong An. (Dr. Geraldine Johnson.) Oxford M.St. (Mod. Hist.)

645 Re-purposing in the Renaissance? A case study of a newly acquired medieval astrolabe at the Museum of the History of Science. Lynn G. Atkin. (Dr. Stephen Johnston and Professor Silke Ackermann.) Oxford M.Sc. (Mod. Hist.)

646 The role of astrology in the cultural interchanges between Portugal, Burgundy and England. Helena Avelar de Carvalho. (Professor Charles S.F. Burnett and Dr. Guido Giglioni.) London Ph.D. (Warburg)

647 On the cusp of *fabula* and *historia*: the myth of Alexander the Great in Italy between the 15th and 16th century. Claudia Daniotti. (Professor Jill A. Kraye and Dr. Alessandro Scafi.) London Ph.D. (Warburg)

648 Identity and integration of the post-Byzantine diaspora in central Italy during the 15th and 16th centuries. Niccolo Fattori. (Dr. Jonathan P. Harris.) London Ph.D. (R.H.U.L. Hist.)

649   The medieval conception of the Greco-Roman goddesses and its impact and reception in the arts, literature and philosophy of the 15th and 16th centuries in Italy. Lorenza Gay. (Dr. Paul Taylor and Dr. Rembrandt Duits.) London Ph.D. (Warburg)

650   Lay devotion and the expansion of *contempus mundi* piety in 15th- and 16th-century Europe. David Harry. (Dr. James Clark and Dr. Anke Holdenried.) Bristol Ph.D. (Hist. Stud.)

651   Image, place and light: towards a typology of the background in Italian Renaissance painting. Ang Li. (Dr. Geraldine Johnson.) Oxford D.Phil. (Mod. Hist.)

652   Possession, consumption and choice: networks of exchange, *c.*1400–1600. Lisa Liddy. (Dr. Sarah R. Rees Jones and Dr. Ailsa Mainman.) York M.Phil./Ph.D. (Hist.)

653   Courtesans in Renaissance Venice and Florence: female networks and family relationships in two republics. Katherine T.A. Lim. (Dr. N.S. Davidson.) Oxford D.Phil. (Mod. Hist.)

654   'Coming of age': youth in England, 1400–1600. Sarah Mawhinney. (Dr. P. Jeremy P. Goldberg.) York Ph.D. (Hist.)

655   The Blount family of Shropshire: a gentry family in the 15th and 16th centuries. Elizabeth Norton. (Dr. Lucy Kostyanovsky and Dr. Laura Gowing.) King's College London M.Phil./Ph.D. (Hist.)

656   Reflections of the Venetian Republic in the 15th- and 16th-century waterfront facades of Murano. Hannah J. Olsen-Shaw. (Dr. Geraldine Johnson.) Oxford M.St. (Mod. Hist.)

657   The Renaissance studio and the development of the self. Peter Scott. (Dr. Kenneth Austin and Dr. Fernando Cervantes.) Bristol M.Litt. (Hist. Stud.)

658   Spirituality and the everyday: a history of the Cistercian convent of Günterstal in the 15th and 16th centuries. Edmund H. Wareham. (Professor Lyndal A. Roper.) Oxford D.Phil. (Mod. Hist.)

659   Forging masculinity: representations of St. George and the dragon in Renaissance Italy. Arthur B. Wells. (Dr. Geraldine Johnson.) Oxford M.St. (Mod. Hist.)

660   The typology and use of staff weapons in Western Europe *c.*1400–*c.*1550. Iason-Eleftherios Tzouriadis. (Dr. Karen Watts and Dr. Alan V. Murray.) Leeds Ph.D. (Med. Stud.)

661   Crown finances in 15th-century England. Alex Brayson. (Professor W. Mark Ormrod.) York Ph.D. (Hist.)

662   The fullness of time: temporalities of the 15th-century Low Countries. Matthew Champion. (Professor Miri E. Rubin.) London Ph.D. (Q.M. Hist.)

663   Illustrated vernacular narratives of the life of Jesus Christ and the Virgin and the characteristics of popular devotion in quattrocento Venice. Lisandra S. Costiner. (Dr. Martin Kauffmann and Dr. A. Gervase Rosser.) Oxford D.Phil. (Mod. Hist.)

664   The business of pilgrimage in 15th-century Venice. Laura Di Stefano. (Dr. Rob Lutton and Dr. Ross Balzaretti.) Nottingham Ph.D. (Hist.)

665 Russian conservatism and populism in the 15th century. George Gilbert. East Anglia Ph.D. (Hist.)

666 Illuminating narrative: an interdisciplinary investigation of the 15th-century St. Cuthbert Window at York Minster. Katharine Harrison. (Ms. Sarah Brown and Professor Tim Ayers.) York Ph.D. (Hist. of Art)

667 'To know a gentilman': men and gentry culture in 15th-century Yorkshire. Alison James. (Dr. P. Jeremy P. Goldberg and Dr. Tim Ayers.) York Ph.D. (Med. Stud.)

668 Collaborative book production in 15th-century London. Holly James-Maddocks. (Professor Linne Mooney and Dr. Jeanne Nuechterlein.) York Ph.D. (Med. Stud.)

669 Reconfiguring the role of credit in 15th-century England. Hannah Robb. (Dr. Charles Insley and Dr. Georg Christ.) Manchester Ph.D. (Hist.)

670 The 15th-century Tocchi lordships in the Adriatic. Robin Shields. (Dr. Jonathan P. Harris.) London M.Phil./Ph.D. (R.H.U.L. Hist.)

671 Blood on the crown: treason among royal kinship groups in 15th-century England. Sarah Stockdale. (Dr. James Ross and Dr. Ellie Woodacre.) Winchester M.Phil./Ph.D. (Hist.)

672 English 'career' soldiers in the 15th century: a socio-economic re-examination. Thomas Wex. (Dr. James Ross and Dr. Ryan Lavelle.) Winchester M.Phil./Ph.D. (Hist.)

673 The history of 15th-century English kingship. Andrew R. Whittle. East Anglia Ph.D. (Hist.)

674 Between Venice and Milan: the making of boundaries and frontiers in 15th-century northern Italy. Luca Zenobi. (Dr. John L. Watts and Dr. Nicholas Davidson.) Oxford D.Phil. (Mod. Hist.)

675 The life and career of Richard Neville, 5th earl of Salisbury (1400–60). Edward A. Shine. (Dr. James A. Ross and Professor Michael A. Hicks.) Winchester M.Phil./Ph.D. (Hist.)

676 How did Christine de Pizan self-consciously construct and illuminate her manuscripts in order to create an authoritative persona as an author? Charlotte E. Cooper-Richardson. (Dr. Helen Swift.) Oxford M.St. (Mod. Hist.)

677 A study of first secretary of the Milanese Ducal Chancery, Cicco Simonetta (1410–80). Oliver Williams. (Dr. Serena Ferente and Dr. Filippo De Vivo.) King's College London M.Phil./Ph.D. (Hist.)

678 Town, crown and urban system: the position of towns in the English polity, 1413–71. Eliza Hartrich. (Dr. John L. Watts.) Oxford D.Phil. (Mod. Hist.)

679 Art and performance in the work of Fra Angelico. Barbara Berrington. (Professor Paul Davies.) Reading Ph.D. (Hist. of Art)

680 Retinue structures in Henry V's army of 1415. Michael Warner. (Professor Anne Curry and Dr. Craig Lambert.) Southampton M.Phil. (Hist.)

682 Religious and racial minorities in the MSS. and cultural milieu of Robert Thornton, Yorkshire gentleman, fl.1418–56. Jennifer Bartlett. (Professor W. Mark Ormrod and Dr. Nicola McDonald.) York Ph.D. (Med. Stud.)

683 Spiritual provision and temporal affirmation: tombs of *les chevaliers*. Anne Adams. (Professor Susie M. Nash.) London Ph.D. (Courtauld Inst.)

684 Representations of donors' children in Bruges panel painting. Harriette Peel. (Professor Susie M. Nash.) London Ph.D. (Courtauld Inst.)

685 The Feuerwekbuch: tradition and change in the early evolution of gunpowder weaponry. Axel Muller. (Professor Tim Thornton.) Huddersfield M.Phil. (Music, Hum. & Media)

686 The reception and implementation of local and parliamentary legislation in England, 1422–*c*.1485. Dean Rowland. (Professor Matthew Davies.) London Ph.D. (Inst. Hist. Res.)

687 Kingship, counsel and service: ideas and practice of government, 1424–1513. Claire Hawes. (Dr. Michael H. Brown.) St. Andrews Ph.D. (Hist.)

688 A civic palimpsest: the fresco paintings of the first floor *salone* of the Palazzo della Ragione, Padua, Italy. Darrelyn Gunzburg. (Dr. Beth Williamson and Professor Ronald Hutton.) Bristol Ph.D. (Hist. Stud.)

689 The politics and ramifications of crusade rhetoric in late medieval and early modern Scottish statecraft, 1437–1542. Katharine Basanti. (Professor William Naphy and Dr. Alastair Macdonald.) Aberdeen Ph.D. (Hist.)

690 Castell Penrhyn. Catrin Wager. (Dr. Lowri Ann Rees.) Bangor Ph.D. (Hist., Welsh Hist. & Archaeol.)

691 The reception of John Chrysostom and the study of ancient Christianity in early modern Europe, *c*.1440–1600. Sam Kennerley. (Scott Mandelbrote.) Cambridge Ph.D. (Hist.)

692 Royal couples and religion, 1445–1536. Hannah Jackson. (Dr. Sarah Bastow.) Huddersfield M.Phil. (Music, Hum. & Media)

693 Patronage, fame and memory in Renaissance Spain: Juan and Diego Pacheco, Marquises of Villena, 1445–1529. Maria Theresa. (Dr. Guido Giglioni and Professor Alastair Hamilton.) London Ph.D. (Warburg)

694 *In modo guerrino*: change and continuity of elite conceptions of violence in England, 1450–1560. Mark R. Geldof. (Dr. Steven J. Gunn.) Oxford D.Phil. (Mod. Hist.)

695 Great Yarmouth: politics and trade, *c*.1450–*c*.1550. Michael Boon. (Professor Caroline M. Barron.) London M.Phil./Ph.D. (R.H.U.L. Hist.)

696 The materiality of physical impairment: mobility and daily living aids, 1450–1550. Rachael Gillibrand. (Dr. Iona M. McCleery and Dr. Eva Frojmovic.) Leeds Ph.D. (Med. Stud.)

697 Vowesses in the province of Canterbury, 1450–1540. Laura Wood. (Dr. Clive R. Burgess.) London M.Phil./Ph.D. (R.H.U.L. Hist.)

698 A comparative study of the impact of civil war on local political society in medieval and early modern Hampshire. Lucy Lynch. (Dr. David Appleby and Dr. Gwilym Dodd.) Nottingham M.Phil. (Hist.)

699 Black powder small arms in the Wars of the Roses – a re-assessment. Sam Wilson. (Dr. Glenn Foard.) Huddersfield M.Phil. (Music, Hum. & Media)

700   The tournament and its role in the court culture of Emperor Maximilian I (1459–1519). Natalie Anderson. (Dr. Alan V. Murray and Dr. Karen Watts.) Leeds Ph.D. (Med. Stud.)

701   Expression and the landscape: the Leicestershire gentry, *c.*1460– *c.*1540. Katie Bridger. (Dr. Richard Jones and Dr. Andrew J. Hopper.) Leicester Ph.D. (Eng. Loc. Hist.)

702   The display of status, authority and nobility in 15th-century manuscripts with specific focus on Flemish manuscript production and the patronage of Louis de Bruges, Lord of Gruuthuse. Justin Sturgeon. (Dr. Craig Taylor and Dr. Jeanne Nuechterlein.) York Ph.D. (Med. Stud.)

703   Public display and the construction of monarchy in Yorkist England, 1460–85. Carolyn Donohue. (Dr. Craig Taylor.) York Ph.D. (Hist.)

704   A study of the *Historia Byzantina* of Doukas. Christopher Hobbs. (Professor Jonathan Harris.) London M.Phil./Ph.D. (R.H.U.L. Hist.)

705   All the queen's jewels: an examination of English queenship through the changing personal and ceremonial collection of royal jewellery, 1464–1547. Nicola Tallis. (Dr. Elena C. Woodacre and Professor Michael A. Hicks.) Winchester M.Phil./Ph.D. (Hist.)

706   The shaping of popular history: the cases of Anne Neville and Elizabeth of York. Lauren Browne. (Dr. James Davis.) Belfast Ph.D. (Hist. & Anthr.)

707   Margaret of Denmark: Scottish queenship, 1469–86. Amy Hayes. (Dr. Jackson Armstrong and Dr. Alastair Macdonald.) Aberdeen Ph.D. (Hist.)

708   Material mnemonics and social relationships in London, 1470–1530. Anna C. Boeles Rowland. (Dr. Ian Forrest.) Oxford D.Phil. (Mod. Hist.)

709   Tucker's Hall. Tamsin Bailey. (Dr. Jonathan Barry.) Exeter M.Phil. (Hist.)

710   Early printing in Catalonia in its political and religious context, 1472–1502. Laura Merino i Pastor. (Professor I.W.F. MacLean and Dr. C.H. Griffin.) Oxford D.Phil. (Mod. Hist.)

711   Chivalry and manhood in late 15th- and early 16th-century England. Emma Levitt. (Professor Keith Laybourn.) Huddersfield Ph.D. (Music, Hum. & Media)

712   Millenarian and reform thought in Renaissance Italy at the end of the 15th century: Giles of Viterbo and Savonarola on church and papacy. Ross Greenhill. (Dr. Matthew Kempshall.) Oxford M.St. (Mod. Hist.)

713   The French campaign of Edward IV in 1475. Michael Lawn. (Professor Nigel E. Saul.) London M.Phil./Ph.D. (R.H.U.L. Hist.)

714   Venetian humanism in the Mediterranean world: writing empire from the margins. Erin N. Maglaque. (Dr. Catherine Holmes and Dr. Nick Davidson.) Oxford D.Phil. (Mod. Hist.)

715   Hernando de Baeza. Teresa Tinsley. Exeter M.Phil. (Hist.)

716   The Mores of Loseley: three generations of a Surrey family. Eliza Wheaton. (Professor Nigel E. Saul.) London M.Phil./Ph.D. (R.H.U.L. Hist.)

717 The integration of the Palatinate of Durham into the Tudor state, c.1484–1547. Edward Geall. (Professor Peter Marshall.) Warwick Ph.D. (Hist.)

718 Martyrs' blood in Reformation England. Anastasia Stylianou. (Professor Rebecca Earle and Peter Marshall.) Warwick M.Phil./Ph.D. (Hist.)

719 The artisan in Tudor Southampton: burgess, freeman or alien. Louise Fairbrother. (Professors Mark Stoyle and Maria Hayward.) Southampton M.Phil. (Hist.)

720 Humanist to godly? Changes in English grammar school education, c.1485–1603. Emily Hansen. (Professor David Wootton.) York Ph.D. (Hist.)

721 Negotiating earthly and spiritual duty: nonconformist women, their families and the path to martyrdom in Tudor England. Charlotte Szepticky. (Dr. Anna French and Professor Melanie J. Ilic.) Gloucestershire M.A. (Hum.)

722 The sunne in splendour: the posthumous reputation of King Edward IV, 1485–1603. Stephanie L. Tracy. (Dr. Tracey Sowerby.) Oxford M.St. (Mod. Hist.)

723 *The Possessions of the Kingdome of Heauen Remaineth to those that Harbour Strangers*: Protestant approaches to hospitality in Elizabethan England. Rebecca Walker. (Dr. Sarah Bastow.) Huddersfield M.A. (Music, Hum. & Media)

724 Tudor noble commemoration and identity: the Howard family in context, 1485–1572. Kirsten Claiden-Yardley. (Dr. Steven J. Gunn.) Oxford D.Phil. (Mod. Hist.)

725 Tudor noble political culture: the changing role of the landed elite in the early modern state, 1485–1572. Allison Kroll. (Dr. Steven J. Gunn.) Oxford D.Phil. (Mod. Hist.)

726 Alleviating the dynastic threat: Henry VII and the Yorkist royal women. Imogene S. Dudley. (Dr. Rowena Archer.) Oxford M.St. (Mod. Hist.)

727 London and the Crown in the reign of Henry VII. Sam Harper. (Professors Matthew Davies and Vanessa A. Harding.) London Ph.D. (Inst. Hist. Res.)

728 Henry VII, 'Ricardianism' and the cautious reassertion of the Crown in northern England, 1485–97. David Yorath. (Professor Ronald Hutton.) Bristol M.Phil. (Hist. Stud.)

729 The dissolution of constitutions: Aristotle and Italian political thought from Niccolò Machiavelli to Giovanni Botero. Nicolas Stone Villani. (Dr. Nicholas S. Davidson.) Oxford D.Phil. (Mod. Hist.)

730 The causes of the 1489 and 1497 rebellions. Karen A.G. Stanley. (Dr. John P.D. Cooper.) York M.Phil./Ph.D. (Hist.)

731 The crown and judicial venality in the parlement of Toulouse, c.1490–1547. Samuel J. Pollack. (Dr. David Parrott and Mr. Robin Briggs.) Oxford D.Phil. (Mod. Hist.)

732 Early modern conceptions of international relations in European peace treaties, 1492–1559. Nicholas A.H. Craft. (Dr. Steven J. Gunn.) Oxford D.Phil. (Mod. Hist.)

733 Rodrigo Borgia: a wolf on the throne of St. Peter. Katharine E. Fellows. (Dr. Nicholas Davidson.) Oxford D.Phil. (Mod. Hist.)

734 The painted glass of Winchester cathedral, c.1495–c.1528. Anya Heilpern. (Ms. Sarah Brown.) York Ph.D. (Hist. of Art)

MODERN EUROPE

General

735 Corporeal signatures of madness in western artistic traditions. Janet Couloute. (Professor David C. Gentilcore.) Leicester Ph.D. (Hist.)

736 Born naked and shameless – an anatomy of shame through early modern art. Valentina Tomassetti. (Professor Rebecca Earle and Dr. Lorenzo Pericolo.) Warwick M.Phil./Ph.D. (Hist.)

737 Early modern European queenship. Marina Tymviou. (Dr. Toby Osborne.) Durham Ph.D. (Hist.)

738 Iconographical representations of women making music, 1500–1650: a study of cultural and social conventions. Laura Ventura. (Dr. Stephen Rose.) London Ph.D. (R.H.U.L. Music)

739 The circulation and collection of Italian printed books in France in the 16th century. Shanti Graheli. (Professor Andrew D.M. Pettegree.) St. Andrews Ph.D. (Hist.)

740 Becoming a queen in France, Poland-Lithuania, and the Holy Roman Empire, 1501–76: ceremonies of marriage, coronation and childbirth. Katarzyna Kosier. (Professor Maria Hayward and Dr. Alice Hunt.) Southampton M.Phil. (Hist.)

741 Authority and practice in Reformation-era medicine, 1520–1650. Mark Elkins. (Professor Andrew D.M. Pettegree.) St. Andrews Ph.D. (Hist.)

742 The printed Greek book production and trade in the eastern Mediterranean in the 16th century: the case of the *editio princeps* of St. Basil's *Syggrammata tina. Opera quaedam beati Basilii Caesariensis episcopi* by Stefano de Sabio (Venice, 1535). Maria Argyrou. (Dr. Charalambos Dendrinos.) London Ph.D. (R.H.U.L. Hist.)

743 Miracles, magic and incorruptible bodies: defining the boundaries of the natural in post-Tridentine legal medicine. Alessandro Laverda. (Professor David C. Gentilcore.) Leicester Ph.D. (Hist.)

744 'Le orrechie si piene di Flandra': Italian news and histories on the revolt in the Netherlands, 1566–1648. Nina Lamal. (Professor Andrew D.M. Pettegree.) St. Andrews Ph.D. (Hist.)

745 'The standard-bearer of the Roman Church': Lorenzo da Brindisi (1559–1619) and the Capuchin missions in the Holy Roman Empire. Andrew Drenas. (Dr. Nicholas S. Davidson.) Oxford D.Phil. (Mod. Hist.)

746 Printed newspapers in 17th-century England, Germany, France and the Netherlands: the impact of new media functionality on the reader. Jan Hillgaertner. (Professor Andrew D.M. Pettegree.) St. Andrews Ph.D. (Hist.)

747 The suspension of the Portuguese inquisitions on trade, religion and cross-cultural politics in 17th-century Europe. Ana P. Lloyd. (Professor Francisco Bethencourt.) King's College London M.Phil./Ph.D. (Hist.)

748 Magical healing and the Greeks in 17th-century Venice. Alexandra Melita. (Dr. Sandra Cavallo.) London Ph.D. (R.H.U.L. Hist.)

749 The influence of English diplomats on 17th-century gardens. Philippa Potts. (Dr. Christine Stevenson.) London Ph.D. (Courtauld Inst.)

750 Seventeenth-century English republican thought in a European context. Amy Shields. (Dr. Rachel Hammersley and Professor Helen Berry.) Newcastle Ph.D. (Hist.)

751 The influence of confessional convictions upon the generalship of Gustav II Adolf and Johann Tserclaes von Tilly during the Thirty Years' War. Michael R. Crimmins. (Dr. David Parrott.) Oxford M.St. (Mod. Hist.)

752 State formation in isolation? A study of the contingent effects of foreign policy upon Brandenburg-Prussia under the Great Elector. Crawford A.R. Matthews. (Dr. Steven J. Gunn and Dr. David Parrott.) Oxford M.St. (Mod. Hist.)

753 Coordinating money: cash, credit and mutual obligation in the Dutch and German countryside, 1650–1850. Sebastian Felten. (Professors Francisco Bethencourt and Anne Goldgar.) King's College London M.Phil./Ph.D. (Hist.)

754 *Louis XIV et le repos de l'Italie*: French policy towards the duchies of Parma, Modena and Mantua-Monferrato, 1659–89. John Condren. (Dr. Guy R. Rowlands.) St. Andrews Ph.D. (Hist.)

755 The public classics: scholarship and education and the rise of two classical cultures in France, Britain and the Dutch Republic, 1670–1739. Floris B. Verhaart. (Professor Laurence Brockliss.) Oxford D.Phil. (Mod. Hist.)

756 International military subsidy treaties during the Nine Years' War and the War of the Spanish Succession. Thomas M. Nora. (Professor Peter Wilson and Dr. Charles Prior.) Hull Ph.D. (Hist.)

757 Bankruptcy legislation in 18th- and 19th-century Europe: notions of failure, opportunities for corruption and institutional dynamics. Frederic J. Bittner. (Professors Avner Offer and Joshua Getzler.) Oxford D.Phil. (Mod. Hist.)

758 Anglo-Irish interactions with Europe: Maria Edgeworth, Lady Morgan and Marguerite, countess of Blessington. Victoria Eberts. (Dr. Thomas Stammers and Dr. Helen O'Connell.) Durham Ph.D. (Hist.)

759 Non-elite women travelling on the continent, 1700–1850. Heather Walker. (Professor Jeremy M. Black.) Exeter M.Phil. (Hist.)

760 How is the term 'sublime' to be understood in a contemporary context? Letice A.S. Littlewood. (Professor Alastair Wright.) Oxford D.Phil. (Mod. Hist.)

761 The navy and the fiscal-military state under Louis XIV: government, private enterprise, and empire during the War of the Spanish Succession, 1701–14. Benjamin G. Darnell. (Dr. David A. Parrott.) Oxford D.Phil. (Mod. Hist.)

762 A partnership for war: England and Austria in the War of the Spanish Succession. Caleb Karges. (Dr. Guy R. Rowlands.) St. Andrews Ph.D. (Hist.)

763 Danger and risk-taking in British travel to the European continent, 1750–1820. Sarah Goldsmith. (Dr. Catriona Kennedy.) York Ph.D. (Hist.)

764 Arranging the canon: keyboard arrangements, publishing strategies and the rise of musical classics, 1750–1820. Elena Pons. (Dr. Stephen Rose.) London Ph.D. (R.H.U.L. Music)

765 Schonenberg, a place in Enlightenment Europe: the summer residence of the governors-general of the Austrian Netherlands, Duke Albert of Saxony-Teschen and Archduchess Marie Christine of Austria at Laeken near Brussels, 1780–94. Wim Oers. (Professor Robert J.W. Evans and Dr. Geoffrey Tyack.) Oxford D.Phil. (Mod. Hist.)

766 Britain, France and the Dutch question, 1785–1815. Graeme E. Callister. (Professor Alan I. Forrest.) York Ph.D. (Hist.)

767 Transnational intellectual history of European socialism in the 19th century. Mateo Arevalo Botero. (Dr. Marc Mulholland.) Oxford M.Phil. (Mod. Hist.)

768 The German spa town as nexus of Russian-European cultural interface, 1814–1914. John B. Layde. (Dr. Julia Mannherz.) Oxford M.St. (Mod. Hist.)

769 The Hapsburg empire from the outside perspective: experiences and encounters of 19th-century travellers, c.1815–1914. Martin Schaller. (Dr. Bernhard Struck.) St. Andrews Ph.D. (Hist.)

770 European rail networks. James Taylor. (Dr. Daniel Laqua.) Northumbria Ph.D. (Hist.)

771 Challenging order: the iconography of normlessness in the revolutions of 1830 and 1848. Philipp Koniger. (Professor Axel Korner.) London Ph.D. (U.C. Hist.)

772 Transnational Jewish relief networks and the emergence of Jewish internationalism in central and eastern Europe, c.1850s–70s. Milena A. Zeidler. (Dr. Abigail Green.) Oxford D.Phil. (Mod. Hist.)

773 The Crimean War: from sanitary disaster to sanitary success. Michael Hinton. (Professor Andrew D. Lambert.) King's College London Ph.D. (War Stud.)

774 Sovereign debt and financial sector stability in monetary unions: the case of Austria-Hungary, 1868–1914. Kilian Rieder. (Dr. Rui Esteves.) Oxford D.Phil. (Mod. Hist.)

775 A league of their own: institutions and networks among Russian artists in Paris, 1870–1917. Anna Winestein. (Dr. J.J.L. Whiteley.) Oxford D.Phil. (Mod. Hist.)

776 Victorian intellectuals and the Eastern Question, 1875–8. William Kelley. (Dr. Brian Young and Dr. Simon Skinner.) Oxford D.Phil. (Mod. Hist.)

777 The representation of East European Jewish migration to Britain. Samuel Hawkins. (Professor Tony Kushner.) Southampton M.Phil. (Hist.)

778 Mythologising the present: theorism and anti-democracy in the work of Georges Sorel. Patricia E. McCabe. (Professor Ruth Harris.) Oxford M.St. (Mod. Hist.)

779 Italian migrants to Germany. Alice Riegler. (Dr. Bernhard Rieger.) London Ph.D. (U.C. Hist.)

780 Nominal rigidities in Europe in a historical perspective. Ligita Visockyte. (Professor Kevin O'Rourke.) Oxford D.Phil. (Mod. Hist.)

781 The meaning of walls: a cultural history of the boundary and the limits of progress. Stephanie Hesz-Wood. (Professor David Cesarani.) London Ph.D. (R.H.U.L. Hist.)

782 Musical modernism in the 'land without music'? Towards an understanding of the phenomenon in Britain and Europe. Annika Forkert. (Dr. J.P.E. Harper-Scott.) London Ph.D. (R.H.U.L. Music)

783 Narrative, identity and intercommunal relations in western Thrace and Cyprus during the 20th century. Huw Halstead. (Dr. Geoffrey T. Cubitt.) York Ph.D. (Hist.)

784 Representing the south Slavonic peasants in popular British discourse, 1900–41. Samuel Foster. East Anglia Ph.D. (Hist.)

785 The rise and fall of the Communist-Syndicalists of the C.N.T. (1917–23). Arturo Zoffman Rodriguez. (Professor Dan Healey and Dr. Graciela Iglesias Rogers.) Oxford M.Phil. (Mod. Hist.)

786 Materiality of Great War remembrance. Jonathan R. Trigg. (Dr. Nyree J. Finlay and Dr. Tony Pollard.) Glasgow Ph.D. (Arts)

787 Henry Moore and the Nordic countries. Anna C. Brandberg. (Professor Alison Yarrington and Dr. Julia Kelly.) Hull Ph.D. (Hist.)

788 Inter-war Europe: emergence and interaction of transnational movements. John Beecher. (Dr. Tom Buchanan.) Oxford M.Phil. (Mod. Hist.)

789 An investigation of the relationship between science and politics in inter-war Europe. Steffan John. (Dr. Jill J. Lewis and Dr. Adam Mosley.) Swansea Ph.D. (Hist.)

790 Pan-Europa: the birth of the supranational in inter-war Europe. Benjamin Thorpe. (Professor Mike Heffernan and Dr. Stephen Legg.) Nottingham Ph.D. (Geog.)

791 The rise of fascism in Austria and Germany, 1919–38. Timothy J. Schmalz. (Dr. Helen Roche.) Cambridge Ph.D. (Hist.)

792 The Devil's paradise: Vilnius conflict in European diplomacy, 1919–23. Donatas Kupciunas. (Professor Robert J.W. Evans and Dr. Patricia M. Clavin.) Oxford D.Phil. (Mod. Hist.)

793 'An unrepentant old Whig': a genealogy of Hayekian liberty. Sean Irving. (Professors Stuart Jones and Bertrand O. Taithe.) Manchester Ph.D. (Hist.)

794 Literary production in Italian pertinent to the Balkan area from fascism to the wars of the 1990s. Claudia Sechi. Bath Ph.D. (Hum & Soc. Sc.)

795 Performing colour and staging sound: revisiting Kandinsky's mulitmedia project. Cecilia Stinton. (Dr. Camille Mathieu.) Oxford M.St. (Mod. Hist.)

796 'Les Belles Années du Plan': mixed economy and supranational integration in European socialism, 1930–45. Tommaso Milani. (Dr. Piers Ludlow.) London Ph.D. (L.S.E. Int. Hist.)

797 A history of Holocaust oral testimony. Madeleine White. (Professor Dan Stone and G. Smith.) London M.Phil./Ph.D. (R.H.U.L. Hist.)

798 Stay behind parties and the Second World War: planning, execution and strategy within the Mediterranean theatre. Nicholas Easingwood. (Dr. Matthew Grant.) Essex Ph.D. (Hist.)

799 Characterising the relationship between Nazi Germany and her south-eastern allies, 1939–45. Scott Fenn. (Dr. Nadine Rossol and Dr. Gerhard Wolf.) Essex Ph.D. (Hist.)

800   The representation of the strategic bombing campaign against Germany in the Allied media and the interpretation and reception of that representation by the general public, 1939–45. Helen Frost. (Professor Richard J. Overy and Dr. David Thackeray.) Exeter M.Phil.

801   The battle for the coast: using oral history to illuminate a forgotten campaign. Nick Hewitt. (Dr. Brad Beavan and Dr. Robert James.) Portsmouth Ph.D. (Soc., Hist. & Lit. Stud.)

802   Stalinism and the Soviet-Finnish War of 1939–40: crisis management, censorship and control. Malcolm L.G. Spencer. (Professor Robert J. Service.) Oxford D.Phil. (Mod. Hist.)

803   Children's experiences of Occupation and post-war demobilisation in Western Europe: France, Germany and Italy. Camille Mahe. (Dr. Pierre Purseigle.) Warwick M.Phil./Ph.D. (Hist.)

804   Women agents in Nazi concentration camps. Mary Miles. (Dr. Sean Lang and Professor Rohan McWilliam.) Anglia Ruskin D.Phil. (Hist.)

805   Homophobia in the Nazi camps. Uta Rautenberg-Thomas. (Dr. Anna Hajkova and Professor Christoph Mick.) Warwick Ph.D. (Hist.)

806   The Jewish councils of Western Europe under Nazi occupation: a comparative analysis. Laurien Vastenhout. (Professor Robert Moore.) Sheffield Ph.D. (Hist.)

807   The Italian occupation of south-eastern France, 1940–3. Niall MacGalloway. (Dr. Stephen Tyre.) St. Andrews Ph.D. (Hist.)

808   France and *el Primer Franquismo*, 1942–5: conflict and continuity. Nick Stevenson. (Professor Julian Jackson.) London Ph.D. (Q.M. Hist.)

809   Fascist Italy's anti-Jewish policy in south-eastern France, 1942–3. Luca Fenoglio. (Dr. Donald Bloxham and Dr. Pertti Ahonen.) Edinburgh Ph.D. (Hist.)

810   Bandiera Rossa: communists in German-occupied Rome, 1943–4. David Broder. (Professor Alan Sked.) London Ph.D. (L.S.E. Int. Hist.)

811   The British way of war in north-west Europe, 1944–5: a study of two infantry divisions. Louis Devine. (Dr. Harry Bennett and Professor Kevin Jefferys.) Plymouth Ph.D. (Hum.)

812   The value and effect in battle of the 6th Airborne Division and Special Service Commando brigades during the Normandy campaign, 6 June–1 September 1944. Andrew Wheale. Buckingham D.Phil. (Hist.)

813   Heidegger, Adorno and the politics of poietic living after Auschwitz. Samuel Elias Sokolsky-Tifft. (Dr. Martin Ruehl.) Cambridge M.Phil. (Hist.)

814   Male homosexuality 1945–70: transnational scientific and social knowledge in British and west European contexts. Julia Maclachlan. (Professor Frank Mort and Dr. Christian Goeschel.) Manchester Ph.D. (Hist.)

815   The united socialist states of Europe: Franco-British socialism and European integration, 1946–9. Benjamin Hecksher. (Dr. N. Piers Ludlow.) London Ph.D. (L.S.E. Int. Hist.)

816 Did England sleep? Transnational networks and self-exclusion from the European coal and steel community, 1948–51. Felix C.O. Klos. (Professor Robert Gildea.) Oxford M.St. (Mod. Hist.)

817 Decolonisation and European integration in the 1950s: a comparison of Britain, France and Belgium. Laura Kottos. (Professor Andrew Knapp.) Reading Ph.D. (French)

818 R.B. Kitaj and the idea of Europe. Francis Marshall. (Professor David Mellor and Dr. Benedict Burbridge.) Sussex D.Phil. (Hist. of Art)

819 The candidacy and promotion of different cities to house the institutions of an integrated Europe, 1952–67. Nathanael Lambot. (Professor Ruth Harris.) Oxford M.Phil. (Mod. Hist.)

820 Art practices at C.E.R.N. Camilla Mørk Røstvik. (Professor David Lomas and Dr. David Kirby.) Manchester Ph.D. (Hist. of Sc., Tech. & Med.)

821 Networks and actors: the Foreign Office and responses to European integration, 1957–73. Adam Rolewicz. (Professor Gaynor Johnson and Dr. Philip Boobbyer.) Kent Ph.D. (Hist.)

822 The soundtrack in European science fiction cinema, 1962–2005. Philip Bird. (Dr. David Gillespie and Mr. Brian Neve.) Bath Ph.D. (Hum & Soc. Sc.)

823 The 'terrorist' underground: political violence and cinema in 1970s Italy and Germany. Maria Christodoulou. (Professors Mercedes Camino and Aristotle Kallis.) Lancaster Ph.D. (Hist.)

824 Art beyond state socialism: transnational networks and alternative spaces in East Germany and Poland in the 1970s. Aneta Jarzebska. (Dr. Juliane Furst and Dr. Josie McLellan.) Bristol M.Litt. (Hist. Stud.)

825 Patriality, work permits and the European Economic Community: the introduction of the 1971 Immigration Act. Callum G.H. Williams. (Dr. Harold Carter.) Oxford M.Phil. (Mod. Hist.)

826 Eastern European women's reflections on the experience of movement and migration in post-1989 Europe. Sabina Fiebig. (Professor Melanie J. Ilic and Dr. Charlotte Beyer.) Gloucestershire Ph.D. (Hum.)

827 National holidays in Budapest and Prague in the post-communist era, 1989–2009. Andrea Talaber. (Dr. Egbert Klautke and Dr. Wendy C. Bracewell.) London M.Phil. (S.S.E.E.S.)

828 Restoration diplomacy in Russia and the Baltic. Thomas A. Henwood. (Dr. Susan Brigden.) Oxford M.St. (Mod. Hist.)

829 French responses to the war in Bosnia. Christopher D. Jones. East Anglia Ph.D. (Hist.)

830 Polish and Ukrainian second generation post-migrant identities in the north of England: social networks, narratives of ancestral land and belonging. Frantisek Grombir. (Dr. Nicholas J. Evans and Dr. Catherine Baker.) Hull Ph.D. (Hist.)

Austria

831 The brief season of the Austrian vice royalty (1707–34). Antonio Mileo. (Dr. Gabriel Guarino and Dr. Éamonn Ó Ciardha.) Ulster Ph.D. (Hist.)

832 The place of my father's sepulchres: the Jewish cemeteries in Vienna. Timothy Corbett. (Dr. Corinna Peniston-Bird and Dr. Thomas Rohkramer.) Lancaster Ph.D. (Hist.)

833 Freud's scalpel: sex reassignment surgery, psychoanalysis, and the fusion of psychiatric paradigms. Andrew S. Lea. (Dr. Sloan Mahone.) Oxford M.Phil. (Mod. Hist.)

834 Representative government, majority rule and Jewish minority representation during the constitutional era in Habsburg Austria, 1895–1914. Larissa C. Douglass. (Dr. D. Rechter.) Oxford D.Phil. (Mod. Hist.)

835 The making of Red Vienna: social democracy in opposition, 1905–14. Frederic G. Shearer. (Dr. Laurence Cole.) East Anglia M.Phil. (Hist.)

836 The emergence of Austrian identity at the Hochschulen, 1945–55. George Neumann. (Professor Elizabeth Harvey and Dr. William Niven.) Nottingham Ph.D. (Hist.)

Balkan states

837 Environmental history and historical geography of woodlands of coastal Dalamatia, Croatia. Ivan Tekic. (Professors Charles Watkins and Georgina Endfield.) Nottingham Ph.D. (Geog.)

838 British diplomatic history with regard to the Balkans prior to the First World War. David Thomas. East Anglia Ph.D. (Hist.)

839 The Albanian question in British foreign policy, 1876–1911. Daut Dauti. (Dr. Nir Arielli and Professor Holger Afflerbach.) Leeds Ph.D. (Hist.)

840 Yugoslavism, rebellion and exile – a political and intellectual biography of Tin Ujevic, 1903–19. Jasmina Knezovic. (Professor James Pettifer.) Oxford M.Litt. (Mod. Hist.)

841 Creating the 'Yugoslav myth'. Benjamin Wynes. East Anglia Ph.D. (Hist.)

842 Macedonian rites of unification. Elisabeth Meijer. (Dr. Emma Aston.) Reading Ph.D. (Classics)

843 The diplomatics of silence: the *foibe*. Luisa Morettin. (Professor Christopher J.H. Duggan.) Reading Ph.D. (Mod. Lang. & Eur. Stud.)

844 The nationalism question in the socialist federal republic of Yugoslavia. Gani Asllani. (Dr. Kenneth Morrison.) De Montfort Ph.D. (Hum.)

845 Siptari to Kosovars: Albanian identity in Kosovo, 1956–2008. Justin Elliott. (Dr. Wendy C. Bracewell.) London M.Phil. (S.S.E.E.S.)

846 The politics, ethics and social implications of hardcore punk in Slovenia during the 1980s. Jack Pitt. East Anglia Ph.D. (Hist.)

847   A culture of nationalism: transformations of culture politics in Tudman's Croatia. Dario Brentin. (Dr. Eric Gordy.) London M.Phil. (S.S.E.E.S.)

848   Uncovering the support networks of devolved violence: irregular armed forces in modern ethnic war, Yugoslavia, 1990–9. Katherine Ferguson. East Anglia Ph.D. (Hist.)

849   Leadership ideology and atrocities in the Bosnian war, 1992–5. Ozren Jungic. (Professor Robert J.W. Evans and Dr. Mark Thompson.) Oxford D.Phil. (Mod. Hist.)

Baltic states

850   Britain and the Grand Duchy of Lithuania: confessional contacts in the early modern period. Hanna Mazheika. (Professors Karin Friedrich and Dr. Marie-Luise Ehrenschwendtner.) Aberdeen Ph.D. (Hist.)

851   Forestry in Lithuania, 1918–40. Loreta Zydeliene. (Professor Greg Bankoff.) Hull Ph.D. (Hist.)

852   Operational art and the Narva front, 1944: Sinimäed and campaign planning. Andrew Del Gaudio. (Dr. Robert Foley.) Liverpool Ph.D. (Hist.)

853   The hippy movement in Latvia, 1967–92. Liva Zolnerovica. (Dr. Juliane Furst and Dr. Josie McLellan.) Bristol M.Litt. (Hist. Stud.)

Belgium

854   The Officina Plantiniana as music publishers and distributors, 1555–95. Louisa Hunter-Bradley. (Dr. Stephen Rose.) London Ph.D. (R.H.U.L. Music)

Bulgaria

855   The dissidence in Bulgaria: between the systems of repression and privileges. Galina Yakova. (Dr. Kelly Hignett and Dr. Heather Shore.) Leeds Beckett Ph.D. (Cultural Stud.)

Czech lands and Slovakia

856   Religious materiality in 17th-century Prague. Suzanna Ivanic. (Professor Ulinka Rublack.) Cambridge Ph.D. (Hist.)

857   Veterans of the Great War in interbellum Czechoslovakia. Adam Luptak. (Professor Robert Evans.) Oxford M.Phil. (Mod. Hist.)

858   Codes and variations in music composed in Terezin. Jory Debenham. (Professors Derek Sayer and Michael Beckerman.) Lancaster Ph.D. (Hist.)

859   Communicating with the occupied and exiled: B.B.C. Czech-language broadcasts, 1940–5. Eric Harrison. (Dr. Rajendra Chitnis and Dr. James Thompson.) Bristol M.Litt. (Hist. Stud.)

860   Education and transition: changes to education in Czechoslovakia as a consequence of the 1989 Velvet Revolution. Zuzana Podracka. (Dr. Alastair Kocho-Williams and Dr. Peter Lambert.) Aberystwyth Ph.D. (Hist. & Welsh Hist.)

Denmark

861   The ritual of the churching of women in early modern Denmark. Mette M. Ahlefeldt-Laurvig. (Professor Lyndal Roper.) Oxford M.St. (Mod. Hist.)

862   The persistence of Catholicism in Denmark after the Protestant Reformation, 1535–1629. Federico Zuliani. (Professors Alastair Hamilton and Jill A. Kraye.) London Ph.D. (Warburg)

Finland

863   Sibelius: post-crisis. Sarah Moynihan. (Dr. Paul Harper-Scott.) London Ph.D. (R.H.U.L. Music)

864   The impact of foreign military volunteers in Finland during the Second World War. Kristo Karvinen. (Dr. Paddy McNally.) Worcester M.Phil./Ph.D. (Hum. & Creative Arts)

865   Finnish diplomacy and the recruitment of foreign volunteers 1939–44. Veikko Karvinen. (Dr. Nir Arielli and Dr. Geoff Waddington.) Leeds Ph.D. (Hist.)

France

866   Divided by La Manche: naval enterprise and maritime revolution in early modern England and France. Benjamin Redding. (Professor Penny Roberts.) Warwick Ph.D. (Hist.)

867   Demonic possession, embodiment, and the life-cycle in early modern England and France. Thomas Wroblewski. (Dr. Jenny Spinks and Dr. Sasha Handley.) Manchester Ph.D. (Hist.)

868   Inventing realities, picturing salvation: making, meaning and patronage of the paintings of Jean Bellegambe, 1470–1535/36. Anna Koopstra. (Professor Susie M. Nash.) London Ph.D. (Courtauld Inst.)

869   Female religious networks in France, 1520–60. Jennifer Tomlinson. (Professor Stuart M. Carroll.) York Ph.D. (Hist.)

870   The succession crisis in France and England: a struggle to power, 1562–1606. Estelle Paranque. (Dr. Jason Peacey.) London Ph.D. (U.C. Hist.)

871   Prince Henry's politics on England and the French civil war. Ariel C. Weber. (Dr. Helen Lacey.) Oxford M.St. (Mod. Hist.)

872   Catholic images of Protestants during the early years of the French Wars of Religion. Josephine D. Rendall-Neal. (Dr. Giora Sternberg.) Oxford M.Phil. (Mod. Hist.)

873   The rhetoric of martyrdom: French hagiographical mission literature of the Society of Jesus, 1632–52. Michael Knox. (Dr. Antoni Ucerler.) Oxford D.Phil. (Mod. Hist.)

874 Antoine Garissoles' Adolphid (1649), a Huguenot Latin epic: an edited text, translation and historical commentary. Sofia Guthrie. (Professor Penny Roberts.) Warwick M.Phil./Ph.D. (Hist.)

875 Popular medical and erotic literature in England and France, 1650–1720. Sara Drake Bennett. (Mr. Robin Briggs and Dr. Faramerz N. Dabhoiwala.) Oxford D.Phil. (Mod. Hist.)

876 Pious sociability: devotional subculture in 17th-century France, c.1650–1680. Jennifer Hillman. (Professor Stuart M. Carroll.) York Ph.D. (Hist.)

877 Tracking the exotic in Paris: pharmacological knowledge, print culture and the marketplace at the turn of the 18th century. Laia Portet i Cordina. (Dr. Emma Spary.) Cambridge Ph.D. (Hist.)

878 Perceptions of the murderess in 18th-century London and Paris, 1674–1789. Anna Jenkin. (Professor Robert B. Shoemaker.) Sheffield Ph.D. (Hist.)

879 The development of French military schools, 1680–1789. Haroldo Guizar. (Professor Alan I. Forrest.) York Ph.D. (Hist.)

880 Monarchy in print: French and English history, 1688–1788. Alexandra Anderson. (Dr. Alexandra E. Bamji and Dr. Richard de Ritter.) Leeds Ph.D. (Hist.)

881 The Huguenots and 18th-century evangelicalism. Chris S. Adams. (Dr. David Ceri Jones and Professor Roger D. Price.) Aberystwyth Ph.D. (Hist. & Welsh Hist.)

882 The embroidery trade in 18th-century France. Tabitha Baker. (Professors Giorgio Riello and Lesley Miller (V&A).) Warwick Ph.D. (Hist.)

883 Conversations on constitution: Jean-Louis De Lolme and his reception in the British, German and American schools of political thought in the 18th century. Ployjaj Pintobtang. (Dr. Iain McDaniel and Dr. Andrew Chitty.) Sussex D.Phil. (Hist.)

884 How does Etienne Bonnot de Condillac's life and oeuvre shed light on the history of metaphysics in France in the years 1700–56? Rory R. Brinkmann. (Professor Laurence Brockliss.) Oxford M.Phil. (Mod. Hist.)

885 Founding and refounding: a problem in Rousseau's political thought and action. Mark Hill. (Professor Laurence W.B. Brockliss.) Oxford D.Phil. (Mod. Hist.)

886 *La maladie honteuse, la maladie vénérienne*: venereal disease in France, 1736–89. Marialana Wittman. (Professor Colin D.H. Jones.) London Ph.D. (Q.M. Hist.)

887 The origins of Marat's revolutionary persona and the creation of a new form of political journalism. Neil Ritchie. (Professor Colin D.H. Jones.) London Ph.D. (Q.M. Hist.)

888 Female portraiture and patronage in the age of Marie-Antoinette and Queen Charlotte. Anne S. Grant. (Dr. Geraldine Johnson and Dr. Linda Whiteley.) Oxford D.Phil. (Mod. Hist.)

889 Political landscapes: self-representation, dissent and the transformation of high noble and princely domains in France, 1770–90. Gabriel Wick. (Professors Colin D.H. Jones and Miles Ogborn.) London Ph.D. (Q.M. Hist.)

890 Ideal beauty in late 18th- and early 19th-century French art and art criticism, with special reference to the role of drapery and costume. Fiona K.A. Gatty. (Dr. J.J.L. Whiteley and Dr. Alistair Wright.) Oxford D.Phil. (Mod. Hist.)

891 Anglo-Jewry and the French Revolution. Jeremy Smilg. (Professor Tony Kushner.) Southampton M.Phil. (Hist.)

892 Industrial utopias in Britain and France, 1789–1900: the scientific and political management of the environment. Amelie Muller. (Professor Pietro Corsi and Dr. Thomas Le Roux.) Oxford D.Phil. (Mod. Hist.)

893 The role of elite women in the reception of French émigrés in England, 1789–1815. Janice Morris. (Professor Rosemary H. Sweet.) Leicester Ph.D. (Hist.)

894 Capturing the whirlwind: Paris depicted through the medium of revolutionary prints. Paul Davidson. (Professor Colin D.H. Jones.) London Ph.D. (Q.M. Hist.)

895 From geology to art history: ceramist Alexandre Brongniart's unexpected contribution. Julia A. Carr-Trebelhorn. (Professor Pietro Corsi.) Oxford D.Phil. (Mod. Hist.)

896 Transnational exchanges: Chartism and French republicanism. Jacob Dengate. (Professor Paul O'Leary and Dr. Peter Lambert.) Aberystwyth Ph.D. (Hist. & Welsh Hist.)

897 British and French military identities during the Revolutionary and Napoleonic Wars. Timothy P. Candlish. (Professor Alan I. Forrest.) York Ph.D. (Hist.)

898 Rumour and popular opinion during the French First Republic. Lindsay Porter. (Professor Alan I. Forrest.) York Ph.D. (Hist.)

899 Political strategies of laughter in the National Convention, 1792–4. Jacob Zobkiw. (Dr. Thomas Biskup.) Hull Ph.D. (Hist.)

900 Fashion merchants and luxury clothing for women: Paris, 1795–1848. Fiona Ffoulkes. (Dr. Joan Tumblety and Professor Maria Hayward.) Southampton Ph.D. (Hist.)

901 Parliamentarianism in the legislative councils of the French Directory, 1795–9. Luke Burgess. (Dr. Ambrogio Caiani and Dr. Philip Boobbyer.) Kent Ph.D. (Hist.)

902 Emotional recovery and reconstruction in the Directory era, 1795–9: the case of La Rochelle. Emily E.A. Honey. (Dr. David Hopkin.) Oxford M.St. (Mod. Hist.)

903 The language question in Napoleonic France. Stewart McCain. (Dr. David M. Hopkin and Dr. Michael Broers.) Oxford D.Phil. (Mod. Hist.)

904 Colonialism and memory in Britain and France. Itay Lotem. (Professor Julian Jackson.) London Ph.D. (Q.M. Hist.)

905 Local reformers and international innovations: a comparative study of approaches to working-class housing in 19th-century France. William Clement. (Dr. Christina de Bellaigue and Dr. William Whyte.) Oxford D.Phil. (Mod. Hist.)

906 Henri Germain: finance, capitalism and politics in 19th-century France. Virginia Crespi de Valldaura. (Professor Ruth Harris.) Oxford M.St. (Mod. Hist.)

907 Parenting the self: welfare, family, and subjectivity in 19th-century France. Tomás A. Cubillas-Gadea. (Dr. Julian Wright and Dr. Thomas Stammers.) Durham Ph.D. (Hist.)

908 Representations of Poland and Polishness in 19th-century France. Mauve Devitt Tremblay. (Dr. Hubertus Jahn and Dr. Emma Spary.) Cambridge Ph.D. (Hist.)

909   The co-creation of champagne in England and France, 1850–1900. Robert G.
      Harding. (Dr. Christina de Bellaigue and Dr. William Whyte.) Oxford D.Phil. (Mod.
      Hist.)

910   Transnational centres of provincial modernity: Manchester and Lille, 1860–1914.
      Harry Stopes. (Professor Axel Körner.) London Ph.D. (U.C. Hist.)

911   Perception in the late work of Pierre Bonnard, 1867–1947. Lucy W. Whelan. (Dr.
      Hanneke Grootenboer.) Oxford D.Phil. (Mod. Hist.)

912   Fraternity in combat: foreigners and resistance in the French republican tradition,
      1870–1945. Gavin Jacobson. (Dr. Sudhir Hazareesingh.) Oxford D.Phil. (Pol.)

913   Folkloric France: the cultural effects of popular tradition, 1870–1914. Daniel DeGroff.
      (Professor Colin D.H. Jones.) London Ph.D. (Q.M. Hist.)

914   The Paris commune and French Revolutionary thought, c.1871–89. Julia Nicholls.
      (Professor Gareth Stedman Jones.) London Ph.D. (Q.M. Hist.)

915   Learning to travel: British tourists in France, 1885–1925. Chloe E. Jeffries. (Dr.
      David M. Hopkin and Dr. William H. Whyte.) Oxford D.Phil. (Mod. Hist.)

916   Capturing the future: cultures of time in radical political movements in France,
      1889–1910. Alexandra C. Paulin-Booth. (Professor Robert N. Gildea.) Oxford
      D.Phil. (Mod. Hist.)

917   French views of Britain and the British in the era of the Boer War. John Blockley.
      (Professor Julian T. Jackson.) London Ph.D. (Q.M. Hist.)

918   Marie Laurencin and the making of avant-garde portraiture. Vanessa Partridge Prill.
      (Dr. Camille Mathieu.) Oxford M.St. (Mod. Hist.)

919   The art of Picabia. Simon Marginson. (Professor Michael White.) York Ph.D.
      (Hist. of Art)

920   The history of the Institut Français in London. Charlotte Faucher. (Professor Julian
      Jackson.) London Ph.D. (Q.M. Hist.)

921   The establishment of the French war machine in the First World War. Alex Bostrom.
      (Professor Hew F.A. Strachan.) Oxford D.Phil. (Mod. Hist.)

922   A comparative analysis of visual propaganda in France and Britain during the First
      World War. Cherie Prosser. (Dr. Timothy P. Baycroft.) Sheffield Ph.D. (Hist.)

923   Muslim intellectual migration to Paris: a study of cultural encounters, 1919–62. Olivia
      A. Holmberg Luce. (Professor Francis Robinson.) Oxford D.Phil. (Mod. Hist.)

924   Militancy and resistance: workers in Le Havre, 1922–45. Rebecca Shtasel. (Dr.
      Christopher M. Warne and Dr. Claudia Siebrecht.) Sussex D.Phil. (Hist.)

925   Psychoanalysis and social change: Francoise Dolto and the French 20th century.
      Richard Bates. (Dr. K. H. Adler and Dr. Colin Heywood.) Nottingham Ph.D. (Hist.)

926   Official British views of the French army, 1933–48. Gareth Mears. (Professor
      Pamela Pilbeam and Dr. Rudolf Muhs.) London M.Phil./Ph.D. (R.H.U.L. Hist.)

927   The French few: French R.A.F. flyers and the British national identity during the
      Second World War. Samantha Black. (Dr. Tom Buchanan.) Oxford M.St. (Mod.
      Hist.)

928 Riencros and Brens, 1939–44: concentration camps for women in the south of France before and during the German occupation of the southern zone. Catherine Robson. (Dr. Joan L. Tumblety.) Southampton M.Phil. (Hist.)

929 Ballet music in France during the Nazi occupation. Abaigh McKee. (Dr. Shirli Gilbert.) Southampton M.Phil. (Hist.)

930 A social history of resistance in upper Normandy. Mason Norton. (Dr. Daniel Gordon.) Edge Hill Ph.D. (English & Hist.)

931 Mental health care in Vichy France. Patricia Legg. (Dr. Joan L. Tumblety.) Southampton Ph.D.-suspended (Hist.)

932 Writing the occupation: the articulation of women's subjectivities, France 1940–4. Sally Palmer. (Dr. Christopher M. Warne and Dr. Claudia Siebrecht.) Sussex M.Phil. (Hist.)

933 Talking to France: radio propaganda from 1940–2. Denis Courtois. (Professor Christoph Mick.) Warwick Ph.D. (Hist.)

934 Inner cities and globalisation: the example of Rheims and Leicester. Ines Hassen. (Professor Simon Gunn.) Leicester Ph.D. (Hist.)

935 Lines of flight: Deleuze, Guattari and the LaBorde Clinic, c.1950–c.1980. Matthew Chan. (Professor Robert Gildea.) Oxford D.Phil. (Mod. Hist.)

936 Private sector influence on public policymaking: Pompidou, Rothschild and immigration in 1969–74 France. Cody Delistraty. (Professor Robert Gildea.) Oxford M.St. (Mod. Hist.)

937 Second wave feminist approaches to sexuality in Britain and France, c.1970–83. Anna Gurun. (Professor Perry Willson and Dr. Anja Johansen.) Dundee Ph.D. (Hist.)

938 The restoration of Chartres cathedral: an examination of the current restoration works from a historical perspective. Andre Holmqvist. (Dr. Gervase Rosser.) Oxford M.St. (Mod. Hist.)

939 Beyond 'Charlie', humour and the freedom to offend: how targeting religion has become emblematic of freedom of speech in contemporary France. Imen Neffati. (Professor M. Mary T. Vincent.) Sheffield Ph.D. (Hist.)

Germany

940 Female patronage of art in the duchy of Württemberg in the 16th and 17th centuries. Roisin Watson. (Dr. Bridget M. Heal.) St. Andrews Ph.D. (Hist.)

941 German-Calvinist musical practices in 16th-century Heidelberg. Matthew Laube. (Dr. Stephen Rose.) London Ph.D. (R.H.U.L. Music)

942 The culture of music printing in 16th-century Augsburg: performing, learning, trading. Amelie Roper. (Professor Andrew D.M. Pettegree.) St. Andrews Ph.D. (Hist.)

943 The impact of the Reformation on the Oberlausitz and the Sechsstädtebund. Martin Christ. (Professor Lyndal A. Roper.) Oxford D.Phil. (Mod. Hist.)

944 Political order and authority in Martin Luther and Philipp Melanchthon, 1525–47. Mads Langballe Jensen. (Dr. Angus Gowland.) London Ph.D. (U.C. Hist.)

945 Mission impossible? Ambassador Karl Harst, Anne of Cleves and their struggles to secure the strategic alliance between Cleves and England. Nicole Bertzen. (Dr. Jan Loop and Professor Kenneth Fincham.) Kent Ph.D. (Hist.)

946 English views of Germany, 1618–1714. Anna-Karina Rühl. (Professor Tony Claydon.) Bangor Ph.D. (Hist., Welsh Hist. & Archaeol.)

947 Life and times of Caroline of Ansbach. Caroline Streek. (Professor Helen Parish.) Reading Ph.D. (Hist.)

948 The works of Johann Georg and Johann Christian Röllig with thematic catalogue. Nigel Springthorpe. (Dr. Stephen Rose.) London Ph.D. (R.H.U.L. Music)

949 Frederick the Great and the Knowledge of War, 1730–55. Adam Storring. (Professor Christopher Clark.) Cambridge Ph.D. (Hist.)

950 Professional identity of army officers in Britain and the Habsburg monarch, 1740–90. Tobias Roeder. (Dr. William O'Reilly.) Cambridge Ph.D. (Hist.)

951 'True Christian edification and greater conformity of the Sunday service': the Mylius Hymnal of 1780 and Prussian enlightened absolutist Church reform. Henrique Laitenberger. (Dr. Jon Parkin.) Oxford M.St. (Mod. Hist.)

952 Managing expectations: the electric telegraph in 19th-century Germany. Jean-Michel Johnston. (Dr. Oliver Zimmer.) Oxford D.Phil. (Mod. Hist.)

953 Early German art in the National Gallery and beyond: the case of the Krüger collection and its reception in Britain in the latter half of the 19th century. Nicola Sinclair. (Dr. Jeanne Nuechterlein.) York Ph.D. (Hist. of Art)

954 A comparative analysis of policy initiatives designed to shape the outlook of German society, highlighting the role of the German military establishment as an educator of society. Alexander Gatos. (Dr. Christoph Dartmann and Dr. Thomas Weber.) Aberdeen Ph.D. (Hist.)

955 A study of the family, background and identity of Rosa Luxemburg, 1871–1919. Rory Castle. (Dr. Jill J. Lewis.) Swansea Ph.D. (Hist.)

956 Democratisation in eastern Germany 1989–1994. Jenny Price. (Professors David Anderson and Jan Palmowski.) Warwick M.Phil./Ph.D. (Hist.)

957 Staging local, acting global: a history of the German circus (1890–1945). Sabine Hanke. (Dr. Dina Gusejnova and Dr. Esme R. Cleall.) Sheffield Ph.D. (Hist.)

958 Economic history of German North Sea ports, 1890–1940. Henning Kuhlmann. (Dr. Gerwin Strobl.) Cardiff Ph.D. (Hist. & Archaeol.)

959 Roland Freisler: an intellectual biography. Thomas Clausen. (Professor Christopher Clark.) Cambridge Ph.D. (Hist.)

960 Competing for the Kaiser's ear: the struggle for control over Germany's England policy, 1898–1914. Michael Hemmersdorfer. (Professor Alan Sked.) London Ph.D. (L.S.E. Int. Hist.)

961 Anti-Marxism and German nationalism in Hof, 1900–33. Alex Burkhardt. (Dr. Riccardo Bavaj.) St. Andrews Ph.D. (Hist.)

962 Weland Smith and Germanic cultural values. Isobel Robertson. (Dr. Alaric Hall and Professor Julia S. Barrow.) Leeds Ph.D. (Hist.)

963 An anthropometric analysis of nutritional deprivation of children in First World War Germany. Mary Cox. (Dr. Deborah J. Oxley.) Oxford D.Phil. (Mod. Hist.)

964 Killing in the German army: organising and surviving combat in the Great War. Brendan Murphy. (Professor Benjamin Ziemann.) Sheffield Ph.D. (Hist.)

965 'Freund' and foe: depicting the enemy in the First World War. Aoife S. O'Gorman. (Dr. Adrian M. Gregory.) Oxford D.Phil. (Mod. Hist.)

966 The German army in the battle of Arras and the Nivelle offensive, April-June 1917: a study in command and control. Anthony Cowan. (Dr. Robert Foley.) Liverpool Ph.D. (Hist.)

967 Assessing the long-term effects of the First World War on trend fertility rates for the U.K. and Germany. Henry S.W. Occleston. (Professor Kevin O'Rourke.) Oxford M.Sc. (Mod. Hist.)

968 Occupational mobility in Germany in the inter-war period. Marie Ladwig. (Dr. Brian A'Hearn.) Oxford M.Sc. (Mod. Hist.)

969 Political elites, the public sphere and the genesis of fascism in Weimar Germany: a prosopographical approach. Simon B. Unger. (Professors Kevin O'Rourke and Nicholas Stargardt.) Oxford D.Phil. (Mod. Hist.)

970 Radical identities inside the Nazi party, 1919–23. Kolja Kroeger. (Dr. Thomas Weber and Dr. Andrew Dilley.) Aberdeen Ph.D. (Hist.)

971 The Volkskartei (People's Card Index): registry for enrolment and segregation. Compiling personal data in national-socialist Germany. Stefan Boberg. (Dr. Gideon Reuveni and Dr. Gerhard Wolf.) Sussex D.Phil. (Hist.)

972 Housing and public policy in England and Germany, c.1930–9: a comparative study. Jörg Filthaut. (Professor J.F. Harris.) Oxford D.Phil. (Mod. Hist.)

973 Educating the National Socialist elite. Dorota Mas. (Professors David Cesarani and Peter Longerich.) London Ph.D. (R.H.U.L. Hist.)

974 Nazi Germany and the morality of war. Jacques Schuhmacher. (Dr. Nicholas Stargardt.) Oxford D.Phil. (Mod. Hist.)

975 Ambulant amateurs – the rise and fade of the Anglo-German fellowship. Charles Spicer. (Professor Lawrence Goldman and Dr. Karina Urbach.) London Ph.D. (Inst. Hist. Res.)

976 The man of confidence in German prisoner-of-war camps during the Second World War. Peter Gregory. Bristol M.Litt. (Hist. Stud.)

977 Jewish refugees from Nazi Germany to East England. Mike Levy. (Dr. Richard Carr and Dr. Jonathan Davis.) Anglia Ruskin D.Phil. (Hist.)

978 A re-evaluation of Field Marshall Alfred Vesseling. Andrew Sangster. East Anglia Ph.D. (Hist.)

979 British women and German prisoners of war in the 1940s. Mary Ingham.
(Professors Richard Grayson and Jan Plamper.) London M.Phil. (Goldsmiths Hist.)

980 Female camp guards in Auschwitz. Charlotte Mears. (Dr. Steve Woodbridge and
Professor Craig Phelan.) Kingston Ph.D. (Econ., Hist. & Pol.)

981 After the Blitz: Luftwaffe operations over the United Kingdom after May 1941.
Stephen Moore. (Dr. Claudia Baldoli and Dr. Martin Farr.) Newcastle Ph.D. (Hist.)

982 The myth of German 'national redoubt': a story of Allied intelligence failure, effective
Nazi propaganda or political spin? Alexander Grant. (Dr. Thomas Weber and Dr.
Andrew Dilley.) Aberdeen Ph.D. (Hist.)

983 The British occupation of Germany and Anglo-German relations after 1945. Daniel
Cowling. (Dr. Henning Grunwald.) Cambridge Ph.D. (Hist.)

984 Treatments of the past: medical memories and experiences in post-war East
Germany. Markus Wahl. (Professor Ulf Schmidt and Dr. Stefan Goebel.) Kent
Ph.D. (Hist.)

985 The fallout: childhood in post-World War II Germany, 1945–55. Julie L. Bailey. (Dr.
Nicholas Stargardt.) Oxford D.Phil. (Mod. Hist.)

986 British attitudes to the German economic miracle, 1948–71. Colin (Ellis)
Chamberlain. (Professor Martin Daunton.) Cambridge Ph.D. (Hist.)

987 National educational reform in the international era: the role of U.N.E.S.C.O. in West
German educational reform, 1950–60. Katherine M. Erickson. (Professor Paul
Betts.) Oxford M.Phil. (Mod. Hist.)

988 State and ritual in a Marxist-Leninist society: East Berlin, 1951. Daniel P. O'Neil.
(Dr. David Priestland.) Oxford M.Phil. (Mod. Hist.)

989 Institutional responses to multiculturalism: networked diversity, the work of the Amt
für Multikulturelle Angelegenheiten and the development of the 'Frankfurt Model'.
Joanna Cagney. (Professor David Gilbert.) London M.Phil./Ph.D. (R.H.U.L. Geog.)

990 Competing emancipations: the West German gay and lesbian movement in the
1970s. Craig Griffiths. (Professor Christina von Hodenberg.) London Ph.D. (Q.M.
Hist.)

991 The German 'aversion' to inflation and 1970s Bundesbank policy. Simon F. Mee.
(Professor Kevin O'Rourke.) Oxford D.Phil. (Mod. Hist.)

992 After the Schonzeit: Jewish life in Germany since 1979. Joseph Cronin. (Dr. Daniel
Wildmann.) London Ph.D. (Q.M. Hist.)

993 Test the West: colonisation, privatisation and identity in a reunified Germany. Myles
Logan Miller. (Dr. Gideon Reuveni and Dr. Gerhard Wolf.) Sussex D.Phil. (Hist.)

994 The politics of memory in united Germany: 9th November and 3rd October
commemorations in comparative perspective. Sidiqa Riazat. (Dr. Anna Saunders
and Dr. Alexander Sedlmaier.) Bangor Ph.D. (Hist., Welsh Hist. & Archaeol.)

Greece

995 Greek and the vernaculars: early modern Greek philology and the *questione della lingua*. Marco Spreafico. (Dr. Guido Giglioni and Professor Jill A. Kraye.) London Ph.D. (Warburg)

996 The Arvanites and the shaping of Greek identity, 1770–1830. Milthiades N.R. Potts. (Professor R.R.M. Clogg.) Oxford M.Litt. (Mod. Hist.)

997 Eastern Orthodoxy and nationalism: a theological and historical approach to the relations between church, nation and state in Greece. Lambros Psomas. (Dr. Andreas Andreopoulos and Dr. Colin M. Haydon.) Winchester M.Phil./Ph.D. (Relig. Stud.)

998 Mortality change in Hermoupolis, Greece, 1859–1940. Michail Raftakis. (Dr. Violetta Hionidou and Professor Jeremy P. Boulton.) Newcastle Ph.D. (Hist.)

999 'Cachexy', fantasy, and exultation; romantic nationalism in early Georgian Greece. Lycourgos Sophoulis. (Professor James Pettifer.) Oxford D.Phil. (Mod. Hist.)

1000 Greece in the European imagination and the formation of Greek identity in the 20th century. Artemis Ignatidou. (Dr. Astrid Swenson and Dr. Alison Carrol.) Brunel Ph.D. (Pol. & Hist.)

1001 The London Greek diaspora and national politics: the Anglo-Hellenic League and the idea of Greece, 1913–19. Georgia Kouta. (Professor Richard Drayton.) King's College London M.Phil./Ph.D. (Hist.)

1002 History of post-Second World War Greek entrepreneurship and a comparison to the U.K. experience. Zoi Pitaaki. (Professors Neil Rollings and Jeff Fear.) Glasgow Ph.D. (Soc. Sc.)

1003 Organised interests and European integration: the course of Greek business towards the E.E.C. Ioannis Vasilopoulos. (Dr. Myrto Tsakatika and Professor Neil Rollings.) Glasgow Ph.D. (Soc. Sc.)

Hungary

1004 The complementarity of nationalism and internationalism in Hungary, 1848. Zsuzanna Lada. (Professor Axel Körner.) London Ph.D. (U.C. Hist.)

1005 No documents, no history: a political biography of Rosika Schwimmer (1877–1948). Dagmar Wernitznig. (Professor Robert J.W. Evans.) Oxford D.Phil. (Mod. Hist.)

1006 The Hungarian Air Service, 1918–45. Stephen Renner. (Professors Robert J.W. Evans and Hew F.A. Strachan.) Oxford D.Phil. (Mod. Hist.)

1007 Bystanders to genocide? The role of building managers in the Hungarian Holocaust. Istvan Adam. (Dr. Tim Cole and Dr. Josie McLellan.) Bristol M.Litt. (Hist. Stud.)

1008 Community, state and identity during the Holocaust: a sociological, conceptual comparative study of Jews in Nyirmada and Budapest, Hungary, 1941–4. Denise Acton. (Dr. Alex Korb.) Leicester Ph.D. (Hist.)

Italy

1009   Creating an urban reading public: cheap print in early modern Bologna. Rebecca Carnevali. (Dr. Rosa Salzberg and Dr. David Lines.) Warwick M.Phil./Ph.D. (Hist.)

1010   The reception of Islamic art in Bologna, Ferrara and Padua in the 16th and 17th centuries. Federica Gigante. (Professors Charles S.F. Burnett and Anna Contadini.) London Ph.D. (Warburg)

1011   Diet, health and identity in early modern England and Italy: a study of reception and assimilation of Galenic principles. Giovanni Pozzetti. (Dr. Alexandra E. Bamji and and Professor Cathy Shrank.) Leeds Ph.D. (Hist.)

1012   Negotiating with things: Olimpia Maidalchini Pamphili and the politics of material culture in early modern Rome. Natalia Rotondo. (Dr. Evelyn Welch and Professor David E.H. Edgerton.) King's College London M.Phil./Ph.D. (Hist.)

1013   The material culture of children and childhood in Bologna, 1550–1600. Michele Robinson. (Dr. Flora Dennis and Professor Michelle O'Malley.) Sussex D.Phil. (Hist. of Art)

1014   Citizenship, *scuole grandi* and artistic patronage in early modern Venice. Guilia Zanon. (Dr. Alexandra E. Bamji and Dr. Richard Checketts.) Leeds Ph.D. (Hist.)

1015   Crafting the Renaissance: the contribution of artisans in Verona to the spread of Renaissance culture throughout Italy and the rest of Europe in the 16th century. Zoe Farrell. (Dr. Mary Laven.) Cambridge Ph.D. (Hist.)

1016   Pierfrancesco Riccio (1501–64): clergyman, bureaucrat, politician and patron of the arts at Cosimo I de Medici's court. Désirée Cappa. (Professor Peter Mack and Dr. Alessandro Scafi.) London Ph.D. (Warburg)

1017   Sculpted identity: the making and display of sculpture in Florence's forgotten centuries. Hannah W. Kinney. (Dr. Geraldine Johnson.) Oxford D.Phil. (Mod. Hist.)

1018   The role of Cardinal Ippolito II d'Este in the politics of his age, with regards to his multifaceted activity as a high exponent of the Church during the years of its inner fights and religious tensions. Giulia Vidori. (Dr. Nicholas Davidson.) Oxford D.Phil. (Mod. Hist.)

1019   The relationship between heresy and literature in the academies of the Venetian republic, 1540–1606. Roberta Giubilini. (Professors Alastair Hamilton and Jill A. Kraye.) London Ph.D. (Warburg)

1020   The representation of angels in counter-Reformation Italy. Aldo Miceli. (Dr. Guido Giglioni and Professor Alastair Hamilton.) London Ph.D. (Warburg)

1021   A Golem in the memory alace: Giordano Bruno and the use of human shaped figures as thinking tools. Hanna Gentili. (Dr. Guido Giglioni and Professor Charles Burnett.) London Ph.D. (Warburg)

1022   Mapping and analysing the clothes worn by male Venetian patrician office holders during the early modern period. Jola Pellumbi. (Professor Evelyn Welch.) King's College London M.Phil./Ph.D. (Hist.)

1023   Unveiling Gregorian Rome: the urban and ecclesiastical patronage of Pope Gregory XIII (1572–85). Evangelia Papoulia. (Dr. Georgia M. Clarke.) London Ph.D. (Courtauld Inst.)

1024   Air as the medium of health, illness and the senses in Tommaso Campanella's medical philosophy. Andrew Manns. (Dr. Guido Giglioni and Professor Peter Mack.) London Ph.D. (Warburg)

1025   The early followers of Caravaggio in Rome. Aron Thom. Aberdeen Ph.D. (Hist. of Art)

1026   'Why tear me from myself?' The depiction of flaying in the art of Jusepe de Ribera. Bogdan Cornea. (Professor Helen Hills.) York Ph.D. (Hist. of Art)

1027   Maps and the Italian Grand Tour, 1660–1824. Jeremy Brown. (Professor Veronica Della Dora.) London M.Phil./Ph.D. (R.H.U.L. Geog.)

1028   Baroque towns built in the Val di Noto area of Sicily, 1700–80. Martin Nixon. (Professor Helen Hills.) York Ph.D. (Hist. of Art)

1029   'Innocent' and 'knowing' children: sexually assaulted girls and boys in Florence in the long 19th century. Christel Radica. (Dr. David Laven and Professor Elizabeth Harvey.) Nottingham Ph.D. (Hist.)

1030   Returned to the ghetto: Jewish encounters with Italian Catholics, 1815–48. Myrna G. Martin. (Dr. Abigail Green.) Oxford D.Phil. (Mod. Hist.)

1031   Camillo Boito and cultural heritage protection in Risorgimento Italy. Guilia Mezzi. (Professor Paul Davies.) Reading Ph.D. (Hist. of Art)

1032   Lorenzo Valerio and the politics of the radical Left. Pat Dalzell. (Dr. Emily West.) Reading Ph.D. (Hist.)

1033   Site-seeing: Rome and the printed ephemera of Victorian tourism. Anne Marie Bush. (Dr. E. Jane Garnett.) Oxford D.Phil. (Mod. Hist.)

1034   Do works of art produced on the island of Capri between 1850 and 1945 share unifying principles besides subject, style and national origin? George Field. (Professor Elizabeth Prettejohn.) York Ph.D. (Hist. of Art)

1035   The construction of the 'mad' female criminal in English, Scottish and Italian medical and legal discourse and practice, c.1850–1913. Fiona MacHugh. (Professor Perry Willson and Dr. Anja Johansen.) Dundee Ph.D. (Hist.)

1036   The international context of later 19th-century Italian ceramic art in Florence. Julia Mellor. (Professor Elizabeth Prettejohn.) York Ph.D. (Hist. of Art)

1037   The Naval Armaments industry in Britain and Italy before 1914. Giulio Marchisio. (Professor Ranald C. Michie and Dr. Andrzej J. Olechnowicz.) Durham Ph.D. (Hist.)

1038   The contribution of St. Frances Xavier Cabrini to Catholic educational practice, 1880–1917. Maria Williams. (Professor Gary McCulloch.) London Ph.D. (Inst. of Educ.)

1039   Italian liberalism and the contradictions of the penal system: between reform and terror, 1887–1914. Danilo Dondici. East Anglia Ph.D. (Hist.)

1040   A de Chirican enigma: the theatricality of *Arte Metafisica*, 1909–19. Anne L. Moore. (Dr. Al Wright.) Oxford D.Phil. (Mod. Hist.)

1041 Anglo-Italian relations during the conflict, 1915–18. Stefano Marcuzzi. (Dr. Robert Johnson and Professor Hew F.A. Strachan.) Oxford D.Phil. (Mod. Hist.)

1042 The relationship between the Italian Jewish communities and the Catholic church during the fascist era. Laura Musker. (Dr. Shirli Gilbert.) Southampton M.Phil. (Hist.)

1043 The Federazione Universitaria Cattolica Italiana, 1925–43. Jorge A. Dagnino. (Dr. Martin H. Conway.) Oxford D.Phil. (Mod. Hist.)

1044 Italy and the League of Nations: nationalism and internationalism, 1926–33. Elisabetta Tollardo. (Dr. Patricia M. Clavin.) Oxford D.Phil. (Mod. Hist.)

1045 The representation of Great Britain in fascist Italy. Jacopo Pili. (Dr. Nir Arielli and Professor Simon J. Ball.) Leeds Ph.D. (Hist.)

1046 Fascist youth organisations and their connections abroad in the 1930s. Tamara Colacicco. (Professor Christopher J.H. Duggan and Dr. Daniela La Penna.) Reading Ph.D. (Mod. Lang. & Eur. Stud.)

1047 The experience of 'confino' and the development of anti-fascists in Italy in the 1930s. Ilaria Poerio. (Professor Christopher J.H. Duggan and Dr. Daniela La Penna.) Reading Ph.D. (Mod. Lang. & Eur. Stud.)

1048 Aldo Moro (1916–78): a statesman with a strategy. Andrea Ambrogetti. (Dr. Ruth Glynn and Dr. Hugh Pemberton.) Bristol M.Litt. (Hist. Stud.)

1049 The British and the brava gente: Italian P.O.W.s and British society during the Second World War. Alexander Henry. (Dr. David Laven and Dr. Rob Lutton.) Nottingham Ph.D. (Hist.)

1050 B.B.C. radio propaganda in Italy in World War II. Ester LoBiundo. (Professor Matt Worley.) Reading Ph.D. (Hist.)

1051 Interactions between the peasantry and the resistance movement in Lombardy, 1943–5. Gian Paolo Ghirardini. (Professor Christopher J.H. Duggan.) Reading Ph.D. (Mod. Lang. & Eur. Stud.)

1052 A comparative study in European social history: co-operation in Italy and England, 1945–90. Corrado Secchi. (Dr. Axel Körner.) London M.Phil. (U.C. Hist.)

1053 Squatting movement in Italy and the U.K. Giulio D'Errico. (Dr. Richard Coopey and Dr. Alastair Kocho-Williams.) Aberystwyth Ph.D. (Hist. & Welsh Hist.)

1054 Italian contemporary popularism and regionalism. George Newth. (Dr. Linda Risso.) Reading Ph.D. (Hist.)

Mediterranean and islands

1055 Messages presented and messages taken: exploring tourist and native perceptions of Malta's early Christian heritage. Glen Farrugia. (Dr. Neil Christie and Dr. Joanna Appleby.) Leicester Ph.D. (Archaeol. & Anc. Hist.)

1056 Challenges to the survival of empires: the Ottoman empire in the 1860s and the Cretan insurrection. Abdurahim Ozer. (Dr. Antony M. Best.) London Ph.D. (L.S.E. Int. Hist.)

1057 Early 20th-century representations of the Mediterranean: to what extent was it a colonial concept? Riccardo Liberatore. (Dr. John Darwin.) Oxford D.Phil. (Mod. Hist.)

1058 The Turkish Cypriots under British rule, 1908–55: from a religious community to an ethnic minority. Ioannis Moutsis. (Dr. Benjamin C. Fortna.) London Ph.D. (S.O.A.S. Hist.)

1059 Competing political spaces in colonial Cyprus, 1931–50. Dimitris Kalantzopoulos. (Dr. David Ricks and Dr. Richard H. Drayton.) King's College London M.Phil./Ph.D. (Hist.)

1060 Readings of colonial insurgency: the British media and E.O.K.A. 'terrorism', 1955–9. Eleni Christou. (Professor Philip Murphy.) London M.Phil. (Inst. C'wealth Stud.)

1061 Foreign policy as a tool for economic development: the case of Malta and Dom Mintoff, 1971–84. Robert Micallef. (Dr. Jonathan Davis and Professor Rohan McWilliam.) Anglia Ruskin D.Phil. (Hist.)

Netherlands

1062 Visual translations of Jerusalem in the early modern Netherlands. Claudia Jung. (Dr. Jeanne Neuchterlein and Dr. Hanna Vorholt.) York Ph.D. (Hist. of Art)

1063 The Catholic nobility in the Dutch Republic, c.1580–1700. Jaap Geraerts. (Professor Ben Kaplan.) London Ph.D. (U.C. Hist.)

1064 Place, space, sight and sound: male anxiety and female conspiracy in Dutch genre paintings of the 17th century. Rachael A. Garrett. (Dr. Geraldine Johnson.) Oxford M.St. (Mod. Hist.)

1065 The concept and image of the Stadhouder in the Dutch Republic, 1650–1702, with special reference to the role of Willem III of Orange. Pauline A. Kiesow. (Mr. Scott Mandelbrote.) Cambridge Ph.D. (Hist.)

1066 Dutch strategies of conflict resolution in the Revolutionary and Napoleonic era. Mark Hay. (Dr. Michael Rowe and Dr. James E. Bjork.) King's College London M.Phil./Ph.D. (Hist.)

1067 Amsterdam Pleyel movement: fascism, anti-fascism, communism. Jasmine Calver. (Dr. Charlotte Alston.) Northumbria Ph.D. (Hist.)

Poland

1068 The lower Oder/Odra region, c.1660–1700. Masatake Wasa. (Professor R.J.W. Evans.) Oxford D.Phil. (Mod. Hist.)

1069 The Polish question in British politics and beyond, 1830–47. Milosz Cybowski. (Professor David Brown.) Southampton Ph.D. (Hist.)

1070 Catholicism, conflict, and the nationalist challenge: the Catholic church and nationalist movements in Ireland and Poland, 1880–1921. Rose Luminiello. (Professors Michael Brown and Robert Frost.) Aberdeen Ph.D. (Hist.)

1071 Polish sexual science in the 20th century. Thom Zawadzki. Exeter Ph.D. (Hist.)

1072   Politics in the shadow of the Holocaust: the Polish government-in-exile and the
       Zionist movement during the Second World War.   Katarzyna Dziekan.   (Dr. Shirli
       Gilbert.)   Southampton M.Phil.   (Hist.)

1073   Reconciling conflicting memories: Poles, Jews, the Holocaust and the Second World
       War.   Anna Solarska.   (Professor Dan Stone.)   London Ph.D.   (R.H.U.L. Hist.)

1074   Dealing with the past: forms of reconstruction of the memory of Jews in Poland.
       Malgorzata Wloszyca.   (Professor Tony Kushner.)   Southampton M.Phil.   (Hist.)

1075   Polish exhibitions between the 1940s and the 1970s.   Katarzuna Jezowska.   (Dr.
       Mikulaj Kunicki and Professor Paul Betts.)   Oxford D.Phil.   (Mod. Hist.)

1076   The rise and fall of the idea of workers' self-management in the Solidarity movement
       in Poland.   Andrew Walters.   (Professor Richard Berry and Dr. Jon Oldfield.)
       Glasgow Ph.D.   (Soc. Sc.)

1077   The Jewish community in contemporary Poland.   Scott Saunders.   (Dr. Shirli
       Gilbert.)   Southampton M.Phil.   (Hist.)

1078   The representation of the Second World War in post-war Polish cinema, 1945–70.
       Lucinda Fenny.   (Dr. Mikolaj Kunicki and Professor Robert J.W. Evans.)   Oxford
       D.Phil.   (Mod. Hist.)

1079   Reshaping bodies, behaviours and minds: Polish displaced persons in refugee camps
       after World War II.   Katarzyna Nowak.   (Professors Bertrand O. Taithe and Peter
       Gatrell.)   Manchester Ph.D.   (Hist.)

1080   A 20th-century enigma – unlocking Leszek Kolakowski.   Hubert Czyzewski.   (Dr.
       Mikolaj Kunicki and Dr. Timothy Garton Ash.)   Oxford D.Phil.   (Mod. Hist.)

1081   The Committee for the Education of Poles in Great Britain.   Agata Blaszczyk-Sawyer.
       (Professor George Kolankiewicz.)   London Ph.D.   (S.S.E.E.S.)

1082   Tobacco harm in Poland – from a non-issue under communist rule to a central focus
       of health advocacy in the post-communist period.   Mateusz Zatonski.   (Dr. Martin
       Gorsky and Professor Martin McKee.)   London M.Phil./Ph.D.   (L.S.H.T.M.)

1083   Solidarity and non-violent resistance, 1980–1.   Graham Harris.   East Anglia Ph.D.
       (Hist.)

Portugal

1084   Modernism and modernity in the Portuguese music of Freitas Branco, 1890–1955.
       Nuno Bettencourt Mendes.   (Professor Nick Cook.)   London Ph.D.   (R.H.U.L.
       Music)

Romania

1085   The 1848 revolutions in the Romanian principalities.   James Morris.   (Professor
       Christopher Clark.)   Cambridge Ph.D.   (Hist.)

1086   Scientific representation of the body of the criminal in modern Romania, 1859–1940.
       Corina-Maria Dobos.   (Professor Roger Cooter.)   London Ph.D.   (U.C. Hist. of Med.)

1087   Re-writing the new man: censorship in communist Romania, 1949–77. Andru Chiorean. (Professors Nick Baron and Elizabeth Harvey.) Nottingham Ph.D. (Hist.)

1088   Romanian foreign policy, 1956–69. Corina Mavrodin. (Professor O. Arne Westad.) London Ph.D. (L.S.E. Int. Hist.)

1089   Opposing communism: the 1956 students' movement in Timisoara. Corina Snitar. (Professors Geoffrey Swain and Terry Cox.) Glasgow Ph.D. (Soc. Sc.)

1090   Escaping the straightjacket: Romania's efforts to limit Soviet influence, 1958–1968. Claudio Biltoc. (Professors Holger H.W. Afflerbach and John Gooch.) Leeds Ph.D. (Hist.)

1091   A constructivist understanding of Romania's foreign policy, 1990–2006. Loretta Salajan. (Dr. Patrick Finney and Dr. Alistair Shepherd.) Aberystwyth Ph.D. (Int. Pol.)

Russia and the U.S.S.R.

1092   The gift-giving culture of Anglo-Muscovite diplomacy: gifts, charters and letters of Elizabeth, James and the Russian tsars, 1566–1623. Tatyana Zhukova. (Dr. Liudmyla Sharipova and Dr. Julia F. Merritt.) Nottingham Ph.D. (Hist.)

1093   The making of an enlightened nation: Europeanisation through scientific knowledge in 18th-century Russia. Alexander Iosad. (Professors Andrew Zorin and Pietro Corsi.) Oxford D.Phil. (Mod. Hist.)

1094   The grand (imperial) strategy of the Russian empire in the Caucasus and Transcaucasia against its southern rivals, 1820–33. Serkan Kececi. (Dr. Antony M. Best.) London Ph.D. (L.S.E. Int. Hist.)

1095   Research into the formation and structure of social networks among the landowning nobility in blacksoil Russia during the Great Reforms: elements of political ideology and the viability of estates after the emancipation (1851–91). Georgios Regkoukos. (Professors Stephen Lovell and Ian McBride.) King's College London M.Phil./Ph.D. (Hist.)

1096   From commune to community: peasants in Voronezh province, 1861–1905. Bartley Rock. (Professor Simon Dixon.) London M.Phil. (S.S.E.E.S.)

1097   Russian revolutionaries in London during the 1890s. Joseph M. Richardson. (Dr. Catherine Andreyev.) Oxford M.St. (Mod. Hist.)

1098   Russian terrorists in emigration, 1881–1917. Lara Green. (Dr. Charlotte Alston.) Northumbria Ph.D. (Hist.)

1099   Outmigration in the Russian village: Perm' province between 1890 and 1914. Jonathan Rowson. (Dr. Nick Baron.) Nottingham Ph.D. (Hist.)

1100   Aleksandr Semenov's Tajik national identity: on Russian orientalism and Soviet nation-building in central Asia. Matthias R. Battis. (Dr. Katya Andreyev and Dr. Alexander Morrison.) Oxford D.Phil. (Mod. Hist.)

1101   From 'yellow ticket' to 'bourgeois evil': female prostitution in urban Russia, 1900–30. Siobhan Hearne. (Dr. Sarah Badcock and Professor Nicholas Baron.) Nottingham Ph.D. (Hist.)

1102 Structures of power and control: the Imperial Russian Navy, 1900–17. Benjamin C. Eacott. (Dr. Katya Andreyev.) Oxford D.Phil. (Mod. Hist.)

1103 Lev Kamenev: a case study in moderate Bolshevism. Nick Coombes. (Dr. Arfan Rees and Dr. Galina Yemelianova.) Birmingham Ph.D. (Russ. Stud.)

1104 Between two powers: Ukrainian intellectuals serving the Bolsheviks. Olena Palko. East Anglia Ph.D. (Hist.)

1105 Internal visions, external changes: Russian religious philosophy, 1905–40. Stephanie Solywoda. (Dr. C. Catherine L. Andreyev and Dr. P. Walters.) Oxford D.Phil. (Mod. Hist.)

1106 British political intelligence gathering and the Zemstvo movement during the Russian revolution of 1905–7. Thomas Jones. (Dr. Shane P. O'Rourke.) York M.A. (Hist.)

1107 The unofficial diplomat: Bernard Pares and the promotion of Anglo-Russian relations, 1906–42. Rebecca Clare. (Professor Michael J. Hughes.) Liverpool Ph.D. (Hist.)

1108 Russian press in the U.K. before and after the Revolution of 1917: from isolated émigré networks to an effective dialogue with the host state and its population. Anastasiia Kudlenko. (Dr. Charlotte Alston.) Northumbria Ph.D. (Hist.)

1109 The mosaic portraits of Boris Anrep, 1913–52. Jane Williams. (Professor Paul Davies.) Reading Ph.D. (Hist.)

1110 War not peace: representations of two world wars by Russian women artists. Natalia Budanova. (Professor John Milner.) London Ph.D. (Courtauld Inst.)

1111 Racism and Russian communism? The Jewish question and the idea of 'race' in Russia, 1914–27. Brendan McGeever. (Professors Terry Cox and Satnam Virdee.) Glasgow Ph.D. (Soc. Sc.)

1112 Reactions to the Russian revolution in British culture, 1916–26. Andrew McIntosh. (Dr. Matthew Grant and Dr. Peter J. Gurney.) Essex Ph.D. (Hist.)

1113 Emancipated from above: women's voices in the early Soviet era. Hannah Parker. (Dr. Miriam J. Dobson.) Sheffield Ph.D. (Hist.)

1114 Emotion and revolution: British socialist responses to the Russian Revolution. Michael Carey. (Dr. Sarah Badcock and Professor Nick Baron.) Nottingham Ph.D. (Hist.)

1115 Ideology and identity: 'knowing' workers in early Soviet Russia, 1917–21. Laura Sumner. (Dr. Sarah Badcock and Dr. Nick Baron.) Nottingham Ph.D. (Hist.)

1116 Soviet foreign trade: 1918–24. Joseph Nicholson. (Dr. Nick Baron and Dr. Sarah Badcock.) Nottingham Ph.D. (Hist.)

1117 Coping with exile: the Zemgor and the Russian emigration, 1919–39. Jennifer Grieve-Laing. (Professor Anthony Heywood and Dr. Elizabeth Macknight.) Aberdeen Ph.D. (Hist.)

1118 Learning to feel Soviet: education and construction of the Soviet community. Aleksandra Kowalska. East Anglia Ph.D. (Hist.)

1119 Reaction to the Soviet Gulag: labour camps. Max Hodgson. (Professor Matt Worley.) Reading Ph.D. (Hist.)

1120   Interpersonal relations in the Stalinist penal system: the 'Urki' and camp authorities. Mark Vincent. East Anglia Ph.D. (Hist.)

1121   The rescue of Jews and Roma in Ukraine during the Holocaust. Hanna Abakunova. (Professor Robert Moore.) Sheffield Ph.D. (Hist.)

1122   The Stalin generation of Communist party leaders: explorations in psychobiography, with case studies of Ernst Thalmann, Harry Pollitt and Maurice Thorez. Theodore Brorza. (Dr. Jill Lewis and Dr. Leighton James.) Swansea M.Res. (Hist.)

1123   Institutions of peace for the Cold War: the history of the Soviet Committee for the Defence of Peace and its affiliated institutions, 1949–91. Vladimir Dobrenko. (Professor O. Arne Westad.) London Ph.D. (L.S.E. Int. Hist.)

1124   Long-term effects of serfdom: could serfdom have engendered a culture of mistrust in modern Russia? Elizaveta Elizarova. (Dr. James Fenske.) Oxford M.Sc. (Mod. Hist.)

1125   Builders of communism, 'defective' children and social orphans: Soviet children in care after 1953. Mirjam Galley. (Dr. Miriam J. Dobson.) Sheffield Ph.D. (Hist.)

1126   Soviet football stadiums of Leningrad, 1956–84: historical spaces of control? Alexander Jackson. (Dr. Leif Jerram and Professor Vera Tolz.) Manchester Ph.D. (Hist.)

1127   Understanding changing Russian nationalism: a cross-generational study. Matthew Blackburn. (Professor Geoffrey Swain and Dr. Moya Flynn.) Glasgow Ph.D. (Soc. Sc.)

1128   The 1965 economic Kosygin reform in the U.S.S.R.: influence of intergenerational learning. Giovanni Cadioli. (Dr. Christopher Davis.) Oxford D.Phil. (Mod. Hist.)

1129   Magnitizdat as a material form of rock music subculture in the U.S.S.R. in the 1970s and 1980s. Anna Kan. Bristol M.Litt. (Hist. Stud.)

1130   The Russian view on Shoah studies: official remembrance versus individual memory of the Holocaust in contemporary Russia. Christina Winkler. (Dr. Olaf Jensen.) Leicester Ph.D. (Hist.)

1131   Russian Orthodox Church between Russian nationalism and the state apparatus in the period of Perestroika, 1985–91. Sophie Kotzer. (Dr. Zoe Knox.) Leicester Ph.D. (Hist.)

1132   Selling the people's game: football's transition from communism to capitalism in the Soviet Union and its successor states. Karl Veth. (Professor Stephen Lovell.) King's College London M.Phil./Ph.D. (Hist.)

1133   Since the collapse of communism how has ideology influenced the built environment in Russia? Scott J. Siggins. East Anglia Ph.D. (Hist.)

1134   Gods, Wandersmanner and the city: post-Soviet literary portrayals of Moscow and the narratives of Moscow's cityscape since 1991. Mark Griffiths. (Dr. Seth Graham.) London M.Phil. (S.S.E.E.S.)

Spain

1135 An archaeological study of a 16th-century Spanish shipwreck. Corey Malcom. (Professor Timothy J. Thornton and Revd. Paul Wilcock.) Huddersfield Ph.D. (Music, Hum. & Media)

1136 The making of imperialism: racism, human rights and authority in 16th-century Spanish debates on empire. Philippe-Andre Rodriguez. (Professor James Belich.) Oxford D.Phil. (Mod. Hist.)

1137 Philip of Spain, king of England: a role overlooked. Gonzalo Berenguer. (Dr. Fernando Cervantes.) Bristol M.Litt. (Hist. Stud.)

1138 Juan de Mariana's place in the history of political thought. Kristoffer M. Hansen. (Dr. Sarah Mortimer.) Oxford M.St. (Mod. Hist.)

1139 Francisco Pacheco: a painter between tradition and innovation in 17th-century Spain. Bernadette Petti. (Dr. Cordula van Wyhe.) York Ph.D. (Hist. of Art)

1140 The role of the *asistente* during Seville's decline in the late 17th century. Oliver Ford. (Dr. Nicholas Davidson.) Oxford D.Phil. (Mod. Hist.)

1141 Spanish naval reform under Ferdinand VI, 1740–63. Catherine Scheybelle. (Professor Andrew D. Lambert and Dr. Alan James.) King's College London Ph.D. (War Stud.)

1142 British public opinion of Spain from 1808 to 1840. John Holsman. Dundee Ph.D. (Hist.)

1143 Writing nations after the break-up of New Spain c.1810–1900. Charles Angelo. (Professor Rebecca Earle.) Warwick M.Phil./Ph.D. (Hist.)

1144 Spanish funerary sculpture, 1850–1920, in an international context. Chloe Sharpe. (Professor Jason Edwards.) York Ph.D. (Hist. of Art)

1145 Josep Puig i Cadafalch and the construction of modern Catalan identity, 1880–1950. Lucila Mallart. (Professor Maiken Umbach.) Nottingham Ph.D. (Hist.)

1146 Anarchist childhoods. Emily Charkin. (Dr. Judith Suissa and Dr. Tom Woodin.) London Ph.D. (Inst. of Educ.)

1147 Centre-right politics in the Spanish province of Valencia, 1931–6. Stephen Lynam. Exeter M.Phil. (Hist.)

1148 The Spanish Civil War and its legacy, 1936–2015: the origins, composition and aims of the Spanish memory movement. Liam Morris. (Dr. Peter Anderson and Dr. Gregorio Alonso.) Leeds Ph.D. (Hist.)

1149 Mentally and physically disabled nationalist veterans and perceptions of masculinity in Franco's Spain, 1936–75. Stephanie Wright. (Professor M. Mary T. Vincent.) Sheffield Ph.D. (Hist.)

1150 The Atlantic Anarchist movement and the Spanish Civil War. Morris Brodie. (Dr. Paul Corthorn.) Belfast M.Phil./Ph.D. (Hist. & Anthr.)

1151 Contested care: medicine and surgery during the Spanish Civil War, 1936–9. Jonathan Browne. (Professor Ulf Schmitt and Dr. Julie Anderson.) Kent Ph.D. (Hist.)

1152 Perspectives, public opinion and coverage of the Spanish Civil War: a thematic approach to Irish newspaper coverage. William Burton. (Dr. P. Emmet J. O'Connor and Dr. James P. Loughlin.) Ulster Ph.D. (Hist.)

1153 The British political cartoon and the Spanish Civil War. Christian Cronin. (Dr. John Bulaitis.) Canterbury Christ Church M.Phil. (Hist.)

1154 Madrid's clandestine women – gender and power in Republican Madrid, 1936–9. Angela T. Flynn. (Dr. Frances Lannon.) Oxford D.Phil. (Mod. Hist.)

1155 The cultural propaganda and social practices of children's evacuation and life in residential homes in Republican Spain during the Spanish Civil War (1936–9). Suan M.J. Sheridan Breakwell. (Dr. Frances Lannon.) Oxford D.Phil. (Mod. Hist.)

1156 The materialisation of identity in the Spanish Civil War. Amy E. Shiel. (Dr. Alex Quiroga and Dr. Jane Webster.) Newcastle Ph.D. (Archaeol.)

1157 The Conde de Mayalde and the Franco regime. Rudolph Savundra. (Dr. Helen E. Graham.) London M.Phil./Ph.D. (R.H.U.L. Hist.)

1158 Labour and nation: welfare, sub-state nationalism and Labour unionism in Galicia and Scotland. Carla Gutierrez Ramos. (Professor M. Mary T. Vincent. and Dr. Eirini Karamouzi.) Sheffield Ph.D. (Hist.)

1159 History of E.T.A. Nicholas Buckley. (Professor Helen E. Graham.) London M.Phil./ Ph.D. (R.H.U.L. Hist.)

Sweden

1160 Anglo-Swedish commercial contact and commodity exchange in the 17th century. Adam Grimshaw. (Professor Steve Murdoch.) St. Andrews Ph.D. (Hist.)

1161 Swedish counter-insurgency warfare against peasants and irregular militias, 1632–48. Olli Backstrom. (Professors Robert Frost and Karin Friedrich.) Aberdeen Ph.D. (Hist.)

1162 British-Swedish relations in the era of the American Revolutionary Wars: a study of diplomatic, military and economic relations, 1773–63. Rikard Drakenlordh. (Dr. Alan Marshall and Professor Elaine Chalus.) Bath Spa Ph.D. (Hist. & Cultural Stud.)

1163 Mapping Jewish life in Stockholm, 1870–1939. Muja Hultman. (Professor Joachim Schlor.) Southampton M.Phil. (Hist.)

1164 Encountering nature and nation on foot: a comparative history of the outdoor movement in Britain and Sweden, 1880–1939. Susanna Blomqvist. (Dr. Paul Readman and Professor Arthur Burns.) King's College London M.Phil./Ph.D. (Hist.)

Switzerland

1165 Mapping rumour: gossip and networks of information in 16th-century St. Gallen. Carla T. Roth. (Professor Lyndal A. Roper.) Oxford D.Phil. (Mod. Hist.)

MODERN BRITAIN AND IRELAND

From c.1500 (long periods)

1166 A journey through space and time: an examination of the reiterative conceptualisation of space in urban Yorkshire. Nicole Harding. (Professor Paul Ward.) Huddersfield M.Phil. (Music, Hum. & Media)

1167 The contextualisation of the social and medical history of osteoarthritis and rheumatoid arthritis in post-medieval Britain. Davina D. Craps. (Dr. Rebecca Gowland and Dr. Pam Graves.) Durham Ph.D. (Archaeol.)

1168 The perils of industrialisation: child health in post-medieval England. Sophie L. Newman. (Dr. Rebecca Gowland, Dr. Pam Graves and Dr. Mike Church.) Durham Ph.D. (Archaeol.)

1169 An environmental history of Whittlesea Mere. Tracey Mooney. (Professors Charles Watkins and Georgina Endfield.) Nottingham Ph.D. (Geog.)

1170 Expressions of occupational identity. Edward Taylor. Exeter M.Phil. (Hist.)

1171 Perceptions of landscape in the Scottish Highlands in the 'period of transition', c.16th–19th century. Kevin J. Grant. (Dr. Christopher Dalglish.) Glasgow Ph.D. (Arts)

1172 Infanticide in south Wales. Shirley A. Smith. (Dr. Owen Roberts and Dr. Steven Thompson.) Aberystwyth Ph.D. (Hist. & Welsh Hist.)

1173 Portrayals of English witchcraft: popular representations from the early modern period through to the Romantic era. Cara V.R. Hanley. (Dr. Andrew Sneddon and Dr. Kyle Hughes.) Ulster Ph.D. (Hist.)

1174 How continental print sources shaped early modern Scottish culture and the delineation of subsequent Scottish print culture. Fern Insh. (Dr. John C. Morrison.) Aberdeen Ph.D. (Hist. of Art)

1175 Mourning jewellery in England, c.1500–1800. Cara Middlemass. (Professor Jeremy Boulton and Dr. Jane Webster.) Newcastle Ph.D. (Hist.)

1176 Early modern London and the rules of business: London merchants and institutions, c.1500–1800. Xu Yang. (Professor Matthew Davies.) London M.Phil./Ph.D. (Birkbeck)

1177 The shaping of Lincolnshire marshland communities: Bradley, Scartho and Humberston, c.1520–c.1850. Martin Watkinson. (Professor Keith D.M. Snell.) Leicester Ph.D. (Eng. Loc. Hist.)

1178 The architectural and social history of Heslington Hall. Katharine Bould. (Professor Anthony Geraghty.) York Ph.D. (Hist. of Art)

1179 Sculpture and the sea: figureheads, ship decoration and Britain's maritime worlds. Erica McCarthy. (Professor Alison Yarrington and Dr. Douglas Hamilton.) Hull Ph.D. (Hist.)

1180 Maritime sculpture and its contexts: 17th–19th-century votive ship models around the North Sea. Meredith Greiling. (Professors Alison Yarrington and David J. Starkey.) Hull Ph.D. (Hist.)

1181 Transpennine crossings. Murray Seccombe. (Dr. Angus J.L. Winchester and Professor Ian Gregory.) Lancaster Ph.D. (Hist.)

1182 Chiltern common waste, c.1650 to the present. Frances Kerner. (Dr. Angus J.L. Winchester.) Lancaster Ph.D. (Hist.)

1183 Preservation and development of rural England. Francesca Church. (Dr. Jeremy Burchardt.) Reading Ph.D. (Hist.)

1184 The evolution of endowment portfolios at Oxford's constituent colleges. Morgan S. Gerlak. (Dr. Rui Esteves.) Oxford M.Sc. (Mod. Hist.)

1185 Women of the great estates of south Wales. Norma E. Tribe. (Dr. Eryn Mant White and Professor Peter Borsay.) Aberystwyth Ph.D. (Hist. & Welsh Hist.)

Sixteenth century

1186 The problem of ornament in early modern architecture. Maria-Anna Aristova. (Professor Helen Hills.) York Ph.D. (Hist. of Art)

1187 Bejewelled: men and adornment in early modern England. Natasha Awais-Dean. (Professor Evelyn Welch and Dr. Dora Thornton.) London Ph.D. (Q.M. Hist.)

1188 Ornamental water (lakes) in the early modern period. Wendy Bishop. East Anglia Ph.D. (Hist.)

1189 The royal touch in early modern England. Stephen Brogan. (Professor Michael Hunter.) London Ph.D. (Birkbeck Hist.)

1190 Domestic servants and domestic space in early modern England. Tessa Chynoweth. (Professor Amanda Vickery.) London Ph.D. (Q.M. Hist.)

1191 Sixteenth- and 17th-century alchemy's place within wider contemporary intellectual frameworks of the occult. John A. Clements. (Professor James A. Sharpe.) York Ph.D. (Hist.)

1192 The invention of addiction in early modern England. Jose Cree. (Professor Phil Withington.) Sheffield Ph.D. (Hist.)

1193 Linen, an early modern necessity. Alice Dolan. (Professor John Styles and Dr. Anne Murphy.) Hertfordshire Ph.D. (Hist.)

1194 The witch's familiar: a study of the familiar spirit in the early modern British Isles. Scott Eaton. (Professor Crawford Gribben.) Belfast Ph.D. (Hist. & Anthr.)

1195 Colour in early modern England. Jenny Ferrando. (Dr. Mark S.R. Jenner.) York Ph.D. (Hist.)

1196 Witchcraft in the early modern home counties. Elizabeth Gardiner. (Professor Ronald Hutton.) Bristol M.Phil. (Hist. Stud.)

1197 'Thou shalt give me body and soul': the witch's familiar in early modern England. Gabriela Leddy. (Professor James A. Sharpe.) York Ph.D. (Hist.)

1198 A material menopause: the cultural and medical negotiation of female middle age in the early modern period. Rebekah Lee. (Dr. Cordula van Wyhe.) York Ph.D. (Hist. of Art)

1199 Early modern British armour and the fashioning of masculinity. Sophie Littlewood. (Dr. Cordula van Wyhe and Dr. John Cooper.) York Ph.D. (Hist. of Art)

1200 Aspects of power and discourse in early modern England. Callum Murrell. (Dr. Adrian Green and Professor Andrew Wood.) Durham Ph.D. (Hist.)

1201 Experimental firing and analysis of impacted early modern lead bullets. Colin Parkman. (Dr. Glenn Foard.) Huddersfield Ph.D. (Music, Hum. & Media)

1202 Crime in early modern Wales. Hollie Powell. (Ms. Nia Powell.) Bangor Ph.D. (Hist., Welsh Hist. & Archaeol.)

1203 Gunpowder and the rise of early modern science. Hailaigh Robertson. (Dr. Sophie Weeks.) York Ph.D. (Hist.)

1204 Living leather: material agency in early modern England. Thomas Rusbridge. (Professor Karen Harvey.) Sheffield Ph.D. (Hist.)

1205 Slaves and the 'new science': natural philosophers and their ideas about black skin in the 16th and 17th centuries. Norris Saakwa-Mante. (Professor Francisco Bethencourt and Dr. Anna Maerker.) King's College London M.Phil./Ph.D. (Hist.)

1206 Food, identity and humoral theory in early modern England: a case study from Leicestershire. Rachel Small. (Dr. Richard Thomas and Dr. Richard Jones.) Leicester Ph.D. (Archaeol. & Anc. Hist.)

1207 Peeping in, peering out: perspective, monocularity and early modern vision. Justina Spencer. (Dr. Hanneke Grootenboer.) Oxford D.Phil. (Mod. Hist.)

1208 Calculating value: using and collecting the tools of early modern mathematics. Kevin Tracey. (Dr. Adam Mosley.) Swansea Ph.D. (Hist.)

1209 Medical practice and its cultural impact in early modern England. Nick Weaver. (Dr. Kenneth Austin.) Bristol M.Litt. (Hist. Stud.)

1210 Fashion, clothing and national identity in early modern Britain. Natalie Williams. (Professor Maria Hayward.) Southampton M.Phil. (Hist.)

1211 The birth of the sporting woman: female embodiment and physical exercise in early modern Europe. Valerio Zanetti. (Professor Ulinka Rublack.) Cambridge Ph.D.

1212 'Vanished comforts': furnishing in Scotland, 1500–1650. Michael Pearce. (Dr. Alan MacDonald, Dr. Stephen Jackson and Dr. Derek Patrick.) Dundee Ph.D. (Hist.)

1213 Property management: a comparative study of three corporate institutions, c.1500–c.1640. Michael B. Saunders. (Dr. R. Evans and Dr. I.W. Archer.) Oxford M.Litt. (Mod. Hist.)

1214 Representation and reception of queenship in 16th-century England and Scotland. Mariana Brockmann. (Dr. Anna Whitelock.) London Ph.D. (R.H.U.L. Hist.)

1215 Identity and culture in 16th-century Scottish neo-Latin histories. Charles Mitchell. (Dr. Steven Reid and Dr. Catherine Steel.) Glasgow Ph.D. (Arts)

1216 The gentry family of south Wales in the 16th century. Anna M. Orofino. (Dr. John Law and Professor Maurice Whitehead.) Swansea Ph.D. (Hist.)

1217 Tudor terror: mental illness in the 16th century. Amelia Sceats. (Dr. Sarah Bastow.) Huddersfield M.Phil. (Music, Hum. & Media)

1218   'Pretty maids all in a row': ruling queens and the language of legitimation in 16th-century England. Lynsey Wood. (Professor Naomi Tadmor.) Lancaster Ph.D. (Hist.)

1219   School education in 16th-century London. Yang Yan. (Dr. Mark Merry and Professor Matthew Davies.) London M.Phil./Ph.D. (Inst. Hist. Res.)

1220   The peace and harmony of the medieval era? Pre-Reformation lay-church relations in the town of Reading. Joseph Chick. (Professor Beat Kumin.) Warwick M.Phil./Ph.D. (Hist.)

1221   Shaping the nation before the Reformation: English national identity up to 1530. Stephanie Collinson. (Dr. Alan V. Murray.) Leeds Ph.D. (Hist.)

1222   St. George in early modern England: continuity and change, 1509–1625. Alice Byrne. (Professor Peter Marshall.) Warwick Ph.D. (Hist.)

1223   The relationship between Henry VIII and the nobility at court. Kathleen Da Graca Pinto. (Dr. Lucy Kostyanovsky and Dr. Laura Gowing.) King's College London M.Phil./Ph.D. (Hist.)

1224   The progress of the Reformation in south Northamptonshire, c.1510–c.1750. Ann Garfield. (Dr. Rob Lutton and Dr. Julia F. Merritt.) Nottingham Ph.D. (Hist.)

1225   Subject to the higher powers: the concept of ordained authority based upon Romans 13:1–7. Steven Foster. (Professor Stephen Alford and Dr. Sarah Baker.) Leeds Ph.D. (Hist.)

1226   English Renaissance drama. Stephen D. Collins. (Professor David Wootton.) York M.Phil./Ph.D. (Hist.)

1227   Authority, clothing and accessories in the Cecil household during the 16th and early 17th centuries, c.1520–1612. Abigail Gomulkiewicz. (Professor Ulinka Rublack.) Cambridge Ph.D. (Hist.)

1228   Patterns of communal conformity: a comparative study of language especially in wills from Reformation Lancashire, 1520–80. David Leach. (Dr. Martin R.V. Heale.) Liverpool Ph.D. (Hist.)

1229   Roots of reform: a contextual interpretation of church fitting in Norfolk during the English Reformation. Jason Ladick. (Deirdre O'Sullivan and Dr. Richard Thomas.) Leicester Ph.D. (Archaeol. & Anc. Hist.)

1230   Power in objects: images, idolatry and recusancy in Yorkshire during the English Reformation. Megan Yadanza. (Dr. Raphael J.L. Hallett and Professor Stephen Alford.) Leeds M.A. (Hist.)

1231   An assessment of the relationship which emerged between young people and evangelicalism during the early English Reformation. Ryan Clayton. (Dr. Martin R.V. Heale.) Liverpool Ph.D. (Hist.)

1232   Languages of power in the early English Reformation. Christine Knaack. (Dr. John P.D. Cooper.) York Ph.D. (Hist.)

1233   Pre-Reformation ecclesiastical justice: the records of courts held between 1527 and 1530 by the vicar-general and the chancellor of John Longland, bishop of Lincoln. Martin Roberts. (Dr. Rob Lutton and Dr. Claire Taylor.) Nottingham Ph.D. (Hist.)

1234 Imagining the devil in Reformation England. Emma Mackie. (Dr. Lucy Kostyanovsky.) King's College London M.Phil./Ph.D. (Hist.)

1235 The afterlife of the dissolution of the monasteries, 1536–1698. Harriet Lyon. (Professor Alexandra Walsham.) Cambridge Ph.D. (Hist.)

1236 The dispersal and use of Welsh monastic lands. Heather Para. (Professor Janet E. Burton.) Wales Ph.D. (Trinity Saint David Hist.)

1237 The draper's company: archive and architecture, c.1540–1640. Sarah Ann Milne. (Dr. John Bold and Dr. Lindsay Bremner.) Westminster Ph.D. (Hist.)

1238 'The course of the gospell interrupted by malicious enemies': religious conservatives at the courts of Henry VIII and Edward VI, c.1540–50. Nasim Tadghighi. (Professor Ronald Hutton.) Bristol Ph.D. (Hist. Stud.)

1239 Manhood and masculinity in counter-Reformation England. Georgina Moore. (Dr. Roberta Anderson and Dr. David Coast.) Bath Spa Ph.D. (Hist. & Cultural Stud.)

1240 Evangelical ecclesiology and the liturgy in the Edwardian Reformation, c.1545–1555. Stephen Tong. (Professor Alexandra Walsham.) Cambridge Ph.D. (Hist.)

1241 'The ornament of a woman is silence': female authorship, censorship and silence in England, c.1546–1640. Alice Ferron. (Dr. Jason Peacey.) London Ph.D. (U.C. Hist.)

1242 Preparing a supper for all England: the eucharist collaboration of Peter Martyr Vermigli and Thomas Cranmer. Laura G. Alexander. (Professors Diarmaid MacCulloch and F.A. James III.) Oxford D.Phil. (Mod. Hist.)

1243 A transcription and study of the church warden's and townsmen's accounts for the parish of Norton-by-Daventry in the county of Northampton for the years 1548–84. Canon James Richardson. (Dr. Nigel R. Aston.) Leicester M.Phil. (Hist.)

1244 English herbs for English bodies: the promotion of native plants remedies, 1549–1659. Graeme Tobyn. (Dr. Stephen Pumfrey.) Lancaster Ph.D. (Hist.)

1245 Defining differences: the religious dimensions of early modern English travel narratives, 1550–1800. Hector Roddan. (Professor Garthine M. Walker.) Cardiff Ph.D. (Hist. & Archaeol.)

1246 An analysis of representation of domestic violence in the Winchester consistory courts between c.1550 and c.1700. Jackie Wilkinson. (Dr. Simon Sandall, Dr. Ellie Woodacre and Dr. Mark Allen.) Winchester M.Phil./Ph.D. (Hist.)

1247 The impact of the regicide of Charles I on contemporary notions of time and the future. Matthias Wong. (Dr. David Smith.) Cambridge Ph.D. (Hist.)

1248 Women's access to justice in Wales, 1550–1640. Elizabeth Howard. (Professor Garthine M. Walker.) Cardiff Ph.D. (Hist. & Archaeol.)

1249 William Cecil, Lord Burghley's use of the media to influence Parliament. Mark Frederick Wilson. (Professors Ted Vallance and Glyn Parry.) Roehampton M.Phil./ Ph.D. (Hist.)

1250 The political thought of Sir Francis Walsingham. Hannah Coates. (Professor Stephen Alford.) Leeds Ph.D. (Hist.)

1251 Propaganda in the reign of Mary Tudor, 1553–8. Corinna Streckfuss. (Dr. Christopher A. Haigh and Dr. Judith S. Pollmann.) Oxford D.Phil. (Mod. Hist.)

1252 An analysis of the Stationers' Register and printing in London, 1557–1640. Alexandra Hill. (Professor Andrew D.M. Pettegree.) St. Andrews Ph.D. (Hist.)

1253 English military institutions, 1558–1690. Graham A. Long. (Dr. Steven J. Gunn.) Oxford M.Phil. (Mod. Hist.)

1254 Brian Darcy and Elizabethan witchcraft. Thomas Davies. (Dr. Ian Archer and Dr. George Southcombe.) Oxford M.St. (Mod. Hist.)

1255 'With my ruling': queenship, gender and the social identity of Elizabeth I. Dustin Neighbors. (Dr. John P.D. Cooper.) York Ph.D. (Hist.)

1256 The intelligence system in Queen Elizabeth I's reign. Hsuan Ying Tu. (Dr. John P.D. Cooper.) York Ph.D. (Hist.)

1257 The sacred space between: the refashioning of belief, community and culture among Midland Catholics, 1558–1603. Laura A. Verner. (Dr. Lucy Kostyanovsky.) King's College London Ph.D. (Hist.)

1258 Recusants in the landscape: the Elizabethan English Catholic community of the Weald and Downland. Haighleagh Winslade. (Dr. Simon Sandall and Dr. Simon Roffey.) Winchester M.Phil./Ph.D. (Hist.)

1259 Sir Nicholas Throckmorton, Thomas Randolph and the political culture of Anglo-Scottish diplomacy. Victoria R. Smith. (Dr. Susan Doran and Dr. Tracey Sowerby.) Oxford D.Phil. (Mod. Hist.)

1260 Population and family in south-east Cambridgeshire, c.1560–1700. Roy Jose. (Professors E. Anne Laurence and Rosemary O'Day.) Open University Ph.D. (Hist.)

1261 Food and religion in Reformation England and Italy, c.1560–1640. Eleanor Barnett. (Dr. Craig Muldrew and Professor Ulinka Rublack.) Cambridge Ph.D. (Hist.)

1262 From pariah to paragon of virtue: the changing status of English bishops' wives, 1560–1640. Rachel Basch. (Dr. Anna Whitelock.) London M.Phil./Ph.D. (R.H.U.L. Hist.)

1263 Bishop John Jewel (1522–71) and the universal Church of England. Angela Ranson. (Dr. John P.D. Cooper.) York Ph.D. (Hist.)

1264 A synoptic study of images of Oxford and its buildings from 1566 to 1751. John W. Hawkins. (Dr. Geoffrey Tyack and Dr. Nicholas Davidson.) Oxford D.Phil. (Mod. Hist.)

1265 George Keith, 4th Earl Marischal, 'godly' humanism, and the Protestant counter-balance in north-east Scotland during the reign of James VI. Miles Kerr-Peterson. (Dr. Steven Reid.) Glasgow Ph.D. (Arts)

1266 Music and post-Reformation English Catholics, 1570–1642: place, sociability and space. Emilie K.M. Murphy. (Dr. Simon R. Ditchfield.) York Ph.D. (Hist.)

1267 Gentry Catholicism in the Thames river valley, 1570–1620. Mary A. Lavin. (Dr. Alexander Gajda.) Oxford M.Phil. (Mod. Hist.)

1268   Marginal poverty: the social and economic lives of the ordinary poor in Ipswich, 1570–1620. Tiffany H. Shumaker. (Dr. Martin J. Ingram.) Oxford D.Phil. (Mod. Hist.)

1269   People on the move in Devon, c.1572–98 to c.1800. Marion Hardy. Exeter M.Phil. (Hist.)

1270   The post-Reformation English Catholic community. John Anthony Hilton. (Dr. Rosamund B.M. Oates and Dr. Anthony J. Adams.) Manchester Metropolitan Ph.D. (Hist.)

1271   'Astrology is higher and nobler than medicine and every physician must be an astrologer': Astrologer-physicians and their working practices c.1580–1680. Barbara Dunn. Exeter Ph.D. (Hist.)

1272   Common consent and public profit: political languages in early modern England, 1580–1649. Hannah Whitfield. (Professor Mark Knights.) Warwick M.Phil./Ph.D. (Hist.)

1273   The pulpit and preaching culture in the dioceses of York and Chester, 1580–1642. Margaret Bullett. (Dr. Sarah Bastow and Dr. Patricia H. Cullum.) Huddersfield Ph.D. (Music, Hum. & Media)

1274   The Northamptonshire network of English Catholics, 1580–1620. Katie McKeogh. (Dr. Susan Brigden and Dr. Alexandra Gajda.) Oxford D.Phil. (Mod. Hist.)

1275   Meanings and experiences of the female body in possession cases of late Elizabethan England. Kyoko Miyake. (Dr. C.A. Holmes.) Oxford D.Phil. (Mod. Hist.)

1276   Plague prevention in early modern London, 1583–1665. Lara Thorpe. (Professors J.N. Peregrine B. Horden and Justin A.I. Champion.) London M.Phil./Ph.D. (R.H.U.L. Hist.)

1277   The exchequer commission into the establishment of the port of Gloucester, 1583. Alexander Higgins. (Dr. Evan Jones.) Bristol M.Litt. (Hist. Stud.)

1278   Diplomacy and deception: James VI's foreign relations, 1586–1604. Cynthia Fry. (Professor Steve Murdoch.) St. Andrews Ph.D. (Hist.)

1279   The abstract imagining of the British state and its relationship to the central figure of government, 1588–1688. Thomas D. Howells. (Dr. Jonathan Parkin.) Oxford D.Phil. (Mod. Hist.)

1280   Christ's Hospital, charity and poor relief in the City of London, c.1590–1670. Gary Jenkins. (Professor Vanessa Harding.) London M.Phil./Ph.D. (Birkbeck Hist.)

1281   Puritans and lay supremacy, 1590–1642. Esther Counsell. (Professor Mark Goldie.) Cambridge Ph.D. (Hist.)

1282   The economic, intellectual and social origins of land ownership in the Fens and colonies in late Elizabethan/Jacobean England. Lynne P. Turner. East Anglia Ph.D. (Hist.)

1283   English attitudes to scripture, 1590–1620, with reference to the works of Richard Hooker. Duncan J. Swan. (Dr. David Crankshaw.) King's College London Ph.D. (Theol. & Rel. Stud.)

1284 The barony of Inishowen, the Nine Years' War and the Ulster Plantation. Janet McGrory. (Dr. William Kelly and Dr. Éamonn Ó Ciardha.) Ulster Ph.D. (Hist.)

Seventeenth century

General and political history

1285 Magical approaches to the passions in 17th-century England. Alex Cummins. (Professor Ronald Hutton.) Bristol M.Litt. (Hist. Stud.)

1286 That colonies have their warrant from God: English Protestant thought and theories of colonisation in the 17th century. Sam Petty. (Dr. Rachel Hammersley and Professor Susan-Mary Grant.) Newcastle Ph.D. (Hist.)

1287 Reimagining England: power and status in 17th-century utopian visions of the new world. Jane Campbell. Exeter Ph.D. (Hist.)

1288 Government by pen (1603–38)? Wayne Cuthbertson. (Professor Roger A. Mason.) St. Andrews Ph.D. (Hist.)

1289 Royal prerogative and parliamentary privilege, 1603–29. Keith Stapylton. (Professor Jason Peacey.) London M.Phil. (U.C. Hist.)

1290 Women at the court of James I. Claire Tremlett. (Dr. Evan Jones and Professor Ronald Hutton.) Bristol M.Litt. (Hist. Stud.)

1291 A social and intellectual biography of Lucius Cary, 2nd Viscount Falkland. Kay Tapply. (Professor Phil Withington and Dr. Thomas Leng.) Sheffield Ph.D. (Hist.)

1292 Sir Julius Caesar and the Great Contract, 1610. Josephine A. Pickard. (Dr. Ian Archer.) Oxford M.St. (Mod. Hist.)

1293 The judiciary and the political use and abuse of the law by the Caroline regime, 1625–40. Christopher St. John-Smith. (Dr. Grant Tapsell and Dr. Clive Holmes.) Oxford D.Phil. (Mod. Hist.)

1294 A reappraisal of the York House Conference, 1626. Joseph Newall. (Dr. Sarah Mortimer.) Oxford M.St. (Mod. Hist.)

1295 The writings of Robert Boreman D.D. in the context of his role in 17th-century society. Helen Kemp. (Dr. David Rundle.) Essex Ph.D. (Hist.)

1296 Popular politics in mid 17th-century London. Geoffrey Meddelton. (Dr. Mark S.R. Jenner.) York M.A. (Hist.)

1297 The publisher Humphrey Moseley and Royalist literature, 1640–60. Nicola M. Whitehead. (Professor Blair Worden.) Oxford D.Phil. (Mod. Hist.)

1298 The visual language of kingship, 1640–53. Rhian Wyn-Williams. (Dr. Edward Vallance.) Liverpool Ph.D. (Hist.)

1299 Popular appeal and political mobilisation: a study of legal pamphlets and the law in the early 1640s. Alexander Hitchman. (Professor Michael J. Braddick.) Sheffield Ph.D. (Hist.)

1300 Propaganda during the English civil wars, 1642–9 – the art of persuasion. Annette H. Walton. (Dr. Steven J. Gunn.) Oxford D.Phil. (Mod. Hist.)

1301 Negotiating defeat: English royalism, 1646–60. Robert Rudge. (Dr. Julia F. Merritt and Dr. David Appleby.) Nottingham Ph.D. (Hist.)

1302 Politics and the economy in England, c.1660–1727. DeAnn de Luna. (Professor Julian Hoppit.) London Ph.D. (U.C. Hist.)

1303 English representations of Wales and Cornwall, 1660–1720. James W. Harris. (Dr. Grant Tapsell.) Oxford D.Phil. (Mod. Hist.)

1304 Courts, commerce and constitutional crisis: Sir John Holt, the law and the English state in the late 17th century. George H. Artley. (Dr. Clive Holmes and Dr. Perry Gauci.) Oxford D.Phil. (Mod. Hist.)

1305 Religion and the Restoration stage. David Fletcher. (Professor Mark Knights and Dr. David Taylor.) Warwick M.Phil./Ph.D. (Hist.)

1306 Thomas Hobbes, *Behemoth* and the dialogue form in Restoration England. Andrew J. Floyd. (Dr. Sarah Mortimer.) Oxford D.Phil. (Mod. Hist.)

1307 Remembering rebellion: communities of memory in the Three Kingdoms, 1660–85. Edward Legon. (Dr. Jason Peacey.) London Ph.D. (U.C. Hist.)

1308 Coronations: the religious, political and social impact of divine right kingship in Britain, c.1661–c.1714. George W.C. Cross. (Dr. David Crankshaw.) King's College London M.Phil. (Theol. & Rel. Stud.)

1309 Policy and power: ideas, policymaking and practice in 1670s England. Michael Cressey. (Dr. Alex Barber and Dr. Stephen Taylor.) Durham Ph.D. (Hist.)

1310 English national identity in political debate, 1678–83. Jonathan D. Finlay. (Dr. Jon Parkin.) Oxford M.St. (Mod. Hist.)

1311 Peers, policy and power under the revolution constitution, 1685–1719. Phillip Loft. (Professor Julian Hoppit.) London Ph.D. (U.C. Hist.)

1312 Imprisonment for debt and women's financial failure in the long 18th century. Alexander Michael Fensome Wakelam. (Dr. Amy Erickson.) Cambridge Ph.D. (Hist.)

1313 The banishment of Hadriaan Beverland (1650–1716): the radical ideas of a humanist scholar on sex, sin and the Bible. Karen E. Hollewand. (Dr. Faramerz Dabhoiwala.) Oxford D.Phil. (Mod. Hist.)

17th century: Local history and government

1314 Hospitality in 17th-century Sussex. Caroline Adams. Chichester M.Phil./Ph.D. (Hist.)

1315 Seventeenth-century Norfolk. Danny Buck. East Anglia Ph.D. (Hist.)

1316 Survival strategies of the clergy of Dorset in the 17th century: economic, political, social and geographical. Trixie Gadd. (Dr. Andrew J. Hopper.) Leicester Ph.D. (Eng. Loc. Hist.)

1317 The trade of Bristol in the 17th century. Richard Stone. (Dr. Evan Jones.) Bristol Ph.D. (Hist. Stud.)

1318 Radical religion and the early development of the Quaker movement in the area of Pendle, the Ribble Valley, Craven and the Yorkshire Dales in the period 1600–60. Roy Hickey. (Dr. Sasha Handley.) Manchester Ph.D. (Hist.)

1319 The forest of Macclesfield in the early 17th century. Thomas Swailes. (Professor Peter G.I. Gaunt.) Chester Ph.D. (Hist. & Archaeol.)

1320 How did Hertfordshire paupers experience poor relief under the Old Poor Law? Carla Herrmann. (Professor Steven A. King.) Leicester Ph.D. (Hist.)

1321 Exeter *c.*1602: illuminating the 'chorus of shadows'. Kate Osborne. (Professors Jonathan Barry and Jane C. Whittle.) Exeter Ph.D. (Hist.)

1322 Impact of civil wars on family economies in Sussex, *c.*1635–80. Helen Whittle. Chichester M.Phil./Ph.D. (Hist.)

1323 Non-aristocratic women's agency in Gloucestershire, 1640–1740. Susan Brown. (Dr. Erin Peters and Professor Melanie J. Ilic.) Gloucestershire Ph.D. (Hum.)

1324 The gentry of north-east Wales *c.*1640–88: power, religion and political networks. Sarah L. Ward. (Dr. Grant Tapsell.) Oxford D.Phil. (Mod. Hist.)

1325 The experience of war widows and orphans in the mid 17th-century Midlands. Stewart Beale. (Dr. Andrew J. Hopper.) Leicester Ph.D. (Eng. Loc. Hist.)

1326 The experience of war widows and orphans in mid 17th-century south-east England. Hannah Worthen. (Dr. Andrew J. Hopper.) Leicester Ph.D. (Hist.)

1327 The role of the castle and town of New Windsor during the English civil wars (1642–50). Elias Kupfermann. (Dr. Andrew J. Hopper.) Leicester Ph.D. (Eng. Loc. Hist.)

1328 The governance of Shropshire, 1645–61. Isabel Jones. (Professor Peter G.I. Gaunt.) Chester Ph.D. (Hist. & Archaeol.)

1329 Industrialising communities in South Yorkshire, 1650–1850: a case study of Cannon Hall. Nicola Walker. (Professor Karen Harvey.) Sheffield Ph.D. (Hist.)

1330 A stream of failures: navigation of the Salisbury Avon and Christchurch Haven, *c.*1650–1750. Stephen Gadd. (Dr. Simon Sandall and Dr. Mark A. Allen.) Winchester M.Phil./Ph.D. (Hist.)

1331 A manly and pious man? Representations and traits of manliness and Quaker notions of masculinity in Essex and East Anglia, *c.*1650–1740. Robert Foulkes. (Dr. Alison Rowlands.) Essex Ph.D. (Hist.)

1332 Protectoral rule in the north-western association: the role and consequence of military and civil governance in the north-west of England, 1655–7. David Williams. (Professor Peter G.I. Gaunt.) Chester Ph.D. (Hist. & Archaeol.)

1333 Restoration Bath, 1658–90. James S. Camp. (Dr. David Coast and Dr. Stephen Gregg.) Bath Spa Ph.D. (Hist. & Cultural Stud.)

1334 My chiefest concern is to see I have enough money: the marriage strategies of the Midland gentry *c.*1660–1820. Gareth Davies. (Professor Mark Knights.) Warwick Ph.D. (Hist.)

1335 The affective communities of protestantism in the north-west of England, 1660–1730. Michael Smith. (Professor Jeremy Gregory and Dr. Sasha Handley.) Manchester Ph.D. (Hist.)

1336   Landscapes of the Bristol Channel region, 1688–1914. Robert Jeffrey Baker. (Professor Louise Miskell.) Swansea Ph.D. (Hist.)

1337   The Wades of New Grange and the lesser gentry in the long 18th century. Keith Rowntree. (Dr. Simon Morgan and Dr. Shane Ewen.) Leeds Beckett Ph.D. (Cultural Stud.)

1338   The religious landscape of Hampshire 1689–1725. Natalie Jennings. (Dr. Simon Sandall and Dr. Colin Haydon.) Winchester M.Phil./Ph.D. (Hist.)

17th century: Ireland

1339   The Skinners Company and the plantation of Ulster, 1609–41. Dearbhaile McCloskey. (Dr. William Kelly and Dr. Éamonn Ó Ciardha.) Ulster Ph.D. (Hist.)

1340   The covenantal structure of James Ussher's theology. Harrison Perkins. (Professor Crawford Gribben.) Belfast M.Phil./Ph.D. (Hist. & Anthr.)

1341   'Protestant martyrs or Irish vagrants?' responses and the organisation of relief to Irish refugees in England, 1641–51. Bethany Marsh. (Dr. David Appleby and Dr. Andrew Hopper.) Nottingham Ph.D. (Hist.)

1342   Charles O'Conor of Belanagare: political ethnographies and historical narratives of early modern Ireland, 1690–1760. Macdara Dwyer. (Professors Ian McBride and Anne Goldgar.) King's College London M.Phil./Ph.D. (Hist.)

1343   An examination of the practices, procedures and operation of the Irish Commons from 1692–1730, including procedural developments and the extent to which the Westminster House of Commons influenced the Irish House. G. McKee. (Professor Ian McBride.) King's College London Ph.D. (Hist.)

17th century: Administrative, military and naval history

1344   Establishing a methodology to unlock the archaeology of attack on siege sites: a case study from 17th-century England. Richard Leese. Huddersfield Ph.D. (Music, Hum. & Media)

1345   Reputation, law, and commercial life in 17th-century England: the case of Thompson and company in 1677. Mabel Winter. (Professor Phil Withington.) Sheffield Ph.D. (Hist.)

1346   The activities, interaction and influence of the Royal Navy on Scotland, c.1603–1760. Colin Helling. (Dr. Andrew MacKillop and Dr. Alastair Macdonald.) Aberdeen Ph.D. (Hist.)

1347   'By the length of their pikes': realities and perceptions of early modern British infantry combat, 1642–1783. Dukhee Yun. Exeter Ph.D. (Hist.)

1348   Sexual violence and rape during the Civil War. Sylvia Broeckx. (Dr. Andrew Heath.) Sheffield Ph.D. (Hist.)

1349   The significance of artillery in sieges in the English Civil War, 1642–51, and its place within the military revolution thesis. Sam Chadwick. (Professor Peter G.I. Gaunt.) Chester Ph.D. (Hist. & Archaeol.)

1350 Supplying the civil war: a case study of supply and logistics in the West Midlands, 1642–6. Glenn Price. (Dr. Ian Atherton and Dr. Siobhan Talbott.) Keele Ph.D. (Hist.)

1351 Analysis and comparison of the function and performance of Charles II's yacht, the *Mary* (1660–75) and her rebuild, *c*.1677–1720. Juan P. Olaberria. (Professor Mary Hayward, Dr. Dominic Hudson and Dr. Graeme Earl.) Southampton M.Phil. (Hist.)

1352 Religion and the late Stuart army, 1660–1714. Ping Liao. (Professor Peter Wilson and Dr. Charles Prior.) Hull Ph.D. (Hist.)

1353 The major-generals in the north: Cromwellian administration in the northern counties during the English Protectorate, 1655–6. Stephen Harper. (Dr. Jonathan Spangler and Professor Melanie Tebbutt.) Manchester Metropolitan M.Phil. (Hist.)

1354 Naumachia and naval commemoration in the British garden during the long 18th century. Dominic C.D. Ingram. (Dr. Hannah Smith.) Oxford M.St. (Mod. Hist.)

1355 The Bloody Code: was it really that? Alan Swinton. (Dr. Drew Gray and Dr. Matthew McCormack.) Northampton Ph.D. (Hist.)

1356 The topography of power of the offices of state, 1689–1750. Lorna Coventry. (Dr. Perry L. Gauci.) Oxford D.Phil. (Mod. Hist.)

1357 Gentlemen of leisure or vital professionals? The officer corps of the British Army, 1689–1739. Neil Sanghvi. (Dr. Hannah Smith.) Oxford D.Phil. (Mod. Hist.)

17th century: Finance, trade and industry

1358 Merchant capital, hybrid knowledge, and the formation of English colonial labour regimes *c*.1600–*c*.1700. Michael Bennett. (Professor Michael J. Braddick.) Sheffield Ph.D. (Hist.)

1359 The Company Director: commerce, state and society, 1600–1708. Aske Laursen Brock. (Dr. William Pettigrew and Dr. Tristan Stein.) Kent Ph.D. (Hist.)

1360 Consumer behaviour and material culture in the south-west peninsula, *c*.1650–1750. Andrew P. Binding. (Professors Mark Overton and Jane Whittle.) Exeter M.Phil. (Hist.)

1361 The social, economic and political development of the West Country woollen manufacturers, 1660–1780. Muhammad Y. Nawaz. (Dr. Perry Gauci.) Oxford D.Phil. (Mod. Hist.)

1362 The Royal Society and the sea: science, expertise and maritime knowledge, *c*.1660–1714. Phillippa Hellawell. (Professors Anne Goldgar and Ian McBride.) King's College London M.Phil./Ph.D. (Hist.)

1363 The making and possessing of quality: the metalware trades in England, *c*.1675–1785. Rachael Morton. (Professor Giorgio Riello.) Warwick Ph.D. (Hist.)

1364 Agency of London beneficiaries, 1688–1830. Megan Webber. (Dr. Sarah Lloyd and Professor Tim Hitchcock.) Hertfordshire Ph.D. (Hist.)

1365 Criminal skill: coining and coiners during the long 18th century. Robert Rock. (Dr. Anne Murphy and Professor John Styles.) Hertfordshire Ph.D. (Hist.)

1366 Seeking success: provincial gentry and middling families in Cumbria encounter the East Indies in the long 18th century. Katherine Saville-Smith. (Dr. Angus J.L. Winchester and Dr. James C. Taylor.) Lancaster Ph.D. (Hist.)

1367 'This little republick': the debtors' sanctuary of Southwark Mint, 1697–1724. John Simon Alex Levin. (Professors Ian S. Gazeley and Tim Hitchcock.) Sussex D.Phil. (Hist.)

17th century: Social history

1368 Accidents, children and death in England and Wales, 1600–1800. Johns Abby. (Professor Garthine M. Walker.) Cardiff Ph.D. (Hist. & Archaeol.)

1369 Betraying bodies and dissembling demeanours in early modern England, 1600–1750. Jasmine Losasso. (Professor Garthine M. Walker.) Cardiff Ph.D. (Hist. & Archaeol.)

1370 Collectors of cheap print in 17th- and early 18th-century England. Tim Somers. (Professor Christopher Marsh.) Belfast M.Phil./Ph.D. (Hist. & Anthr.)

1371 'Treacherous Glass': counterfeit jewels in the 17th century and the illusion of splendour, an examination of gemstone enhancement and imitation, the acceptability of inferior materials and perceptions of value. Anna Lisa Jensen. (Dr. Evelyn Welch and Professor David E.H. Edgerton.) King's College London M.Phil./Ph.D. (Hist.)

1372 Motherhood examined in 17th-century legal and bureaucratic records. Carolanne Selway. (Dr. Laura Gowing and Professor Anne Goldgar.) King's College London M.Phil./Ph.D. (Hist.)

1373 Dealing in smoke: the trade, consumption and regulation of tobacco in early modern England, 1624–85. Alexander Taylor. (Professor Phil Withington.) Sheffield Ph.D. (Hist.)

1374 The city lady in the godly city: gender, religion and social obligations in London, c.1600–30. Ioanna Z. Tsakiropoulou. (Dr. Ian W. Archer and Dr. Susan E. Brigden.) Oxford D.Phil. (Mod. Hist.)

1375 Alternative discourses: religious toleration in context, 1603–47. Thomas Luttrell. (Professor Peter Marshall.) Warwick M.Phil./Ph.D. (Hist.)

1376 Public ritual in English towns, 1630–70. Amy Calladine. (Dr. Julia F. Merritt and Dr. Liudmyla Sharipova.) Nottingham Ph.D. (Hist.)

1377 Lady Ranelagh and her circle. Elaine Josephs. (Professor Justin A.I. Champion.) London M.Phil./Ph.D. (R.H.U.L. Hist.)

1378 Children's emotional responses to the English civil war. Jessica Champion. (Dr. Ian Archer.) Oxford M.St. (Mod. Hist.)

1379 Scottish chapbooks and popular culture, 1650–1800. Daliah Bond. (Professor William Naphy and Dr. Michael Brown.) Aberdeen Ph.D. (Hist.)

1380 Noblemen and furnishing the home, 1650–1730. Antonia Brodie. (Professor Amanda Vickery.) London Ph.D. (Q.M. Hist.)

1381 'Intimate crime' in early modern England and Wales, 1660–1760. Anna Field. (Professor Garthine M. Walker.) Cardiff Ph.D. (Hist. & Archaeol.)

1382   News in late Stuart England. Samuel Garland. (Professor Tony Claydon.) Bangor Ph.D. (Hist., Welsh Hist. & Archaeol.)

1383   Becoming a man in Restoration England: two young diarists and their social environments, 1663–78. Daniel Patterson. (Professor Christopher Marsh.) Belfast M.Phil./Ph.D. (Hist. & Anthr.)

1384   The trouble with tennis – the conduct of the game in Oxford from 1680–1720, in the context of moral concerns. Margaret R. Henderson-Tew. (Dr. Hannah Smith.) Oxford M.St. (Mod. Hist.)

1385   The history of emotion, analysed through a study of providentialism in late 17th- and early 18th-century England. Victoria Lewis. East Anglia Ph.D. (Hist.)

1386   Continuity and tradition: popular behaviour between birth and baptism in the long 18th century. Sarah Fox. (Professor Hannah Barker and Dr. Sasha Handley.) Manchester Ph.D. (Hist.)

1387   Leisured women and the English spa town in the long 18th century: a case study of Bath and Tunbridge. Rose McCormack. (Professor Peter Borsay and Dr. Martyn J. Powell.) Aberystwyth Ph.D. (Hist. & Welsh Hist.)

1388   Alternative masculinities and their settings in Britain, 1689–1702. Owen Brittan. (Dr. Lawrence Klein.) Cambridge Ph.D. (Hist.)

1389   'Powerful and active atoms': scent and smelling in Britain, 1690–1800. William Tullett. (Professor Laura Gowing.) King's College London Ph.D. (Hist.)

17th century: Ecclesiastical and religious history

1390   The bishop of Durham's castles in the 17th and 18th centuries. Seif El Rashidi. (Dr. Adrian G. Green and Dr. Toby Osborne.) Durham Ph.D. (Hist.)

1391   French Anglicanism: a religious history of Jersey in the 17th century. Frances M. Jeune. (Dr. Grant Tapsell.) Oxford M.Litt. (Mod. Hist.)

1392   Touch and space in 17th-century mission narratives. Robin MacDonald. (Dr. Mark S.R. Jenner and Dr. Simon R. Ditchfield.) York Ph.D. (Hist.)

1393   Irenicism in matters of fact and matters of faith: rethinking the relationship between the Anglican via media and natural philosophy in 17th-century England. Martin Walker. (Dr. Stephen Pumfrey.) Lancaster Ph.D. (Hist.)

1394   The reception of Calvinist resistance theory in early 17th-century Scotland. Karie Schultz. (Dr. Ian Campbell.) Belfast Ph.D. (Hist. & Anthr.)

1395   Orthodox radicals: Baptist identity formation in Stuart England. Matthew Bingham. (Professor Crawford Gibben.) Belfast M.Phil./Ph.D. (Hist. & Anthr.)

1396   Puritanism, emotion and moderation, Samuel Clarke (1599–1682): the shaping and moderation of emotion in 17th-century puritan culture. Martyn Cutmore. (Professor Mark Knights.) Warwick M.Phil./Ph.D. (Hist.)

1397   Perceptions of English cathedrals, 1625–1714. Alice Soulieux-Evans. (Professor Alexandra Walsham.) Cambridge Ph.D. (Hist.)

1398   Religious attitudes in Somerset, 1625–60.   John Reeks.   (Professor Ronald Hutton.)
       Bristol Ph.D.   (Hist. Stud.)

1399   The experience of discipline amongst the community of the faithful in Lothian,
       Scotland, 1640–70.   Claire McNulty.   (Professor Crawford Gribben.)   Belfast Ph.D.
       (Hist. & Anthr.)

1400   Anti-popery and the politics of English Protestantism, 1640–2.   Emma C. Turnbull.
       (Dr. Alexandra Gajda and Dr. Sarah Mortimer.)   Oxford D.Phil.   (Mod. Hist.)

1401   Representations of hell in post-Reformation England.   Richard Dhillon.   (Dr. Tara
       Hamling and Dr. Jonathan Willis.)   Birmingham Ph.D.   (Hist.)

1402   Thomas Manton among Interregnum and Restoration Presbyterians.   Adam
       Richardson.   (Professor John R.D. Coffey.)   Leicester Ph.D.   (Hist.)

1403   The crisis of Calvinism in Cromwellian England: Arminian soteriology in Anglican
       and Puritan thought.   Andrew Ollerton.   (Professor John Coffey.)   Leicester Ph.D.
       (Hist.)

1404   Identities and networks of nonconformist ministers (1658–74).   Kinda Skea.
       (Professor John R.D. Coffey.)   Leicester Ph.D.   (Hist.)

1405   Gender and religious dissent, 1660–1720.   Sue Haines.   (Professor John Miller.)
       London M.Phil.   (Q.M. Hist.)

1406   The rational apocalypse of Latitudinarians in Restoration England.   Jeongkyu Park.
       (Professor John Spurr.)   Swansea Ph.D.   (Hist.)

1407   Conscience, grace and religious liberty in Restoration England: the nature of the
       argument around liberty of conscience.   Richard Billinge.   (Dr. Sarah Mortimer.)
       Oxford D.Phil.   (Mod. Hist.)

1408   The political thought of John Owen.   Gregory McManus.   (Professor John R.D.
       Coffey.)   Leicester Ph.D.   (Hist.)

1409   Furnishing Sir Christopher Wren's churches: Anglican identity in late 17th-century
       London.   Mark Kirby.   (Dr. Anthony Geraghty.)   York Ph.D.   (Hist. of Art)

1410   Investigating the tradescant cabinet.   Christopher Hunt.   (Professor Claudia Stein.)
       Warwick M.Phil./Ph.D.   (Hist.)

1411   The Scottish Episcopal church and the Jacobite rebellions.   Jonathan McClintock.
       Dundee Ph.D.   (Hist.)

1412   Edmund Calamy (1671–1732) and the history of English dissent.   Paul McMenemy.
       (Professor John R.D. Coffey.)   Leicester Ph.D.   (Hist.)

17th century: Education, the arts, science and medicine

1413   The dark side of ivory: an analysis of a 17th-century ivory cabinet and its implications
       for the 21st century.   Jamee L. Bender.   (Dr. Camille Mathieu.)   Oxford M.St.   (Mod.
       Hist.)

1414   John Evelyn and the visual arts.   Marc de Knighton.   (Scott Mandelbrote.)
       Cambridge Ph.D.   (Hist.)

1415   Man, God and knowledge: anatomical investigation in 17th-century England. Anna Payne. (Dr. Kenneth Austin and Dr. Fernando Cervantes.) Bristol M.Litt. (Hist. Stud.)

1416   Love and the object: the English in the 17th century. Sarah A. Robin. (Dr. Sarah E. Barber and Dr. Corinna Peniston-Bird.) Lancaster Ph.D. (Hist.)

1417   Murderesses, mothers and martyrs: popular representations of violent women in 17th-century English prints. Molly I. Smith. (Dr. Geraldine Johnson.) Oxford M.St. (Mod. Hist.)

1418   The reception of Titian in 17th-century Britain. Madeline Ward. Aberdeen Ph.D. (Hist. of Art)

1419   Reflections of the New World in English secular music c.1600. Katherine Bank. (Dr. Helen Deeming.) London Ph.D. (R.H.U.L. Music)

1420   Master John Hall's *Little Book of Cures*: a critical edition. Greg Wells. (Dr. Claudia Stein and Dr. David Lines.) Warwick Ph.D. (Hist.)

1421   The serial press and partisan culture in early modern Britain, c.1641–1720. Edward Taylor. (Professor Mark Knights.) Warwick M.Phil./Ph.D. (Hist.)

1422   Sickness in correspondence: gentry letter writing and the subject of health in 18th-century Yorkshire and the north-east. Kathleen Reynolds. (Dr. Cathy McClive and Dr. Adrian Green.) Durham Ph.D. (Hist.)

1423   Mental capacity in the early Royal Society and beyond: intelligence and the new science in England, c.1650–1750. Thomas Colville. (Dr. Adam Sutcliffe and Professor Anne Goldgar.) King's College London M.Phil./Ph.D. (Hist.)

1424   The country house in English women's poetry, 1650–1750: genre, power, identity. Sharon Young. (Dr. David Arnold, Professor Jean Webb and Dr. Andreas Mueller.) Worcester Ph.D. (Hum. & Creative Arts)

1425   Samuel Pepys's diaries: a historical and psychological analysis. Anna Blundy. (Professor Barbara Taylor and Dr. Kate Hodgkin.) East London Ph.D. (Hist.)

1426   Mary Beale and her 'paynting room' in London, 1655–65 and 1670–99. Helen Draper. (Professor Matthew Davies and Dr. Joanna Woodall.) London Ph.D. (Inst. Hist. Res.)

1427   Constructing cultural memories: a mnemohistorical study of print culture in Restoration England, 1658–66. Erin Peters. (Dr. Paddy McNally and Dr. Darren Oldridge.) Worcester Ph.D. (Hum. & Creative Arts)

1428   Exquisite sense: sexual reproduction, nervous physiology and the culture of sensibility in Britain, c.1660–1780. Darren Wagner. (Dr. Mark S.R. Jenner.) York Ph.D. (Hist.)

1429   Collecting and correspondence in the papers of Sir Hans Sloane (1660–1753): creating and exchanging natural historical knowledge in early 18th-century Britain. Alice Marples. (Professor Anne Goldgar.) King's College London M.Phil./Ph.D. (Hist.)

1430   Decorative wrought iron in England, Wales and Scotland, 1660–1720. Samantha Twomey. (Professors Elizabeth A. James and Maurice Howard.) Sussex D.Phil. (Hist. of Art)

1431 Interchange and appropriation: Roman vocal music in the British Isles, 1660–1710. Ester Lebedinski. (Dr. Stephen Rose.) London Ph.D. (R.H.U.L. Music)

1432 Making nations, Englishness and otherness in the works of Daniel Defoe. Frauke Jung. (Dr. Paddy McNally, Dr. Mario Lorenzo-Modia and Professor Alan Downie.) Worcester M.Phil./Ph.D. (Hum. & Creative Arts)

1433 Dr John Radcliffe and the architecture of Oxford. Glenis Kerr-Elliott. (Dr. Simon Lee.) Reading Ph.D. (Hist. of Art)

1434 The creation of the knowledge of the calculus in the long 18th century. Kevin Baker. (Dr. Benjamin Wardhaugh.) Oxford D.Phil. (Mod. Hist.)

1435 The treatment of mental illness among current and ex-servicemen in England during the long 18th century. Michael Joseph. (Professor Mark Harrison.) Oxford M.Sc. (Mod. Hist.)

1436 The Poets Laureate of the long 18th century. Leo Shipp. Exeter Ph.D. (Hist.)

1437 Ancient history in British universities and public life, 1688–1810. James Marsden. (Dr. Brian Young.) Oxford D.Phil. (Mod. Hist.)

1438 Sixteen Moons: expanding the story of the company of Scotland expeditions to Darien, 1698–1700. Julie Orr. Dundee Ph.D. (Hist.)

Eighteenth century

General and political history

1439 Animals in 18th-century London. Thomas Almeroth-Williams. (Dr. Mark S.R. Jenner.) York Ph.D. (Hist.)

1440 National identity, popular culture and 18th-century chapbooks. Gervase French. (Professor Rosemary H. Sweet.) Leicester Ph.D. (Urban Hist.)

1441 Scottish scepticism towards the empire in the 18th century. Gains Murdoch. (Dr. Andrew MacKillop and Professor Thomas Bartlett.) Aberdeen Ph.D. (Hist.)

1442 Political economy and the shadow of war, 1741–1834. Stephen P. Brosha. (Dr. Brian Young.) Oxford D.Phil. (Mod. Hist.)

1443 Theological bearings on the influence of Newtonism on Adam Smith's systematic understanding of society. James W. Storrs Cullis. (Professor Vinita Damodaran and Dr. Iain McDaniel.) Sussex M.Phil. (Hist.)

1444 Spines of the thistle: findings from the Jacobite database of 1745. Darren Layne. (Professor Steve Murdoch.) St. Andrews Ph.D. (Hist.)

1445 Liberal language, imperial cause: rhetoric, empire and the liberal tradition in British politics. Simon Mackley. Exeter M.Phil. (Hist.)

1446 Divergent timescapes: Britain's changing experience of time in the long 19th century (1750–1914). Marie Ventura. (Dr. Bernhard Struck.) St. Andrews Ph.D. (Hist.)

1447 The international political thought of the Scottish Enlightenment. Oliver Krentz. (Dr. Peter Schroder.) London M.Phil. (U.C. Hist.)

1448 A north British interest in London: late 18th-century Scottish lobbying in Westminster, 1760–1832. Andrew J. Mackley. (Dr. Bob Harris.) Oxford D.Phil. (Mod. Hist.)

1449 The crowd in Britain 1780–1850: Unruly riots or orderly rational/legitimate gatherings? David Steel. (Professor Sarah Richardson.) Warwick M.Phil./Ph.D. (Hist.)

1450 'Sir, I was much disgusted': Conservative thought and the war of ideas for moral reform, 1780–1832. Miranda Reading. (Professor Arthur Burns.) King's College London Ph.D. (Hist.)

1451 Henry Bate, the *Morning Herald* and political/patriotic loyalism in the 1780s. Lance Chase. (Dr. Martyn J. Powell and Dr. Peter Borsay.) Aberystwyth Ph.D. (Hist. & Welsh Hist.)

1452 Re-thinking petitions, Parliament and people in the long 19th century. Gary Blank. (Dr. Sarah Richardson.) Warwick M.Phil./Ph.D. (Hist.)

18th century: Local history and government

1453 The experience of being poor in the Fens between 1700 and 1834. Tamar Moore. (Dr. Elizabeth Hurren.) Leicester Ph.D. (Hist.)

1454 The middling sort of Catholic in 18th-century Warwickshire. Ruth Barbour. (Professors Beat Kümin and Peter Marshall.) Warwick Ph.D. (Hist.)

1455 Social relations in 18th-century Norwich. Daniel R. Howse. (Dr. Andrew Wood.) East Anglia Ph.D. (Hist.)

1456 Poaching and criminals in the East Midlands in the 18th century. Rosemary Muge. (Professor John V. Beckett and Dr. Richard Goddard.) Nottingham Ph.D. (Hist.)

1457 Representing 18th-century Norwich: perceptions of the past in a declining present. Roger Woods. (Dr. Andrea Tanner and Professor Lawrence Goldman.) London M.Phil./Ph.D. (Inst. Hist. Res.)

1458 Patronage, party and protest: the political culture of Georgian Hampshire, *c.*1715–*c.*1830. David Roberts. (Dr. Simon Sandall, Dr. Colin M. Haydon and Dr. Louise H. Curth.) Winchester M.Phil./Ph.D. (Hist.)

1459 Petty constables in Hertfordshire, 1730–1800. Elaine Saunders. (Dr. Amanda Goodrich and Dr. Chris A. Williams.) Open University Ph.D. (Hist.)

1460 Luxury and locality: supply and demand for high-end goods in England's north-west, *c.*1730–*c.*1785. Benjamin Wilcock. (Professor Hannah Barker and Dr. Aashish Velkar.) Manchester Ph.D. (Hist.)

1461 The business of smuggling in south-east Scotland, *c.*1740–96. Derek Janes. Exeter M.Phil. (Maritime Hist.)

1462 Industrialising communities: a case study of Elsecar, *c.*1750–1860. Nigel Cavanagh. (Professor Karen Harvey.) Sheffield Ph.D. (Hist.)

1463 The local origins of the Industrial Revolution: the case study of the Derbyshire lead industry, *c.*1750–1830. Matthew Pawelski. (Professor Naomi Tadmor.) Lancaster Ph.D. (Hist.)

1464   Country house consumption and material culture and Audley End, c.1750–1830. Hannah Waugh. (Professor Jon V. Stobart and Dr. Matthew McCormack.) Northampton Ph.D. (Hist.)

1465   The seaborne trade of Southampton, 1772–1815. Maria Newbery. (Dr. John McAleer and Dr. Helen Paul.) Southampton M.Phil. (Hist.)

1466   Association and reassurance: local responses to the French Revolution in the Bath newspapers, 1789–1802. Kevin Grieves. (Dr. Alan Marshall, Professor Elaine Chalus and Dr. Olivette Otele.) Bath Spa Ph.D. (Hist. & Cultural Stud.)

1467   Politics and print in the East Midlands constituencies, c.1790–1832. Hannah Nicholson. (Dr. R.A. Gaunt and Professor John V. Beckett.) Nottingham Ph.D. (Hist.)

1468   A microhistory of poor relief response to crisis and death: Quainton, 1796–1804. Valerie Bagnas. (Professor Keith D.M. Snell.) Leicester Ph.D. (Eng. Loc. Hist.)

18th century: Ireland

1469   Irish migration and return migration. Rian Holland. (Professor David Gleeson.) Northumbria Ph.D. (Hist.)

1470   From land to parliament: the management of late 18th-century County Donegal, 1750–1800. Emma Wright. (Dr. Allan Blackstock and Dr. Robert McNamara.) Ulster Ph.D. (Hist.)

1471   Elite women and material culture in Ireland, 1760–1840. Ruth Thorpe. (Professor Mary O'Dowd.) Belfast Ph.D. (Hist. & Anthr.)

1472   People in subjugation: the bearing of arms and the legacy of volunteering in late 18th-century Ireland. Stephen Dean Jr. (Professors Ian McBride and Arthur Burns.) King's College London M.Phil./Ph.D. (Hist.)

1473   Discourse and debate on anti-slavery in Ulster: British or Irish, 1779–1865. Krysta Beggs-McCormick. (Dr. Allan Blackstock and Dr. Gabriel Guarino.) Ulster Ph.D. (Hist.)

18th century: Administrative, military and naval history

1474   Colonial influences on the development of the English prison. John Moore. (Dr. Kirsty Reid and Dr. James Thompson.) Bristol Ph.D. (Hist. Stud.)

1475   The administration of the out-pension of the Royal Hospital, Chelsea, in the early 18th century. Andrew Cormack. (Professor Chris Woolgar and Dr. John McAleer.) Southampton Ph.D. (Hist.)

1476   Charles Middleton – Britain's first policy-maker. Matthew Cheetham. (Dr. Kevin B. Linch.) Leeds Ph.D. (Hist.)

1477   Death, execution and the criminal corpse: understanding post-mortem punishment in Scotland, 1745–1832. Rachel Bennett. (Professor Clare Anderson.) Leicester Ph.D. (Hist.)

1478 A comparison of the civil and military penal codes of England for influence upon each other from 1749 to 1957. Terry Patton. (Dr. Chris A. Williams and Dr. Rosalind Crone.) Open University Ph.D. (Hist.)

1479 The social and spatial worlds of Old Bailey convicts, 1750–1800. Lucy Huggins. (Professor Robert B. Shoemaker.) Sheffield Ph.D. (Hist.)

1480 Patronage in the Royal Navy, 1771–1815. Catherine Beck. (Professor Stephen Conway and Dr. James Davey.) London Ph.D. (U.C. Hist.)

1481 The sea officers: gentility and professionalism in the Royal Navy, 1775–1815. Evan Wilson. (Professor Nicholas A.M. Rodger.) Oxford D.Phil. (Mod. Hist.)

1482 Policing and the identification of offenders in Metropolitan London, 1780–1850. Eleanor C. Bland. (Professor Robert B. Shoemaker.) Sheffield Ph.D. (Hist.)

1483 Between state and subject: discourses on British security and surveillance in the 1790s. Christopher Gibbs. (Dr. Catriona A.L. Kennedy and Dr. Geoffrey T. Cubitt.) York Ph.D. (Hist.)

1484 Billets to barracks: the barrack building programme in England, 1792–1815. Stephen King. (Dr. Kevin B. Linch.) Leeds Ph.D. (Hist.)

1485 The 1797 naval mutinies at Spithead and the Nore. Callum Easton. (Renaud Morieux, James Davey and Bruno Pappalardo..) Cambridge Ph.D. (Hist.)

18th century: Finance, trade and industry

1486 Coal, shipping and empire: the triumvirate of British power. Christopher Allan. (Professors Ranald C. Michie and Justin Willis.) Durham Ph.D. (Hist.)

1487 The experience of commercial society: consumer mentality in 18th- and 19th-century Britain. Hazel Tubman. (Dr. Faramerz Dabhoiwala.) Oxford D.Phil. (Mod. Hist.)

1488 Changing perceptions: the effects of Enlightenment thought on the identity of a mercantile city. Alison Bolitho. (Dr. Madge J. Dresser and Dr. Steven W. Poole.) West of England Ph.D. (Hist.)

1489 The undertaking business in the 18th-century west of England. Daniel O'Brien. (Dr. Richard Sheldon and Dr. James Thompson.) Bristol M.Litt. (Hist. Stud.)

1490 The impact of John, 2nd duke of Montagu's colonial, industrial and commercial ventures on his national estates, with a particular focus on how his Northamptonshire estates were affected (1700–70). Helen Bates. (Professor Peter J.R. King.) Leicester Ph.D. (Hist.)

1491 Women workers in Sheffield's metal trades, c.1742–1867. Laura Bracey. (Professor Karen Harvey.) Sheffield Ph.D. (Hist.)

1492 Ideas and practice in British taxation policy, 1743–1816. Shane Horwell. (Dr. Julian Hoppit.) London Ph.D. (U.C. Hist.)

1493 The Royal Mint in crisis? Public offices, private enterprises and technical innovation: the career of Assay Master Alchorne (1727–1800). Joseph Payne. (Dr. Stephen Pumfrey.) Lancaster Ph.D. (Hist.)

1494 Shipped out? Pauper apprentices of port towns during the Industrial Revolution, 1750–1870. Caroline Withall. (Professor Jane Humphries.) Oxford D.Phil. (Mod. Hist.)

1495 The urban coaching inn, c.1750–c.1850. Karen Green. (Dr. Mark S.R. Jenner.) York M.A. (Hist.)

1496 Creative destruction in the British industrial revolution: hand spinning to mechanisation, c.1750–1830. Benjamin M. Schneider. (Professor Jane Humphries.) Oxford M.Sc. (Mod. Hist.)

1497 Sir William Hamilton (1731–1803): networks and knowledge within an 18th-century context. Geoffrey Stone. (Dr. Michael Brown and Dr. Marta Garcia Morcillo.) Roehampton M.Phil./Ph.D. (Hist.)

1498 Female enterprise and entrepreneurship in the north-east of England, 1778–1801. Susan Beaumont. (Dr. Joan Allen and Professor Helen Berry.) Newcastle Ph.D. (Hist.)

1499 The Bristol hatting industry. Christopher Heal. (Dr. Evan Jones and Dr. Richard Sheldon.) Bristol M.Phil. (Hist. Stud.)

18th century: Agriculture

1500 The impact of game shooting on the 18th and 19th century landscape. William S. Cassidy. East Anglia Ph.D. (Hist.)

1501 The impact of severe weather conditions on designed landscapes and their planting. Sandra E. Morris. East Anglia Ph.D. (Hist.)

1502 How did the farm livestock painting and prints from the 18th and 19th centuries function within society? Hilary Matthews. (Dr. Jeremy Burchardt.) Reading Ph.D. (Hist.)

1503 The meaning and experience of agricultural work in 18th-century England. James Fisher. (Professor Arthur Burns and Dr. Alexandra Sapoznik.) King's College London M.Phil./Ph.D. (Hist.)

1504 Agrarian land law and the 18th-century commonwealth tradition. Emily Mitchelson. (Dr. Rachel Hammersley and Professor Helen Berry.) Newcastle Ph.D. (Hist.)

18th century: Social history

1505 The village shop in the 18th and 19th centuries: image and reality. Lucy Bailey. (Professor Jon V. Stobart and Dr. Phillippa Bennett.) Northampton Ph.D. (Hist.)

1506 The consumption and life-cycle of English papers, 1700–1834. Joseph Harley. (Professor Peter J.R. King.) Leicester Ph.D. (Eng. Loc. Hist.)

1507 Women's negative emotions and micro-emotional communities, 1700–1830: examining experiential possibilities through emotional linguistics. Laura Alston. (Professor Karen Harvey.) Sheffield Ph.D. (Hist.)

1508 Perceptions and experiences of illegitimate birth, c.1700–1830. Kate Gibson. (Dr. Karen Harvey.) Sheffield Ph.D. (Hist.)

1509 The trade and consumption of English wallpapers, 1700–1830. Phillippa Mapes. (Professor Rosemary H. Sweet.) Leicester Ph.D. (Hist.)

1510 Lust, marriage and murder in 18th-century Scotland: the trial of Katharine Nairn and Patrick Ogilvie. Theresa Antoff. (Dr. Elizabeth Macknight and Dr. Michael Brown.) Aberdeen Ph.D. (Hist.)

1511 Women, celebrity and the public sphere in 18th-century England. Amy Clarke. (Dr. Stephen Bending and Dr. Julie Gammon.) Southampton M.Phil. (Hist.)

1512 The emergence of the concept of respectability during the 18th century. Jonathan Darby. (Professor Joanna Innes.) Oxford M.Phil. (Mod. Hist.)

1513 Public representations and secret lives of 18th-century actresses: Mrs. Dorothy Jordan and her questionable locks. Lorraine Droney. (Dr. Amanda Capern.) Hull Ph.D. (Hist.)

1514 Gang crime and moral panics in 18th-century England. Christopher Hammerton. (Dr. Julie Gammon.) Southampton M.Phil. (Hist.)

1515 Bankruptcy in 18th-century England: a social account. Robert Nantes. (Professors Henry French and Dr. Jonathan Barry.) Exeter M.Phil. (Hist.)

1516 The role of domestic knowledge in an era of professionalisation: 18th-century manuscript medical recipe collections. Sally Osborn. (Dr. Sara Pennell, Dr. Michael Brown and Dr. Edward Vallance.) Roehampton Ph.D. (Hist.)

1517 Shoplifting in 18th-century England. Shelley Tickell. (Professor John Styles and Dr. Sarah Lloyd.) Hertfordshire Ph.D. (Hist.)

1518 Gender, sartorial politics and the politics of making in 18th-century Britain. Rosanne Waine. (Professors Elaine Chalus and Maria Hayward.) University of Southampton Ph.D. (Hist. & Cultural Stud.)

1519 Ulterior identity in 18th-century London and transatlantic public spheres: anonymity, psuedonyms, and disguise. Megan Kobza. (Dr. Rachel Hammersley, Dr. Matthew Grenby and Professor Helen Berry.) Newcastle Ph.D. (Hist.)

1520 Houses and homes: the management of a network of great households, c.1709–1827. Emma Purcell. (Professor Rosemary H. Sweet.) Leicester Ph.D. (Hist.)

1521 The bachelor in Georgian Britain. Helen Metcalfe. (Professor Hannah Barker and Dr. Hal Gladfelder.) Manchester Ph.D. (Hist.)

1522 Trained to Consume: dress and the female consumer in England, 1720–1820. Serena Dyer. (Professor Giorgio Riello.) Warwick Ph.D. (Hist.)

1523 Capital mapping: geographies of enlightened Edinburgh. Phillip Dodds. (Professor C.W.J. Withers.) Edinburgh Ph.D. (Geog.)

1524 Eating the imperial: London's food culture and metropolitan identity, 1747–1860. Elspeth Dow. (Professor Stephen Conway.) London Ph.D. (U.C. Hist.)

1525 Romany families in eastern England: social geography and lineage, 1750–1950. Matthew Sears. (Professor Keith D.M. Snell.) Leicester Ph.D. (Eng. Loc. Hist.)

1526 Murder in the metropole: the changing nature of homicide in London and Middlesex, 1750–1900. Julian Raynor. (Professor Peter J.R. King.) Leicester Ph.D. (Eng. Loc. Hist.)

1527 An examination of the country houses and architectural and landscaping activities of selected landowning families and of their reliance on non-landed sources of income to fulfil their aspirations. Andrew Wells. (Professor Lawrence Goldman.) London M.Phil./Ph.D. (Inst. Hist. Res.)

1528 The social and cultural history of the English fair, c.1750–1850. Jessica A. Davidson. (Dr. Bob Harris.) Oxford M.St. (Mod. Hist.)

1529 Understandings of habitual criminality and the trajectory of criminal stereotyping in England from 1770 to 1870. Helen Churcher. (Professor Robert B. Shoemaker.) Sheffield Ph.D. (Hist.)

1530 Social and commercial influences on early black writing in Britain, 1770–1830. Ryan J. Hanley. (Dr. Douglas Hamilton and Dr. Nicholas Evans.) Hull Ph.D. (Hist.)

1531 Emotionalism and violence amongst male elites, 1770–1820. Caroline Davies. East Anglia Ph.D. (Hist.)

1532 Conspicuous consumption in fashionable clothing in urban Scotland, c.1780–1830. Louisa Cross. (Professor James Livesey and Dr. Matthew C. Ward.) Dundee Ph.D. (Hist.)

1533 The ménage à trois and other unconventional relationships, c.1780–1830. Natalie Hanley-Smith. (Professor Mark Philp and Dr. Sarah Richardson.) Warwick Ph.D. (Hist.)

1534 Newspaper reporting and robbery in London, c.1780–1830. Robert Hopps. (Dr. Paul Lawrence, Dr. Amanda Goodrich and Professor Peter King.) Open University Ph.D. (Hist.)

1535 Hipolito Jose da Costa (1774–1823): a Luso-Brazilian man of letters in English freemasonry (1807–23). Paulo Henrique De Magalhaes Arruda. (Professor Francisco Bethencourt and Dr. Anthony Pereira.) King's College London M.Phil./ Ph.D. (Hist.)

1536 British masculinities and material culture in the armies of India, 1799–1900. Holly Winter. (Professor Maxine Berg and Dr. Rebecca Earle.) Warwick M.Phil./Ph.D. (Hist.)

18th century: Ecclesiastical and religious history

1537 Cambridge bell ringing. Gareth Davis. (Professor Rohan McWilliam and Dr. Sean Lang.) Anglia Ruskin D.Phil. (Hist.)

1538 The social and ecclesiastical significance of church seating plans, 1700–1900. Paul Owens. (Professor Keith D.M. Snell.) Leicester Ph.D. (Eng. Loc. Hist.)

1539 Contesting human knowledge and God: George Berkeley and the challenges of religious heterodoxy. Alvin Chen. (Dr. Brian Young.) Oxford D.Phil. (Mod. Hist.)

1540 John Cennick – Moravian evangelist? Robert Cotter. (Dr. Scott Dixon.) Belfast Ph.D. (Hist. & Anthr.)

1541 The history and development of the Moravian church in the United Kingdom, 1722–2012. James Rollo. (Dr. Stefanie Sinclair and Professor John Wolffe.) Open University Ph.D. (Hist.)

1542   Evangelicalism and student missionary work. Adam Baron. (Dr. Dominic Erdozain.)
       King's College London M.Phil. (Theol. & Rel. Stud.)

1543   Evangelicalism and the gnostic impulse. Robin Phillips. (Dr. Dominic Erdozain.)
       King's College London M.Phil. (Theol. & Rel. Stud.)

1544   'Rational dissent' in England c.1770–c.1800: definitions, identity and legacy. Valerie
       Smith. (Professors Kenneth Fincham and Grayson M. Ditchfield.) Kent M.Phil.
       (Hist.)

1545   An examination of the words and influences of the Revd. Isaac Taylor (1759–1829)
       and his immediate family. Georgina Bailey. (Professor James R. Raven.) Essex
       Ph.D. (Hist.)

18th century: Education, the arts, science and medicine

1546   Barrett family of artists. Logan M.K. Morse. (Professor Geoff Quilley and Dr.
       Francesco Ventrella.) Sussex D.Phil. (Hist.)

1547   Recipe books and the exchange of medical knowledge in 18th-century English
       households. Katherine Allen. (Dr. Erica Charters and Dr. Perry Gauci.) Oxford
       D.Phil. (Mod. Hist.)

1548   Paralysis in 18th-century England. Stan Booth. (Professors Chris Mounsey and
       Louise Curth.) Winchester M.Phil./Ph.D. (Hist.)

1549   Eighteenth-century house interiors in north-east Scotland. Lorraine Hesketh-
       Campbell. (Professor Jane Geddes.) Aberdeen Ph.D. (Hist. of Art)

1550   The marketing techniques of William Hogarth (1697–1764), artist and engraver,
       together with an account of his artistic relationship with the novelist Henry Fielding
       (1707–54). Mark McNally. (Dr. Adrian G. Green and Dr. David Craig.) Durham
       Ph.D. (Hist.)

1551   The care of sick children in 18th-century England. Claire Rennie. (Dr. Alexandra E.
       Bamji and Dr. Adrian F. Wilson.) Leeds Ph.D. (Hist.)

1552   Eighteenth-century aristocratic men and domestic music-making. Sheila Thomas.
       (Professors Chris Woolgar and Jeanice Brooks.) Southampton M.Phil. (Hist./Mus.)

1553   Aspects of deafness in 18th-century England. Rachel Wilks. (Professor David
       Turner.) Swansea M.Res. (Hist.)

1554   Christian Wolff's oeconomica methodo scientifica pertractata – household economics
       as the foundation for the welfare state? Antonia Karaisl von Karais. (Dr. Guido
       Giglioni.) London Ph.D. (Warburg)

1555   Charles Bridgeman: a reappraisal from a landscape history perspective. Susan
       Haynes. East Anglia Ph.D. (Hist.)

1556   'That noble possessor': knowledge and its materials in the collection of Margaret
       Cavendish Bentinck, duchess of Portland, 1715–85. Madeleine Pelling. (Dr.
       Richard Johns.) York Ph.D. (Hist. of Art)

1557   'No enemy more powerful than pleasure': The English Malady and the politics of
       sensibility in the mid 18th century. Steven B. Server. (Dr. Sloan Mahone and Dr.
       Erica Charters.) Oxford M.Sc. (Mod. Hist.)

1558   Gender and nationhood in Scottish family group portraits, c.1740–90. Helen Whiting. (Professors Mary Modeen and Chris Whatley.) Dundee Ph.D. (Hist.)

1559   The problem with John Witherspoon: reassessing the Presbyterian pastor-president and his relationship to the Scottish Enlightenment. Kevin De Young. (Professor John R.D. Coffey.) Leicester Ph.D. (Hist.)

1560   The medical response to the 'alcohol question' in Scotland, 1750–2000. Iain Smith. (Dr. Rose Elliot, Dr. Kenneth Mullen and Professor Malcolm A. Nicolson.) Glasgow M.D. (Soc. Sc.)

1561   Making an impression: printed book illustration, 1750–1850. William Finley. (Professor Karen Harvey.) Sheffield Ph.D. (Hist.)

1562   Medical print and the communication of medical knowledge in the 'age of improvement' in Scotland, 1750–1850. Liz Neesam. (Dr. Ben Marsden and Professor Ralph O'Connor.) Aberdeen Ph.D. (Hist.)

1563   The death of allegory: problems of the funerary monument, 1750–1850. Rebecca Senior. (Professor Jason Edwards.) York Ph.D. (Hist. of Art)

1564   Reading associations in Britain, 1750–1830. Christy Ford. (Dr. Faramerz Dabhoiwala.) Oxford D.Phil. (Mod. Hist.)

1565   Philanthropists, entrepreneurs and culture, c.1770–1840. Roshan Allpress. (Dr. E. Jane Garnett.) Oxford D.Phil. (Mod. Hist.)

1566   Efficacy and professionalism: resuscitation in the late 18th and early 19th centuries. George P. Head. (Dr. Erica Charters.) Oxford M.Sc. (Mod. Hist.)

1567   One last glance: art, death and memory in late 18th- to early 19th-century British posthumous portraiture. Emily A. Knight. (Dr. Hanneke Grootenboer.) Oxford D.Phil. (Mod. Hist.)

1568   Venus in tights: *tableaux vivants* in Britain in the long 19th century. Elena Stevens. (Dr. Jonathan Conlin.) Southampton Ph.D. (Hist.)

1569   The influence of romanticism on the thought of Edward Irving, 1792–1834. Nicholas J. Tucker. (Professor David W. Bebbington and Dr. Jacqueline L.M. Jenkinson.) Stirling Ph.D. (Hist.)

Nineteenth century

General and political history

1570   Female anarchists. Lidia Iazzolino. (Professors Lucy Bland and Rohan McWilliam.) Anglia Ruskin D.Phil. (Hist.)

1571   Space, place and urban contentious politics in London. Hannah Awcock. (Dr. Innes Keighren and Professor David Gilbert.) London M.Phil./Ph.D. (R.H.U.L. Geog.)

1572   The empire in the garden: the British Empire, British gardens and national identity in 19th and early 20th century Britain. Keith Alcorn. (Professor Felix Driver and Dr. Zoe Laidlaw.) London M.Phil./Ph.D. (R.H.U.L. Geog.)

1573 Mary Gurney and her circle. Mary Campbell-Day. (Professor Gary McCulloch and Dr. Mark Freeman.) London M.Phil. (Inst. of Educ.)

1574 Continental refugees and British politics in the 19th century. Matthew I. Brand. East Anglia Ph.D. (Hist.)

1575 Open space, enclosure and popular protest in London in the 19th century – the case of Epping Forest. Mark Gorman. (Dr. Christopher Thornton.) London M.Phil./Ph.D. (Inst. Hist. Res.)

1576 Constructing a conservative: the reception of Edmund Burke in 19th-century Britain. Emily Jones. (Mr. Peter Ghosh.) Oxford D.Phil. (Mod. Hist.)

1577 Law and emigration in 19th-century England. Patricia Peal. Chichester M.Phil./Ph.D. (Hist.)

1578 Disraeli and Bentinck: a personal and political relationship in history and memory. Thomas Pritchard. (Professors Malcolm S. Chase and Simon J.D. Green.) Leeds Ph.D. (Hist.)

1579 Sir George Harrison: a 19th-century 'statesman in disguise'? Paul McIntyre. (Professor Arthur Burns.) King's College London Ph.D. (Hist.)

1580 Robert Peel and his recommendations for mercy as home secretary from 1822–7, 1828–30. Brenda G. Mortimer. (Professor Peter J.R. King.) Leicester Ph.D. (Eng. Loc. Hist.)

1581 Remember the rights of the savage: the ethical dimensions of British colonial warfare, 1823–1902. Nicole M. Hartwell. (Dr. Jane Garnett.) Oxford D.Phil. (Mod. Hist.)

1582 George Canning, the 'Canningites' and the quest for the liberal centre, c.1825–30. Shaun J. Lawson. (Dr. S.A. Skinner.) Oxford D.Phil. (Mod. Hist.)

1583 Botanical education and civic science: the work of John Hutton Balfour, 1808–74. Laura Stoddart. (Professor C.W.J. Withers.) Edinburgh Ph.D. (Geog.)

1584 Armchair geography: speculation, synthesis and the culture of British exploration, c.1830–80. Natalie Cox. (Dr. David Lambert.) Warwick Ph.D. (Hist.)

1585 Building the fullest fountain of advancing civilisation: constructing the space of British parliament, c.1830–80. Edward J. Gillin. (Dr. William H. Whyte.) Oxford D.Phil. (Mod. Hist.)

1586 Parliamentary boundaries and reform in England, 1830–68. Martin Spychal. (Professor Miles Taylor.) London Ph.D. (Inst. Hist. Res.)

1588 The influence of the 'Little Circle' and the Manchester press on the passage of the 1832 Reform Act. David Knott. (Professor Hannah Barker and Dr. Henry Miller.) Manchester Ph.D. (Hist.)

1589 'Of magic and misery': representations of witchcraft, spiritualism and the dark arts in Victorian and Edwardian Britain. Alexandra Denman. (Professor Elizabeth Prettejohn.) York Ph.D. (Hist. of Art)

1590 The Victorians under siege. Brian Wallace. (Dr. David Todd and Dr. Paul Readman.) King's College London M.Phil./Ph.D. (Hist.)

1591   The ideological convergence and divergence of Richard Cobden and the Quakers in mid 19th-century radical politics. Austin D.W. Haight. (Professor Norman Vance and Dr. Iain McDaniel.) Sussex D.Phil. (Hist.)

1592   The political career of Arthur Wellesley, first duke of Wellington, between 1841 and 1846. Thomas Goldsmith. East Anglia Ph.D. (Hist.)

1593   Sidney & Beatrice Webb and the welfare state. Yanwei Han. Exeter Ph.D. (Hist.)

1594   Westminster-on-Sea: Osbourne House and geographies of the monarchy. Lee Butcher. (Professor David Green and Dr. Ruth Craggs.) King's College London Ph.D. (Geog.)

1595   Foreign immigration into northern England and Wales, 1851–1911. James Perry. (Professor Ian Gregory.) Lancaster Ph.D. (Hist.)

1596   Sir Edward Grey's critics. David Yates. (Professor Stuart Ball.) Leicester Ph.D. (Hist.)

1597   The emergence of libertarian conservatism in Britain, 1867–1914. Alastair Paynter. (Dr. Jonathan Conlin.) Southampton Ph.D. (Hist.)

1598   The National Library of Wales and national identity, 1870–1916. Calista Williams. (Dr. Paul Lawrence, Dr. Rosalind Crone and Professor Lorna Hughes.) Open University M.Phil./Ph.D. (Hist.)

1599   From liberalism to nationalism: women and political change in Wales, 1870–1925. Anys Wood. (Professor Bill Jones.) Cardiff Ph.D. (Hist. & Archaeol.)

1600   The politics, culture and reception of British invasion scares, c.1870–1914. Christian Melby. (Dr. Paul Readman and Professor David E.H. Edgerton.) King's College London M.Phil./Ph.D. (Hist.)

1601   Religion and the emergence of New Liberalism, 1870–1910. Nicholas Loizou. (Professor Stuart Jones and Dr. Henry Miller.) Manchester Ph.D. (Hist.)

1602   The power of friends: Reginald Brett, 2nd Viscount Esher, and the political influence of social networks in Edwardian Britain. Michael Humphries. (Dr. Paul Readman and Professor Richard C. Vinen.) King's College London M.Phil./Ph.D. (Hist.)

1603   The Chamberlains, Conservatism and foreign policy. Dominic M. Bray. East Anglia Ph.D. (Hist.)

1604   Blavatsky and time: sources and implications of temporality in modern theosophy. Jeffrey Lavoie. Exeter M.Phil. (Stud. of Esotericism)

1605   Utopianism in British political thought, 1880–1930. Peter Evans. (Dr. Richard Sheldon and Dr. James Thompson.) Bristol M.Litt. (Hist. Stud.)

1606   Visions of empire: a history of the ideas of social-imperialism, 1880–1922. Graeme Bradstreet. East Anglia Ph.D. (Hist.)

1607   Scottish Unionist and Tory ideas in the late 19th and early 20th centuries. Jonathan Paquette. (Professor Colin Kidd.) St. Andrews Ph.D. (Hist.)

1608   A Labour sect? Primitive Methodism in parliament, 1886–1924. Melvin Johnson. (Dr. Douglas Reid and Dr. Alan G.V. Simmonds.) Hull Ph.D. (Hist.)

1609 The Liberal Unionists and British politics, 1886–1912. Timothy O'B. Moore.
(Professor R.F. Foster.) Oxford D.Phil. (Mod. Hist.)

1610 Perceptions of future war in the British press, 1890–1914. David Bangert. (Dr. Brad
Beavan and Dr. Robert James.) Portsmouth Ph.D. (Soc., Hist. & Lit. Stud.)

1611 The referendum in British new liberal and socialist thought, 1890–1910. Michael L.J.
Hindmarsh. (Dr. Ben Jackson.) Oxford M.St. (Mod. Hist.)

1612 A forgotten statesman: Douglas McGarel Hogg, the 1st Viscount Hailsham.
Christopher Cooper. (Professor David J. Dutton.) Liverpool Ph.D. (Hist.)

1613 The Women's Total Abstinence Union and Periodical Wings, 1892–1910: a study
of gender and politics. Gemma Outen. (Dr. Bob Nicholson.) Edge Hill Ph.D.
(English & Hist.)

1614 Jewish identity and attitudes to militarism in Scotland, c.1899–1939. Kirk Hansen.
(Dr. William Kenefick and Professor Graeme Morton.) Dundee Ph.D. (Hist.)

19th century: Local history and government

1615 Stone decay in cleaned and non-cleaned sandstone buildings in west Scotland.
Marta Zurakowska. (Dr. Simon Cuthbert and Dr. Richard Lang.) West of Scotland
Ph.D. (Sci. and Sport.)

1616 Memory of slavery: public discourse in Liverpool from the 19th to the 21st centuries.
Jessica Moody. (Dr. Geoffrey T. Cubitt.) York Ph.D. (Hist.)

1617 Social and economic changes in the Pontardawe area in the 19th and 20th centuries
with specific reference to the Lloyd and Gilbertson families. Elizabeth J. McSloy.
(Professor Louise Miskell.) Swansea Ph.D. (Hist.)

1618 Judgement, taste, propriety and economy or how to succeed in church building in
Victorian England's manufacturing towns: the example of Mallinson and Healey of
Halifax and Bradford. Colin Canfield. (Professor Martin Hewitt.) Huddersfield
M.Phil. (Music, Hum. & Media)

1619 Bradford's urban sporting culture, 1800–1914. David Pendleton. (Professor Tony
Collins.) De Montfort Ph.D. (Hum.)

1620 The rise and fall of Hathersage hacklepin making and its effect on the community in
the long 19th century. Christopher Side. (Professor Keith D.M. Snell.) Leicester
Ph.D. (Eng. Loc. Hist.)

1621 A comparison of core family survival in Swaledale and York in the 19th century.
Philip Batman. (Professor Keith D.M. Snell.) Leicester Ph.D. (Eng. Loc. Hist.)

1622 Law enforcement and social order in 19th-century west Wales. David Bowmer. (Dr.
Eryn M. White and Dr. Owen Roberts.) Aberystwyth Ph.D. (Hist. & Welsh Hist.)

1623 Economic and social change in the 19th century in south-west Middlesex and north-
west Surrey: a comparative study of seven parishes bordering the Thames. Mike
Brownlee. (Professor Miles Taylor.) London Ph.D. (Inst. Hist. Res.)

1624 Urban enlightenment: class, culture and the industrial spirit, Derby, c.1720–1900.
Michael Crane. (Professor John V. Beckett and Dr. Richard Gaunt.) Nottingham
Ph.D. (Hist.)

1625　Sailors in a merchant port: the maritime and urban interface in 19th-century Bristol. Joe Davey. (Dr. Brad Beavan and Dr. Karl Bell.) Portsmouth Ph.D. (Soc., Hist. & Lit. Stud.)

1626　An urban history of Holyhead in the 19th century. Gareth Hughes. (Professor Paul B. O'Leary and Dr. Iwan Morus.) Aberystwyth Ph.D. (Hist. & Welsh Hist.)

1627　The changing nature of landownership in the Glamorgan valleys in the 19th century. Jeremy Morgan. Cardiff M.Phil. (Hist. & Archaeol.)

1628　Land agents and aristocratic estates in 19th-century Staffordshire: a comparison of Longton and Walsall. Cathal Rogers. (Dr. Alannah Tomkins and Dr. Nigel Tringham.) Keele Ph.D. (Hist.)

1629　The patients of the Bristol lunatic asylum in the 19th century. Paul Tobia. (Dr. Michael R. Richards and Dr. Martin Simpson.) West of England Ph.D. (Hist.)

1630　The urbanisation of Harwich during the 19th century. Gerald Reilly. (Professor Edward Higgs.) Essex Ph.D. (Hist.)

1631　Women's employment in Bath and Cheltenham, c.1800–30. Diana Russell. (Professor Elaine Chalus and Dr. Roberta Anderson.) Bath Spa M.Phil. (Hist. & Cultural Stud.)

1632　The provision of poor relief in Maldon and the adjacent parishes of Woodham Mortimer/Woodham Walter, c.1824–44. David Thomas. (Dr. Christopher Thornton and Professor Lawrence Goldman.) London M.Phil./Ph.D. (Inst. Hist. Res.)

1633　The outdoor-poor of Leeds, 1829–51. Graham Rawson. (Professor Malcolm S. Chase.) Leeds Ph.D. (Hist.)

1634　Contention and collaboration: the development of municipal government in the Potteries, c.1830–1910. Stephanie Maksimovic. (Professor Richard G. Rodger.) Edinburgh Ph.D. (Hist.)

1635　The anti-Poor Law movement in Preston, Lancashire in the 1830s. Bernard Melling. (Dr. Sally B. Sheard.) Liverpool Ph.D. (Hist.)

1636　The influence of Derbyshire railways on leisure travel in the 19th century. Andrew Wager. (Professor Keith D.M. Snell.) Leicester Ph.D. (Eng. Loc. Hist.)

1637　The expansion of institutions for the medical relief of the poor, c.1834–94: a comparative study of two poor law unions in Leicestershire. Kimberley Pullen. (Professor Keith D.M. Snell.) Leicester Ph.D. (Eng. Loc. Hist.)

1638　The workhouse system in Suffolk, from the 1834 Poor Law Amendment Act, to its takeover by the Local Government Board in 1871. Angela Miller. (Dr. Peter J. Gurney.) Essex Ph.D. (Hist.)

1639　Child poverty in Shropshire, 1834–70. Jeffrey Sumbler. (Dr. Nigel Tringham and Dr. Alannah Tomkins.) Keele Ph.D. (Hist.)

1640　People, power and pauperism: the implementation of the new Poor Law in Hertfordshire. Karen Rothery. (Dr. Katrina Navickas and Dr. Alysa Levene.) Hertfordshire Ph.D. (Hist.)

1641　Somerset: the journey from parish constable to county police, 1835–56. Robert Love. (Professor Peter J.R. King.) Leicester Ph.D. (Eng. Loc. Hist.)

1642 The animal history of Bristol Zoo. Andy Flack. (Professor Peter A. Coates and Dr. Timothy J. Cole.) Bristol M.Litt. (Hist. Stud.)

1643 Social histories of Bristol Zoo. Sarah-Joy Maddeaux. (Professor Peter A. Coates and Dr. Timothy J. Cole.) Bristol M.Litt. (Hist. Stud.)

1644 The socio-economic impacts of the coming of the railways to Hertfordshire, Bedfordshire and Buckinghamshire in the 19th century. Friedrich Newman. (Professor Nigel Goose and Dr. Katrina Navickas.) Hertfordshire Ph.D. (Hist.)

1645 Unifiers and dividers in a north Staffordshire parish: Audley, 1840–1939. Ian Bailey. (Professor Keith D.M. Snell.) Leicester Ph.D. (Eng. Loc. Hist.)

1646 Resort development on the Cambrian coast, 1840–1914. John Hirst. (Professor Peter Borsay and Dr. Owen Roberts.) Aberystwyth Ph.D. (Hist. & Welsh Hist.)

1647 Property and population growth in Northampton in the mid 19th century. F. Clifford German. (Professor Richard J. Dennis.) London Ph.D. (U.C. Geog.)

1648 Migration and integration – an example: Fletton, 1841–1911. Sadie McMullon. (Professor Kevin Schurer.) Leicester Ph.D. (Eng. Loc. Hist.)

1649 Work, school and play: childhood in south Wales, 1842–1914. Mary J. Stephenson. (Dr. Owen Roberts and Dr. Steven Thompson.) Aberystwyth Ph.D. (Hist. & Welsh Hist.)

1650 A godly nation: presbyterianism, dissent and Scottish society in the decade after disruption. Ryan Mallon. (Dr. Andrew Holmes.) Belfast M.Phil./Ph.D. (Hist. & Anthr.)

1651 Negotiating the asylum: Lancaster Moor Hospital, 1844–1946. Natalie Mullen. (Dr. John Welshman and Professor Paolo Palladino.) Lancaster Ph.D. (Hist.)

1652 Waterscapes: history and heritage in the Washburn Valley since c.1850. Andrew McTominey. (Dr. Shane Ewen and Dr. Robert Ellis.) Leeds Beckett Ph.D. (Cultural Stud.)

1653 The development of Rutland as a county community in the modern age. Hilary Crowden. (Professor Keith D.M. Snell.) Leicester Ph.D. (Eng. Loc. Hist.)

1654 The popularisation of football games in Winchester, 1850–1914. Ian Denness. (Dr. Mark Allen, Dr. Simon Sandall and Dr. Colin Haydon.) Winchester M.Phil./Ph.D. (Hist.)

1655 Associational networks and urban identities: Swansea, 1850–1914. Barry J. Rees. (Professors Paul B. O'Leary and Peter Borsay.) Aberystwyth Ph.D. (Hist. & Welsh Hist.)

1656 Aspects of the development of the South Wales ports, 1850–1914. John Young. (Professors Christine Macleod and Roger Middleton.) Bristol M.Litt. (Hist. Stud.)

1657 'Our sailor lads': identity, citizenship and empire in Portsmouth, 1850–1900. Louise Moon. (Dr. Brad Beavan and Dr. Karl Bell.) Portsmouth Ph.D. (Soc., Hist. & Lit. Stud.)

1658 Crime reporting in the 19th-century provincial press: a study of two Essex newspapers, 1850–1900. Isobel Moore. (Professor Peter J.R. King.) Leicester Ph.D. (Eng. Loc. Hist.)

1659   A study of migratory patterns of four settlements in Lincolnshire, 1851–1901.   Jill
        Caine.   (Professor Steven A. King.)   Leicester Ph.D.   (Eng. Loc. Hist.)

1660   Juvenile crime and punishment in the West Riding of Yorkshire, 1856–1914.   Lucie
        Wade.   (Dr. Heather Shore and Dr. Helen Johnston.)   Leeds Beckett Ph.D.
        (Cultural Stud.)

1661   The history of Salters', the Thames boat firm based at Folly Bridge in Oxford,
        1858–c.1970.   Simon Wenham.   (Dr. Mark Smith.)   Oxford D.Phil.   (Mod. Hist.)

1662   Palmerston and anti-slavery.   Robert McGregor.   (Professor David Brown.)
        Southampton M.Phil.   (Hist.)

1663   Origins of football in Nottinghamshire, c.1860–1914.   Andy Dawes.   (Professor
        Matthew Taylor.)   De Montfort M.Phil.   (Hum.)

1664   Managing pauperism and poverty in Axminster Union, 1860–1901.   Joan Hornsby.
        (Dr. Donna Loftus and Dr. Megan Doolittle.)   Open University M.Phil./Ph.D.   (Hist.)

1665   'From the battles of the bridge to the battle of the gates': the labour and trade union
        movement in Perth, c.1867–1922.   Paul Philippou.   (Dr. William Kenefick and
        Professor Christopher A. Whatley.)   Dundee Ph.D.   (Hist.)

1666   Corruption in public life: a study of the exercise of power in Manchester and Salford in
        the late Victorian period.   Pamela Nutton.   (Professor Martin Hewitt.)   Huddersfield
        M.Phil.   (Music, Hum. & Media)

1667   Women and drink in the Manchester region, c.1870–81.   Craig Stafford.   (Dr. Andrew
        Davies.)   Liverpool Ph.D.   (Hist.)

1668   More than the Pankhursts: an examination of women's suffrage movements in the
        East Yorkshire region.   Marie Holmes.   (Dr. Douglas Reid and Dr. Rosemary Wall.)
        Hull Ph.D.   (Hist.)

1669   Church Broughton: a cultural and oral history, 1880–1980.   Janet Arthur.   (Professor
        Robert Colls.)   De Montfort Ph.D.   (Hum.)

1670   Popular political continuity in urban England, 1867–1918: the case studies of Bristol
        and Northampton.   Matthew Kidd.   (Dr. Sascha Auerbach and Dr. Dean Blackburn.)
        Nottingham Ph.D.   (Hist.)

1671   Social and economic change in Chelmsford and Colchester, 1880–1914.   Julia
        Marsh.   (Professor Rohan McWilliam and Dr. Sean Lang.)   Anglia Ruskin D.Phil.
        (Hist.)

1672   A comparative analysis of attempts to provide policing in Salford and Manchester
        between 1880 and 1905.   David Daniels.   (Dr. Craig Horner and Dr. Anthony J.
        Adams.)   Manchester Metropolitan Ph.D.   (Hist.)

1673   Prostitution, gender and society in Cardiff, 1885–1950.   Simon Jenkins.   (Dr. Keir
        Waddington.)   Cardiff Ph.D.   (Hist. & Archaeol.)

1674   Cotton and the community: exploring changing concepts of identity and community
        on Lancashire's cotton frontier, c.1890–1950.   Jack Southern.   (Dr. Stephen Caunce
        and Dr. Andrew Gritt.)   Central Lancashire Ph.D.   (Hum.)

1675 Carnivals in Greater London, 1890–1914: locality, leisure and voluntary action on the metropolitan periphery. Dionysius Georgiou. (Professor Gareth Stedman Jones.) London M.Phil. (Q.M. Hist.)

19th century: Ireland

1676 The Irish in 19th-century Coventry: immigration and adjustment. Thomas Prendergast. (Professor Donald M. MacRaild and Dr. Kyle Hughes.) Ulster Ph.D. (Hist.)

1677 The supernatural in Catholic Ireland, 1800–1900. Jodie Shevlin. (Dr. Andrew Sneddon and Professor Ian D. Thatcher.) Ulster Ph.D. (Hist.)

1678 Adolescent sibling relationships in 19th-century Ulster. Shannon Devlin. (Dr. Elaine Farrell.) Belfast Ph.D. (Hist. & Anthr.)

1679 Poverty, poor relief and public health in Belfast and its region, c.1800–51. Robyn Atcheson. (Professor Peter Gray.) Belfast Ph.D. (Hist. & Anthr.)

1680 Women in the district mental asylums in Ulster, 1825–1921. Seaneen Larkin. (Dr. Leanne McCormick.) Ulster Ph.D. (Hist.)

1681 The rise of Bangor as a seaside resort, 1830–99. Sandra Millsopp. (Professor Sean J. Connolly.) Belfast Ph.D. (Hist. & Anthr.)

1682 A study of Ireland's elderly female population, 1845–1908. Sarah McHugh. (Dr. Elaine Farrell.) Belfast Ph.D. (Hist. & Anthr.)

1683 A 19th-century Irish coroner: William Charles Waddell, 1846–76. Michelle McCann. (Professor Peter Gray.) Belfast M.Phil./Ph.D. (Hist. & Anthr.)

1684 Cricket in Victorian Ireland, 1847–78: a social history. Sean Reid. (Dr. Peter Davies.) Huddersfield Ph.D. (Music, Hum. & Media)

1685 Musical culture and the spirit of Irish nationalism, 1848–1998. Richard E. Parfitt. (Professor Roy Foster.) Oxford D.Phil. (Mod. Hist.)

1686 Public perceptions of women religious: Irish and British dialogue, 1849–1912. Bridget Harrison. (Professor Mary O'Dowd.) Belfast M.Phil./Ph.D. (Hist. & Anthr.)

1687 Yorkshire and Ireland, 1850–1950: nationality, land ownership and identity. Catherine Badley. (Dr. Allen J. Warren.) York Ph.D. (Hist.)

1688 The welfare of children and childhood under the Irish Poor Law. Simon Gallaher. (Professor Eugenio Biagini and Dr. Samantha Williams.) Cambridge Ph.D. (Hist.)

1689 Irish childcare, 1850–1913: attitudes & approaches. Cecilia Hallström. (Professor Maria Luddy.) Warwick Ph.D. (Hist.)

1690 Margaret Anne Cusack, the Nun of the North. Marietta Farrell. (Dr. Leanne McCormick and Dr. Andrew Sneddon.) Ulster Ph.D. (Hist.)

1691 Irish nationalism in the West Riding, c.1870–1922. Andrew Maguire. (Dr.James P. Loughlin and Dr. J. Devlin Trew.) Ulster Ph.D. (Hist.)

1692 The British Army officer corps in Irish society, 1870–1920. Loughlin Sweeney. (Professor Eugenio Biagini.) Cambridge Ph.D. (Hist.)

1693 The Irish in Leeds and their politics 1870 to 1914. David Robatham. (Professor Malcolm S. Chase.) Leeds M.A. (Hist.)

1694 Belfast Corporation, 1880–1914: managing a mature industrial city. Stuart Irwin. (Professor Sean J. Connolly.) Belfast M.Phil./Ph.D. (Hist. & Anthr.)

1695 Protestants and progress: some aspects of Irish Catholic thought, c.1880–1914. Richard P. Mann. (Dr. S. Paseta and Dr. Marc Mulholland.) Oxford D.Phil. (Mod. Hist.)

1696 Deconstructing Westminster: a four nations history of the Irish Home Rule crisis, c.1886–93. Naomi Lloyd-Jones. (Dr. Paul A. Readman.) King's College London M.Phil./Ph.D. (Hist.)

1697 Popular politics in the Queen's County, Ireland, 1898–1914. Philip Sheppard. (Dr. Fergus Campbell and Dr. Joan Allen.) Newcastle Ph.D. (Hist.)

19th century: Administrative, military and naval history

1698 Popular perceptions of common British soldiers across the 19th century. Daniel C. Chaplin. (Professor Laurence Brockliss.) Oxford M.St. (Mod. Hist.)

1699 The role of the army and navy in influencing civilian public health policy and application in 19th-century England. Hilary Morris. (Dr. Karl Bell, Dr. Brad Beavan and Dr. Robert James.) Portsmouth Ph.D. (Soc., Hist. & Lit. Stud.)

1700 The myth of the 95th Rifles. Brian Wreglesworth. (Professor Charles J. Esdaile.) Liverpool M.Phil. (Hist.)

1701 Primitive Methodism on the Yorkshire Wold, 1819–1932. Priscilla Truss. (Professor Malcolm S. Chase and Dr. Simon J.D. Green.) Leeds Ph.D. (Hist.)

1702 Chronometry and British maritime exploration, c.1820–c.1845. Emily Akkerman. (Professor C.W.J. Withers.) Edinburgh Ph.D. (Geog.)

1703 Reform of the British Army in the Victorian/Edwardian period. Edward Gosling. (Professors Harry Bennett and Kevin Jefferys.) Plymouth Ph.D. (Hum.)

1704 Certification of the British Merchant Service: origins, development and impact, 1840–1914. Victoria Culkin. (Dr. Richard C. Gorski.) Hull Ph.D. (Hist.)

1705 The Victorian army and the cadet colleges: Woolwich and Sandhurst, 1840–1902. Sebastian Puncher. (Professor Mark Connelly and Dr. Timothy Bowman.) Kent Ph.D. (Hist.)

1706 The development of the British Royal Naval sailor uniform and its influence on civilian fashion in Victorian England, 1846–1901. Jennifer Daley. (Professor Andrew D. Lambert.) King's College London Ph.D. (War Stud.)

1707 Besmirching Britannia's good name: the reception of military scandals in mid Victorian Britain. Margery Masterson. (Dr. Kirsty Reid and Dr. James Thompson.) Bristol Ph.D. (Hist. Stud.)

1708 Medicalising the military: the British soldier and modern medicine, 1853–1918. Simon Walker. Glasgow Caledonian Ph.D (Hist.)

1709 Great Britain, international law and the evolution of maritime strategic thought, 1856–1914. Gabriela A. Frei. (Professor Hew F.A. Strachan.) Oxford D.Phil. (Mod. Hist.)

1710 An evaluation of the rifles issued to the British Army between 1866 and 1900. Tom Hepstinall. (Revd. Paul Wilcock.) Huddersfield M.Phil. (Music, Hum. & Media)

1711 'We shall sail the ocean blue': sailors in the Royal Navy and British imperial sentiment, 1870–1939. Simon Smith. (Dr. Brad Beavan and Dr. Robert James.) Portsmouth Ph.D. (Soc., Hist. & Lit. Stud.)

1712 The military thought of Charles E. Callwell. Daniel Whittingham. (Dr. Alan James and Professor William J. Philpott.) King's College London Ph.D. (War Stud.)

1713 Brabazon and the early politics of air power. Sophy Gardner. Exeter Ph.D. (Hist.)

1714 Patriotic pessimists and liberal internationalists: the defence debate in Britain, 1880–1900. Peter Keeling. (Professor Mark Connelly and Dr. Peter Donaldson.) Kent Ph.D. (Hist.)

19th century: Finance, trade and industry

1715 National policy, banking and finance in 19th-century England: towards an understanding of the causes and effects of the English crisis of 1866. Zhihui Yu. (Professor Kevin O'Rourke.) Oxford M.Sc. (Mod. Hist.)

1716 The paisley shawl loom: a study of the draw loom as adapted and developed for the weaving of paisley shawls during the first half of the 19th century. Daniel Coughlan. (Professor Sam McKinstry and Dr. J. Wood.) West of Scotland Ph.D. (Sci. and Sport.)

1717 Tracing policy by ports: the economic growth of port cities and British colonial development policy. Kevin A. Tang. (Professor Gregg Huff.) Oxford D.Phil. (Mod. Hist.)

1718 Spaces of industrial heritage: a history of uses, perceptions and remaking of the Liverpool Road Station site, Manchester. Erin Beeston. (Dr. James Sumner.) Manchester Ph.D. (Hist. of Sc., Tech. & Med.)

1719 Railway architecture and the development of the tunnel portal in the early history of the British railway system, c.1830–70. Hubert J. Pragnell. (Professor Colin Divall.) York Ph.D. (Hist.)

1720 Incorporation of the first English railways into the existing freight transport system. Carolyn Dougherty. (Professor Colin Divall.) York Ph.D. (Hist.)

1721 A history of Siemens in the north of England. Katherine Platt. (Dr. Jeff A. Hughes.) Manchester Ph.D. (Hist. of Sc., Tech. & Med.)

1722 The finance-growth Nexus in Britain, 1850–1913. Walter Jansson. (Dr. Cristiano Ristuccia.) Cambridge Ph.D. (Hist.)

1723 Britain's seafaring men and women: an analysis of the maritime labour force, 1850–1911. Joanna Thomas. (Professor Maria Fusaro and Dr. David Thackeray.) Exeter M.Phil. (Maritime Hist.)

1724 Through the looking glass: spectacle and the social real, 1851–1914. Josh Poklad. (Dr. Rosemary Mitchell and Dr. Di Drummond.) Leeds Trinity Ph.D. (Hist.)

1725 The introduction of general limited liability in England, 1855–6. Julia Chaplin. East Anglia Ph.D. (Hist.)

1726 Impact of the decline of the Cleveland ironstone industry on Cleveland. Elizabeth C. Marsh. (Professor Lawrence Black and Dr. James Symonds.) York Ph.D. (Hist.)

1727 Trends in invention: the paper industry, 1875–1945. Pauline Stern. (Dr. Florian Ploeckl.) Oxford M.Sc. (Mod. Hist.)

1728 The development and quality of management on the London and South Western Railway, 1876–1911. David A. Turner. (Professor Colin Divall.) York Ph.D. (Hist.)

1729 Matters of smell: a history of the fragrance industry, 1880–1960. Galina Shyndriayeva. (Professor David E.H. Edgerton.) King's College London Ph.D. (Hist.)

1730 Photography, engineers and business practices: a study of the S. Pearson & Son photographic albums. Noeme Santana. (Dr. Innes Keighren and Professor Felix Driver.) London M.Phil./Ph.D. (R.H.U.L. Geog.)

1731 Crefydd, Copr a Chymreictod – Anghydffurfiaeth Abertawe diwydiannol 1800–1914. [Religion, copper and Welshness – the nonconformity of industrial Swansea, 1800–1914.] (*In Welsh medium*). Christian Williams. (Mr. Robert Rhys.) Swansea Ph.D. (Hist.)

1732 Female professionals in Wales, 1881–1945. Beth Jenkins. (Dr. Stephanie Ward.) Cardiff Ph.D. (Hist. & Archaeol.)

1733 The Railway and Canal Commission. Simon G. Gibbs. (Professor Colin Divall.) York Ph.D. (Hist.)

1734 Co-operative contradictions: business, labour and gender in the British co-operative movement, 1889–1920. Rachael E. Vorberg-Rugh. (Dr. K.J. Humphries.) Oxford D.Phil. (Mod. Hist.)

1735 The rise and fall of the Manchester motor industry, 1896–1939. Joshua Butt. (Dr. Craig Horner, Professor Melanie Tebbutt and Jan Shearsmith.) Manchester Metropolitan Ph.D. (Hist.)

1736 London taxicabs. Fu-Chia Chen. (Dr. Barbara Schmucki.) York Ph.D. (Hist.)

19th century: Agriculture

1737 Watercress – archaeology/landscape history. Barrie Hawkins. (Professor Tom M. Williamson.) East Anglia Ph.D. (Hist.)

1738 Land settlement in Suffolk and Norfolk, 1850–1950. Penelope J. Macdonald. (Professor Tom M. Williamson.) East Anglia Ph.D. (Hist.)

1739 Gifted amateurs: the contribution of British artists to garden design, 1870–1951. Jean Cornell. (Dr. Barbara Simms and Professor Lawrence Goldman.) London M.Phil./Ph.D. (Inst. Hist. Res.)

1740   Agricultural landholding in Devon, 1876–1939. Kevin Cahill. (Professor Henry French.) Exeter M.Phil. (Hist.)

1741   The Welsh tithe war: a study in agrarian discontent. Sion Jones. (Dr. Lowri Ann Rees.) Bangor Ph.D. (Hist., Welsh Hist. & Archaeol.)

19th century: Social history

1742   An oral history of rugby union. Joe Hall. (Professor Tony Collins.) De Montfort Ph.D. (Hum.)

1743   A history of English women's hockey. Joanne Halpin. (Dr. Jean Williams.) De Montfort Ph.D. (Hum.)

1744   The female music fan in sociological and historical discourse since the 19th century. Nancy Bruseker. (Dr. Marion Leonard.) Liverpool Ph.D. (Hist.)

1745   Histories of soup kitchens. Lewis Smith. (Professor Rebecca Earle.) Warwick M.Phil./Ph.D. (Hist.)

1746   Cultural negotiations of empire: gender and race in juvenile missionary literature. Julie McColl. (Dr. Mark Towsey.) Liverpool Ph.D. (Hist.)

1747   The British only child, 1800–1950. Alice Violett. (Professor Edward Higgs.) Essex Ph.D. (Hist.)

1748   Investigation of the development of living standards during the 19th and early 20th century using anthropometric evidence. Caspar Henle. (Dr. Brian A'Hearn.) Oxford M.Sc. (Mod. Hist.)

1749   From suffragette to citizen: an exploration of female experience of political spaces in the 19th and early 20th centuries. Amy Galvin. (Dr. Laura Schwartz and Dr. Sarah Richardson.) Warwick M.Phil./Ph.D. (Hist.)

1750   Gardeners: their accommodation and remuneration, 1800–1914. Peter J. Denby. (Professor Jane Humphries.) Oxford D.Phil. (Mod. Hist.)

1751   Masculine display of exotic luxury goods. Charlotte Brown. (Dr. Jane Hamlett.) London Ph.D. (R.H.U.L. Hist.)

1752   A corpus-based investigation of the representation of places in 19th-century British newspapers. Amelia Joulain-Jay. (Professor Ian Gregory and Dr. Andrew Hardie.) Lancaster Ph.D. (Hist.)

1753   By reason of insanity; marriage, divorce, and the madness of violent female criminals in 19th-century Britain. Kaitlin J. Lloyd. (Dr. Sloan Mahone.) Oxford M.Sc. (Mod. Hist.)

1754   Picturing the Antipodes: race, image and empire in 19th-century Britain. Mary McMahon. (Dr. Zoe Laidlaw and Dr. G. Sculthorp.) London M.Phil./Ph.D. (R.H.U.L. Hist.)

1755   Education and the poor on Merseyside in the 19th century. Judith Taylor. (Dr. Peter Shapely.) Bangor Ph.D. (Hist., Welsh Hist. & Archaeol.)

1756   Morality and 19th-century British female emigration. Brooke Weber. (Dr. Zoe Laidlaw.) London M.Phil./Ph.D. (R.H.U.L. Hist.)

1757 Inside the 'homes of mercy': the domestic, the material and the moral in the reform of 'fallen' women in 19th-century England. Susan Woodall. (Dr. Jane Hamlett.) London M.Phil./Ph.D. (R.H.U.L. Hist.)

1758 Representations of celebrity, sex and power in Regency England: Harriette Wilson and her memoirs. Katarzyna W. Brzezinska. (Dr. Erica Charters.) Oxford M.St. (Mod. Hist.)

1759 Refiguring radicalism: exploring gender, class and 'the body' in popular protest, 1819–48. Katharine Mutlow. (Dr. Kathryn Gleadle.) Oxford D.Phil. (Mod. Hist.)

1760 The clothing of Charlotte Bronte and a study of 'plainness'. Eleanor Houghton. (Professor Maria Haywayd.) Southampton M.Phil. (Hist.)

1761 The vigilante in British culture, 1829–1967. Courtney Stickland. (Dr. Max Jones and Dr. Eloise Moss.) Manchester Ph.D. (Hist.)

1762 Children who kill: Victorian responses to the passionate child, 1830–95. Eleanor Betts. (Dr. Thomas M. Dixon.) London Ph.D. (Q.M. Hist.)

1763 'A deed at which humanity shudders': mad mothers, the law and the asylum in England, 1845–90. Alison Pedley. (Dr. Margaret L. Arnot and Dr. Michael Brown.) Roehampton M.Phil./Ph.D. (Hist.)

1764 'On a shiny night': the representation of the poacher in English culture, c.1831–1920. Stephen Ridgwell. (Professor Claire L. Langhamer.) Sussex D.Phil. (Hist.)

1765 Gender and institutional confinement in England: from the New Poor Law to the 1912 Lunacy Act. Lucy Williams. (Dr. Andrew Davies.) Liverpool Ph.D. (Hist.)

1766 A social history of Scottish homicide, 1836–60. Alison Brown. (Professor Peter J.R. King.) Leicester Ph.D. (Eng. Loc. Hist.)

1767 The Boys' Brigade in the Victorian and Edwardian city. Chris Spackman. (Dr. Brad Beavan and Dr. Karl Bell.) Portsmouth Ph.D. (Soc., Hist. & Lit. Stud.)

1768 An investigation of the social and cultural history of the apple during the Victorian era (1837–1901), with consideration of how its status influenced, and was affected by, its commercial value. Joanna Crosby. (Dr. Peter J. Gurney.) Essex Ph.D. (Hist.)

1769 A social history of Turkish baths in Victorian London. Charlotte Jones. (Professor Richard J. Dennis and Dr. James Kneale.) London Ph.D. (U.C. Geog.)

1770 Welfare and patronage in the Victorian Post Office. Kathleen McIlvenna. (Professor Miles Taylor and Dr. Adrian Steel.) London Ph.D. (Inst. Hist. Res.)

1771 A social history of swimming and the working classes in Victorian England. Keith Myerscough. (Dr. Jean Williams.) De Montfort Ph.D. (Hum.)

1772 Digging in Victorian newspapers: a study of the Other in Victorian newspapers through computer analysis. Quintus Van Galen. (Dr. Bob Nicholson.) Edge Hill Ph.D. (English & Hist.)

1773 Modern British social history focussing upon the Chartists. Christian Radley. (Professor Keith Laybourn.) Huddersfield M.Phil. (Music, Hum. & Media)

1774 'The song of the pen': popular romantic literature, 1839–89. Cheryl Deedman. (Dr. Vivienne Richmond and Professor Richard Grayson.) London Ph.D. (Goldsmiths Hist.)

1775 Leisure activities of the rural working class, 1840–1940, with particular reference to Norfolk. Carole V. King. East Anglia Ph.D. (Hist.)

1776 Working-class female agency in 'outcast London': the East End of London, 1840–1914. Dianne Shepherd. (Dr. Katrina Navickas and Dr. Sarah Lloyd.) Hertfordshire Ph.D. (Hist.)

1777 Captives of the system: the commissioners in lunacy as regulators of services for pauper lunatics and idiots, 1845–1914. Frank Hughes. (Dr. Deborah Brunton and Dr. Donna Loftus.) Open University M.Phil./Ph.D. (Hist.)

1778 Cricket crowds: a social and cultural history. Nigel Hancock. (Professor Tony Collins.) De Montfort Ph.D. (Hum.)

1779 The cultural and historical geography of pigeon fancying in Britain. Kate Whiston. (Professors Charles Watkins and David Matless.) Nottingham Ph.D. (Geog.)

1780 A history of policing same-gendered sexual relations in north-west England, 1850s–1980s. Jeffrey G. Evans. (Ms. Patricia Ayres and Dr. Anthony J. Adams.) Manchester Metropolitan Ph.D. (Hist.)

1781 Oxford college servants, 1850–1950. Kathryne Crossley. (Professor Jane Humphries.) Oxford D.Phil. (Mod. Hist.)

1782 Sex, suffrage and the music hall, 1850–1919. Fern Riddell. (Dr. Paul Readman and Professor Arthur Burns.) King's College London M.Phil./Ph.D. (Hist.)

1783 From 'pugs' and 'outlaws' to the 'gentlemanly art of self defence': notions of masculinity and violence in England, 1850–1914. Liam Hannan. (Dr. Max Jones and Professor Julie-Marie Strange.) Manchester Ph.D. (Hist.)

1784 Passengers, emigrants and modern men: a social history of the 1852 voyage of S.S. *Great Britain* from Liverpool to Melbourne. Claire Connor. (Dr. Tim Cole and Dr. Simon Potter.) Bristol Ph.D. (Hist. Stud.)

1785 Cracking cribs: representations of burglars and burglary in London, 1860–1939. Eloise Moss. (Dr. Matt Houlbrook.) Oxford D.Phil. (Mod. Hist.)

1786 Baby minding and baby murder: paid childcare in England and Scotland, c.1860–1910. James Hinks. (Dr. Andrew Davies.) Liverpool Ph.D. (Hist.)

1787 The 1860s garrotting crisis: crime culture and power in north-west England. Zoe Alkers. (Dr. Helen Rogers and Dr. Mike Benbough-Jackson.) Liverpool John Moores Ph.D. (Hist.)

1788 Property, crime and the home in London, c.1861–1914. Krissie Glover. (Dr. Jane Hamlett.) London M.Phil./Ph.D. (R.H.U.L. Hist.)

1789 The discursive limits of lesbian sexuality: Sapphic aestheticism in the lives and work of Vernon Lee and Virginia Woolf. Soozi Mead. (Dr. Susan Morgan and Dr. Hugo Frey.) Chichester M.Phil./Ph.D. (Hist.)

1790 Pain, childhood and the emotions: a cultural history, 1870–1950. Leticia Fernandez Fontecha Rumeu. (Dr. Mary Clare Martin, Professors Ian McNay and Sarah Palmer.) Greenwich Ph.D. (Educ. & Community Studies)

1791 Welfare outside the workhouse: outdoor relief and the New Poor Law, 1870–1930. Nicola Blacklaws. (Professor Keith D.M. Snell.) Leicester Ph.D. (Eng. Loc. Hist.)

1792   Constructing woman: medical discourse, popular culture and society in Yorkshire, 1870–1930. Claire Martin. (Dr. Kate M. Dossett and Dr. Jessica Meyer.) Leeds Ph.D. (Hist.)

1793   Working-class homes in three urban communities, 1870–1918. Oliver Betts. (Professor Richard J. Bessel.) York Ph.D. (Hist.)

1794   The development of education in central and east Lancashire for children with disabilities from the late 19th century to the Second World War. Claire Hadwen. (Dr. Keith Vernon and Dr. Martin Atherton.) Central Lancashire M.Phil./Ph.D. (Hum.)

1795   Sir Frederic Leighton: imperialism and concepts of masculinity. Madeline Boden. (Professor Jason Edwards.) York Ph.D. (Hist. of Art)

1796   Arthur Conan Doyle and sport. James McPherson. (Dr. Jean Williams.) De Montfort Ph.D. (Hum.)

1797   Changing conceptions of the sense of touch in Britain, c.1880–1970. Simeon Koole. (Dr. Matthew Houlbrook.) Oxford D.Phil. (Mod. Hist.)

1798   Landscape, travel, and literary tourism in the western British-Irish Isles, c.1880–1939. Gareth Roddy. (Dr. Adrian C. Bingham.) Sheffield Ph.D. (Hist.)

1799   Breaking the shackles of convention: Elizabeth Le Blond in the mountains, 1880–1920. Madeline Armstrong. (Dr. Jean Williams.) De Montfort Ph.D. (Hum.)

1800   Collecting magic in late 19th- and early 20th-century England. Tabitha Cadbury. (Professor Ronald Hutton and Dr. James Thompson.) Bristol M.Litt. (Hist. Stud.)

1801   Segregation or assimilation? Assessing the impact of English migration upon national and cultural identities in Wales, c.1880–1914. Lewis Owen. (Professor Paul B. O'Leary and Dr. Steven Thompson.) Aberystwyth Ph.D. (Hist. & Welsh Hist.)

1802   Philanthropy: a benefit or a burden? The dual face of Anglo-Jewish philanthropic organisations, 1880–1912. Micheline Stevens. (Professor Tony Kushner.) Southampton Ph.D. (Hist.)

1803   The history of Scottish public policy in relation to travelling communities, 1885–2014. Andrea Salvona. (Professors Paul Cairney and Douglas Robertson.) Stirling Ph.D. (Hist.)

1804   The Whitechapel murders and degeneration: an investigation of biological and class anxiety. Kathryn Phillips. (Dr. Darren Oldridge.) Worcester M.Phil./Ph.D. (Hum. & Creative Arts)

1805   Leisure, society and marginal communities – fairground folk and outdoor pleasure-seeking in Britain, 1890–1950. Elijah Bell. (Dr. Matthew Grant.) Essex Ph.D. (Hist.)

19th century: Ecclesiastical and religious history

1806   Denominational responses to the religious content of 19th-century novels. Anthony J. Coles. (Dr. Mark Smith and Dr. Simon Skinner.) Oxford D.Phil. (Mod. Hist.)

1807   Nineteenth-century evangelicalism and children's literature. Irene Smale. (Dr. Susan Morgan and Professor D. Hugh McLeod.) Chichester M.Phil./Ph.D. (Hist.)

1808 'Christianity personified': religion, politics and Spencer Perceval. Edward Hicks. (Dr. Simon Skinner.) Oxford D.Phil. (Mod. Hist.)

1809 Primitive Methodism in Hertfordshire. David Noble. (Dr. Katrina Navickas, Dr. Sarah Lloyd and Professor Owen Davies.) Hertfordshire Ph.D. (Hist.)

1810 The Commissioners' Churches on a Lancashire religious frontier: vital bastions of a 19th-century Anglican 'counter Reformation'? William Walker. (Dr. Stephen Caunce and Dr. Andrew Gritt.) Central Lancashire M.Phil./Ph.D. (Hum.)

1811 Urban church closure and the redefining of Church of England mission from 1833 to 2011. Steven Saxby. (Professor Arthur Burns.) King's College London M.Phil./Ph.D. (Hist.)

1812 The creation of the diocese of Shrewsbury. Vincent Roper. (Professor Robert Lee.) Liverpool M.Phil. (Hist.)

1813 Doctrine, progress and history: British religious debate, c.1845–1914. Joshua M.R. Bennett. (Dr. E. Jane Garnett.) Oxford D.Phil. (Mod. Hist.)

1814 'We claim to be a kingdom': Roman Catholic social and political thought in England, c.1848–c.1914. Colm O Siochru. (Dr. E. Jane Garnett.) Oxford D.Phil. (Mod. Hist.)

1815 Religious heritage in transition: Sikh places of worship in England. Clare Canning. (Deirdre O'Sullivan and Dr. Ruth Young.) Leicester Ph.D. (Archaeol. & Anc. Hist.)

1816 The impact of church disestablishment campaigns on religion and society in south-east Wales in the second half of the 19th century. Canon Arthur Edwards. (Professor Bill Jones.) Cardiff Ph.D. (Hist. & Archaeol.)

1817 Methodism as designed space, 1851–1932? Ruth Mason. (Dr. James Kneale.) London Ph.D. (U.C. Geog.)

1818 The life and influence of John Wilbur Chapman, 1859–1918. Ross Purdy. (Professor David W. Bebbington and Dr. Colin Nicolson.) Stirling Ph.D. (Hist.)

1819 Historical perceptions of Roman Catholicism and national identity, 1869–1919. Alec Corio. (Professor John R. Wolffe, Dr. Marion Bowman and Dr. Carol Richardson.) Open University Ph.D. (Relig. Stud.)

1820 John William Graham (1859–1932), Quaker apostle of progress. Joanna Dales. (Professors Ben Pink Dandelion and D. Hugh McLeod.) Birmingham Ph.D. (Theol.)

1821 The English use: liturgy and the arts in the Church of England, 1895–1965. Evan McWilliams. (Dr. Anthony Geraghty.) York Ph.D. (Hist. of Art)

19th century: Education

1822 The development of pharmacy in Scotland. Susan Osbaldstone. Glasgow Caledonian Ph.D. (Hist.)

1823 Routes into consumption: the student economy in 19th-century Oxford. Sabine S. Chaouche. (Professor Jane Humphries.) Oxford D.Phil. (Mod. Hist.)

1824 The university question and the 19th-century British Catholic hierarchy. Bridget Randolph. (Dr. Matthew Grimley.) Oxford M.Phil. (Mod. Hist.)

1825 Bullying in English schools, 1820–1900. Catherine G. Sloan. (Dr. Christina de Bellaigue and Dr. Kathryn Gleadle.) Oxford D.Phil. (Mod. Hist.)

1826 Middle-class, professional and utilitarian: the foundation of the London University and the socio-cultural status of English liberal education, 1825–36. Mohd Helmi Mohd Sobri. (Dr. Niall O'Flaherty and Professor Ian McBride.) King's College London M.Phil./Ph.D. (Hist.)

1827 Mechanics institutes in Victorian England. Douglas Watson. (Dr. James Gregory, Dr. Daniel Grey and Professor James Daybell.) Plymouth M.Phil./Ph.D. (Hum.)

1828 History of British school uniform. Katherine E.P. Stephenson. (Dr. Elizabeth A. Buettner.) York Ph.D. (Hist.)

1829 The School Board for London and the training ship tradition: the T.S. *Shaftesbury's* literal, metaphorical, and institutional spaces. Jamie Nightingale. (Dr. Jane Hamlett.) London Ph.D. (R.H.U.L. Hist.)

1830 The first women at St. Andrews: the L.L.A. from 1877 to 1904. Elisabeth Smith. (Dr. David Allan.) St. Andrews Ph.D. (Hist.)

19th century: The arts, science, medicine and public health

1831 The local history of lunatic asylums/mental health institutions in Scotland: archival inquiries and contemporary resonances. Kim Ross. (Professors Chris Philo and Malcolm A. Nicolson.) Glasgow Ph.D. (Soc. Sc.)

1832 Art and the anthropocene. Bergit Arends. (Professors Felix Driver and Helen Gilbert.) London M.Phil./Ph.D. (R.H.U.L. Geog.)

1833 The history of peptic ulcer disease in the 19th and 20th centuries. Alexander Pollock. (Professors Malcolm A. Nicolson and Lawrence Weaver.) Glasgow M.D. (Soc. Sc.)

1834 Correcting vision in 19th-century Britain. Gemma Almond. (Professor David Turner.) Swansea Ph.D. (Hist.)

1835 A queer quarry: 19th-century female sculptors outside the bounds of Victorian heteronormativity. Melissa Gustin. (Professor Elizabeth Prettejohn.) York Ph.D. (Hist. of Art)

1836 Exploring the eccentricities and anachronisms of Gothic revival sculpture in the 19th century. Claire Hildreth. (Professor Jason Edwards.) York Ph.D. (Hist. of Art)

1837 Painter, place and presence: Joseph Wright's afterlives, 1800–1900. Alice Insley. (Professors Stephen Daniels and Nicholas Alfrey.) Nottingham Ph.D. (Geog.)

1838 The caryatid in 19th-century Britain. Ciarán Rua O'Neill. (Professor Elizabeth Prettejohn.) York Ph.D. (Hist. of Art)

1839 Entertaining the insane: rethinking the role of social activities in British asylums (*c.*1800–1900). Ute Oswald. (Professor Hilary Marland.) Warwick M.Phil./Ph.D. (Hist.)

1840 Nineteenth-century music and English nationalism. James D.C. Shearer. (Dr. Joanna de Groot and Dr. Catriona A.L. Kennedy.) York M.A. (Hist.)

1841   Rethinking the history of anorexia nervosa: a critical analysis of the historiography of 19th-century anorexia.   Rhea V. Sookdeosingh.   (Dr. Sloan Mahone.)   Oxford D.Phil.   (Mod. Hist.)

1842   Alice's glass: mirrors in 19th-century painting.   Claire Yearwood.   (Professor Elizabeth Prettejohn.)   York Ph.D.   (Hist. of Art)

1843   Entrepreneurship allied to the history of theatre, 1800–30.   Elizabeth Tames.   (Professor James R. Raven.)   Essex Ph.D.   (Hist.)

1844   Canonising British sculpture: Sir Francis Chantrey and the Chantrey bequest.   Amy Harris.   (Professor Jason Edwards.)   York Ph.D.   (Hist. of Art)

1845   The apprentice, the aristocrat, and the analyst: a comparative schematic study of the posthumous impact, shared biographical traits and changing literary fortunes of Faraday, Lovelace and Turing.   Thomas Redpath.   (Professor Pietro Corsi and Dr. Stephen Johnston.)   Oxford M.Sc.   (Mod. Hist.)

1846   Henning's moulds in the British Museum.   Alan Hiscutt.   (Professor Amy Smith.)   Reading Ph.D.   (Classics)

1847   The relationship of the work of G.A. Henty, 'the boy's historian', to historical fiction for children in Britain, 1814–1903.   Laura Jones.   (Professor Jean Webb, Dr. Paddy McNally and Dr. Andreas Mueller.)   Worcester M.Phil./Ph.D.   (Hum. & Creative Arts)

1848   Charles Roberson, London colourman, and the supply of painting materials, 1820–1920.   Sally Woodcock.   (Professor Peter Mandler.)   Cambridge Ph.D.   (Hist.)

1849   The contested rise of dispensaries: their contribution to health care in Warwickshire 1820–80.   John Wilmot.   (Professors Hilary Marland and Sarah Richardson.)   Warwick M.Phil./Ph.D.   (Hist.)

1850   Death and the disposal of the dead in the world's first industrial city, 1820–70.   Michala Hulme.   (Professor Melanie Tebbutt and Mr. Terry Wyke.)   Manchester Metropolitan Ph.D.   (Hist.)

1851   The primacy of architectural patronage: incorporating a case study of Joseph Aloysius Hansom, 1809–82.   Penelope Harris.   (Dr. Peter Shapely.)   Bangor Ph.D.   (Hist., Welsh Hist. & Archaeol.)

1852   Geography and periodicals: the *Geographical Journal* and the making of geographic knowledge, 1830–1930.   Ben Newman.   (Dr. Innes Keighren and Professor Klaus Dodds.)   London M.Phil./Ph.D.   (R.H.U.L. Geog.)

1853   William Lauder Lindsay and the animal mind: a 19th-century comparative psychology.   Elizabeth Gray.   (Dr. Rhodri Hayward.)   London Ph.D.   (Q.M. Hist.)

1854   The donated dead: body donation in the UK, 1832–2004.   Lindsay Dalgarno.   Glasgow Caledonian Ph.D.   (Hist.)

1855   William Benjamin Carpenter (1813–85), forgotten protagonist of Victorian science.   Shannon Delorme.   (Professor Pietro Corsi.)   Oxford D.Phil.   (Mod. Hist.)

1856   The scientific rationality of the early statistics, 1833–77.   Yasuhiro Okazawa.   (Professor Simon Szreter.)   Cambridge Ph.D.   (Hist.)

1857 The construction of the Airy Transit Circle: the role of the relations between men of science and instrument makers in the field of astronomy in 19th-century Britain. Daniel Belteki. (Dr. Rebekah Higgitt and Professor Charlotte Sleigh.) Kent Ph.D. (Hist.)

1858 The medicalisation of the 19th-century coroner's inquest, 1836–1906. Yvonne Fisher. (Dr. Silvia de Renzi and Dr. Deborah Brunton.) Open University Ph.D. (Hist.)

1859 Between fact and imagination: *tableaux vivants*, fancy dress and the Victorian imagination. Hannah Jordan. (Dr. Meaghan E. Clarke and Professor Geoffrey Quilley.) Sussex D.Phil. (Hist. of Art)

1860 Science in the kitchen in Victorian England. Katie Carpenter. (Dr. Jane Hamlett.) London M.Phil./Ph.D. (R.H.U.L. Hist.)

1861 An investigation into the introduction and use of coal-tar derived dyes to colour Victorian food. Carolyn Cobbold. (Dr. Emma Spary.) Cambridge Ph.D. (Hist.)

1862 Victorian street life: browsing, performance and interaction in the museum. Jack Gann. (Professor Karen Sayer and Dr. Rosemary Mitchell.) Leeds Trinity Ph.D. (Hist.)

1863 Canine contexts: understanding the role of the dog in British Victorian art. Amy Robson. (Dr. James Gregory and Dr. Gemma Blackshaw.) Plymouth M.Phil./Ph.D. (Hum.)

1864 Household medicine in a century of change: Victorian domestic healthcare, c.1837–1901. Irene Stirling. Glasgow Caledonian Ph.D. (Hist.)

1865 Queen Victoria's reign as mediated through portraiture, 1837–61. Ann Poulson. (Professor Ludmilla J. Jordanova.) King's College London M.Phil./Ph.D. (Hist.)

1866 Sir George Scharf and the problem of authenticity at the National Portrait Gallery. Paula E. Freestone Mellor. (Dr. J.J.L. Whiteley and Dr. A. Peach.) Oxford D.Phil. (Mod. Hist.)

1867 Negotiating ovariotomy: innovation, intellectual property and operative risk in Victorian surgery, 1842–95. Sally Frampton. (Professor Roger Cooter and Dr. Nick D. Hopwood.) London Ph.D. (U.C. Hist. of Med.)

1868 Man of nonsense: Alfred Russel Wallace and the vaccination question. Ahren Lester. (Dr.Jonathan Conlin.) Southampton Ph.D. (Hist.)

1869 Abraham Solomon (1823–62). Thomas Woodhouse. (Professor Elizabeth Prettejohn.) York Ph.D. (Hist. of Art)

1870 A comparative study of the Jewish hospital in London and the German hospital in London. Howard Rein. (Professor Tony Kushner.) Southampton Ph.D. (Hist.)

1871 Dealing with lunatic children: a comparative regional study of child lunatic admissions to pauper lunatic asylums in the period 1845–1907. Michael Tedd. (Professor Keith D.M. Snell.) Leicester Ph.D. (Eng. Loc. Hist.)

1872 Victorian illustration: Arthur Hughes and Frederick Sandys. Rebecca Gibbons. (Professor Caroline H. Arscott.) London Ph.D. (Courtauld Inst.)

1873 History of ergonomics. Roland Edwards. (Dr. Jeff A. Hughes.) Manchester Ph.D. (Hist. of Sc., Tech. & Med.)

1874 The role of business, religious, academic and kinship networks in the establishment of publicly accessible natural history collections in East Anglia. Ann Nix. East Anglia Ph.D. (Hist.)

1875 John Hollingshead and the Victorian theatre. Helen Innes. (Professors Rohan McWilliam and John Gardner.) Anglia Ruskin D.Phil. (Hist.)

1876 Theories of Impressionism across painting and literature: R.A.M. Stevenson and Ford Madox. Jennifer R. Pitt. (Dr. Hanneke Grootenboer.) Oxford M.St. (Mod. Hist.)

1877 John Skelton and the development of herbal medicine in the 19th century. Allison Denham. (Dr. Mark S.R. Jenner.) York M.A. (Hist.)

1878 Imagining gender in the art of Elizabeth Siddal. Rachael Morris. (Dr. Geraldine Johnson.) Oxford M.St. (Mod. Hist.)

1879 A new perspective on the cholera epidemic of 1853–4 in London, England. Rebecca D. Stieva. (Professor Mark Harrison.) Oxford M.Sc. (Mod. Hist.)

1880 Sir George Scharf and the early National Portrait Gallery: reconstructing an intellectual and professional artistic world, 1857–95. Elizabeth Heath. (Dr. Meaghan E. Clarke and Dr. Benedict Burbridge.) Sussex D.Phil. (Hist. of Art)

1881 Works of travel in an age of high empire: John Murray III and domestic markets for the far away, c.1859–92. Anne Peale. (Professor C.W.J. Withers.) Edinburgh Ph.D. (Geog.)

1882 Cottage hospitals: their foundation, development and contribution to community health in England and Wales, 1860–1949. Keith Atkins. (Dr. Sue Hawkins and Professor Craig Phelan.) Kingston Ph.D. (Econ., Pol. & Hist.)

1883 Instruments of exploration: technologies of geographical enquiry, c.1860–1939. Jane Wess. (Professor C.W.J. Withers.) Edinburgh Ph.D. (Geog.)

1884 The abdominal abyss: the surgical exploration of maternal medicine, 1860–90. Laura Neff. (Dr. Graham Smith.) London M.Phil. (R.H.U.L. Hist.)

1885 The 'generation of 1863' as transnational network. Nicholas Shaddick. (Professor Elizabeth Prettejohn.) York Ph.D. (Hist. of Art)

1886 Julia Margaret Cameron: portraits of representative men. Nichole J. Fazio-Veigel. (Dr. G. Johnson and Dr. M. Weaver.) Oxford D.Phil. (Mod. Hist.)

1887 The Victoria Institute 1865–1930: a case study in the relationship between science and religion. Stuart Mathieson. (Dr. Andrew Holmes.) Belfast M.Phil./Ph.D. (Hist. & Anthr.)

1888 John Tenniel's *Alice in Wonderland* illustrations. Klara Wagner. (Dr. Geraldine Johnson.) Oxford M.St. (Mod. Hist.)

1889 Trauma, gender and the treatment of epilepsy, 1870–1948. Rachel Hewitt. (Professor Oonagh Walsh, Dr. Vicky Long and Dr. Janet Greenlees.) Glasgow Caledonian M.Sc. (Hist.)

1890 Gardening and gardens in urban schools in England, 1870–1939. Florence Pinard-Nelson. London M.Phil./Ph.D. (R.H.U.L. Hist.)

1891 Rationale, identity and legacy: the collection of Maurice, 4th and last Baron Egerton of Tatton Park, 1874–1958. Sarah G. Marden. (Dr. Jonathan Spangler and Dr.Faye Sayer.) Manchester Metropolitan Ph.D. (Hist.)

1892 Esoteric thought in the life and work of H. Rider Haggard. Simon Magus. Exeter M.Phil. (Stud. of Esotericism)

1893 From antiquarians to archaeologists: the development of archaeology in Wales, c.1880–1940. John Gould. (Professors Nancy Edwards, A. Huw Pryce and Raimund Karl.) Bangor Ph.D. (Hist., Welsh Hist. & Archaeol.)

1894 Making germs real: germ work in Britain, c.1880–1930. Laura Newman. (Dr. Anna Maerker and Professor David E.H. Edgerton.) King's College London M.Phil./Ph.D. (Hist.)

1895 The Scottish medical community in London during the late 19th and early 20th centuries. Alistair Haggarty. (Professor Marjory Harper and Dr. Ben Marsden.) Aberdeen Ph.D. (Hist.)

1896 Racehorse training, nutrition, management and health in England between 1880 and 1920. Esther Harper. (Dr. Abigail Woods and Dr. Chris Garibaldi.) King's College London M.Phil./Ph.D. (Hist.)

1897 Industrial health foods and culture during Britain's 'decadent era', 1880–1920. Lesley Steinitz. (Dr. Emma Spary and Dr. Anne Secord.) Cambridge Ph.D. (Hist.)

1898 Concerning venereal disease, to what extent had the discourse of 'blame' altered since the abolition of the Contagious Diseases Acts in Britain, c.1880–1914? Rachel Ross. (Professor Mark Harrison.) Oxford M.Sc. (Mod. Hist.)

1899 The Newlyn School. Christopher Guy. (Dr. Lee Simon.) Reading Ph.D. (Hist. of Art)

1900 William and Evelyn De Morgan and the art of ceramic. Rosalie Garry. (Professor Paul Davies.) Reading Ph.D. (Hist.)

1901 Negotiating intimacy: sexuality and the body in the history of physiotherapy, 1890–1994. Kayleigh Nias. Exeter M.Phil. (Medical Hist.)

1902 A critical re-evaluation of the historic articled pupil training system for aspiring professional musicians, with particular reference to how it operated under Dr. Herbert Brewer (organist of Gloucester Cathedral, 1898–1928). Simon Carpenter. (Dr. Christian O'Connell and Professor Melanie J. Ilic.) Gloucestershire M.A. (Hum.)

1903 External threats mask internal fears: British invasion literature, 1899–1914. Harry Wood. (Dr. Robert Foley.) Liverpool Ph.D. (Hist.)

Twentieth century

General and political history

1904 The Labour party in west London. Barbara Humphries. (Professor Matt Worley.) Reading Ph.D. (Hist.)

1905 A second 'century of co-operation': the fall of mutualism in the first part of the 20th century and the rise of mutualism in the first part of the 21st century. Nicholas Janes. (Professor Keith Laybourn and Dr. Rebecca Gill.) Huddersfield Ph.D. (Music, Hum. & Media)

1906 Public open spaces. Lesley Kant Cunneen. East Anglia Ph.D. (Hist.)

1907 Remedies of decline? An investigation into the memorialisation of key 20th-century English myths. Vanessa Morrell. (Professor Barry Doyle.) Huddersfield Ph.D. (Music, Hum. & Media)

1908 Myth and political parties. Emily Robinson. (Dr. Richard Grayson.) London Ph.D. (Goldsmiths Pol.)

1909 The traffic problem: geographies, politics and technologies of congestion in 20th-century London. David Rooney. (Professor David Gilbert.) London Ph.D. (R.H.U.L. Geog.)

1910 The House of Lords in the 20th century. Neville Shack. Exeter Ph.D. (Hist.)

1911 Roads and modernity in 20th-century Britain, 1900–63. Justine Cook. (Professor Charlotte Sleigh and Dr. Rebekah Higgit.) Kent Ph.D. (Hist.)

1912 British maritime history, national identity and film, 1900–60. Victoria Carolan. (Dr. Daniel Todman.) London Ph.D. (Q.M. Hist.)

1913 Poor Law to welfare law in the first part of the 20th century. Hayley Whitaker. (Dr. Matthew Garrett.) Chester M.Phil. (Hist. & Archaeol.)

1914 Race and the communist movement in Britain, c.1900–29. Daniel Edmonds. (Professors Kevin Morgan and Stuart Jones.) Manchester Ph.D. (Hist.)

1915 From mills to militants: the Kenney sisters and the suffragettes. Lyndsey V. Jenkins. (Dr. Senia Paseta and Dr. Selina Todd.) Oxford D.Phil. (Mod. Hist.)

1916 Centre and periphery: woman's suffrage discourse and cultural hegemony in Britain, 1900–18. John G. Barr. (Dr. Christopher M. Warne and Professor Claire L. Langhamer.) Sussex D.Phil. (Hist.)

1917 Constance Lytton: upper class suffragette. Wendy Tuxill. (Professors Lucy Bland and Mary Joannou.) Anglia Ruskin D.Phil. (Hist.)

1918 'Fires smouldering in the English spirit': dissent, civil disobedience, radicalism and conscientious objection in the Edwardian era. Alison Wilcox. (Dr. Mark A. Allen and Dr. Stephanie Spencer.) Winchester M.Phil./Ph.D. (Hist.)

1919 Rose Lamartine Yates and Wimbledon W.S.P.U.: reconfiguring suffragette history from the local to the national. Alexandra Hughes-Johnson. (Dr. Alex Windscheffel.) London Ph.D. (R.H.U.L. Hist.)

1920 London Jewry and the First World War: patriotism, identity and the politics of integration. Christopher Smith. (Dr. Adam Sutcliffe and Dr. Paul A. Readman.) King's College London M.Phil./Ph.D. (Hist.)

1921 Internal security in Britain 1918–31. Patrick Kiernan. (Professor Simon J. Ball.) Leeds Ph.D. (Hist.)

1922 The changing official mind of British imperialism, 1918–22. Ben Markham. (Dr. Jeremy Krikler.) Essex Ph.D. (Hist.)

1923 Governmental perceptions of, and reactions to, the origins of political discontent in British society in the immediate aftermath of the First World War. Calum White. (Dr. Adrian Gregory.) Oxford D.Phil (Mod. Hist.)

1924 'Save the Children': humanitarianism, human rights and constructions of international responsibility in inter-war Britain. Emily Baughan. (Dr. James Thompson and Dr. Kirsty Reid.) Bristol M.Litt. (Hist. Stud.)

1925 The political economy of the inter-war years. Alan E. de Bromhead. (Professor Kevin O'Rourke.) Oxford D.Phil. (Mod. Hist.)

1926 Fitness for citizenship: feminist perspectives on gender, education and the politics of biology in the inter-war years. Janice Tripney. (Professor Jane Martin.) London M.Phil. (Inst. of Educ.)

1927 The cultural politics of Englishness: John Hargrave, the Kibbo Kift and social credit, 1920–39. Hana Qugana. (Dr. Michael Collins.) London Ph.D. (U.C. Hist.)

1928 Sir Orme Sargent and British policy towards Europe, 1926–49. Adam Richardson. (Dr. Geoffrey G.T. Waddington.) Leeds Ph.D. (Hist.)

1929 'Luddites in this day and age?' The Communist party of Great Britain's engagement with the rationalisation of labour, 1926–41. Michael Weatherburn. (Professor David E.H. Edgerton.) Imperial College London Ph.D. (Hist. of Sc.)

1930 The representation of the North of England in British fiction feature film, 1927 to c.2000. Alan Hughes. (Dr. Annemarie McAllister and Professor Wendy Webster.) Central Lancashire M.Phil./Ph.D. (Hum.)

1931 The Nancy Astor papers. Kate Meanwell. (Professor David Stack.) Reading Ph.D. (Hist.)

1932 The effect of the Great Depression on gender inequality in U.K.'s labour market in the 1930s. Rick N. Ashworth. (Dr. Julie Marfany.) Oxford M.Sc. (Mod. Hist.)

1933 Pro-Americanism and the British left, 1931–55. Catherine Kinchin. (Dr. Andrew C. Edwards and Dr. Alexander Sedlmaier.) Bangor Ph.D. (Hist., Welsh Hist. & Archaeol.)

1934 Trade unions and the political culture of the British Labour party, 1931–40. James Parker. Exeter M.Phil. (Hist.)

1935 The management of the parliamentary supporters of the U.K. National Government, 1935–40. Tim Roll-Pickering. (Professor John A. Ramsden.) London Ph.D. (Q.M. Hist.)

1936 'There can be no doubt he united the country': British public opinion and appeasement, 1935–9 – continuity and change. Paul Horsler. (Professor David Stevenson.) London Ph.D. (L.S.E. Int. Hist.)

1937 Lord Lothian and the country houses scheme. Sarah Bruce-Lockhart. East Anglia Ph.D. (Hist.)

1938 Class, gender and consumerism in industrial Scotland, c.1939–90. Hayley Cross. (Dr. Annmarie Hughes and Dr. Jim Phillips.) Glasgow Ph.D. (Soc. Sc.)

1939 The impact of temporary immigrants on the Welsh identity and culture in World War II. Martin Hanks. (Dr. Andrew Edwards.) Bangor Ph.D. (Hist., Welsh Hist. & Archaeol.)

1940 British political culture and the press in wartime Britain, 1939–45. Kristopher Lovell. (Dr. Siân H. Nicholas and Professor Thomas O'Malley.) Aberystwyth Ph.D. (Hist. & Welsh Hist.)

1941 The Conservatives and conceptions of British power from Churchill to Macmillan. James O. Bloom. East Anglia Ph.D. (Hist.)

1942 Eden, the Foreign Office and British foreign policy, 1941–5. David M. Hall. East Anglia Ph.D. (Hist.)

1943 The geography of power: the role of the Boundary Commissioners in shaping the electoral representation of Britain. Rebekah Moore. (Professor Lawrence Goldman and Dr. Philip Salmon.) London Ph.D. (Inst. Hist. Res.)

1944 Utopian dreams or peacetime pragmatism? The successes and constraints of post-war reconstruction in the south west. Clare L. Maudling. (Professor Richard J. Overy.) Exeter M.Phil. (Hist.)

1945 The effectiveness of Whitehall planning in the Cold War era. Teresa Stirling. (Professor Ian S. Gazeley and Dr. Hester Barron.) Sussex D.Phil. (Hist.)

1946 From co-operation to confrontation: trade unionism, British politics and the media, 1945–79. Lucy Bell. (Professor Adrian C. Bingham.) Sheffield Ph.D. (Hist.)

1947 Newton Park: memory and place 1945–68. Kathryn James. (Dr. Roberta Anderson and Dr. Alison Hems.) Bath Spa Ph.D. (Hist. & Cultural Stud.)

1948 The influence of the Holocaust on British anti-fascism, 1945–17. Joshua Cohen. (Dr. Paul Moore.) Leicester Ph.D. (Hist.)

1949 Nostalgia and the post-war Labour party. Richard Jobson. (Dr. Hugh Pemberton and Professor Mark Wickham-Jones.) Bristol Ph.D. (Hist. Stud.)

1950 Re-launching fascism: British fascist ideologies in the immediate post-war period, 1945–65. Joe Mulhall. (Professor Dan Stone.) London M.Phil./Ph.D. (R.H.U.L. Hist.)

1951 Michael Young, social science and the British left, 1945–63. Lise Butler. (Dr. Ben Jackson.) Oxford D.Phil. (Mod. Hist.)

1952 The monarch as intercessor: an historical analysis of the role of Queen Elizabeth II in the 'special relationship' between the United Kingdom and the United States. Robert Traynham. (Professor Thomas Weber and Dr. Andrew Dilley.) Aberdeen Ph.D. (Hist.)

1953 Ordering expended mobility: the designation and display of British railway heritage, 1948–present. Mark Lambert. (Professors David Matless and Mike Heffernan.) Nottingham Ph.D. (Geog.)

1954 Hijacking the Olympic spirit: Britain's appropriation of the 1948 London Games. Teresa J. Thomas. (Dr. John Davis.) Oxford M.St. (Mod. Hist.)

1955 The Festival of Britain 1951: identities of place in the industrial north. Caterina Benincasa. (Professor Paul J. Ward.) Huddersfield Ph.D.-suspended (Music, Hum. & Media)

1956 A social and intellectual history of British socialism from New Left to New Times. Alexandre Campsie. (Dr. Jon Lawrence.) Cambridge Ph.D. (Hist.)

1957 Peggy Duff and the anti-Vietnam War movement. Sophie Roberts. (Professor Sylvia Ellis.) Northumbria Ph.D. (Hist.)

1958 A sinister cloud: propaganda and information around nuclear weapons in Britain, 1957–63. Philip Cohen. (Professors Tony Shaw and Jon Morris.) Hertfordshire Ph.D. (Hist.)

1959 The British Labour party and the restriction of Commonwealth immigration c.1958–c.1968. Amy Cross. (Dr. David Stewart and Dr. Stephen Meredith.) Central Lancashire M.Phil./Ph.D. (Hum.)

1960 Cultures of Labour militancy in Britain, 1960–79. Jack Saunders. (Dr. Michael Collins.) London Ph.D. (U.C. Hist.)

1961 British traffic planning and the urban environment in the 1960s: the cases of Leicester and Milton Keynes. Richard Harrison. (Professor Simon Gunn.) Leicester Ph.D. (Urban Hist.)

1962 Duncan Sandys and the informal politics of decolonisation, 1960–8. Peter Brooke. (Professor Richard Drayton and Dr. Sarah Stockwell.) King's College London M.Phil./Ph.D. (Hist.)

1963 Never had it so good? Surviving decline, narrating collapse: negotiating deindustrialisation in working-class Britain, 1964–79. Antony Lockley. (Dr. Leif Jerram and Dr. Charlotte Wildman.) Manchester Ph.D. (Hist.)

1964 The ministerial career of Anthony Crosland, 1964–77. Stephen King. (Dr. Martin Farr and Dr. Nicholas Randall.) Newcastle Ph.D. (Hist.)

1965 Pavement politics: community action in urban Britain, c.1965–90. David Ellis. (Dr. Mark C. Roodhouse.) York Ph.D. (Hist.)

1966 Liberal party in Wales, 1966–88. Nicholas Alderton. (Professor Scott Newton.) Cardiff Ph.D. (Hist. & Archaeol.)

1967 The origins of Scotland's country parks. Philip Back. (Dr.Timothy P. Baycroft.) Sheffield Ph.D. (Hist.)

1968 The libertarian milieu – Britain's forgotten autonomists. Seth Wheeler. (Dr. Graham Smith.) London Ph.D. (R.H.U.L. Hist.)

1969 Riots and 'Rivers of Blood': race and class identity formation in Britain, 1968–92. Emma Craddock. (Dr. Karen Salt and Professor Andrew Blaikie.) Aberdeen Ph.D. (Hist.)

1970 Legislating gender equality in England: the political and cultural context and the ramifications of the 1970 Equal Pay Act and 2010 Equality Act. Terri Bickford. (Dr. Mark Allen and Dr. Simon Sandall.) Winchester M.Phil./Ph.D. (Hist.)

1971 Margaret Thatcher's politics: the cultural and ideological forces of domestic femininity. Jessica Prestidge. (Professors Ludmilla Jordanova and Philip Williamson.) Durham Ph.D. (Hist.)

1972 The ideological element of British foreign policy, 1970–80. James A. Hollis. (Dr. Ben Jackson.) Oxford M.Phil. (Mod. Hist.)

1973 Feminisms and politics in 1970s Britain. Liz Homans. (Dr. Peter Shapely and Dr. Andrew C. Edwards.) Bangor Ph.D. (Hist., Welsh Hist. & Archaeol.)

1974 The shaping of ideas in the Conservative and Labour parties, 1970–9. Mikko M. Lievonen. (Dr. Ben Jackson.) Oxford D.Phil. (Mod. Hist.)

1975 A study of the causes and the progress of the 1972 miners' strike. Barnaby Moores. (Professors Richard Vinen and Ian McBride.) King's College London M.Phil./Ph.D. (Hist.)

1976 Governing the ungovernable: Sir John Hunt as cabinet secretary. Ian Beesley. (Professor Peter J. Hennessy.) London Ph.D. (Q.M. Hist.)

1977 The dying flame: the decline of Welsh political violence in the late 20th century. Ben M. Lake. (Dr. Marc Mulholland.) Oxford M.St. (Mod. Hist.)

1978 British party politics, 1975–97: a study in ideology. Richard Mellalieu. (Dr. Lawrence Black and Professor Philip A. Williamson.) Durham M.A. (Hist.)

1979 'Verbal combat': Margaret Thatcher's set-piece speeches, 1979–90. Thomas Hurst. (Professor Richard C. Vinen and Dr. Paul A. Readman.) King's College London M.Phil./Ph.D. (Hist.)

1980 The S.D.P. breakaway and the Labour party. Paul Bloomfield. (Dr. Jonathan Davis and Professor Rohan McWilliam.) Anglia Ruskin D.Phil. (Hist.)

1981 The Thatcher government and multilateral diplomacy during the 1982 Falklands crisis. Jeremy Young. (Professor John W. Young and Dr. Spencer Mawby.) Nottingham Ph.D. (Hist.)

20th century: Local history and government

1982 The experiences of women in agriculture in Pembrokeshire during the first half of the 20th century. Donnah E. Lewis. (Dr. Steven Thompson.) Aberystwyth Ph.D. (Hist. & Welsh Hist.)

1983 The role of the press in the development of new communities in the Rhymney valley in the early 20th century. Hannah Price. (Professor Bill Jones.) Cardiff Ph.D. (Hist. & Archaeol.)

1984 The Great War and the people of Wirral in Cheshire, c.1911–25. Stephen Roberts. (Dr. Sam Edwards, Professor Melanie Tebbutt, Dr. Craig Horner and Dr. Nick Mansfield.) Manchester Metropolitan Ph.D. (Hist.)

1985 The 1913 Mental Deficiency Act and its implications for Meanwood Park Colony, Leeds. Tom Allen. (Dr. Robert Ellis.) Huddersfield M.Phil. (Music, Hum. & Media)

1986 The construction history of war memorials in Leicestershire and Rutland. Elizabeth Blood. (Dr. Sally Horrocks.) Leicester Ph.D. (Hist.)

1987 The impact of the First World War on the landscape of Norfolk. Lucy Poulter. East Anglia Ph.D. (Hist.)

1988 The First World War and the industry and town of Barrow-in Furness. Peter Schofield. (Dr. Keith Vernon and Dr. Mairtin O'Cathain.) Central Lancashire M.Phil./Ph.D. (Hum.)

1989   Cinema ownership in the south Wales valleys, 1916–76. Angela Evans. (Professor Bill Jones.) Cardiff Ph.D. (Hist. & Archaeol.)

1990   Trench art of the north-east: material culture, memory and perception from the First World War to the present. Andrew Marriott. (Dr. Jane Webster and Dr. Martin Farr.) Newcastle Ph.D. (Archaeol.)

1991   Vision and practice: the Westfield War Memorial Village, Lancaster, from 1918 to the present. Martin Purdy. (Dr. Corinna Peniston-Bird and Mrs. Amanda Stretch.) Lancaster Ph.D. (Hist.)

1992   Collective memory in the mining communities of South Wales, 1919–74. David Selway. (Dr. Hester Barron and Professor Robert Cook.) Sussex D.Phil. (Hist.)

1993   Women's social and political activism in Manchester and Salford, 1918–39. Suzanne Bradshaw. (Dr. Joanna C. de Groot.) York Ph.D. (Hist.)

1994   A study of how mixed farming fared financially in the inter-war years in the area of the Midland Clays. Michael Heaton. (Professor Keith D.M. Snell and Dr. Richard Jones.) Leicester Ph.D. (Eng. Loc. Hist.)

1995   An environmental history of the Dukeries. Susan Bestwick. (Dr. Robert A. Lambert and Dr. Susanne Seymour.) Nottingham Ph.D. (Geog.)

1996   Local political cultures and the Communist party of Scotland, 1920–37. Malcolm Petrie. (Dr. Bill Knox.) St. Andrews Ph.D. (Hist.)

1997   The community unit and government agency: Speke, Wythenshawe and New Addington estates, c.1930–80. Jonathan A. McDonagh. (Dr. William H. Whyte.) Oxford D.Phil. (Mod. Hist.)

1998   An oral history project on the social impact of the introduction of television into Norfolk. Samuel Cross. East Anglia Ph.D. (Hist.)

1999   Troubled families: discourse, policy and intervention in north-west England since 1939. Michael H. Lambert. (Dr. John Welshman.) Lancaster Ph.D. (Hist.)

2000   Conscientious objection in the north-east during the Second World War. Stuart Anderson. (Dr. Charlotte Alston.) Northumbria Ph.D. (Hist.)

2001   The police in Edinburgh in the Second World War. Edward G. Goodwin. (Dr. Louise A. Jackson and Professor Richard G. Rodger.) Edinburgh Ph.D. (Hist.)

2002   'We all had to do our bit': women and the Second World War in Portsmouth and the Isle of Wight. Daniel Swan. (Dr. Sue Bruley.) Portsmouth Ph.D. (Soc., Hist. & Lit. Stud.)

2003   Local government in south Wales in World War II. Evonne Wareham. (Dr. Stephanie Ward.) Cardiff Ph.D. (Hist. & Archaeol.)

2004   The heritage of home: the role of history in the socio-economic development of Leicester, 1945–2013. Sally Hartshorne. (Professor Simon Gunn.) Leicester Ph.D. (Hist.)

2005   The conception, development and social consequences of Telford New Town, 1945–2000: 60 years of progress? F. Verity. (Dr. Keith Gildart.) Wolverhampton M.Phil./Ph.D. (Hist.)

2006 Economic development and the provision of transport services in the Highlands and Islands of Scotland, 1945–c.1980. Mike Macdonald. (Professor Raymond G. Stokes and Dr. Duncan M. Ross.) Glasgow Ph.D. (Soc. Sc.)

2007 Fashion for the high street: the design and making of menswear in Leeds, 1945–80. Danielle Sprecher. (Dr. Kate M. Dossett and Ms. Natalie Raw.) Leeds Ph.D. (Hist.)

2008 Making the city mobile: the place of the car in the planning of post-war Birmingham, 1945–73. Matthew Parker. (Professor Simon Gunn.) Leicester Ph.D. (Urban Hist.)

2009 The British Black Power Movement: a documented and oral history. Frank Harding. (Dr. Kate M. Dossett, Dr. Say Burgin and Dr. Will Jackson.) Leeds Ph.D. (Hist.)

2010 The African descent experience in Huddersfield/Kirklees since the 1950s. Milton Brown. (Professor Paul Ward.) Huddersfield Ph.D. (Music, Hum. & Media)

2011 Social networks and migration: Jamaicans in Wolverhampton since the 1950s. Michelle L. Buchanan. (Professor Paul B. O'Leary and Dr. Richard C. Coopey.) Aberystwyth Ph.D. (Hist. & Welsh Hist.)

2012 Women in the Rhondda in the 1950s: education, career aspirations and paid work. Christine Chapman. (Dr. Timothy Jones and Professor Gareth Williams.) Glamorgan Ph.D. (Hist.)

2013 Port Talbot and its steelworkers: an oral history, 1951–88. Bleddyn Penny. (Dr. Louise Miskell.) Swansea Ph.D. (Hist.)

2014 The Conservative party in south Wales, 1951–83. Sam Blaxland. (Dr. Martin O. Johnes.) Swansea Ph.D. (Hist.)

2015 'Bogged down in housing': politics and planning in residential Leeds, 1954–79. Ben Philliskirk. (Professors Simon J.D. Green and Richard C. Whiting.) Leeds Ph.D. (Hist.)

2016 The history of caste in Leicester. Vimal Patel. (Professor Panikos Panayi.) De Montfort Ph.D. (Hum.)

2017 Youth culture in Sheffield: spaces and behaviours of young people, 1962–90. Sarah Kenny. (Dr. Adrian C. Bingham.) Sheffield Ph.D. (Hist.)

2018 Socio-economic change, contested memories and the cultural re-configuration of Hull during the decline of distant water trawling. Joanne Bryne. (Professor David J. Starkey.) Hull Ph.D. (Hist.)

2019 'This is the North – where we do what we want': an investigation into the culture and practices of South Yorkshire police during the miners' strike of 1984–5. Philip Rawsthorne. (Roger Spalding.) Edge Hill Ph.D. (English & Hist.)

20th century: Ireland

2020 Ethnic minority communities in 20th-century Queen's University Belfast. Jack Crangle. (Professor Sean O'Connell.) Belfast Ph.D. (Hist. & Anthr.)

2021   A comparative study of the socio-economic and religious backgrounds of nurses working at the R.V.H. Belfast and the Royal Infirmary Glasgow, 1900–20, and their training within those institutions and subsequent careers. Sean Graffin. (Professor Greta J. Jones and Dr. Leanne McCormick.) Ulster Ph.D. (Hist.)

2022   The relationship between coalition of nationalist interests in County Monaghan, pre–1919. Robert T. Ryan. (Dr. Colin Reid.) Oxford M.St. (Mod. Hist.)

2023   A study of Ernest Blythe (1889–1975). Marjorie McKay. (Dr. P. Emmet J. O'Connor and Dr. James P. Loughlin.) Ulster Ph.D. (Hist.)

2024   The political career of William T. Cosgrove. Seamus MacSuibhne. (Dr. G. O'Brien and Dr. James P. Loughlin.) Ulster Ph.D. (Hist.)

2025   From the Conciliation Bill to the Free State: gender in the Irish national press. Holly Dunbar. (Dr. Matthew Kelly.) Southampton M.Phil. (Hist.)

2026   Nationalist masculinities and the Irish Revolution, 1912–23. Rebecca Mytton. (Dr. Caoimhe Nic Dháibhéid.) Sheffield Ph.D. (Hist.)

2027   The north-west in a time of war and revolution, 1912–23. Okan Ozseker. (Dr. Robert McNamara and Dr. Allan Blackstock.) Ulster Ph.D. (Hist.)

2028   The struggle for the capital: revolutionary urban warfare in Dublin during the 'Irish Troubles', 1919–23. Paul Lavery. (Dr. Robert McNamara and Dr. P. Emmet J. O'Connor.) Ulster Ph.D. (Hist.)

2029   Asymmetric war finance: how was the I.R.A. financed in the Irish War of Independence? Robin J.C. Adams. (Dr. Senia Paseta and Professor Kevin O'Rourke.) Oxford D.Phil. (Mod. Hist.)

2030   The relationship between the army and police in Ireland, 1919–21. Christopher Powis. (Dr. Stuart R. Ball.) Leicester Ph.D. (Hist.)

2031   'Great War' veterans' organisations, commemoration and remembrance in the south of Ireland from partition to the Good Friday Agreement. Pauline Mitchell. (Dr. James P. Loughlin and Dr. Allan Blackstock.) Ulster Ph.D. (Hist.)

2032   The relation between Northern and Southern nationalists in Ireland, 1920–32. Cecilia Biaggi. (Dr. Marc Mulholland.) Oxford D.Phil. (Mod. Hist.)

2033   The split: the N.A.C.A. and political division in Irish athletics and cycling. Pearse Reynolds. (Professor Richard Holt.) De Montfort Ph.D. (Hum.)

2034   The Irish soccer split: a reflection of the politics of Ireland? Cormac Moore. (Professor Martin Polley.) De Montfort Ph.D. (Hum.)

2035   Northern nationalists and the Boundary Commission in Ireland. Clive Abbott. (Dr. James Thompson and Dr. Jim McPherson.) Bristol M.Litt. (Hist. Stud.)

2036   Abortion in Northern Ireland. Mark Benson. (Professor Mary O'Dowd.) Belfast Ph.D. (Hist. & Anthr.)

2037   Emyr Esty Evans and the cultural identity of Ulster, c.1929–69. Lauren Taylor. (Professor Peter Gray.) Belfast M.Phil./Ph.D. (Hist. & Anthr.)

2038   The Irish labour movement and social partnership. Patrick Patton. (Dr. P. Emmet J. O'Connor and Dr. James P. Loughlin.) Ulster Ph.D. (Hist.)

2039 The fullness of time: the cult of Collins in De Valera's Ireland, 1932–73. Harry McGeehan. (Professor Stephen Royle.) Belfast Ph.D. (Geog., Archaeol. & Palaeoecology)

2040 The development of oral history in Ireland, 1935–2011. Regina Fitzpatrick. (Dr. Neil Carter.) De Montfort Ph.D. (Hum.)

2041 A cross-border study of boundary-region censorship as applied in Éire and Northern Ireland during the Second World War. Conor Campbell. (Professor Fearghal McGarry.) Belfast M.Phil./Ph.D. (Hist. & Anthr.)

2042 Derry City in World War II. Lawrence Hughes. (Dr. P. Emmet J. O'Connor.) Ulster Ph.D. (Hist.)

2043 The post-war Irish community in Bristol. Nick Conway. (Dr. Madge J. Dresser and Dr. Philip G. Ollerenshaw.) West of England Ph.D. (Hist.)

2044 The reception of Enoch Powell in Northern Ireland, 1968–98. Paul Lundy. (Dr. Paul Corthorn.) Belfast Ph.D. (Hist. & Anthr.)

2045 A history of the people's democracy, 1968–91. Matthew Collins. (Dr. P. Emmet J. O'Connor and Dr. James P. Loughlin.) Ulster Ph.D. (Hist.)

2046 Irish communities in England during the troubles, 1968–85. Nicholas A. Megaw. (Dr. Matthew Grimley.) Oxford M.St. (Mod. Hist.)

2047 The Catholic Church and the Northern Irish troubles, 1969–98. Margaret Scull. (Professor Ian McBride.) King's College London M.Phil./Ph.D. (Hist.)

2048 British government counter terrorism policy in Northern Ireland. Oliver Mattock. (Dr. Thomas Freeman.) Essex M.A. by Dissertation (Hist.)

2049 Operation Motorman. Laurence Townsend. (Dr. Richard Grayson.) London Ph.D. (Goldsmiths Pol.)

2050 Margaret Thatcher, Charles Haughey and Anglo-Irish relations. Fiona McKelvey. (Dr. Kyle Hughes and Dr. Robert McNamara.) Ulster Ph.D. (Hist.)

2051 Strategic starvation: use of the body as a political instrument during the I.R.A. hunger strikes of the late 20th century. Rasheed Ayesha. (Dr. Sloan Mahone.) Oxford M.Sc. (Mod. Hist.)

2052 Irish identities in sport after the 1998 Belfast Agreement. Seamus Morris. (Professor Martin Polley.) De Montfort Ph.D. (Hum.)

2053 The failure of dissent: public opposition to prevailing economic policy in Ireland, 2000–6. Ciaran M. Casey. (Professors Roy Foster and Kevin O'Rourke.) Oxford D.Phil. (Mod. Hist.)

20th century: Administrative, military and naval history

2054 The early military thought of Winston S. Churchill. Judson Alphin. (Professor Hew F.A. Strachan.) Oxford D.Phil. (Mod. Hist.)

2055 British policy on underwater weapons, 1900–14. Richard Dunley. (Professor Andrew D. Lambert.) King's College London Ph.D. (War Stud.)

2056　Locating crime and criminality in Edwardian London: a G.I.S.-based approach. Kallum Dhillon. (Professors Richard J. Dennis and Paul Longley.) London Ph.D. (U.C. Geog.)

2057　Fact or fiction: the British spy novel and British intelligence, 1903–91. Jonathan Best. (Dr. Paul Corthorn.) Belfast M.Phil./Ph.D. (Hist. & Anthr.)

2058　Part-time defenders of the realm: an historical consideration of past Territorial Army training and operations in relation to the proposed reorganisation laid down in *Future Reserves 2020*. Shaun Allan. (Professor Greg Bankoff and Dr. Catherine Baker.) Hull Ph.D. (Hist.)

2059　Unit cohesion in battalions of the London Regiment, 1908–18. Tom Thorpe. (Dr. Helen McCartney.) King's College London Ph.D. (War Stud.)

2060　Aspects of the British forces during the First and Second World Wars. Sarah McCook. (Professor Joanne C. Fox and Dr. Andrzej J. Olechnowicz.) Durham Ph.D. (Hist.)

2061　A history of the Women's Royal Naval Service, 1914–45. Hannah Roberts. (Dr. Alan James.) King's College London Ph.D. (War Stud.)

2062　Chasing shadows: British intelligence and internal security, 1914–19. Harry Richards. (Professor Karen Hunt and Dr. Anthony Kauders.) Keele Ph.D. (Hist.)

2064　Children of the 42nd military district and the Great War. Norman Fraser Brown. (Dr. Derek Patrick and Dr. William Kenefick.) Dundee Ph.D. (Hist.)

2065　British combined arms warfare doctrine, 1914–18. James Cook. (Dr. Helen McCartney and Professor William J. Philpott.) King's College London Ph.D. (War Stud.)

2066　Cambridgeshire regiment in the First World War. Joanna Costin. (Dr. Sean Lang.) Anglia Ruskin D.Phil. (Hist.)

2067　More than just bombing: a critical examination of the official history of the war in the air, 1914–18. Julia Dawson. (Dr. David Jordan and Dr. Jonathan Farrell.) King's College London Ph.D. (War Stud.)

2068　Training for war: life in First World War training camps in England. Jennifer Flood. (Dr. Hester Barron and Dr. Claudia Siebrecht.) Sussex D.Phil. (Hist.)

2069　War registers in the Leeds area during World War I: a rare and vilified breed. Eve Haskins. (Professor Holder H.W. Afflerbach and Dr. Ingrid Sharp.) Leeds Ph.D. (Hist.)

2070　The men who planned the war: a study of the senior staff officers of the British Army on the Western Front. Paul Havins. (Professors William J. Philpott and Brian Holden Reid.) King's College London Ph.D. (War Stud.)

2071　How successfully were the procedures instituted by the army during the First World War to improve the health of the troops implemented by the soldiers and the medical officers? Catherine Hickman. (Professor Michael Roper.) Essex M.Phil. (Hist.)

2072　Trench warfare in the First World War, 1914–18: the practice and the reality. Heather Montgomery. (Dr. Colm Donnelly.) Belfast Ph.D. (Geog., Archaeol. & Palaeoecology)

2073 British army miner operations in the First World War. Christopher Newton. (Professor William J. Philpott.) King's College London Ph.D. (War Stud.)

2074 Scotland's Great War wounded. Emily Rootham. (Professor Elaine W. McFarland and Dr. Ben H. Shepherd.) Glasgow Caledonian Ph.D. (Hist.)

2075 A study of the Air Ministry, techno-military invention and the bomb aiming problem, 1916–44. Stephen Marsh. (Professor David E.H. Edgerton.) King's College London M.Phil./Ph.D. (Hist.)

2076 The work of the Middlesex military service and appeals tribunals, 1916–18. Peter Harris. (Professor Panikos Panayi.) De Montfort Ph.D. (Hum.)

2077 A naval travesty: the dismissal of Admiral Jellicoe, 1917. Allan Macfarlane. (Professor Gerard J. De Groot.) St. Andrews Ph.D. (Hist.)

2078 How did official British propaganda and the social expectations it created affect young R.A.F. pilots' psychological makeup. Emma K. Doyle. (Dr. Adrian M. Gregory.) Oxford M.Phil. (Mod. Hist.)

2079 The care provided for facially-wounded and shell-shocked ex-servicemen in Britain after the First World War. Ellis Boyle. (Dr. Jessica K. Meyer and Dr. Alison Fell.) Leeds Ph.D. (Hist.)

2080 Examining the influence of the First World War on attitudes to service in the Second World War. Joel Morley. (Dr. Dan Todman.) London Ph.D. (Q.M. Hist.)

2081 Women in the Metropolitan Police, 1919–45: on the front line. Helen Barnard. (Dr. Mary Clare Martin.) Greenwich M.Phil. (Educ. & Community Studies)

2082 'All work, no play, is not the Territorial way?': the role and organisation of the Territorial Army, 1919–40. Alexander Oates. (Dr. Rob Johnson.) Oxford D.Phil. (Mod. Hist.)

2083 Military parades in inter-war England. Bill Dickson. (Dr. Dan Todman.) London Ph.D. (Q.M. Hist.)

2084 An examination of British and Indian army staff training, 1919–39. Iain Farquharson. (Professor Matthew Hughes and Dr. Matthew Seligmann.) Brunel Ph.D. (Pol. & Hist.)

2085 The British Fleet Air Arm in the inter-war period: a question of decline? Anthony Heslop. (Dr. Richard Gorski.) Hull M.Phil. (Hist.)

2086 The political economy of the British naval arms industries between the wars. Christopher W. Miller. (Dr. Phillips O'Brien and Professors Simon Ball, Raymond G. Stokes and Nicholas A.M. Rodger.) Glasgow Ph.D. (Soc. Sc.)

2087 'Citizens in khaki': the army, mutiny and labour relations in Britain, c.1919–25. Owen Sellers. (Dr. Ben Jackson.) Oxford M.St. (Mod. Hist.)

2088 The Royal Air Force and the provision of naval aviation, 1920–30. Alexander Clarke. (Professor Andrew D. Lambert.) King's College London Ph.D. (War Stud.)

2089 The impact of financial cutbacks and restrictions upon the ability of the Royal Navy to realign itself, during the 1920s, to meet the challenges of the early inter-war period. Matthew Heaslip. Exeter M.Phil. (Maritime Hist.)

2090   Disabled soldiers and the material culture of charity in 1920s Britain.   Emily Bartlett.
        (Dr. Julie Anderson and Dr. Stefan Goebel.)   Kent Ph.D.   (Hist.)

2091   The Supermarine Spitfire: a history of an object as a memory.   T. Pratley.   (Dr.
        Stefan Goebel and Professor Ulf Schmidt.)   Kent Ph.D.   (Hist.)

2092   Representations of community in second world war civil defence.   Jessica Hammett.
        (Dr. Hester Barron and Professor Robert Cook.)   Sussex D.Phil.   (Hist.)

2093   'No Pakis at Dunkirk': remembering and forgetting force K6 in Europe, 1939–45.
        Ghee Bowman.   Exeter Ph.D.   (Hist.)

2094   The contribution made by the development of target marking techniques to the
        prosecution of the bomber offensive during World War II.   Paul Freer.   Exeter M.Phil.
        (Hist.)

2095   The British chiefs of staff during the Second World War, 1939–45.   Colin McDowall.
        (Professor Peter Jackson and Dr. Phillips O'Brien.)   Glasgow Ph.D.   (Soc. Sc.)

2096   'Doing their bit': dogs in the British armed forces and London civil defence region in
        the Second World War.   Kimberley B. O'Donnell.   (Professor Dr. David A. McLean
        and Dr. Abigail Woods.)   King's College London M.Phil./Ph.D.   (Hist.)

2097   The development of command and control in naval home commands in the Second
        World War.   John Ross.   (Professors Andrew D. Lambert and Joseph Maiolo.)
        King's College London Ph.D.-suspended   (War Stud.)

2098   Charity, rehabilitation and religion: the experience of disabled veterans in Britain after
        the First World War.   Bethany Rowley.   (Dr. Jessica K. Meyer and Professor Simon
        J. Ball.)   Leeds Ph.D.   (Hist.)

2099   'The trick cyclists': neuropsychiatry and the management of aerial warfare, 1939–45.
        Lynsey Shaw.   (Professor Mark Harrison.)   Oxford D.Phil.   (Mod. Hist.)

2100   Banged up in Britain, 1939–45.   Sarah R. Shelmerdine.   (Dr. Mark C. Roodhouse.)
        York M.A.   (Hist.)

2101   Jewellery of loyalty, love and loss: the sweetheart brooch in Second World War
        Britain.   Penelope S. Street.   (Dr. Meaghan Clarke and Professor Geoffrey Quilley.)
        Sussex D.Phil.   (Hist. of Art)

2102   Aerial defeat? The R.A.F. and the Luftwaffe in Operation Dynamo, May-June 1940.
        Harry Raffal.   (Dr. David Omissi.)   Hull Ph.D.   (Hist.)

2103   The development of nuclear propulsion for H.M. submarines in the post-war period.
        Gareth Jones.   (Dr. Harry Bennett and Dr. Elaine Murphy.)   Plymouth Ph.D.   (Hum.)

2104   The influence of limiting casualties on British military operations since 1945.   Richard
        Hughes.   (Dr. Douglas Ford and Dr. Alaric Searle.)   Salford M.Phil./Ph.D.-suspended
        (Cen. Eur. Sec.)

2105   The impact of participating in British counterinsurgency campaigns, 1945–97, on the
        psyche of British armed forces personnel.   Kathryn Butler.   (Dr. Karl Hack, Dr. Alex
        Tickell and Dr. Simon Robbins.)   Open University M.Phil./Ph.D.   (Hist.)

2106   Deterrence or defence? The British Army and tactical nuclear weapons, 1945–57.
        Simon Moody.   (Dr. Robert Foley.)   Liverpool Ph.D.   (Hist.)

2107 A history of the development of the British techno-surveillance state in the context of British policing, 1950–2000. Benjamin Taylor. (Professor David E.H. Edgerton and Dr. Dan Matlin.) King's College London M.Phil./Ph.D. (Hist.)

2108 Concepts of military and civilian 'gallantry' in British culture and society, 1958–1982. Matthew Lord. (Professor Simon J. Ball.) Leeds Ph.D. (Hist.)

2109 The U.K. Polaris programme. James Jinks. (Professor Peter J. Hennessy.) London Ph.D. (Q.M. Hist.)

2110 From civilian to soldier: British heath professional veterans' perceptions of their miltary, social and health experiences from the Gulf War, 1990–1. Deirdre Wild. (Dr. Angela Kydd and Professor Colin Martin.) West of Scotland Ph.D. (Health, Nursing and Midwifery)

20th century: Finance, trade and industry

2111 Doing business underwater: flooding, entrepreneurship and resilience. Rebecca L. Messham. (Professor Greg Bankoff.) Hull Ph.D. (Hist.)

2112 The cultural and historical geographies of onshore oil exploration in 20th-century Britain. Andrew Naylor. (Professors Mike Heffernan and Charles Watkins.) Nottingham Ph.D. (Geog.)

2113 Women and the 'railway family', 1900–48. Hannah Reeves. (Dr. Alannah Tomkins and Dr. Tim Proctor.) Keele Ph.D. (Hist.)

2114 The road from industrialism to post-industrialism: a reappraisal of the guild social theory of A. J. Penty. Deric L. O'Huallachain. (Dr. Siân H. Nicholas and Dr. Steven Thompson.) Aberystwyth Ph.D. (Hist. & Welsh Hist.)

2115 Did investors anticipate the First World War? Christoph J. Weisser. (Professor Kevin O'Rourke.) Oxford M.Sc. (Mod. Hist.)

2116 Driftermen and the silver darlings: responses to the crises suffered by the British herring fishing industry, c.1914–50. William Jewell. (Professor Sam Davies, Dr. Nicholas J. White and Dr. Ian Cook.) Liverpool John Moores M.Phil./Ph.D. (Hist.)

2117 The impact of the two world wars on the London livery companies. Peter Davies. (Dr. Andrew Edwards.) Bangor Ph.D. (Hist., Welsh Hist. & Archaeol.)

2118 Railways in the First World War. Tanya Kenny. (Professor Anthony Heywood and Dr. Ben Marsden.) Aberdeen Ph.D. (Hist.)

2119 An examination of the decline of shipbuilding on the north-east coast and the west coast of Scotland during the inter-war period, 1918–39. William Paxton. (Dr. Matt Perry and Dr. Martin Farr.) Newcastle Ph.D. (Hist.)

2120 Economic discourse during depression: a study of newspapers in inter-war Britain. Aaron Ackerley. (Professor Adrian C. Bingham.) Sheffield Ph.D. (Hist.)

2121 Business attitudes to macroeconomic policy in the U.K. in the inter-war period. Ruairi Cullinane. (Professor Kevin O'Rourke.) Oxford M.Phil. (Mod. Hist.)

2122 The Southern Railway response to road competition in the 1920s and 1930s. Reginald Davies. (Professor Colin Divall.) York Ph.D. (Hist.)

2123 Deindustrialisation and industrial communities: the Lanarkshire coalfields, 1947–83. Ewan Gibbs. (Dr. Jim Phillips and Dr. Duncan Ross.) Glasgow Ph.D. (Soc. Sc.)

2124 The impact of organisation structure, locality, culture, and employment legislation on gender in employment, 1950–80. Susan E. Granshaw. (Professor Jane Humphries.) Oxford D.Phil. (Mod. Hist.)

2125 Bankside power station: planning, politics and pollution. Stephen Murray. (Professor Simon Gunn and Dr. Sally Horrocks.) Leicester Ph.D. (Hist.)

2126 Technological development of the British motorways. Jonathan Winkler. (Professor Avner Offer.) Oxford D.Phil. (Mod. Hist.)

2127 Constructing Leviathan: studies on the left and the rise of corporate liberalism, 1959–79. Chris Olewicz. (Dr. Andrew Heath.) Sheffield Ph.D. (Hist.)

2128 An economic history of association football, 1960–2010. Andrew Arvends. (Professor Peter J. Hennessy.) London Ph.D. (Q.M. Hist.)

2129 The inhibition of militancy in the West Yorkshire woollen textile industry, c.1960–c.1990. Laura Price. (Dr. Elizabeth A. Buettner and Professor David Howell.) York Ph.D. (Hist.)

2130 Business, the environment and the consumer 1968–92: the case of Marks and Spencer. Jessica Gray. (Dr. Kate M. Dossett and Professor Richard C. Whiting.) Leeds Ph.D. (Hist.)

2131 The rise and demise of women's sections in the Union of Shop, Distributive and Allied Workers, 1970–c.2000. Esther Quinn. (Professor Eleanor Gordon.) Glasgow Ph.D. (Soc. Sc.)

2132 'I feel I am in control of my own little area': agency and emotion in women's financial management, c.1980–2000. Katherine M. Wall. (Professor Claire Langhamer and Dr. Lucy Robinson.) Sussex D.Phil. (Hist.)

2133 Imperial Chemical Industries: a history. The final quarter-century (1982–2007). Geoffrey Pyke. (Professor Richard Roberts and Dr. Michael Kandiah.) King's College London M.Phil./Ph.D. (Hist.)

20th century: Agriculture

2134 The farming community in Yorkshire, 1914–51, through oral history. Jane Rowling. (Professor Keith D.M. Snell.) Leicester Ph.D. (Eng. Loc. Hist.)

20th century: Social history

2135 Aftershave: a cultural history of pubic hair removal in 20th- and 21st-century Britain. Laura Cofield. (Dr. Lucy Robinson and Professor Claire L. Langhamer.) Sussex D.Phil. (Hist.)

2136 A history of the Cornish male voice choir: the relationship between music, place and culture. Susan Skinner. (Professor Kevin Jefferys, Dr. Michael McInerney and Professor Roberta Mock.) Plymouth Ph.D. (Hum.)

2137 Heroines, queens, goddesses and glamazons: theatrical male cross-dressing performance in 20th-century London. Jacob Bloomfield. (Professors Laura Doan and Frank Mort.) Manchester Ph.D. (Hist.)

2138 Mythology and politics in 20th-century British music. Jessica Collins. (Dr. Paul Harper-Scott.) London Ph.D. (R.H.U.L. Music)

2139 The effect of parental marital status and family form on experiences of childhood in 20th-century Scotland. Felicity Crawley. (Dr. Annmarie Hughes and Dr. Rose Elliot.) Glasgow Ph.D. (Soc. Sc.)

2140 Little wars: the geopolitics of 20th-century board games. Alexander Harby. (Dr. Alex Vasudevan and Dr. Isla Forsyth.) Nottingham Ph.D. (Geog.)

2141 Same-sex sexualities in public history. Claire Hayward. (Dr. Nicola Phillips and Dr. Sue Hawkins.) Kingston Ph.D. (Econ., Pol. & Hist.)

2142 The role of sport in the creation of female identities, 1900–2000. Katherine A. Nutman. (Dr. Selina Todd.) Oxford M.Phil. (Mod. Hist.)

2143 Freaks at the beach: freak shows, seaside resorts and 20th-century British culture. Emma Purce. (Dr. Julie Anderson and Dr. Karen Jones.) Kent Ph.D. (Hist.)

2144 Espionage in British popular culture of the 20th century: gender, moral ambiguity and the inextricability of fact and fiction. Kirsten Smith. (Dr. Corinna Peniston-Bird.) Lancaster Ph.D. (Hist.)

2145 Home, love, belonging and selfhood for women in relationships together, 1900–60: a study of Vera 'Jack' Holme (1881–1969) and friends. Jane Mackelworth. (Dr. Rhodri Hayward and Professor Alison Blunt.) London Ph.D. (Q.M. Hist.)

2146 'A curious process of action and reaction': the Webbs, the Poor Law Commission, the campaign for the Minority Report and Edwardian social reform, 1905–14. Vanessa Byham. (Dr. David Feldman.) London M.Phil. (Birkbeck Hist.)

2147 Emotional interactions of male family members in the First and Second World Wars. Linda Maynard. (Professor Joanna Bourke.) London M.Phil./Ph.D. (Birkbeck Hist.)

2148 The impact of First World War conscription on British society. Jim Barker. (Dr. James Thompson and Dr. Hugh Pemberton.) Bristol M.Litt. (Hist. Stud.)

2149 The 'women and war' debate in British feminism: 1914–18. Marc Calvini-Lefebvre. (Dr. Richard Grayson.) London Ph.D. (Goldsmiths Pol.)

2150 Opposition to the Great War in Wales. Aled Eiryg. (Professor Chris Williams.) Cardiff Ph.D. (Hist. & Archaeol.)

2151 The funny side of war: a study of British cartoon humour in the First World War. Phillippa Gregory. (Dr. Stefan Goebel and Dr. Peter Donaldson.) Kent Ph.D. (Hist.)

2152 How was female same-sex desire understood in Britain during the First World War? Victoria A. Hemmingway. (Dr. Sian Pooley.) Oxford M.St. (Mod. Hist.)

2153 Widening horizons – female participation in the organisation and deployment of the wartime workforce in Yorkshire, 1914–18. Gail Ledgard. (Dr. Rebecca Gill.) Huddersfield Ph.D. (Music, Hum. & Media)

2154 Cinema in Cambridgeshire in World War I. Amanda Randall. (Professor Rohan McWilliam and Dr. Sean Lang.) Anglia Ruskin D.Phil. (Hist.)

2155 Volunteering for World War I: a case study of influences and values on young men as evident from a school magazine. Charles Whitney. (Dr. Vicky Morrisroe and Professor Melanie J. Ilic.) Gloucestershire M.A. (Hum.)

2156 Joe Beckett: a study in identity. Jennifer Lewis. (Professor Tony Kushner.) Southampton M.Phil. (Hist.)

2157 Curating women: historical representations of women's wartime work at the Imperial War Museum. Alyson Mercer. (Professor Patricia M. Thane.) King's College London M.Phil./Ph.D. (Hist.)

2158 Histories of the everyday and democratic culture in England, c.1918–69. Laura Carter. (Professor Peter Mandler.) Cambridge Ph.D. (Hist.)

2159 Natives and newcomers, marriage and belonging – South Asian migration, settlement and working-class tolerance in the Sheffield area during the early 20th century. David Holland. (Professor Adrian C. Bingham.) Sheffield Ph.D. (Hist.)

2160 A history of sport and the B.B.C. Craig W. Thomas. (Professor Tony Collins.) De Montfort Ph.D. (Hum.)

2161 Veterinary training and work: a female perspective, c.1919–2000. Julie Hipperson. (Dr. Abigail Woods.) King's College London M.Phil./Ph.D. (Hist.)

2162 Reactions to crime, criminality and class in Hull and East Yorkshire during the inter-war period. Ashley Borrett. (Dr. Alan G.V. Simmonds.) Hull Ph.D. (Hist.)

2163 A sociology without sociologists? The development of a British sociological tradition in the inter-war years, 1919–39. Baudry Rocquin. (Dr. Lawrence Goldman.) Oxford D.Phil. (Mod. Hist.)

2164 The outdoor movement. Mel Reid. (Professor Tony Collins.) De Montfort Ph.D. (Hum.)

2165 Constructions of race, gender and empire on the extreme right in Britain, 1920s to 1960s. Liam Liburd. (Dr. Julie Gottlieb.) Sheffield Ph.D. (Hist.)

2166 The silence of labour: a study of the women's sexual liberation campaign and the reaction of the labour movement, 1920–51. Vanessa Aiken. (Dr. Nicole Robertson.) Northumbria Ph.D. (Hist.)

2167 The London Labour Choral Union, 1920–40: a musical institution of the left. Maria Kiladi. (Mr. Erik Levi.) London Ph.D. (R.H.U.L. Music)

2168 Saving Old England: voluntary groups, historic buildings and urban redevelopment, 1925–70. Michael Nelles. (Dr. Eve Colpus.) Southampton M.Phil. (Hist.)

2169 The British documentary movement and social and political change, 1926–45. Erica K. Read. (Professor Mark Harrison.) Oxford M.Sc. (Mod. Hist.)

2170 Growing well: dirt, health and the home gardener in Britain, 1930–70. Sophie Greenway. (Professor Hilary Marland.) Warwick M.Phil./Ph.D. (Hist.)

2171 Childhood and the emotion of corporal punishment, 1938–86. Owen Emmerson. (Dr. Lucy Robinson and Professor Claire L. Langhamer.) Sussex D.Phil. (Hist.)

2172 Popular representations of the internment of 'enemy aliens' in wartime Britain, 1939–present. Darren Davies. (Professors Penny Summerfield and Frank Mort.) Manchester Ph.D. (Hist.)

2173 Bletchley Park social history. Margaret Lenton. (Professor David Cesarani.) London Ph.D. (R.H.U.L. Hist.)

2174 Time and social change in everyday British language, c.1939–90. Cowan David. (Jon Lawrence.) Cambridge Ph.D. (Hist.)

2175 Renegotiating identity: continental incomers to Britain at the time of the Second World War. Hannah Burton. (Dr. Rudolf Muhs.) London Ph.D. (R.H.U.L. Hist.)

2176 Welfare of Scottish evacuees in World War II. Josephine Jack. (Dr. Jacqueline L.M. Jenkinson and Dr. James J. Smyth.) Stirling Ph.D. (Hist.)

2177 'The people's war' in British film propaganda, 1939–45. Anna R. Jones. (Professor Joanne C. Fox and Dr. Sarah R. Davies.) Durham Ph.D. (Hist.)

2178 Consumption in the Second World War. Elspeth King. (Professor Maggie Andrews.) Worcester M.Phil./Ph.D. (Hum. & Creative Arts)

2179 Rationed food in Second World War Britain: experience and memory. Kelly Spring. (Professor Penny Summerfield.) Manchester Ph.D. (Hist.)

2180 Remembering the First World War in Britain, 1939–45. Samuel Tranter. (Professor Gerard J. De Groot.) St. Andrews Ph.D. (Hist.)

2181 A history of women and rugby league. Victoria Dawson. (Professor Tony Collins.) De Montfort Ph.D. (Hum.)

2182 A history of women's cricket: a case study of the north. Judy Threlfall. (Professor Tony Collins.) De Montfort Ph.D. (Hum.)

2183 Women under the jackboot: representations of women in the public history of the Channel Islands occupation. Nicolle Watkins. (Dr. Matthew Grant and Dr. Nadine Rossol.) Essex Ph.D. (Hist.)

2184 Why did the co-operative movement go into decline after the Second World War with reference to London and eastern England? Percy Lomax. (Professor Peter Gurney.) Essex Ph.D. (Hist.)

2185 'Finding our own solutions': the women's movement and mental health provision in post-War England. Kate Mahoney. (Professor Matthew Thomson.) Warwick Ph.D. (Hist.)

2186 Oral histories of peace and environmental activism in Scotland since the end of World War II. Imogen Michel. (Dr. Louise A. Jackson.) Edinburgh Ph.D. (Hist.)

2187 Toy soldiers in Britain since 1945: a cultural history. Piotr Czosnyka. (Professor Rohan McWilliam and Dr. Jonathan Davis.) Anglia Ruskin D.Phil. (Hist.)

2188 The spatialisation of social policy in Britain since 1945. Alistair Kefford. (Dr. Leif Jerram and Dr. Iain Deas.) Manchester Ph.D. (Hist.)

2189 Creating the past on film: re-enactment, performance and popular memory of the home front. Benjamin Knowles. (Dr. Ana Carden-Coyne and Dr. Johannes Sjoberg.) Manchester Ph.D. (Hist.)

2190　The delinquent youth as the antithesis of true Britishness: cultural representations of national decline, race and class in post-war Britain. Magnus B. Niklasson. (Dr. Elizabeth A. Buettner.) York Ph.D. (Hist.)

2191　Elisabeth Frink's heroes and thugs: a study in conceptions of masculinity in the post-war era. Emily L. Arbis. (Dr. Geraldine Johnson.) Oxford M.St. (Mod. Hist.)

2192　Learning not to know your place: post-war British cinema and early social realism. Alistair Billam. (Professor Paul J. Ward.) Huddersfield M.A. (Music, Hum. & Media)

2193　A social and emotional history of fathers and sons in Britain, 1945–70. Richard Hall. (Dr. Lucy Delap and Dr. Simon Sleight.) Cambridge Ph.D. (Hist.)

2194　'The joke's on who?' Comedy and the construction of English identities, c.1945–70. Michael Potter. (Professor Frank Mort and Dr. Max Jones.) Manchester Ph.D. (Hist.)

2195　The racialisation of belonging: representations of the British north-west's non-white communities in the popular press, 1945–70. Matthew Young. (Dr. Andrew Davies.) Liverpool Ph.D. (Hist.)

2196　Metropolitan masculinities: gender and space in London in the aftermath of war and decolonisation, c.1945–65. Kevin Guyan. (Dr. Michael Collins.) London Ph.D. (U.C. Hist.)

2197　Post-war cinema-going in the U.K.: a comparative analysis of Belfast and Sheffield. Sam Manning. (Dr. Sean O'Connell.) Belfast Ph.D. (Hist. & Anthr.)

2198　The visualisation of communism in British culture, 1945–63. Jacqueline Clulow. (Professor Michael J. Hughes.) Liverpool Ph.D. (Hist.)

2199　The culture of death in Scotland. Edward Small. (Professors Callum G. Brown and Jim Tomlinson.) Dundee Ph.D. (Hist.)

2200　The public lives of two royal women in the second half of the 20th century: Princess Mary, the Princess Royal, Countess of Harwood, and H.R.H. The Princess Margaret, Countess of Snowdon. Wendy Tebble. (Professors David N. Cannadine and Lawrence Goldman.) London M.Phil./Ph.D. (Inst. Hist. Res.)

2201　Peace protest before Greenham: the women's peace movement in Britain, 1950–70. Susan Allen. (Professors Barbara Taylor and Mica Nava.) East London Ph.D. (Hist.)

2202　How did women balance the competing demands of motherhood, marriage, domesticity and employment in England in the 1950s? Lucy A. Golding. (Dr. Selina Todd.) Oxford D.Phil. (Mod. Hist.)

2203　Women in the 1950s: politics and subjectivity. Eve M. Worth. (Dr. Selina Todd.) Oxford D.Phil. (Mod. Hist.)

2204　Shattered 'consensus': the regression of British society on black immigration in the post-war period, 1951–62. Robert Kalonian. (Dr. Ben Jackson.) Oxford M.St. (Mod. Hist.)

2205　Encountering each other: love and emotional relationships between men and women in Britain, 1950s–1970s. Lucy Brown. (Dr. Adrian C. Bingham.) Sheffield Ph.D. (Hist.)

2206 Men's hair in Britain, c.1958–c.1974. Mark Anderson. (Dr. Nick Thomas and Dr. Richard Hornsey.) Nottingham Ph.D. (Hist.)

2207 The narratives of British women and men who posed for *Playboy* and *Playgirl* magazine between the 1960s and the early 2000s. Marjolein van Bavel. (Dr. Helga Satzinger and Dr. Henk De Smaele.) London Ph.D. (U.C. Hist.)

2208 A history of urban decline in Britain: Glasgow and Liverpool, c.1960–90. Aaron Andrews. (Professor Simon Gunn.) Leicester Ph.D. (Urban Hist.)

2209 'Will never marry': gender, sexuality and singleness in Britain, 1960–90. Emily Priscott. (Dr. Lucy Robinson and Professor Claire L. Langhamer.) Sussex D.Phil. (Hist.)

2210 Women, love and anarchism: British counter-culture in the 1960s and 1970s. Emma Dixon. (Dr. Alexander Sedlmaier.) Manchester Ph.D. (Hist.)

2211 The image and experience of youth in 1960s England. Helena C. Mills. (Dr. Selina Todd.) Oxford D.Phil. (Mod. Hist.)

2212 Dangerous sexualities, cultural geographies and the Moors murders. Ian Field. (Dr. Max Jones and Professor Frank Mort.) Manchester Ph.D. (Hist.)

2213 Screening Jews and Jewishness in British television comedy, 1965–90. Christopher Byrne. (Dr. James Jordan.) Southampton M.Phil. (Hist.)

2214 *Nova*, 1965–75: a new kind of magazine for the new kind of woman. Alice Beard. (Professor Sally A. Alexander and Dr. Vivienne Richmond.) London M.Phil. (Goldsmiths Hist.)

2215 The history of the English pro-life movement, 1967–2012. Livi Dee. (Dr. Stella Moss.) London Ph.D. (R.H.U.L. Hist.)

2216 The persuasion industries in the U.K. and the inculcation of persuasion within British society from 1969 to 1997. Steven McKevitt. (Dr. Adrian C. Bingham.) Sheffield Ph.D. (Hist.)

2217 Changing attitudes to British pet dog training: 1970s to the present day. Natalie Light. (Professors Louise Curth and Christopher Aldous.) Winchester M.Phil./Ph.D. (Hist.)

2218 Changing the people's game: football in England, 1970–2010. Mark Sampson. (Dr. Peter P. Catterall.) London M.Phil. (Q.M. Hist.)

2219 From friendship clubs to match.com: a London study of metropolitan courtship, 1970 to the present. Zoe Strimpel. (Professor Claire L. Langhamer.) Sussex D.Phil. (Hist.)

2220 Marriage and marriage breakdown in late 20th-century Scotland. Andrea Thomson. (Dr. Annemarie Hughes and Professor Eleanor J. Gordon.) Glasgow Ph.D. (Soc. Sc.)

2221 Bussing out and in: racism and anti-racism in the 1970s. Joe Hopkinson. (Professor Paul Ward.) Huddersfield M.Phil. (Music, Hum. & Media)

2222 Identities in post-industrial northern towns, c.1975–2010. Adam Blackburn. (Dr. Selina Todd.) Oxford M.St. (Mod. Hist.)

2223   Architectural geographies of the British public house, from 1979 to the present day. Jonathan Moses. (Professors Philip Crang and David Gilbert.) London M.Phil./ Ph.D. (R.H.U.L. Geog.)

2224   Overcoming colonial and post-colonial ethnic and racial prejudices: the construction of a Zimbabwean community in Britain. Christopher Zembe. (Professor Panikos Panayi.) De Montfort Ph.D. (Hum.)

2225   Working class men, education and achievement in Britain, 1980–2010. Grantley Greene. (Dr. Tom Woodin and Dr. Michela Franceschelli.) London Ph.D. (Inst. of Educ.)

2226   Talk of the south: teenage culture in Essex in the 1980s. Laura Whittle. (Professor Gary McCulloch and Dr. Alice Sullivan.) London Ph.D. (Inst. of Educ.)

2227   Gender, psychology and emotions: investigating selfhood in women's popular advice literature, 1982–7. Charlotte A. Mackenzie. (Dr. Matthew Grimley.) Oxford M.St. (Mod. Hist.)

20th century: Ecclesiastical and religious history

2228   Queering paganism: sexual orientation and paganism in the 20th century. Brian Paisley. (Professor Ronald Hutton.) Bristol Ph.D. (Hist. Stud.)

2229   Faith and good works: congregationalism in Edwardian Hampshire. Roger Ottewill. (Professor D. Hugh McLeod.) Birmingham Ph.D. (Hist.)

2230   Bishops as legislators: the lords spiritual, c.1904–74. Thomas Rodger. (Professors Philip Williamson and Stephen Taylor.) Durham Ph.D. (Hist.)

2231   English Catholic press and foreign affairs in the inter-war period. Julianna Johnson. (Dr. Sean Lang and Dr. Jonathan Davis.) Anglia Ruskin D.Phil. (Hist.)

2232   George Bell and the World Council of Churches. John Richardson. Chichester M.Phil./Ph.D. (Hist.)

2233   What makes a church or chapel redundant or marked for closure in the modern era in England? Denise Bonnette-Anderson. (Professor Keith D.M. Snell.) Leicester Ph.D. (Eng. Loc. Hist.)

2234   An investigation into influences on modern pagan witchcraft. Lynn Reglar. (Professor Ronald Hutton and Dr. James Thompson.) Bristol M.Litt. (Hist. Stud.)

20th century: Education

2235   Education and older learners: the politics of experience. Grace Rose. (Dr. Tom Woodin.) London Ph.D. (Inst. of Educ.)

2236   The relationship between education and socioeconomic mobility among impoverished communities. James K. McGraw. (Dr. Deborah J. Oxley.) Oxford M.Phil. (Mod. Hist.)

2237   Violence, mental mealth and the British school child: theory, practice and representation in an era of war, peace and social change. Andrew Burchell. (Professor Mathew Thomson.) Warwick Ph.D. (Hist.)

2238 Public schoolboys' identities in early 20th-century England. Edward Whiffen. (Professor Gary McCulloch and Dr. Mark Freeman.) London Ph.D. (Inst. of Educ.)

2239 Memorialisation of the second Boer War in British public and private schools and its implications for World War I remembrance. Dennis Huggins. (Dr. Margaret L. Arnot and Professor John Tosh.) Roehampton M.Phil./Ph.D. (Hist.)

2240 Policy-making in secondary education: evidence from two local authorities. Dorothy A. Makin. (Dr. Harold Carter and Professor Jane Humphries.) Oxford D.Phil. (Mod. Hist.)

2241 Rural education in the inter-war years. Alice Kirke. (Dr. Tom Woodin and Professor Gary McCulloch.) London Ph.D. (Inst. of Educ.)

2242 A century of student life: town and gown in Swansea, 1920–2020. Jay Leigh Rees. (Professor Louise Miskell.) Swansea Ph.D. (Hist.)

2243 'A spectacle for angels and the laughing stock of men': an exploration of student insurgence at the Bible churchmen's missionary and theological college, 1925–32. Rosalind Janssen. (Dr. Tom Woodlin.) London Ph.D. (Inst. of Educ.)

2244 Learning parenthood: family, schooling and childhood, 1930–80. Eleanor Murray. (Dr. Laura King, Dr. Jessica Meyer and Dr. Kate M. Dossett.) Leeds Ph.D. (Hist.)

2245 A pupil perspective of progressive education at King Alfred School, 1930–60. Katherina Grant. (Professor Gary McCulloch.) London Ph.D. (Inst. of Educ.)

2246 The educational experiences of children in England during the Second World War. Emma Lautman. (Dr. Nick Thomas and Professor Colin Heywood.) Nottingham Ph.D. (Hist.)

2247 The history of the Polish School of Medicine at the University of Edinburgh, 1941–9. Michal A. Palacz. (Dr. Pertti Ahonen and Dr. Gayle Davis.) Edinburgh Ph.D. (Hist.)

2248 The impact of an Oxford education on women's class and gender identities, 1948–63. Bethany A. White. (Dr. Selina Todd.) Oxford M.St. (Mod. Hist.)

2249 Technical and vocational training of young women in the north-west, 1950–65: underachievement and opportunities missed? Veronica M. Jackson. (Ms. Patricia Ayers and Professor Melanie Tebbutt.) Manchester Metropolitan Ph.D. (Hist.)

2250 Educational reforms in Wales, c.1955–75. Kerstin A. Olsson-Rost. (Dr. Andrew Edwards and Dr. Lowri Rees.) Bangor Ph.D. (Hist., Welsh Hist. & Archaeol.)

2251 Pupil experiences at Westminster School, 1957–86. Rudolf Lockhart. (Professor Gary McCulloch.) London Ed.D. (Inst. of Educ.)

2252 The diploma in art and design and British art schools, 1958–68. Frederika J. Adam. (Mr. M. Archer.) Oxford D.Phil. (Mod. Hist.)

2253 From right to read to access for all: how was the relationship between adult literacy and education for adults with non-specific learning difficulties reflected in adult literacy theory, policy and practice in the U.K., 1970–2010? Judith Rose. (Dr. Tom Woodin and Dr. Sam Duncan.) London Ph.D. (Inst. of Educ.)

2254 Multicultural education and the teaching of history, 1976–88. Marlene Laing. (Professor Gary McCulloch.) London Ph.D. (Inst. of Educ.)

2255 The influence of teacher media images on professional teacher identities. Davina Kirby. (Professors Gary McCulloch and Jon Swain.) London Ph.D. (Inst. of Educ.)

20th century: The arts, science, medicine and public health

2256 Patients, therapy and multiple sclerosis in 20th-century Britain. Katrina Gately. (Dr. Michael R. Neve and Dr. Stephen Jacyna.) London Ph.D. (U.C. Hist. of Med.)

2257 History and health inequalities in 20th-century west of Scotland. Ellen Glasgow. (Professor Marguerite W. Duprée and Dr. Michaela Benzeval.) Glasgow Ph.D. (Soc. Sc.)

2258 Shakespeare and modern British opera: two *Tempests*. Michael Graham. (Dr. Paul Harper-Scott.) London Ph.D. (R.H.U.L. Music)

2259 Providing education for children with cerebral palsy and related disabilities: how policy and collective action brought about change during the second half of the 20th century. Teresa Hillier. (Professor David Turner.) Swansea M.Res. (Hist.)

2260 Man made: creating life in the 20th century. Bethany Logan. (Dr. Jim Endersby and Dr. Sue Currell.) Sussex D.Phil. (Hist.)

2261 The social history of medical self-help in 20th-century England: a micro-history of a rural community. Fiona Mantle. (Professor Owen Davies and Dr. Ciara Meehan.) Hertfordshire Ph.D. (Hist.)

2262 The role of women, female artists in particular, and the depiction of women in modern and contemporary art. Katherine A. Mato. (Dr. Geraldine Johnson.) Oxford M.St. (Mod. Hist.)

2263 British brass bands and their music in the 20th century. Christopher Osborn. (Dr. Corinna Peniston-Bird and Professor Jeffrey Richards.) Lancaster Ph.D. (Hist.)

2264 Performing bodies: anatomical display in the 20th-century fairground. Vicki Pugh. (Professor M. Mary T. Vincent.) Sheffield Ph.D. (Hist.)

2265 British Jews and radical theatre in Britain in the 20th century. Isabelle Seddon. (Professor Tony Kushner.) Southampton M.Phil. (Hist.)

2266 The advantages and disadvantages of 'living in' on identity and perpetuation of a standard of care. Claire Brough Shearer. (Dr. Catherine Mills and Dr. James J. Smyth.) Stirling Ph.D. (Hist.)

2267 Medical professional misconduct in the 20th century. Roz Sullivan. (Professor Malcolm A. Nicolson, Dr. Kenneth Mullen and Dr. Angus Ferguson.) Glasgow Ph.D. (Soc. Sc.)

2268 Medical understandings of alcohol and the liver in the 20th century. Ryosuke Yokoe. (Professor Phil Withington.) Sheffield Ph.D. (Hist.)

2269 'Work amongst the sick poor': home medical missions and the transition from Victorian charity to the welfare state. Sarah J. Bodell. (Professor Hilary Marland.) Warwick Ph.D. (Hist.)

2270 Materiality, medium and meaning in the aesthetics of Jacques Maritain and the paintings of Georges Rouault. Jennifer J. Johnson. (Dr. Alastair Wright.) Oxford D.Phil. (Mod. Hist.)

2271 Stillbirth in Glasgow: medical, legal and religious perspectives, 1901–92. Maelle J. Duchemin-Pelletier. (Dr. Rose Elliot and Professor Malcolm A. Nicolson.) Glasgow Ph.D. (Soc. Sc.)

2272 From Shund to Kunst? London Yiddish theatre, 1906–50. Katie Power. (Dr. Claire Le Foll and Dr. James Jordan.) Southampton M.Phil. (Hist.)

2273 G.P.s, politics and the evolution of state-funded healthcare in Britain, 1909–49. Christopher Locke. (Dr. Julia Moses.) Sheffield Ph.D. (Hist.)

2274 Networking the modern: Roger Fry and the Contemporary Art Society c.1910–39. Julia Musgrave. (Professor Elizabeth Prettejohn.) York Ph.D. (Hist. of Art)

2275 Dislocation: regarding Dante in T.S. Eliot. Carey Karmel. (Dr. Wim Van Mierlo and Dr. Alessandro Scafi.) London Ph.D. (Inst. Eng. Stud.)

2276 The role of paediatric dental care in Britain's public health, 1914–48. Helen Franklin. (Dr. Andrea Tanner.) London M.Phil./Ph.D. (Inst. Hist. Res.)

2277 'These horrible and splendid times': English musical life during the Great War. Jane Angell. (Mr. Erik Levi.) London Ph.D. (R.H.U.L. Music)

2278 An examination of male perpetrated domestic violence, 1914–39. Rebecca Crites. (Dr. Pierre Purseigle.) Warwick Ph.D. (Hist.)

2279 Hospitals in stately homes in the south-east in the First World War. Jack Davies. (Dr. Julie Anderson and Professor Mark Connelly.) Kent Ph.D. (Hist.)

2280 Victorian artists during the Great War. Antonio Noh. (Professor Elizabeth Prettejohn.) York Ph.D. (Hist. of Art)

2281 Astudiaeth o'r wasg Gymreig yn ystod y Rhyfel Byd Cyntaf. [A study of the Welsh press during the First World War.] (In Welsh medium). Meilyr Powel. (Mr. Robert Rhys.) Swansea Ph.D. (Hist.)

2282 Art and order: the culture and work of a London general hospital during the Great War: an evaluation of the life and community of the 3rd London General Hospital in Wandsworth. Pippa Sharp. (Dr. Sue Hawkins and Professor Craig Phelan.) Kingston Ph.D. (Econ., Hist. & Pol.)

2283 Script doctors and drug cultures: the prescribing of controlled drugs to addicts and U.K. drug culture, 1916–60. Christopher Hallam. (Professor Virginia Berridge.) London Ph.D. (L.S.H.T.M.)

2284 Viral insanity: the medical formation of encephalitis lethargica into an epidemic, 1917–30. Sarah Savage. (Dr. Helga Satzinger.) London Ph.D. (U.C. Hist.)

2285 Women's sport and leisure in the workplace: a cultural case study of gender and class construction in inter-war England. Adam McKie. London M.Phil./Ph.D. (R.H.U.L. Hist.)

2286 Inter-war British art and the apocalypse. Thomas Bromwell. (Professor Liz Prettejohn.) York Ph.D. (Hist. of Art)

2287 Women and depression in inter-war Britain: case notes, narratives and experiences, 1923–38. Jean Hye-Hwang. (Professor Hilary Marland.) Warwick Ph.D. (Hist.)

2288 Education, social mobility and the inter-war labour movement: building socialism or conforming to tradition? A British case study. Christine Kumbhat. (Professors Malcolm S. Chase and Richard C. Whiting.) Leeds Ph.D. (Hist.)

2289 Male attitudes towards deafness in soldiers who fought at the Battle of the Somme. Melissa Dawson. (Dr. Jessica K. Meyer and Dr. Kevin B. Linch.) Leeds M.A. (Hist.)

2290 Unearthing the 'medical encounter'. Gartnavel Royal Asylum, 1918–28: exploring the intersection of scientific and social discourses which negotiated the boundaries of psychiatric diagnoses. Hazel Morrison. (Professors Malcolm A. Nicolson and Chris Philo.) Glasgow Ph.D. (Soc. Sc.)

2291 Networks, connections and ambition: the work of Sir William Goscombe John, 1899–1942. Melanie Polledri. (Professor Jason Edwards.) York Ph.D. (Hist. of Art)

2292 The photography of working people, 1919–39. Michael Nolan. (Professor Keith Laybourn.) Huddersfield M.Phil. (Music, Hum. & Media)

2293 Architecture and the public in inter-war Britain. Neal E. Shasore. (Dr. Alastair Wright and Dr. William Whyte.) Oxford D.Phil. (Mod. Hist.)

2294 History of the theory of comics. Ian Hague. (Dr. Hugo Frey and Professor Keith W. Jenkins.) Chichester M.Phil./Ph.D. (Hist.)

2295 Rex Whistler. Nikki Frater. (Professors Daniel Maudlin and Sam Smiles.) Plymouth Ph.D. (Hum.)

2296 The history of antibiotics, antibiotic resistance and infection control in Scottish hospitals, c.1930–70. Susan Gardiner. (Professors Marguerite Duprée and Malcolm A. Nicolson.) Glasgow Ph.D. (Soc. Sc.)

2297 'Enter the dream-house': evaluating the role of British cinemas in public emotion, spatial appropriation and notions of modernity, c.1930–60. James Jones. (Professor Claire Langhamer and Mr. Andy Medhurst.) Sussex D.Phil. (Hist.)

2298 Penguin Book Specials and the centre-left. Dean Blackburn. (Dr. Hugh Pemberton.) Bristol Ph.D. (Hist. Stud.)

2299 War neurosis and civilian mental health in Second World War Britain. Hazel Croft. (Professor Joanna Bourke.) London Ph.D. (Birkbeck Hist.)

2300 Occupational health in Scotland during the Second World War. Nicola Graham. Glasgow Caledonian Ph.D. (Hist.)

2301 British exploitation of German science and technology from war to post-war, 1943–8. Charlie Hall. (Professor Ulf Schmidt and Dr. Stefan Goebel.) Kent Ph.D. (Hist.)

2302 Music and nation in World War II London. Eleanor Thackrey. (Dr. Rachel Beckles Willson.) London Ph.D. (R.H.U.L. Music)

2303 The history of Alcoholics Anonymous and the rise of self-help in Britain. Ashley Wilkinson. (Professor Bertrand Taithe and Dr. Eloise Moss.) Manchester Ph.D. (Hist.)

2304 Expeditionary film, geographical science and media culture. Jan Faull. (Professor Felix Driver.) London M.Phil./Ph.D. (R.H.U.L. Geog.)

2305 A volitional regulation of the marriage state: the dissemination of contraceptive knowledge, 1940–75. Kenneth MacAulay. (Professor Malcolm A. Nicolson and Dr. Kenneth Mullen.) Glasgow M.D. (Soc. Sc.)

2306 Sexual 'deviance', mental illness and the medical profession in mid 20th-century Britain. Janet Weston. (Professor Joanna Bourke.) London M.Phil./Ph.D. (Birkbeck Hist.)

2307 Remploy: the changing face of disability employment in Britain, 1944–2014. Andrew Holroyde. (Dr. Robert Ellis.) Huddersfield M.Phil. (Music, Hum. & Media)

2308 Under-, over- and mis-represented: representations of Victorian women in contemporary museums. Lauren Padgett. (Dr. Rosemary Mitchell and Dr. Nathan Uglow.) Leeds Trinity Ph.D. (Hist.)

2309 The world through their lens: the Walter Gardiner photographic archive and the cultures of modernism in Britain. Carly Vaughan. (Dr. Benedict Burbridge and Professor David Mellor.) Sussex D.Phil. (Hist. of Art)

2310 British medical education, post-1945. Caroline Torres. (Professor David Smith, Dr. Anna Jones and Professor Oonagh Walsh.) Glasgow Caledonian Ph.D. (Hist.)

2311 Biomedical research policy in Britain: the Medical Research Council, 1945–2000. Andrew Black. (Dr. Carsten Timmermann.) Manchester Ph.D. (Hist. of Sc., Tech. & Med.)

2312 The rise of the leisure painter: artistic creativity within the experience of ordinary life in post-war Britain, c.1945–2000. Ruth Brown. (Professor Avner Offer.) Oxford D.Phil. (Mod. Hist.)

2313 The healthy body ideal in medicine: media and conceptions of the healthy body in Britain, 1945–2000. Martha Kirby. (Professor Malcolm A. Nicolson and Dr. Rose Elliot.) Glasgow Ph.D. (Soc. Sc.)

2314 The face(s) of science: narrating lives in science since c.1945. Ruth Wainman. (Dr. Charlotte Sleigh and Dr. Juliette Pattinson.) Kent Ph.D. (Hist.)

2315 The rise of the art and antiquities business, 1945–65. Alycen Mitchell. (Professor Donald Sassoon.) London M.Phil. (Q.M. Hist.)

2316 Progressive ideals and the promotion of 'high' culture in Britain, 1945–c.1964. Beau A.H. Woodbury. (Dr. Matthew Grimley.) Oxford D.Phil. (Mod. Hist.)

2317 The British comedy industry: prosperity and decline in live comedy performance, 1945–65. Leo Bird. (Dr. Adrian C. Bingham.) Sheffield Ph.D. (Hist.)

2318 Fashion in a time of austerity: London, 1945–51. Bethan Bide. (Professor David Gilbert and Ms. Beatrice Behlen.) London M.Phil./Ph.D. (R.H.U.L. Geog.)

2319 A thematic study on the planning and actualisation of three English towns of the New Town Movement: Letchworth, Milton Keynes and Harlow. Melissa Stanley. (Professor Michael White.) York Ph.D. (Hist. of Art)

2320 Archival or scientific? The role of contemporary biology at the Museum of Natural History, Oxford, from 1946–79. Robyn S. Haggard. (Professor Pietro Corsi and Dr. Stephen Johnston.) Oxford M.Sc. (Mod. Hist.)

2321 Health care choices and market values. Andrew D. Lawson. (Professor Avner Offer.) Oxford M.Phil. (Mod. Hist.)

2322 Health education in modern Scotland. David Black. (Professor Elaine W. McFarland and Dr. Janet Greenlees.) Glasgow Caledonian Ph.D. (Hist.)

2323 Epidemiology, heart disease and the British public, 1948–2010. Peder Clark. (Dr. Alex Mold.) London M.Phil./Ph.D. (L.S.H.T.M.)

2324 Lung cancer and tobacco consumption in urban Scotland, 1948–97. Nicola Rennie. (Professor Elaine W. McFarland and Dr. Janet Greenlees.) Glasgow Caledonian Ph.D. (Hist.)

2325 Photographers in the making: what motivations for photography are provided by practice-based photography courses in U.K. higher education. Tim P. Stephens. (Dr. Benedict Burbridge and Professor John Pryor.) Sussex D.Phil. (Hist. of Art)

2326 Visualising A.I.D.S.: re-codify the body to re-codify society. Ilaria Grando. (Dr. James Boaden and Dr. Jo Applin.) York Ph.D. (Hist. of Art)

2327 The use of text in conceptual art. Hyunji Jang. (Dr. Hanneke Grootenboer.) Oxford M.St. (Mod. Hist.)

2328 A gene's eye view: W.D. Hamilton, the science of society, and the new biology of enlightened self-interest, 1950–90. Sarah A. Swenson. (Professor Pietro Corsi.) Oxford D.Phil. (Mod. Hist.)

2329 Conservatives and the politics of art, 1950–88. Karen P. Heath. (Dr. Gareth B. Davies and Dr. Stephen G.N. Tuck.) Oxford D.Phil. (Mod. Hist.)

2330 National prestige, in(ter)dependence and the technopolitics of British space research, 1955–75. Stuart Butler. (Dr. Jeff Hughes.) Manchester Ph.D. (Hist. of Sc., Tech. & Med.)

2331 Research, development and commercialisation of cannabis-based medicine in the U.K.: controversies, contradictions and resistance. Yewande Okuleye. (Dr. Sally Horrocks.) Leicester Ph.D. (Hist.)

2332 Esotericism and quantum theories, 1960–2010: a study of David Bohm. Gustavo O. Fernandez. (Professor Andew Pickering.) Exeter M.Phil. (Stud. of Esotericism)

2333 Popular culture and sci-fi in Britain, 1960–79. Charlotte Rockey. (Dr. Daniel Grey, Dr. James Gregory and Dr. Sandra Barkhof.) Plymouth Ph.D. (Hum.)

2334 Genius of the slums: a biography of Andrea Dunbar. Adelle Stripe. (Professor Paul Ward.) Huddersfield Ph.D. (Music, Hum. & Media)

2335 Organisation and policy for research and development: the health department for England and Wales, 1961–88. Stephen Davies. (Dr. Martin Gorsky.) London M.Phil./Ph.D. (L.S.H.T.M.)

2336 Conceptual art in Britain, 1964–79. Louisa Lee. (Dr. Jo Applin.) York Ph.D. (Hist. of Art)

2337 Experiencing crime and punishment: emotions, perceptions and responses to crime and penal heritage in courtroom and prison museums. Rhiannon Pickin. (Dr. Heather Shore and Dr. Helen Johnston.) Leeds Beckett Ph.D. (Cultural Stud.)

2338 From mental patient to service user: deinstitutionalisation and the emergence of the mental health service user/survivor movement in Scotland, 1970–2010. Mark Gallagher. (Professor Malcolm A. Nicolson and Dr. Gavin Miller.) Glasgow Ph.D. (Soc. Sc.)

2339 Wall painting and the conjuncture: London's exterior murals, 1970–86. Ben Wiedel-Kaufmann. (Dr. Jody Patterson and Dr. Gemma Blackshaw.) Plymouth Ph.D. (Hum.)

2340 Advertising, addictions and health advice: understanding 'tanorexia' in contemporary Britain, 1978–2016. Fabiola Creed. (Professor Roberta Bivins.) Warwick M.Phil./Ph.D. (Hist.)

2341 Lay epidemiology and political campaigning: the role of the Society for the Prevention of Asbestosis and Industrial Diseases (S.P.A.I.D.), 1978–2008. William McDougall. Glasgow Caledonian Ph.D. (Hist.)

2342 Ethics discourse as an influence on the development of Assisted Reproductive Technologies (A.R.T.) and embryo research regulation in Britain, 1978–90. Imogen L. Goold. (Dr. M. Harrison and Dr. S.M. Liao.) Oxford D.Phil. (Mod. Hist.)

2343 The Holocaust in British popular culture: interpretations of recent feature films. Stefanie Rauch. (Dr. Olaf Jensen.) Leicester Ph.D. (Hist.)

2344 Conspiracy in British film and television, 1980–90. Paul Lynch. (Professor Tony Shaw and Dr. Steven Peacock.) Hertfordshire Ph.D. (Hist.)

2345 The creation, dissemination and reception of representations of H.I.V.-positive identities in children's media in Britain, 1981–97. Hannah Kershaw. (Dr. David Kirby and Professor Frank Mort.) Manchester Ph.D. (Hist. of Sc., Tech. & Med.)

2346 Grayson Perry and British cultural identity. Anna Murphy. (Dr. Alastair Wright.) Oxford D.Phil. (Mod. Hist.)

2347 The new art of the botanic garden: landscape design in an age of biodiversity conservation, climate change and cultural diversity. Belinda Hawkins. (Professor David Gilbert and Ms. Julia Willison (Kew Gardens).) London M.Phil./Ph.D. (R.H.U.L. Geog.)

2348 Performing images in the Vanessa Beecroft metanarrative. Eleanor Dilloway. (Dr. Alastair Wright.) Oxford M.St. (Mod. Hist.)

INTERNATIONAL HISTORY

2349 The experience of childhood in Mamluk society (Egypt and Syria, 1250–1517). Catherine Rose. (Dr. Yossef Rapoport.) London Ph.D. (Q.M. Hist.)

2350 Encountering difference in the age of discovery: understanding indigenous perceptions of Europeans, 1492–1572. Claudia Rogers. (Dr. Anyaa J. Anim-Addo and Professor Manuel Barcia Paz.) Leeds Ph.D. (Hist.)

2351 Disputed frontiers: entangled territories between Spanish and British rule in colonial Central America. Ben Fuggle. (Dr. Matthias Röhrig Assunção.) Essex Ph.D. (Hist.)

2352 From astrology to aliens: a shift in early modern cosmology. James Christie. (Dr. Guido Giglioni and Professor Charles Burnett.) London Ph.D. (Warburg)

2353   Early modern theories and modes of conquest in the 16th and 17th century.   Jonas
       P. Pollex.   (Dr. Jon Parkin.)   Oxford D.Phil   (Mod. Hist.)

2354   'Heathenism' in the Protestant Atlantic world, c.1500–c.1650.   Patrick Seamus
       McGhee.   (Professor Alexandra Walsham.)   Cambridge Ph.D.   (Hist.)

2355   Italians in the opening of the Atlantic world.   Matteo Salonia.   (Dr. Harald Braun.)
       Liverpool Ph.D.   (Hist.)

2356   The development of numeracy and the dissemination of Hindu-Arabic numerals in the
       early modern period, 1550–1750.   Cheryl Periton.   (Professor Jacqueline S. Eales.)
       Canterbury Christ Church Ph.D.   (Hist.)

2357   The long space age: essays on the economic history of space exploration from
       Galileo to Gagarin.   Alexander C. MacDonald.   (Professor Avner Offer.)   Oxford
       D.Phil.   (Mod. Hist.)

2358   History and implication of the principles of authentication in art.   Rita Akkari.
       (Professor M.J. Kemp and Dr. M. Baker.)   Oxford D.Phil.   (Mod. Hist.)

2359   Perspectives in flux: scenes of knowledge and entertainment in the 17th-century
       Dutch and Edo-Japanese material culture and encounter.   Dayeon Oh.   (Dr.
       Hanneke Grootenboer.)   Oxford D.Phil.   (Mod. Hist.)

2360   Alchemy's role in the reception and reproduction of prototypical Chinese porcelain
       in 17th-century Europe.   Morgan Wesley.   (Mr. Timothy Wilson and Professor Craig
       Clunas.)   Oxford D.Phil.   (Mod. Hist.)

2361   Religious governance in England and 17th-century overseas companies, c.1601–
       1702.   Haig Smith.   (Dr. William Pettigrew and Dr. Tristan Stein.)   Kent Ph.D.
       (Hist.)

2362   Catholicism in Scotland and the Atlantic world, 1603–1745.   Mary Hardy.   (Dr. Colin
       Barr.)   Aberdeen Ph.D.   (Hist.)

2363   Saving the empire: the stability of the Portuguese colonies in the face of growing
       competition during the years 1630–68.   Nuno Silva.   (Dr. Gabriel Guarino and Dr.
       Éamonn Ó Ciardha.)   Ulster Ph.D.   (Hist.)

2364   'The world must be peopled': mercantilism and citizenship in the English and French
       empires, 1660–1770.   Daisy Gibbs.   (Professor Julian Hoppit.)   London Ph.D.
       (U.C. Hist.)

2365   The economics of philanthropy: Halle pietism and the international medical trade.
       Anne Moeller.   (Dr. Claudia Stein.)   Warwick Ph.D.   (Hist.)

2366   Pirate executions and British maritime sovereignty in the Atlantic world, 1677–1800.
       Rebecca Simon.   (Professor Richard H. Drayton and Dr. Laura Gowing.)   King's
       College London M.Phil./Ph.D.   (Hist.)

2367   Studying the life cycle of the British slave trade, 1680–1807.   Michael Smith.   (Dr.
       Jane Webster and Dr. Andrea Dolfini.)   Newcastle Ph.D.   (Archaeol.)

2368   Africans, Euro-Africans, and Europeans as middlemen in the West and West Central
       Africa slave trade in 1680–1720 .   Maria Ines Guarda.   (Professor Francisco
       Bethencourt and Dr. Tobias Green.)   King's College London M.Phil./Ph.D.   (Hist.)

2369 An analysis of the global economy in National Socialist memorabilia. Michael Hughes. (Professor Raymond G. Stokes.) Glasgow Ph.D. (Soc. Sc.)

2370 Britain's experience of empire. Jody Crutchley. (Dr. Neil Fleming, Dr. Paddy McNally and Dr. Stephen Porter.) Worcester M.Phil./Ph.D. (Hum. & Creative Arts)

2371 Literary opposition to evangelical revivalism in the British Atlantic world, c.1735–50. Simon J. Lewis. (Dr. Brian Young.) Oxford D.Phil. (Mod. Hist.)

2372 Seeds of the future. Elizabeth Scott. East Anglia Ph.D. (Hist.)

2373 Classify and conquer? Religious intellectual discovery and empire. Nicole M. Apostol. (Dr. E. Jane Garnett.) Oxford D.Phil. (Mod. Hist.)

2374 British colonial atrocities. Michelle Gordon. (Professor Dan Stone.) London M.Phil./Ph.D. (R.H.U.L. Hist.)

2375 The relationship between art and the British Empire: the Palace of Arts at the imperial exhibitions. Jiyi Ryu. (Professor Jason Edwards.) York Ph.D. (Hist. of Art)

2376 Fashion across borders and seas: print culture, women's networks and the creation of feminine identities in the British Atlantic world, 1750–1900. Anna Bonewitz. (Professor Elizabeth Prettejohn.) York Ph.D. (Hist. of Art)

2377 Globalising communities: the Atlantic slave trade and the socio-economic development of northern Scotland, 1750–1850. Michael Hopcroft. (Dr. S. Karly Kehoe, Dr. Annie Tindley and Dr. Maria Castrillo (National Museums of Scotland).) Glasgow Caledonian Ph.D. (Hist.)

2378 Trade, reform and communication: the Ottoman relations with Britain and France from 1750 to 1808. Ali Bayindir. (Professor James Livesey and Dr. Christopher Storrs.) Dundee Ph.D. (Hist.)

2379 Comparative responses to royal deaths in Britain and the Atlantic world, 1751– 1817. Jennifer Scammell. (Professor Helen Berry and Dr. Rachel Hammersley.) Newcastle Ph.D. (Hist.)

2380 Scottophobia in Britain and the empire, 1760–1815. Timothy Worth. (Dr. Christer Petley.) Southampton M.Phil. (Hist.)

2381 Beyond Corsairs: the role of the Barbary States and the relationship with Britain and Spain, 1770–1815. Caitlin M. Gale. (Professor Nicholas A.M. Rodger.) Oxford D.Phil. (Mod. Hist.)

2382 Edward Gibbon and perceptions of decline in the late 18th-century British empire. Hamish S. Roberts. (Dr. Brian Young.) Oxford M.St. (Mod. Hist.)

2383 'The great desideratum in government': James Madison, Benjamin Constant and the theory and establishment of liberal-republican constitutional neutrality. James Shaw. (Professor Stuart Jones and Dr. Francisco Eissa-Barroso.) Manchester Ph.D. (Hist.)

2384 European influences at the genesis of the continental army and United States armed services in the late 18th to early 19th centuries. Nathatai Manadee. (Dr. Kevin B. Linch.) Leeds Ph.D. (Hist.)

2385 Revisiting America's 'Old China Trade'. Jonathan W. Sudbury. (Professor Richard J. Carwardine.) Oxford D.Phil. (Mod. Hist.)

2386 Britain and the fur trade: commerce and consumers in the north Atlantic world, 1783–1821. David Hope. (Professor Tony Webster.) Northumbria Ph.D. (Hist.)

2387 Coerced migration systems in comparative perspective: an analysis of the British slave trade and convict transportation, 1786–1815. Lauren Bell. (Dr. Douglas Hamilton and Dr. Nicholas J. Evans.) Hull Ph.D. (Hist.)

2388 An econometric examination of paintings of rural France, England and the United States. Diana S. Greenwald. (Professors Kevin O'Rourke and Michael Hatt.) Oxford D.Phil. (Mod. Hist.)

2389 Global market integration in industrial commodities during the 19th and 20th centuries. Peter A. Wegerich. (Professor Kevin O'Rourke and Dr. Rui Esteves.) Oxford D.Phil. (Mod. Hist.)

2390 Comparing the underlying social and economic circumstances in Mexico and Russia before their respective revolutions. Jan H. Cortes. (Dr. Brian A'Hearn.) Oxford M.Phil. (Mod. Hist.)

2391 *La France algérienne*: colonialism and the making of the Third Republic. Avner Ofrath. (Professor Robert Gildea.) Oxford D.Phil. (Mod. Hist.)

2392 Diseases, diaspora and discourse: Irish and Italian migration, 1832–1907. Lee Cook. (Dr. John Welshman.) Lancaster Ph.D. (Hist.)

2393 Comparative indentures: experiences of indentured labour and transnational identity in Mauritius and Fiji. Reshaad Durgahee. (Professor Mike Heffernan and Dr. Stephen Legg.) Nottingham Ph.D. (Geog.)

2394 African indentured labourers and their descendants in Grenada and St. Lucia: belief, identity and memory, c.1836–2011. Shantelle George. (Dr. John Parker.) London Ph.D. (S.O.A.S. Hist.)

2395 The international sphere in Victorian conservative political thought. Richard Smittenaar. (Dr. Georgios Varouxakis.) London Ph.D. (Q.M. Hist.)

2396 Masculinity and missions: Irish Presbyterian missionaries in India, China and Nigeria, 1840–1910. Catherine Jamieson. (Dr. Eric Morier-Genoud.) Belfast Ph.D. (Hist. & Anthr.)

2397 Kuwaiti business relationships with India: trade, merchants and cultural impact, mid 19th century–1945. Madeha al Fadhli. (Dr. Christian Koller.) Bangor Ph.D. (Hist., Welsh Hist. & Archaeol.)

2398 Consumption and colonial expansion: dining habits and food practices in literatures of empire. James Collinge. (Dr. Rob Burroughs and Dr. Grainne Goodwin.) Leeds Beckett Ph.D. (Cultural Stud.)

2399 The friendly planet: friendly societies, 'fraternals' and mutual aid associations in the English-speaking world and Argentina, 1850–1920. Arthur Downing. (Professor James Belich.) Oxford D.Phil. (Mod. Hist.)

2400 Penal Sakhalin: forging identity in the Euro-Asian borderlands. Carrie Crockett. (Professor Clare Anderson.) Leicester Ph.D. (Hist.)

2401 Convenient imperialism: Britain and France in Japan, 1858–69. Scott Gilfillan. (Dr. Antony M. Best.) London Ph.D. (L.S.E. Int. Hist.)

2402   J.S. Mill and the language of reform within the British empire, c.1859–71. Jake C. Richards. (Dr. Brian Young.) Oxford M.St. (Mod. Hist.)

2403   Recollections and movements: Murray Marks's translations of Chinese porcelain and Italian Renaissance bronzes, c.1860–1918. Eunmin Lim. (Professor Elizabeth Prettejohn.) York Ph.D. (Hist. of Art)

2404   From the marginalist revolution to neoclassical mainstream. Joseph Schwarz. (Dr. George Bitsakakis.) Oxford M.Sc. (Mod. Hist.)

2405   Sir Basil Zaharoff: modern merchant of armaments or 'merchant of death'? Virginia Hart Ezell. (Professor Richard Roberts.) King's College London Ph.D. (Hist.)

2406   Ottoman emigration to the U.S.A., Argentina and Chile in the age of mass migrations, 1870–1914. Muhammet K. Baycar. (Professor Kevin O'Rourke.) Oxford D.Phil. (Mod. Hist.)

2407   Liberating the coolie: moralising narratives on Chinese indentured labour in British Guiana and South Africa, 1870–1911. Edward C. Carins. (Professor James Belich.) Oxford M.St. (Mod. Hist.)

2408   The U.S.-Korean confrontation of 1871. Christoph G. Nitschke. (Dr. Jay Sexton.) Oxford M.St. (Mod. Hist.)

2409   Pox, docks and entrepôts – infectious disease, threats and responses across a British imperial maritime network, 1872–1912. Rhian Crompton. (Professor Mark Harrison.) Oxford D.Phil. (Mod. Hist.)

2410   Ph.D. candidates in the humanities in the late 19th/early 20th century in Berlin, London and at Columbia University, New York. Daniel Hardegger. (Professor Alan Sked.) London Ph.D. (L.S.E. Int. Hist.)

2411   The defence policy of the Royal Navy in the Far East and the Pacific, 1880–1914. Hiraku Yabuki. (Professor Andrew D. Lambert and Dr. Alessio Patalano.) King's College London Ph.D. (War Stud.)

2412   Soldiers, politics and empire: Ireland, Egypt and the Sudan, 1882–1900. Fergal O'Leary. (Professor Peter Gray.) Belfast M.Phil./Ph.D. (Hist. & Anthr.)

2413   Birdie *soul of Anzac*: the military and public career of Field Marshal Lord Birdwood. Richard Farrimond. (Professor Carl Bridge.) King's College London M.Phil./Ph.D. (Hist.)

2414   Ottoman and North African émigré intellectuals in Paris, 1890–1914. David Beamish. (Dr. Konrad Hirschler.) London Ph.D. (S.O.A.S. Hist.)

2415   Slums, squatters and urban redevlopment schemes in Bombay, Hong Kong and Singapore, 1894–1960. Michael Sugarman. (Dr. Tim Harper.) Cambridge Ph.D. (Hist.)

2416   Queen Victoria's diamond jubilee celebrations in Cape Town and Hong Kong. Richard Morris. (Dr. Prashant Kidambi.) Leicester Ph.D. (Urban Hist.)

2417   Competition and co-operation: Diederichsen, Jebsen & Company in German Qingdao and its hinterland of Shandong, 1898–1908. So Wai Ling. (Dr. Andrea Janku.) London Ph.D. (S.O.A.S. Hist.)

2418 An Anglo-American perception of difference: the war powers debate on the Spanish-American war. Cole R. Kosydar. (Dr. Sebastian Page.) Oxford M.St. (Mod. Hist.)

2419 Does inequality lower social mobility? Historical evidence from the U.S., U.K. and Scandinavia. Jerod K. Coker. (Professor Kevin O'Rourke.) Oxford M.Sc. (Mod. Hist.)

2420 A critical re-evaluation of 20th-century visual formalism. Jinhee Choi. (Professor M.J. Kemp and Dr. P.D. Crowther.) Oxford D.Phil. (Mod. Hist.)

2421 Lapsed intelligence: the fate of evolutionary theories of learning in 20th-century psychology. John M. Lidwell-Durnin. (Professor Pietro Corsi and Dr. Sloan Mahone.) Oxford D.Phil. (Mod. Hist.)

2422 Selling health on the world stage. Patricia Yewande Okuleye. (Dr. Sally Horrocks.) Leicester Ph.D. (Hist.)

2423 The role of political and cultural discursive conflict in 20th-century transport transitions: a refinement of the multi-level perspective. Cameron Roberts. (Professor Frank Geels and Dr. James Sumner.) Manchester Ph.D. (Hist. of Sc., Tech. & Med.)

2424 Melville Mackenzie and the history of international health organisations. David MacFayden. (Professors Marguerite W. Duprée and Lawrence Weaver.) Glasgow M.D. (Soc. Sc.)

2425 Gathering limbs: photomontage as a contemporary response to war. Clare Robson. (Dr. Geraldine Johnson.) Oxford M.St. (Mod. Hist.)

2426 The disintegration of the system: far-right terrorism, fascist mythicism and metapolitics. Anna Castriota. (Dr. Paul Jackson and Dr. Jim Beach.) Northampton Ph.D. (Hist.)

2427 The limitations in the use of hard power for humanitarian intervention. Thomas P. Hughes. (Professor Hew F.A. Strachan.) Oxford D.Phil. (Mod. Hist.)

2428 The long-term impact of the Italian colonial expenditures in the Horn of Africa. Mattia C. Bertazzini. (Dr. James Fenske.) Oxford M.Phil. (Mod. Hist.)

2429 Across the deserts and the seas: Cairo, Delhi and Britain's informal empire in the Middle East, 1914–48. Erin M.B. O'Halloran. (Professor Margaret MacMillan.) Oxford D.Phil. (Mod. Hist.)

2430 British, French and American attitudes and policies towards the rebirth of Poland, 1914–21. Denis Clark. (Professor Margaret O. MacMillan.) Oxford D.Phil. (Mod. Hist.)

2431 The question of the South Pacific in war and diplomacy, 1914–19. Bartholomaeus Zielinski. (Professor Carl Bridge.) King's College London M.Phil./Ph.D. (Hist.)

2432 The British world, the empire and dominion interactions in Britain's First World War propaganda. Gregory W. Hynes. (Dr. Adrian Gregory and Professor James Belich.) Oxford D.Phil. (Mod. Hist.)

2433 Forestry, the British empire and the First World War: supply networks, logistics and environmental sustainability. Robert Newman. (Professor Mark Connelly and Dr. Karen Jones.) Kent Ph.D. (Hist.)

2434   Britain's trade relations with Germany in China during the First World War.   Sarah Shipway.   (Professor Robert Bickers.)   Bristol M.Litt.   (Hist. Stud.)

2435   Feminism, pacifism and the international women's movement, 1915–39.   Sarah Hellawell.   (Dr. Nicole Robertson.)   Northumbria Ph.D.   (Hist.)

2436   Britain and France in the Middle East: re-examining the motives behind policies, 1915–22.   Louise Pyne-Jones.   (Dr. Nir Arielli and Professor William R. Gould.)   Leeds Ph.D.   (Hist.)

2437   An unexpected ending: Allied strategic thought about how to end the First World War.   Meighen McCrae.   (Professor Hew F.A. Strachan.)   Oxford D.Phil.   (Mod. Hist.)

2438   The east is white: Sino-Russian conflict in the Russian civil war, 1917–20.   Yuexin R. Lin.   (Dr. Katya Andreyev.)   Oxford D.Phil.   (Mod. Hist.)

2439   A global university? L.S.E., empire and the shaping of post-colonial elites, 1918–47.   Brant Moscovitch.   (Dr. Anna-Maria S. Misra and Dr. Nicholas Owen.)   Oxford D.Phil.   (Mod. Hist.)

2440   'Women of all races and nations welcome'? British feminists and the empire, 1918–38.   Ester M. Pink.   (Professor James Belich.)   Oxford M.St.   (Mod. Hist.)

2441   Coalition war: America, France and the battle of St. Mihiel, September 1918.   Bryon Smith.   (Professor William J. Philpott.)   King's College London M.Phil.   (War Stud.)

2442   Divided we fall: continuity or discontinuity in close air support, 1919–39.   Simon Coningham.   (Professor Philip A.G. Sabin and Dr. David Hall.)   King's College London Ph.D.   (War Stud.)

2443   'Civil emergencies': the langauges and methods of state responses to 'communal violence' in the inter-war years.   Charles J.P. Parker.   (Dr. Faisal Devji.)   Oxford M.St.   (Mod. Hist.)

2444   Intellectual co-operation and international relations between the World Wars.   Jan Stoeckmann.   (Dr. Patricia Clavin.)   Oxford D.Phil.   (Mod. Hist.)

2445   Empire and Europe: a reassessment of British foreign policies, 1919–25.   Chris Crook.   (Professors Stephen Burman and Clive Webb.)   Sussex D.Phil.   (Hist.)

2446   Mass media and the first Red scare.   Claire M. Corkery.   (Dr. Jay Sexton.)   Oxford M.St.   (Mod. Hist.)

2447   Sentiments of the lost land: the rise of Argentine tango in Japan.   Yuiko Asaba.   (Dr. Henry Stobart.)   London Ph.D.   (R.H.U.L. Music)

2448   Becoming global race women: the travels and networks of black female activist-intellectuals, 1920–60.   Imaobong D. Umoren.   (Dr. Stephen G.N. Tuck and Dr. Mara Keire.)   Oxford D.Phil.   (Mod. Hist.)

2449   Surrealism and advertising.   James Wedlake.   (Dr. Hanneke Grootenboer.)   Oxford M.St.   (Mod. Hist.)

2450   Mexican diplomats in Europe during the 1920s.   Itzel Toleda Garcia.   (Dr. Brian Hamnett and Dr. Matthias Röhrig Assunção.)   Essex Ph.D.   (Hist.)

2451   The British imperial response to the refugee problem: the Jewish and Chinese cases.   Jennifer S. Reeve.   East Anglia Ph.D.   (Hist.)

2452 The 1927 events that occurred in China and the response of Stalin and Trotsky. Angela Blackbun. (Dr. James Harris and Dr. Adam Cathcart.) Leeds M.A. (Hist.)

2453 How did the Great Depression affect African trade? Frank Flight. (Dr. Jan-Georg Deutsch.) Oxford M.Sc. (Mod. Hist.)

2454 An international history of unemployment through the International Labour Organization and League of Nations. Mark E. Timpson. (Dr. Patricia M. Clavin.) Oxford D.Phil. (Mod. Hist.)

2455 Imperial justice at the sunset of empire: a study of the evolving role and ideology of the British Colonial Legal Service, 1933–66. Mark O'Connor. (Dr. Joanna E. Lewis.) London Ph.D. (L.S.E. Int. Hist.)

2456 The International Committee on the Christian approach to Jews and its role in ecumenical understanding of anti-semitism and the Jewish question during the Hitler years. Carolyn Sanzenbacher. (Professor Tony Kushner.) Southampton M.Phil. (Hist.)

2457 Friends and foes, 1933–9: British perceptions of Germany, Japan, Russia, France and America. Nicholas Graham. (Professor Holger H.W. Afflerbach and Dr. James Harris.) Leeds Ph.D. (Hist.)

2458 The entangled sites of memory: the significance of photography for the contentious movements of May 1968 and June 1936. Ben Partridge. (Dr. Matt Perry and Dr. Sarah Leahy.) Newcastle Ph.D. (Hist.)

2459 I.M. Pei's museum architecture and internationalism. Sa Xiao. (Professor Michael White.) York Ph.D. (Hist. of Art)

2460 Questioning neutrality: Sino-Portuguese relations during the war and the post-war periods, 1937–49. Helena Ferreira Santos Lopes. (Professor Rana S.R. Mitter.) Oxford D.Phil. (Mod. Hist.)

2461 British government and the Inter-Governmental Committee on Refugees, 1938–43. Diana Packer. (Professor Tom Lawson.) Northumbria Ph.D. (Hist.)

2462 Transit routes and destinations: civilian evacuation within the British Empire during World War II. Bridget Deane. (Dr. Kent Fedorowich and Dr. Philip G. Ollerenshaw.) West of England Ph.D. (Hist.)

2463 Food and dining in the German defence: subsistence, logistics and American strategic culture in World War II. Jill Russell. (Professor Brian Holden Reid.) King's College London Ph.D. (War Stud.)

2464 War memory of World War II in Singapore: Australian, British and Singaporean perspectives. Emily Sharp. (Dr. Adam Cathcart and Dr. Jay Prosser.) Leeds M.A. (Hist.)

2465 Employing the enemy's enemy: a comparative study of the use of indigenous forces in the east African and Levantine campaigns of the Second World War. Jacob Stoil. (Dr. Rob Johnson and Dr. Peter Claus.) Oxford D.Phil. (Mod. Hist.)

2466 The foundations of modern food aid: field practice and values in complex emergencies, 1940–50. Alice Tligui. (Professor Peter Gatrell and Dr. Jen Peterson.) Manchester Ph.D. (Hist.)

2467 The Indian army in Africa and Italy, 1940–5. Alexander Wilson. (Professor Brian Holden Reid.) King's College London Ph.D. (War Stud.)

2468 Zen Buddhism in the Cold War Order between Japan and the U.S.A. (1941–73). Alice J. Freeman. (Dr. Sho Konishi.) Oxford D.Phil. (Mod. Hist.)

2469 Search for a common purpose: Commonwealth prime ministers' conferences, 1944–69. Robert J. O'Shea. (Dr. John G. Darwin.) Oxford D.Phil. (Mod. Hist.)

2470 Canadian civil affairs administration in north-west Europe, 1944–5. Michelle Fowler. (Professors Ian D. Thatcher and Donald M. MacRaild.) Ulster Ph.D. (Hist.)

2471 Medicine, famine and catastrophe in the shadow of World War II. Jan Lambertz. (Professor David Cesarani.) London Ph.D. (R.H.U.L. Hist.)

2472 Post-war theatrical images of Anne Frank in Britain, United States and France. Anna Scanlon. (Dr. Olaf Jensen.) Leicester Ph.D. (Hist.)

2473 The culture of international development in the United Kingdom, 1945–2000. Christopher Timms. (Dr. Peter Gurney.) Essex Ph.D. (Hist.)

2474 The consequences of forces overseas: a look at post-World War II U.S.-Philippine relations. Katie D. Whitcombe. (Professor Gregg Huff.) Oxford M.Phil. (Mod. Hist.)

2475 The commercialisation of mountain climbing, 1945–90. Thomas P. Barcham. (Dr. Jean Williams.) De Montfort Ph.D. (Hum.)

2476 Cold War animated film production. Natasha Neary. (Dr. Randall Stephens.) Northumbria Ph.D. (Hist.)

2477 The influence of Admiral Gorshkov and the U.S.-Soviet naval rivalry upon American naval thought. Jessica Huckabey. (Professors John Gooch and Holger H.W. Afflerbach.) Leeds Ph.D. (Hist.)

2478 The British empire and the Cold War. Christopher J. Sutton. East Anglia Ph.D. (Hist.)

2479 England and the end of the empire. Nicholas J. Swatman. East Anglia Ph.D. (Hist.)

2480 Abolishing capital punishment in the common law world, 1945–79. Thomas J. Wright. (Dr. Mark C. Roodhouse.) York Ph.D. (Hist.)

2481 The African Inland Mission, the African Inland Church and the development of global evangelicalism, 1945–75. Revd. Fleetwood L. Young. (Professor David W. Bebbington and Dr. Phia Steyn.) Stirling Ph.D. (Hist.)

2482 A changing world: colonial violence in Kenya and Cyprus and the emergence of a human rights 'conscious' Britain, 1945–65. Kate L.E. Kennedy. (Dr. John G. Darwin.) Oxford D.Phil. (Mod. Hist.)

2483 Cold War secret intelligence co-operation between Turkey and the West, 1945–60. Egemen Bezcei. (Professor John W. Young and Dr. Rory Cormac.) Nottingham Ph.D. (Hist.)

2484 Fighting over Nazis? Anglo-American intelligence rivalry in occupied Germany, 1945–55. Luke Daly-Groves. (Professor Simon J. Ball and Dr. Elisabeth Leake.) Leeds Ph.D. (Hist.)

2485 From forced labourers to displaced persons: experiences of Poles in the British zone of occupation, 1945–51. Samantha Knapton. (Professor T. Kirk and Dr. F. Schulz.) Newcastle Ph.D. (Hist.)

2486 The United States and the concentration camp trials at Dachau, 1945–7. Greta Louise Lawrence. (Professor Sir Richard J. Evans.) Cambridge Ph.D. (Hist.)

2487 Redisplaying the modern: a history of art exhibitions, artistic networks and institutions in the Middle East and North Africa, 1947–89. Amina Diab. (Dr. Jo Applin.) York Ph.D. (Hist. of Art)

2488 Sino-Indian relations, 1947–62. Anton Harder. (Professor O. Arne Westad.) London Ph.D. (L.S.E. Int. Hist.)

2489 British Foreign Office perspectives on the admission of Turkey and Greece to N.A.T.O., 1947–52. Norasmahani Hussain. (Dr. Elisabeth Leake and Dr. Will Jackson.) Leeds Ph.D. (Hist.)

2490 U.S. politics of betrayal: the Urdu press on Pakistan-U.S. relations since the 1971 war. Shakil Akhtar. (Dr. Philip Constable and Dr. Jonathon Colman.) Central Lancashire Ph.D. (Hum.)

2491 The international context of the art of St. Ives, 1948–60. Rachel Smith. (Professor Michael White.) York Ph.D. (Hist. of Art)

2492 Malaysia vs. Nigeria: palm oil and development, British business interests in the colonies post-independence. Gavin Purdie. (Professor Ray Stokes and Dr. Sumita Mukherjee.) Glasgow Ph.D. (Soc. Sc.)

2493 'What's past is prologue': the two Germanies and Israel, 1949–65. Lorena Devita. (Professor Jenny Edkins and Dr. Gerry Hughes.) Aberystwyth Ph.D. (Int. Pol.)

2494 Pyrrhic progress: agricultural antibiotics in Western agriculture, 1950–2013. Claas Kirchhelle. (Professor Mark Harrison.) Oxford D.Phil. (Mod. Hist.)

2495 Chinese foreign relations: the case of the port of Piraeus, 1950s–2000s. Gina Balta. (Professor Chris Bellamy and Dr. Martin Wilcox.) Greenwich M.Phil./Ph.D. (Greenwich Maritime Inst.)

2496 Female artists' fantasy of home-making in the world: Mona Hatoum, Yin Xiuzhen and Nikki S. Lee. Kuang Sheng. (Dr. Jo Applin.) York Ph.D. (Hist. of Art)

2497 American war journalism in Korea and Vietnam. Oliver Elliott. (Dr. Steven Casey.) London Ph.D. (L.S.E. Int. Hist.)

2498 'To supplement but not to supplant': the U.S. Embassy in Saigon and the American effort in Vietnam, 1950–7. Alex Ferguson. (Professor Kendrick Oliver.) Southampton Ph.D. (Hist.)

2499 Stalin's role in the origins of the Korean War. Yun Kim. (Dr. Jonathan Davis.) Anglia Ruskin D.Phil. (Hist.)

2500 End of empire policies and the politics of local elites: the British exit from south Arabia and the Gulf, 1951–72. Dennis Sammut. (Dr. James McDougall.) Oxford D.Phil. (Mod. Hist.)

2501 American foreign policy and de-Stalinisation, 1953–6. Weston Ullrich. (Dr. Steven Casey.) London Ph.D. (L.S.E. Int. Hist.)

2502 Conversations in clay: ceramic art and activity in Albisola, Italy and along the West Coast, L.A. (1954–66). Helen Shaw. (Dr. Jo Applin.) York Ph.D. (Hist. of Art)

2503 Counter-insurgency in Vietnam. Darren Poole. (Dr. Donna Jackson.) Chester Ph.D. (Hist. & Archaeol.)

2504 U.S. intervention in Lebanon, 1958. Michael Joel. (Professor Matthew Hughes.) Brunel Ph.D. (Pol. & Hist.)

2505 The U.S. pacification advisory effort in the Vietnam War from the perspective of the advisors. William N. Pulliam. (Dr. Gareth B. Davies and Dr. Robert Johnson.) Oxford D.Phil. (Mod. Hist.)

2506 The antiretroviral gay body: the production and governance of sexual subjectivities in the realm of H.I.V. prevention. Alvaro Martínez Lacabe. (Dr. Carrie Hamilton and Dr. Mike Brown.) Roehampton M.Phil./Ph.D. (Hist.)

2507 The commune movement during the 1960s and 1970s in Britain, Denmark and the United States. Sangdon Lee. (Professor Simon D. Hall and Dr. Stephan Petzold.) Leeds Ph.D. (Hist.)

2508 The American opposition to the Vietnam War which existed in Britain during the 1960s and 70s. Toby Lanyon Jones. (Professor Simon D. Hall.) Leeds Ph.D. (Hist.)

2509 U.S. cold war policy towards the Philippines in the 1960s. Ben Walker. (Dr. Aaron Moore and Dr. Pierre Fuller.) Manchester Ph.D. (Hist.)

2510 In defence of democracy: the political role of U.S. Special Operations in South Vietnam, 1961–75. Christopher Hoekstra. (Professor Jonathan Bell and Dr. Tony McCulloch.) U.C.L. M.Phil./Ph.D. (Inst. Amer.)

2511 Soviet and American covert and political actions in Portugal's Southern Africa, 1961–74. Petr Labrentsev. (Dr. Martin Folly and Dr. Kristian Gustafson.) Brunel Ph.D. (Pol. & Hist.)

2512 Placing knowledge in a decolonising world: the Commonwealth Fund for Technical Co-operation (C.F.T.C.) and the histories of expertise for development, 1965–90. Matthew Battey. (Professor Philip Murphy.) London Ph.D. (Inst. C'wealth Stud.)

2513 Victory and strategic culture: the Marines, the army and Vietnam – First Corps tactical zone, 1965–71. Arrigo Velicognia. (Professors Brian Holden Reid and Philip A.G. Sabin.) King's College London Ph.D. (War Stud.)

2514 'Reds in Space': American perceptions of the Soviet space programme from Apollo to Mir, 1967–91. Thomas Ellis. (Professor Kendrick Oliver.) Southampton M.Phil. (Hist.)

2515 Christian gay rights groups, 1967–80. Liam F. Fleming. (Dr. Matthew Grimley.) Oxford M.St. (Mod. Hist.)

2516 The United States and mediation strategies in the Egyptian-Israeli peace process, 1967–76. Ksenia Wesolowska. (Professor John W. Young and Dr. Nick Thomas.) Nottingham Ph.D. (Hist.)

2517 The Sino-American bilateral exchange programme and U.S. support for China's reform and opening, 1969–89. Peter Millwood. (Professor O. Arne Westad.) London Ph.D. (L.S.E. Int. Hist.)

2518 Britain, the United States and the radicalisation of Qaddafi's Libya, 1969–86. Amal Tarhuni. (Dr. Kirstin E. Schulze and Professor O. Arne Westad.) London Ph.D. (L.S.E. Int. Hist.)

2519 The changing character of war and terrorist network adaptation. Melissa L. Skorka. (Dr. Robert Johnson.) Oxford D.Phil. (Mod. Hist.)

2520 Orthodox economics, social norms and the financial services, 1970 to the present. Masud Ally. (Professor Avner Offer.) Oxford D.Phil. (Mod. Hist.)

2521 Contemporary Jewish responses to interfaith dialogue. Wendy Fidler. (Professor Tony Kushner.) Southampton Ph.D. (Hist.)

2522 'Voices from Slough': a socio-historic empirical analysis of Somali refugees and 'Accession Eight' Polish economic migrants. Mel Cox. (Professor K. Humayun Ansari.) London Ph.D. (R.H.U.L. Hist.)

2523 British world influence in the 1970s. Andrew Southam. (Professor Philip Murphy.) London M.Phil. (Inst. C'wealth Stud.)

2524 U.S.-Egyptian 'joint strategy', 1972–6: planning and implementation/history of U.S. foreign relations, Cold War, Middle East. Aidan Condron. (Dr. Andrew Priest and Dr. James Vaughan.) Aberystwyth Ph.D. (Int. Pol.)

2525 Britain and American foreign policy concerning Cyprus, 1973–80. Marilena Varnava. (Professor Philip Murphy.) London M.Phil. (Inst. C'wealth Stud.)

2526 U.S. foreign policy towards Afghanistan: identity and geostrategy. Anthony Teitler. (Professor Iwan Morgan and Dr. Tony McCulloch.) U.C.L. Ph.D. (Inst. Amer.)

2527 The American influence on Sino-British relations: from recognition to full diplomatic relations. Emily Stephens. (Dr. Michael Hopkins.) Liverpool Ph.D. (Hist.)

2528 Clinging like barnacles to the old hull of empire: Anglo-American relations and British foreign policy and the Rhodesian crisis, 1976–80. Todd Carter. (Dr. Ben Jackson.) Oxford M.Phil. (Mod. Hist.)

2529 The politics of monetarism, 1978–87. Adam Broadbent. (Professor Peter J. Hennessy.) London M.Phil. (Q.M. Hist.)

2530 The impact of state polices on growth through innovation: an analysis of Germany and China. Nasira Bradley. (Professor Ray Stokes and Dr. Celine Azemar.) Glasgow Ph.D. (Bus.)

2531 Turning tables: interrogating silence and violence in war-related artistic practice since 1980. Konstantinos Stasinopoulos. (Dr. Jo Applin.) York Ph.D. (Hist. of Art)

2532 The legacies of colonialism and the Final Solution: an intellectual history of British and French anti-racist memory culture, c.1981–2001. Patrick Soulsby. (Dr. Daniel Gordon.) Edge Hill Ph.D. (English & Hist.)

2533 The consequences of the Reagan doctrine wars in Central America, Angola and Afghanistan. Todd R. Greentree. (Dr. Robert Johnson and Professor Hew Strachan.) Oxford D.Phil. (Mod. Hist.)

2534 Britain and the Falklands crisis: international perspectives, 1982–90. John Bagnall. (Dr. Martin Farr and Dr. Sarah Campbell.) Newcastle Ph.D. (Hist.)

2535 The relationship between anti-semitism and Islamophobia. Doerte Letzmann. (Professor David Cesarani.) London Ph.D. (R.H.U.L. Hist.)

2536 The '"cork" in the bottle': explaining Reagan's failure to confront Iran. Nicholas Cummins. (Dr. Andrew Johnstone.) Leicester Ph.D. (Hist.)

2537 Squaring the circle: shaping cultural tourism policy and practice in UNESCO World Heritage cities. Courtney Fleming. (Dr. Alison Hems and Dr. Darren Hoad.) Bath Spa Ph.D. (Hist. & Cultural Stud.)

2538 Pop Goth: transgressive fandom in contemporary art. Ana F. Honigman. (Dr. Alastair Wright.) Oxford D.Phil. (Mod. Hist.)

2539 The reshaping of U.S. foreign policy and the Yugoslav crises, 1990–5. David Berman. (Dr. Svetozar Rajak.) London Ph.D. (L.S.E. Int. Hist.)

2540 Gendered rememberings: sexual violence in the aftermath of conflict. Lydia Cole. (Dr. Patrick Finney and Dr. Jenny Mathers.) Aberystwyth Ph.D. (Int. Pol.)

2541 'Trouble at the top': the U.N., Rwanda and genocide. Herman Salton. (Professor Michael Foley and Dr. Simon Rushton.) Aberystwyth Ph.D. (Int. Pol.)

2542 To what extent does the 'Barcelona Process: Union for the Mediterranean' offer real partnership and equal economic benefits to the Middle East partners? Madlen Rabadi. (Professor Martin Evans and Dr. Hilary Kalmbach.) Sussex D.Phil. (Hist.)

2543 U.S. foreign policy and the 'war on terror': Iraq, Iran and Saudi Arabia. Stephanie Cassidy. (Dr. Leonie Murray and Dr. Dianne Kirby.) Ulster Ph.D. (Hist.)

2544 S.O.F. landing: U.S. special operations forces and the Battle of Tora Bora. James O'Connell. (Professor Stephen Tuck.) Oxford M.St. (Mod. Hist.)

2545 'Behavioural selves'. An epigraph for social media information, identity, selfhood: Facebook as a technology of the self. Chris Fletcher. (Dr. Yoke-Sum Wong.) Lancaster Ph.D. (Hist.)

2546 Failure by design: responses to, and implications of, the Arab Spring on U.S. foreign policy. Stephanie Kutshcmann. London M.Phil./Ph.D. (R.H.U.L. Hist.)

2547 The commemoration of the abolition of the transatlantic slave trade and the memorialisation of historical trauma. Marian Gwynn. (Professor Raimund Karl and Dr. Christian Koller.) Bangor Ph.D. (Hist., Welsh Hist. & Archaeol.)

AFRICA

General

2548 Missionary agendas, slavery and identity in Belgian colonial Africa, 1880–1939. David Whitehouse. Exeter Ph.D. (Hist.)

2549 Belgian Africa at war: Europeans in the Belgian Congo and Ruanda-Urundi, 1940–5. Guy Bud. Oxford M.Phil (Mod. Hist.)

North Africa

2550 Civic epigraphy and Roman Cyrenaica. Muna H. Haroun H.H. Abdelhamed. (Professors David J. Mattingly and David Edwards.) Leicester Ph.D. (Archaeol. & Anc. Hist.)

2551 Death is another country: mortuary rituals and cultural identity in Fazzan, Libya. Mireya González Rodríguez. (Professor David J. Mattingly and Dr. David Edwards.) Leicester Ph.D. (Archaeol. & Anc. Hist.)

2552 Pseudo-Chrysostom texts and the formation of patristic authority in North Africa (c.450–c.550). Sukanya Raisharma. (Dr. Conrad Leyser and Dr. Neil McLynn.) Oxford D.Phil. (Mod. Hist.)

2553 Conquests of Egypt: making history in the Abbasid period. Edward P. Zychowicz-Coghill. (Dr. Robert Hoyland and Dr. Mark Whittow.) Oxford D.Phil. (Mod. Hist.)

2554 Treasure hunting and grave robbery in Islamic Egypt – an analysis of Arabic manuals for treasure hunters. Christopher Braun. (Professor Charles S.F. Burnett and Dr. Konrad Hirschler.) London Ph.D. (Warburg)

2555 The other Christian warriors: the north-east African influence on the crusades. Adam Simmons. (Professor Andrew Jotischky.) Lancaster Ph.D. (Hist.)

2556 Olive presses and oil production in Cyrenaica (north-east Libya). Ahmed M. Buzaian. (Professor David Mattingly and Dr. Daniel Stewart.) Leicester Ph.D. (Archaeol. & Anc. Hist.)

2557 Environmental and climatic history of south Sinai, Egypt. Caroline Servaes. (Professors Georgina Endfield and Francis Gilbert.) Nottingham Ph.D. (Geog.)

2558 British diplomatic engagement in north Africa: a study of consular activity in Tripoli, 1795–1835. Sara ElGaddari. (Dr. David J. Starkey.) Hull Ph.D. (Hist.)

2559 Slavery and social life in Libya during the 19th and early 20th centuries. Amal al Taleb. (Dr. Laurence Brown and Dr. Steven Pierce.) Manchester Ph.D. (Hist.)

2560 'The falcon and the falconer': state, society and politics in colonial Egypt, 1872–1919. Hussein Omar. (Dr. Eugene L. Rogan.) Oxford D.Phil. (Mod. Hist.)

2561 Repercussions: international news in colonial Algeria, 1881–1940. Arthur Asseraf. (Dr. James McDougall.) Oxford D.Phil. (Mod. Hist.)

2562 International health, water and the political economy of development: Uganda and Sudan, 1898–1995. Joanna Lunt. (Professor Sanjoy Bhattacharya.) York Ph.D. (Hist.)

2563 The social history of Benghazi under Italian colonial rule through the judicial records. Aisha Mossa Soleman. (Dr. Christian Koller.) Bangor Ph.D. (Hist., Welsh Hist. & Archaeol.)

2564 The rise of Egyptian nationalism: the case of the 1919 Egyptian revolution. Nabila Ramdani. (Dr. Kirsten E. Schulze.) London Ph.D. (L.S.E. Int. Hist.)

2565 Outside the walls (suburban zones of towns in Cyrenaica). Mohammed Omar M. Abdrbba. (Professor David Mattingly and Dr. Jeremy Taylor.) Leicester Ph.D. (Archaeol. & Anc. Hist.)

Africa

2566   From Tobruk to Tunis: the impact of topography and improvisation on British military doctrine and tactics, North Africa, 1940–3. Neal Dando. (Dr. Harry Bennett and Professor Kevin Jefferys.) Plymouth Ph.D. (Hum.)

2567   The political influence of the British military administration on the Libyans in Tripolitana, 1943–51. Mohammed Esseqaire. (Dr. Christian Koller.) Bangor Ph.D. (Hist., Welsh Hist. & Archaeol.)

2568   The cultural life in Libya under the British military administration, 1943–51. Yousef Madi. (Dr. Christian Koller.) Bangor Ph.D. (Hist., Welsh Hist. & Archaeol.)

2569   Development narratives in south Sudan since c.1945. Sarah Marriott. (Professor Justin Willis and Dr. Donna Leonardi.) Durham Ph.D. (Hist.)

2570   Revolutions confined: a social history of political imprisonment in Egypt, 1949–2009. Hannah E. Ashmawi. (Dr. Lucie Ryzova and Professor Robert Gildea.) Oxford D.Phil. (Mod. Hist.)

2571   Banking and finance in Sudan, 1956–77. Harry Cross. (Dr. Cherry Leonardi and Professor Justin Willis.) Durham Ph.D. (Hist.)

2572   Critical responses to globalisation in contemporary North African and diaspora art. Katarzyna W. Falecka. (Dr. Hanneke Grootenboer.) Oxford M.St. (Mod. Hist.)

2573   Nation-building remembered: social memory in contemporary Algeria. Edward J. McAllister. (Dr. James McDougall.) Oxford D.Phil. (Mod. Hist.)

2574   The fourth ordeal: history of the Muslim Brotherhood, 1973–2013. Victor J. Willi. (Dr. James McDougall.) Oxford D.Phil. (Mod. Hist.)

2575   S.P.L.A. Oyee! The Sudan People's Liberation Movement and army in exile, 1983–98. Sebabatso C. Manoeli. (Professor Jocelyn Alexander.) Oxford D.Phil. (Mod. Hist.)

West Africa

2576   The English West African experience in the early modern era, 1587–1672. Lior Blum. (Dr. Christer Petley.) Southampton M.Phil. (Hist.)

2577   Slavery, memory and orality: a case study of 19th-century Ghana. Emmanuel Saboro. (Professors David Richardson and John Oldfield.) Hull Ph.D. (Hist.)

2578   Cotton growing and textile production in northern Nigeria: from caliphate to protectorate, c.1804–1914. Marisa Candotti. (Dr. John Parker.) London Ph.D. (S.O.A.S. Hist.)

2579   The export of British printed textiles to West Africa, 1850–1914. Josephine Tierney. (Professor Giorgio Riello and David Anderson.) Warwick M.Phil./Ph.D. (Hist.)

2580   Treates as the diplomatic tool in the pacification, legalisation and colonisation of the lower Niger, 1885–1914. Charles Ariye. (Dr. Rachel Bright and Dr. Shalini Sharma.) Keele Ph.D. (Hist.)

2581   Between famine and malnutrition: Spatial aspects of nutritional health during Ghana's long 20th century, c.1890–2000. John Nott. (Dr. Shane Doyle.) Leeds Ph.D. (Hist.)

2582 'Budding forth in its nascent growth': English-language and Yoruba-language newspapers in the Lagos printing sphere. Katharina A. Oke. (Dr. Jan-Georg Deutsch.) Oxford D.Phil. (Mod. Hist.)

2583 The history of childhood in colonial Ghana, c.1900–57. Jack Lord. (Dr. John Parker.) London Ph.D. (S.O.A.S. Hist.)

2584 Sex, race and health in fascist colonial policy: the fight against venereal disease in Italian Africa, 1922–43. Meredith Carew. (Dr. M. Harrison and Dr. J. Pollard.) Oxford D.Phil. (Mod. Hist.)

2585 Political press in southern Ghana and southern Nigeria: nationalism, visuality and professionalism, c.1937–66. Rouven Kunstmann. (Dr. Jan-Georg Deutsch.) Oxford D.Phil. (Mod. Hist.)

2586 The business of empire in late colonial Nigeria: Shell-B.P. and the politics of decolonisation, c.1946–67. Christopher Minton. (Dr. Spencer W. Mawby and Dr. A. Greenward.) Nottingham Ph.D. (Hist.)

2587 Islamic associations and economic development in Niger. Ignatius Anipu. (Dr. John S. Parker.) London Ph.D. (S.O.A.S. Hist.)

2588 The West African Students' Union and its relationship with the British government, the African diaspora and West African independence movements at home. Imachibundu Onuzo. (Dr. Sarah Stockwell and Professor Richard H. Drayton.) King's College London M.Phil./Ph.D. (Hist.)

2589 The road to ruin – Sierra Leone, 1961–99. Richard Stowell. (Dr. Heike Schmidt.) Reading Ph.D. (Hist.)

2590 Footprints on the neoliberal frontier: PMSCs and resource extraction. Jethro Norman. (Dr. Raymond C. Bush and Dr. Nir Arielli.) Leeds Ph.D. (Hist.)

East and central Africa

2591 Legacies of British imperial administrators working in postcolonial East Africa. Robert Joy. (Dr. Christopher Prior.) Southampton M.Phil. (Hist.)

2592 Lake Tanganyika: commercial frontier in the era of long-distance commerce, east and central Africa, c.1830–90. Philip Gooding. (Professor Richard Reid.) London Ph.D. (S.O.A.S. Hist.)

2593 Masculinities and violence in Acholiland, 1860 to the present. Lucy Taylor. (Dr. Shane D. Doyle.) Leeds Ph.D. (Hist.)

2594 Uganda, the politics of identity and landscape in Uganda's Albertine Rift Valley since c.1860. Adrian J. Browne. (Professor Justin Willis and Dr. Cherry Leonardi.) Durham Ph.D. (Hist.)

2595 Religious encounter in the Nyungwe region of the middle Zambezi, c.1870–1950. Antonio Marizane. (Dr. John Parker.) London Ph.D. (S.O.A.S. Hist.)

2596 British collecting in East Africa 1880–1940, with special focus on the British Museum. Alison Bennett. (Professor Margot Finn and Dr. Sarah Longair.) London Ph.D. (U.C. Hist.)

2597 Unity is strength? The construction of political community in Kenya and Tanzania, 1900–70. Edward K. Goodman. (Dr. Jan-Georg Deutsch.) Oxford D.Phil. (Mod. Hist.)

2598 Freedom as fiction: the ending of legal-status slavery in Mombasa, Kenya, 1907–63. Feisal Farah. (Professors David Richardson and Michael Turner.) Hull Ph.D. (Hist.)

2599 Mwomboko: performing historical narratives of Kenya between the 1920s and today. Cecile Feza Bushidi. (Dr. John Parker.) London Ph.D. (S.O.A.S. Hist.)

2600 The pursuit of the 'good forest' in colonial Kenya: the interaction between state-led scientific forestry, private enterprise and African labour. Ben Fanstone. (Dr. Phia Steyn and Dr. Paul Adderley.) Stirling Ph.D. (Hist.)

2601 British church and state in Tanganyika, 1920–61. John S. Stubbings. (Dr. Jan-Georg Deutsch.) Oxford D.Phil. (Mod. Hist.)

2602 Colonialisms, markets and power: a transnational approach to state formation in the Somalia-Kenya borderlands, c.1925–63. Anna Bruzzone. (Professors David Anderson and Daniel Branch.) Warwick Ph.D. (Hist.)

2603 Imperial and international responses to forced and early marriage in British colonial Africa, c.1926–62. Rhian Keyse. (Dr. Stacey Hynd and Professor Kate Fisher.) Exeter Ph.D. (Hist.)

2604 Consuming communities: the making of an African middle class in Nairobi, 1930s–70s. Andrea Scheibler. (Professor David Anderson.) Oxford D.Phil. (Mod. Hist.)

2605 Women and childbirth in Haile Selassie's Ethiopia. Julianne R. Weis. (Dr. Sloan C. Mahone.) Oxford D.Phil. (Mod. Hist.)

2606 The Koinange dynasty and the development of Kenyan politics. Daniel Ostendorff. (Dr. Sloan Mahone.) Oxford D.Phil. (Mod. Hist.)

2607 The Kenyan financial system: from motionless to rashless, 1950–90. Christian Velasco-Reyes. (Professors David Anderson and Daniel Branch.) Warwick Ph.D. (Hist.)

2608 The state of the Somali State-Society Foundation, formation and formulation, 1950–69. Mohamed Haji Abdullahi. (Dr. Jan-Georg Deutsch.) Oxford D.Phil. (Mod. Hist.)

2609 British colonial identity in Northern Rhodesia and Kenya: emotions, race, and violence at the end of empire, 1945–65. Joshua Doble. (Dr. Shane D. Doyle and Dr. Will Jackson.) Leeds Ph.D. (Hist.)

2610 'Walking the talk'? Kenya, Oxfam and development, 1955–97. James C. Morris. (Dr. Gerald McCann.) York Ph.D. (Hist.)

2611 The Anglo-American special relationship and decolonisation in the Central African Federation, 1957–63. Claire Melland. (Dr. Andrew Johnstone.) Leicester Ph.D. (Hist.)

2612 A historical and contemporary study of adult literacy and language in Kenya. Riaz Manji. (Professor Gary McCulloch and Dr. Tom Woodin.) London Ph.D. (Inst. of Educ.)

2613 Women's running and the political economy of gender in Kenya. Michelle Sikes.
(Dr. Jan-Georg Deutsch and Dr. Nicholas Cheeseman.) Oxford D.Phil. (Mod. Hist.)

Southern Africa

2614 Violence, race and civilisation: the premises and self-assertion of trusteeship
and imperial control in Anglo-German southern Africa. Mads Bomholt Nielsen.
(Professors Francisco Bethencourt and Richard H. Drayton.) King's College London
M.Phil./Ph.D. (Hist.)

2615 The Griqua and their neighbours: trading, raiding and relationships on the margins of
Cape society, 1800–74. Peter McKean. (Dr. Zoe Laidlaw.) London M.Phil./Ph.D.
(R.H.U.L. Hist.)

2616 Persistence of French influence on Mauritius after 1810. Michael Allan. (Professor
Clare Anderson.) Leicester Ph.D. (Hist.)

2617 A social history of gentlemen and their clubs in South Africa, c.1860–1960. Danielle
Dunbar. (Dr. John G. Darwin.) Oxford D.Phil. (Mod. Hist.)

2618 Chiefship, power and state in the Bakgatla community in Botswana, 1870–2014.
Louisa Cantwell. (Emma Hunter.) Cambridge Ph.D. (Hist.)

2619 South African Jews in British entertainment and culture. Danielle Lockwood. (Dr.
James Jordan and Dr. Shirli Gilbert.) Southampton M.Phil. (Hist.)

2620 Ireland and the South African war, 1899–1902: nationalist and unionist responses.
Lewis Hendrick. (Professor Thomas Hennessey.) Canterbury Christ Church M.Phil.
(Hist.)

2621 Metropolitan actors and men on the spot: explaining the refugee camp crisis in the
Second Boer War. Timothy Ross. (Dr. Miles Larmer.) Oxford M.St. (Mod. Hist.)

2622 Land, settlement and competing narratives of history in northern Bushbuckridge,
1900–70. James Cockfield. (Professor William J. Beinart.) Oxford D.Phil. (Mod.
Hist.)

2623 White workers and the production of race in colonial Zimbabwe, 1910–80. Nicola
Ginsburg. (Dr. Will Jackson and Dr. Shane D. Doyle.) Leeds Ph.D. (Hist.)

2624 A social history of Copperbelt settlers, 1926–74. Duncan J. Money. (Dr. Jan-Georg
Deutsch.) Oxford D.Phil. (Mod. Hist.)

2625 Resistance and complicities: literature and the history of postcolonial Angola.
Dorothee Boulanger. (Dr. Vincent Hiribarren.) King's College London M.Phil./Ph.D.
(Hist.)

2626 Colouring the Cape: how did the National Party's city planning policies help realise
the ideology of apartheid and racially organise the Cape Townian community,
1950–70? James W. Hutton. (Dr. Miles Larmer.) Oxford M.St. (Mod. Hist.)

2627 Urban growth and decline on the Copperbelt in Zambia, c.1955–2000. Daniel F. Hall.
(Dr. James Fenske.) Oxford M.Sc. (Mod. Hist.)

2628 Race and non-black Africanists in the emergence of Zimbabwean mass nationalist
politics, 1957–66. Joshua Pritchard. (Professor David Maxwell.) Cambridge Ph.D.
(Hist.)

2629 Populism and the rise of Michael Sata in Zambia, 1962–2011. Dipak Sishuwa. (Dr. Jan-Georg Deutsch and Dr. Nicholas Cheeseman.) Oxford D.Phil. (Mod. Hist.)

2630 Invisible labourers: histories of female domestic workers in post-colonial Zambia. Sacha M. Hepburn. (Dr. Miles Larmer.) Oxford D.Phil. (Mod. Hist.)

2631 Britain and the U.D.I.-era Rhodesia: kith and kin? David W. Kenrick. (Professor Jocelyn Alexander.) Oxford D.Phil. (Mod. Hist.)

2632 Soothsayers and troublemakers: opposition party mobilisation strategies in Zimbabwe, Zambia and Uganda. Nicole Beardsworth. (Professors Gabrielle Lynch and David Anderson.) Warwick Ph.D. (Pol.)

2633 On the edge of history: small political parties and groupings in South Africa's transition, 1990–6. Jason T. Robinson. (Professor William J. Beinart.) Oxford D.Phil. (Mod. Hist.)

AMERICA AND WEST INDIES

General

2634 The cultural history of the voodoo doll. Natalie Armitage. (Dr. Natalie Zacek.) Manchester Ph.D. (English, Amer. Stud. & Creative Writing)

2635 Antebellum black-Indian history of the Caribbean South. Mandy Izadi. (Professor Richard J. Carwardine and Dr. Jay Sexton.) Oxford D.Phil. (Mod. Hist.)

2636 The experience of slave soldiers in the war of independence in New York State and the Mexican region of Corboda. Liam Physick. (Professor Manuel Barcia Paz and Dr. Andrea Major.) Leeds Ph.D. (Hist.)

2637 'A luminous constellation pointing the way'? North Americans, federalism and Rioplatense and Chilean federative republics, 1810–19. David M. Jones. (Dr. Natasha Glaisyer.) York M.A. (Hist.)

2638 Fear, honour and bravado: slave rebellions in the elite white male psyche in South Carolina and Cuba, 1830–50. Liana-Beatrice Valerio. (Professor Tim Lockley and Dr. Camilia Cowling.) Warwick M.Phil./Ph.D. (Hist.)

2639 Metropolitan British perceptions of Canada and British North America, 1837–90. Christopher P. Morash. (Dr. John Darwin.) Oxford M.St. (Mod. Hist.)

2640 Structural features of U.S. empire in Central America. Josh Hollis. (Professors Richard H. Drayton and Ian McBride.) King's College London M.Phil./Ph.D. (Hist.)

2641 The process of memory: Native American massacre sites, 1863–90. Susannah Hopson. (Professors Joy Porter and David Crouch.) Hull Ph.D. (Hist.)

2642 George and Florence Blumenthal: a collecting partnership in the gilded age. Rebecca Tilles. (Dr. Flora Dennis and Dr. Francesco Ventrella.) Sussex D.Phil. (Hist. of Art)

2643   Health on distant shores: the American intervention in Puerto Rican public health, 1898–1952. Linda C. Magana. (Professor Mark Harrison and Dr. Gareth Davies.) Oxford D.Phil. (Mod. Hist.)

2644   The impact of World War I on Native Americans. Emily Magrath. (Dr. Karen Salt and Dr. Thomas Weber.) Aberdeen Ph.D. (Hist.)

2645   Theodore Roosevelt and U.S.-Latin American relations. Elizabeth Davidson. (Dr. Michael Cullinane.) Northumbria Ph.D. (Hist.)

2646   The totalitarian disease: the American intellectual left, body politics and the image of America in the world from the Cold War to the War on Terror. Sophie Louise Josceleyne. (Professor Robert Cook and Dr. Katharina Rietzler.) Sussex D.Phil. (Hist.)

2647   Senator Jesse Helms in central America, 1973–92. Andrew Stead. (Dr. Alex Goodall.) York Ph.D. (Hist.)

2648   Promoting democracy? The role of U.S. N.G.O.s in inter-American relations, 1980–93. Mara Sankey. (Professor Nicola A. Miller.) London Ph.D. (U.C. Hist.)

Canada

2649   The Hudson Bay Company, 1666–1821: entrepreneurship of the individual and entrepreneurship of the firm. Dean Lymath. (Dr. Sheryllynne Haggerty and Dr. David Appleby.) Nottingham Ph.D. (Hist.)

2650   Migration of British and Irish military veterans to the Canadian colonies and the development of settler societies, 1760–1826. Shane Smith. (Dr. Joe Hardwick.) Northumbria Ph.D. (Hist.)

2651   Hidden voices of the Nuu'Chah'Nulth women from Captain Cook to the present day. Jacky Moore. (Dr. Sam Hitchmough.) Canterbury Christ Church M.Phil. (Hist.)

2652   The Butler Homesta site: the archaeology of a loyalist homestead in early upper Canada, 1784–1813. Denise McGuire. (Dr. Jane Webster and Professor Susan-Mary Grant.) Newcastle Ph.D. (Archaeol.)

2653   Upper Canada foodways: an analysis of faunal remains recovered from urban household and rural farmsteads in York, Toronto, 1794–1900. Eric Tourigny. (Dr. Richard Thomas and Professor Marijke van der Veen.) Leicester Ph.D. (Archaeol. & Anc. Hist.)

2654   The Saugeen Ojibway Nation and Canada: indigenous and immigrant transnationals and the ends of settler colonialism. Christopher Wright. (Professor Richard H. Drayton and Dr. Simon Sleight.) King's College London M.Phil./Ph.D. (Hist.)

2655   Mapping and charting the Canadian Arctic: from Franklin to Harper. Rosanna White. (Professor Klaus Dodds.) London M.Phil./Ph.D. (R.H.U.L. Geog.)

2656   Memory of residential schools in Canada: naming and remembering atrocity. Tricia Logan. (Professor Dan Stone.) London M.Phil./Ph.D. (R.H.U.L. Hist.)

2657   Jingoism and its discontents: statecraft and political thought in British-Canadian imperial relations, 1887–1914. Graeme Thompson. (Professor James Belich.) Oxford D.Phil. (Mod. Hist.)

2658　'A most lamentable state of affairs': Canada, Ireland, and the imperial conscription crises, 1915–18. Alexandre Angle. (Dr. John Darwin.) Oxford M.St. (Mod. Hist.)

Colonial America and the U.S.A.

2659　Understanding a ritual landscape: an investigation into the rock art of the Jornada Mogollon region of the American Southwest. Belinda Mollard. (Dr. Mark Gilling and Dr. Huw Barton.) Leicester Ph.D. (Archaeol. & Anc. Hist.)

2660　The late woodland period (A.D. 900–1607) in coastal Virginia: dietary adaptation and population mobility. Dane Magoon. (Dr. Joanna Appleby and Dr. Huw Barton.) Leicester Ph.D. (Archaeol. & Anc. Hist.)

2661　Savagery and civilisation: representations of Americans in English print culture, 1492–1607. Rachel Winchcombe. (Dr. Sasha Handley and Dr. Jenny Spinks.) Manchester Ph.D. (Hist.)

2662　Variation in the architecture and design of gravemarkers in Great Britain and British North America, 1600–1800. Jonathan Kewley. (Dr. Adrian Green.) Durham Ph.D. (Hist.)

2663　An exploration into the daily life, social conditions and social integration of white indentured servitude in colonial America in the 17th and 18th centuries. Leanne McMullan. (Dr. Gabriel Guarino and Professor Donald M. MacRaild.) Ulster Ph.D. (Hist.)

2664　Transplanted puritan networks in the 17th century: the English roots of an American controversy. Sarah K. Hall. East Anglia Ph.D. (Hist.)

2665　Anglo-American perceptions of Christian Indians in colonial New England, 1607–1780. Tumi Belo. (Professor Pekka Hämäläinen.) Oxford M.St. (Mod. Hist.)

2666　Fit to put on the face of Commonwealth? Commonwealth discourse, politics and culture in England and Virginia, c.1607–42. Misha Ewen. (Professor Jason Peacey.) London Ph.D. (U.C. Hist.)

2667　The public sphere and political culture in New England, 1630–1710. John S. Springford. (Dr. P.J. Thompson.) Oxford D.Phil. (Mod. Hist.)

2668　Black serfs: the influence of feudalism, religious conflict and Englishness on the institutionalisation of slavery in Maryland under the proprietorship of the Lords Baltimore, 1634–89. Helen Kilburn. (Dr. Natalie Zacek.) Manchester Ph.D. (English, Amer. Stud. & Creative Writing)

2669　Comparing attitudes toward infertility in early modern England and colonial New England, c.1650–1750. Marisa Benoit. (Dr. Erica Charters and Dr. Margaret Pelling.) Oxford D.Phil. (Mod. Hist.)

2670　A comparative study of American and British towns, 1660–1840. Sarah Collins. (Professor David Gleeson.) Northumbria Ph.D. (Hist.)

2671　The border states and their response to free people of colour. Julia Lawton. (Dr. Laura Sandy and Dr. Kathleen Cushing.) Keele Ph.D. (Hist.)

2672　English guns, gun components and the role of firearms in colonial North America. John Stewart. Dundee Ph.D. (Hist.)

2673　Transatlantic consumerism in the 18th century: a comparative study of the material culture of ordinary people in Britain and its American colonies.　Catherine Talbot.　Exeter M.Phil. (Hist.)

2674　The cultural paradigms of British imperialism in the militarisation of Scotland and North America, 1715–75.　Nicola Martin.　(Dr. Colin Nicolson and Dr. Alastair Mann.)　Stirling Ph.D. (Hist.)

2675　Privateers of the American Revolution from the New England ports of Salem and Newbury Port, Massachusetts.　Maria Pride.　(Dr. Colin Nicolson and Dr. Emma MacLeod.)　Stirling Ph.D. (Hist.)

2676　Did military honour hinder the effective use of American Indians by the British in the Sixty Years' War?　T.J. Linzy.　(Dr. Alan James and Dr. Wayne Lee.)　King's College London Ph.D. (War Stud.)

2677　Construction of American identity in Boston, New York and Philadelphia, 1754–83.　Angel O'Donnell.　(Dr. Keith Mason.)　Liverpool Ph.D. (Hist.)

2678　Intrepid and loyal: the highland regiments in the French and Indian war.　Richard Loutzenheiser.　(Dr. Matthew Ward and Dr. Derek Patrick.)　Dundee Ph.D. (Hist.)

2679　Edward Braddock, Lord Loudoun and the British war effort in North America, 1755–7.　Richard Hall.　(Dr. Stephen J. Sarson.)　Swansea Ph.D. (Hist.)

2680　Lost horizons: the United States and the challenge of British North America, 1760–1871.　Gareth Davis.　(Professor Stephen Conway and Dr. Adam Smith.)　London Ph.D. (U.C. Hist.)

2681　The asylum and the Church: religion, madness and medical practice in England and America, 1760–1850.　Mark W. Lee.　(Dr. Jane Garnett.)　Oxford D.Phil. (Mod. Hist.)

2682　Liverpool merchants, British imperialism and the American revolution, 1763–83.　Simon Hill.　(Dr. Nicholas J. White, Dr. Anthony Webster and Dr. Sheryllynne Haggerty.)　Liverpool John Moores Ph.D. (Hist.)

2683　Liberty, property, and no excise: the cider excise and the American Stamp Act crisis, 1763–6.　Trent DeW. Taylor.　(Dr. Peter Thompson and Dr. Nicholas Cole.)　Oxford M.St. (Mod. Hist.)

2684　Spies, civil liberties and the Senate.　Daffyd Townley.　(Dr. Mara Oliva.)　Reading Ph.D. (Hist.)

2685　Making Louisiana a slave state, making the U.S. a slave nation: new perspectives on the Louisiana Purchase, 1769–1820.　Kathryn Olivarius.　(Professors Lawrence Goldman and Pekka Hämäläinen.)　Oxford D.Phil. (Mod. Hist.)

2686　Extralegal, religious, and legal discipline in Harvard, Massachusetts from 1772 to 1812.　Kristine Tomlinson.　(Dr. Simon Middleton.)　Sheffield M.Phil. (Hist.)

2687　Paine and Hitchens: prophets of American messianism.　Bum Sun Jun.　(Dr. Brian Young.)　Oxford M.St. (Mod. Hist.)

2688　John Adams: friendship and politics, c.1774–1801.　Jamie Macpherson.　(Dr. Colin Nicolson and Dr. Emma Macleod.)　Stirling Ph.D. (Hist.)

2689 Music and political culture in the United States from the early republic to the civil war era. William Coleman. (Dr. Adam Smith.) London Ph.D. (U.C. Hist.)

2690 Environmental history of the middle Missouri river valley, 1779–1840. Jason Kaufman. (Professor Pekka Hämäläinen.) Oxford M.St. (Mod. Hist.)

2691 'A new promised land'? Faith, power, wealth and the slavery question in early Kentucky, 1780–1830. Jonathan De Vries. (Dr. Matthew C. Ward and Professor James Livesey.) Dundee Ph.D. (Hist.)

2692 Enslaved wet nurses in antebellum America. Rosie Knight. (Dr. Emily R. West.) Reading Ph.D. (Hist.)

2693 Fear of the armed black man in the white male psyche: the extent to which slave rebellions were 'unthinkable' events in the antebellum old South. Liana B. Valerio. (Dr. Peter Thompson.) Oxford M.St. (Mod. Hist.)

2694 Thomas Jefferson and slavery in Virginia, c.1785–1821. Stuart McBratney. (Mr. Neil Curtin and Professor Christopher Aldous.) Winchester M.Phil./Ph.D. (Hist.)

2695 Beyond removal: Indians, states and sovereignties in the American South during the long 19th century. Jane Dinwoodie. (Professor Pekka Hämäläinen.) Oxford D.Phil. (Mod. Hist.)

2696 Black literacy and slave rebelliousness in the United States South between c.1790–1810. Shaun Wallace. (Dr. Colin Nicolson and Dr. E. Hart.) Stirling Ph.D. (Hist.)

2697 Cancer in Britain, 1792–1914. Agnes Arnold-Forster. (Dr. Abigail Woods.) King's College London M.Phil./Ph.D. (Hist.)

2698 Cruelty discourses on abusive marriages: a comparative study of 19th-century central Scotland and New York, U.S.A. Meagan Butler. (Dr. Annemarie Hughes and Professor Eleanor J. Gordon.) Glasgow Ph.D. (Soc. Sc.)

2699 'The style of politics and the politics of style': an analysis of early Washington society and the political culture of the nation's capital. Joseph C. Hepplewhite. (Professor Pekka Hämäläinen and Dr. Peter Thompson.) Oxford M.St. (Mod. Hist.)

2700 Racialised boundaries: a study of rape and consensual relationships between white men and black women in antebellum Louisiana, 1803–65. Andrea Livesey. (Dr. Michael Tadman.) Liverpool Ph.D. (Hist.)

2701 William Shiels, R.S.A. (1783–1857): identity, scientific enquiry and his cross-cultural art world in Edinburgh, London, New York and Charleston. Fiona Salvesen Murrell. (Dr. John C. Morrison.) Aberdeen Ph.D. (Hist. of Art)

2702 A British/imperial-based study of the post-1812 development of Anglo-American relations. Andrew Elrick. (Dr. Andrew MacKillop and Dr. Andrew Dilley.) Aberdeen Ph.D. (Hist.)

2703 Conflict, collusion and identity in the lower Mississippi Valley during the war of 1812. Hugh Roberts. (Dr. Ben Marsh and Dr. Tim Bowman.) Kent Ph.D. (Hist.)

2704 'Those who lie in barns and wash their cravats in hog trough': vagrants, criminality, mobility, and subsistence in the mid Atlantic, 1820–45. Kristin O'Brassill-Kulfan. (Dr. James Campbell.) Leicester Ph.D. (Hist.)

2705   New Orleans 1820–32: a spatial, social and demographic profile. Matthew Stallard. (Dr. Natalie Zacek.) Manchester Ph.D. (English, Amer. Stud. & Creative Writing)

2706   Anglo-American kinship and ethnic nationalism in the discourses of the American South, 1830–77. Alison S. Montgomery. (Dr. Jay Sexton.) Oxford D.Phil. (Mod. Hist.)

2707   The influence of the London money market on different types and the centre of American railroad finance c.1830–c.1870 and lessons for industrial policy. Lewis J. Willcocks. (Dr. Jay Sexton.) Oxford M.Phil. (Mod. Hist.)

2708   'Perpetuating fear: representations of the armed black man in the Antebellum Southern Press, 1830–60. Rosalyn Narayan. (Professor Tim Lockley.) Warwick M.Phil./Ph.D. (Hist.)

2709   Born to rule the seas: the 1830s and the genesis of the U.S. Navy as a professional, global power. Claude Berube. (Professors Holger H.W. Afflerbach and John Gooch.) Leeds Ph.D. (Hist.)

2710   Linked memories: slavery, race and remembrance in the United States and the United Kingdom. Jennifer Davison. (Professor Sean O'Connell.) Belfast Ph.D. (Hist. & Anthr.)

2711   Thomas Wilson Dorr, the people's governor: a life of politics and sacrifice in the early American Republic. Raymond J. Lavertue. (Professor Richard J. Carwardine.) Oxford D.Phil. (Mod. Hist.)

2712   Gender, the household, and child human capital formation: evidence from Victorian England and Depression-era America. Vellore S. Arthi. (Professor Jane Humphries.) Oxford D.Phil. (Mod. Hist.)

2713   Irish-American emigrant letters, 1845–1900. Claire M. McGowan. (Professor Martin Polley.) De Montfort Ph.D. (Hum.)

2714   Diffusion against centralisation: centralisation and its discontents in America, 1848–60. Charles Thompson. (Dr. Andrew Heath.) Sheffield Ph.D. (Hist.)

2715   Executive clemency in Texas, 1849–65. Daniel Hale. (Dr. Emily R. West.) Reading Ph.D. (Hist.)

2716   The Protestant Episcopal Church (P.E.C.) within the culture of the late antebellum South and the Confederacy. Sam Aldred. (Professor Pekka Hämäläinen.) Oxford M.St. (Mod. Hist.)

2717   The Mountain Meadows massacre and the making of the Mormons in the American mind. Janiece Johnson. (Dr. George D.G. Lewis.) Leicester Ph.D. (Hist.)

2718   The forgotten tycoon: James McHenry, the Atlantic and Great Western Railroad, and the gilded age of robber barons, 1858–91. Barry Henderson. (Professor Catherine Clinton.) Belfast M.Phil./Ph.D. (Hist. & Anthr.)

2719   Fenian influences in Worcester, Massachusetts, 1858–75. Barry Ward. (Dr. Neil Fleming.) Worcester M.Phil./Ph.D. (Hum. & Creative Arts)

2720   Ecclesiastical politics and the role of women in African-American Christianity, 1860–1900. George Scratcherd. (Professor Richard J. Carwardine.) Oxford D.Phil. (Mod. Hist.)

2721 Race, democracy and the American Civil War in the county of Yorkshire. Mark Bennett. (Dr. Matthew Johnson and Dr. David Craig.) Durham Ph.D. (Hist.)

2722 U.S. Civil War: the ironclad C.S.S. *Mississippi*. Andrew English. (Professor Jeremy Black and Dr. Laura Rowe.) Exeter M.Phil. (Maritime Hist.)

2723 Dissent and discontent in the Confederate South, 1861–5. Brian Langley. (Dr. David Gleeson.) Northumbria Ph.D. (Hist.)

2724 William James and psychopathology: degeneration and regeneration. Emma Sutton. (Professor Sonu Shamdasani and Dr. Stephen Jacyna.) London Ph.D. (U.C. Clinical Psychology)

2725 The gentlemen's clubs of New York City: a social and architectural history, 1865–1914. Henry H. Joyce. (Dr. William H. Whyte.) Oxford D.Phil. (Mod. Hist.)

2726 Whose nation? Post-civil war southern and black American nationalism. Jack Noe. (Professor Simon D. Hall.) Leeds Ph.D. (Hist.)

2727 Gender and family life among African Americans in reconstruction-era North and South Carolina. Michelle Wallis. (Dr. Natalie Zacek.) Manchester Ph.D. (Hist.)

2728 United we stand, divided we fall? The American Equal Rights Association and the pursuit of universal suffrage, 1866–70. Stuart Galloway. (Dr. Elizabeth J. Clapp.) Leicester Ph.D. (Hist.)

2729 Executive power and Republicanism: the battle to define Ulysses S. Grant's presidency, 1868–80. Annabelle Grenville-Mathers. (Dr. Andrew D. Heath.) Sheffield Ph.D. (Hist.)

2730 A brief moment in the sun: Francis Cardozo and reconstruction in South Carolina. Neil Kinghan. (Professor Iwan Morgan and Dr. Tony McCulloch.) U.C.L. M.Phil./ Ph.D. (Inst. Amer.)

2731 Scholarly solutions: American political science and the challenge of democracy, 1870–1970. Louisa K.A. Hotson. (Dr. Gareth Davies.) Oxford D.Phil. (Mod. Hist.)

2732 Civic improvements in Philadelphia and London: municipal patriotisms in Britain and America, 1870–1925. John Ingram. (Dr. Paul Readman and Professor David E.H. Edgerton.) King's College London M.Phil./Ph.D. (Hist.)

2733 A special relationship: Anglo-American aristocratic marriages, 1870–1914. Melissa Aaron. (Dr. Paul Readman and Professor Patricia M. Thane.) King's College London M.Phil./Ph.D. (Hist.)

2734 Zionism in American evangelicalism. Kelly Agler. (Dr. Michael Ledger-Lomas.) King's College London M.Phil. (Theol. & Rel. Stud.)

2735 'Feebleminded victims': eugenics, miscegenation and lynching in Virginia, 1880–1930. Nicola Price. (Dr. Bruce Baker.) London M.Phil./Ph.D. (R.H.U.L. Hist.)

2736 'A humanising eye': situating the snapshot photography of Jennie Ross Cobb, 1880–1910. Emma Doubt. (Dr. Meaghan E. Clarke and Professor David Mellor.) Sussex D.Phil. (Hist. of Art)

2737 Governing Jim Crow: Louisiana, 1890–1965. Catherine H. McLaughlin-Stonham. (Dr. Dianne Kirby and Dr. Nerys Young.) Ulster Ph.D. (Hist.)

2738 Progressive plans and urban realities in St. Louis, 1890–1930. Katie Myerscough. (Dr. Natalie Zacek and Dr. David Brown.) Manchester Ph.D. (English, Amer. Stud. & Creative Writing)

2739 Chicago's criminal children: a study of juvenile delinquency in the progressive era, 1890–1920. Oenone Kubie. (Dr. Mara Keire and Dr. Stephen Tuck.) Oxford D.Phil. (Mod. Hist.)

2740 John Singer Sargent's British and American sitters, 1890–1910: interpreting cultural identity within society portraits. Emily Moore. (Professor Elizabeth Prettejohn.) York Ph.D. (Hist. of Art)

2741 'The living and dying': the rise of the United States, the Spanish-American War and European visions of decline. Ben Rhode. (Dr. Patricia Clavin.) Oxford D.Phil. (Mod. Hist.)

2742 Politics, personalities, purpose and propaganda: sustaining the U.S. Marine Corps' mission and birth of the Fleet Marine Force, 1898–1939. Brian McCrary. (Professors Holger H.W. Afflerbach and John Gooch.) Leeds Ph.D. (Hist.)

2743 Political wives to political lives: the evolution of women in American politics on screen. Sharon Betts. (Professor Iwan Morgan and Dr. Nick Witham.) U.C.L. M.Phil./Ph.D. (Inst. Amer.)

2744 A comparative study of the health impact of social housing, Glasgow and Baltimore. Nick Sharrer. (Professors Malcolm A. Nicolson and Ade Kearns.) Glasgow Ph.D. (Soc. Sc.)

2745 William Burrell, Thomas & Drake, and the transatlantic trade in stained glass, 1900–50. Marie-Helene Groll. (Ms. Sarah Brown.) York Ph.D. (Hist. of Art)

2746 In full colour or black and white? White ethnicity and American citizenship in the newspaper comic strip, 1900–32. Hilary Hall (Fraser). (Dr. Andrew Heath.) Sheffield Ph.D. (Hist.)

2747 The San Francisco plague epidemics and the influence of race, politics, science and the press. Judith Anderson. (Professor Mark Harrison.) Oxford D.Phil. (Mod. Hist.)

2748 The impact of Hubert Henry Harrison on African-American radicalism, 1909–27. Brian Kwoba. (Dr. Stephen Tuck.) Oxford D.Phil. (Mod. Hist.)

2749 A comparison: the development of veteran identity and First World War memory in the U.S. and U.K. Ashley E. Garber. (Dr. Adrian M. Gregory.) Oxford D.Phil. (Mod. Hist.)

2750 Coloured cosmopolitanism on the Pacific coast, 1918–41. Owen Walsh. (Dr. Kate M. Dossett and Dr. Gina Denton.) Leeds Ph.D. (Hist.)

2751 Rockstar games and American history. Esther Wright. (Professor Jennifer Smyth.) Warwick M.Phil./Ph.D. (Hist.)

2752 Eugenics according to geneticists – how geneticists perceived eugenics in the United States from the 1920s to the 1960s. Melissa B. Alberts. (Professor Pietro Corsi.) Oxford M.Sc. (Mod. Hist.)

2753 Murder and male control in American roots records of the '20s and '30s. Allan Symons. (Professor Brian Ward.) Northumbria Ph.D. (Hist.)

2754   An urban history: the impact of cultural entrepreneurship in jazz in 1920s Boston, Massachusetts. Craig Doughty. (Dr. Shalini Sharma and Dr. Kathleen Cushing.) Keele Ph.D. (Hist.)

2755   Religious opposition to mainstream science in the United States: 1925 to the present. Ben Huskinson. (Professor Crawford Gribben.) Belfast M.Phil./Ph.D. (Hist. & Anthr.)

2756   Huey P. Long and the 1929 impeachment. Diane Smith. (Dr. Niall Palmer and Dr. Martin Folly.) Brunel Ph.D. (Pol. & Hist.)

2757   The white disease that became black: how polio both re-enforced and challenged racial medicine, as told through the newspapers of the African American community, 1930–59. Caitlin R. Page. (Dr. Sloan Mahone.) Oxford M.Sc. (Mod. Hist.)

2758   George G. Meade: from Gettysburg to Appomattox. Zakary Powell. (Dr. George Conyne and Dr. Ben Marsh.) Kent M.A. (Hist.)

2759   The Welles of loneliness: Sumner Welles and the creation of U.S. foreign policy. Christopher Parkes. (Dr. Steven Casey.) London Ph.D. (L.S.E. Int. Hist.)

2760   'For the future peace of the world': the wartime alliance and the Anglo-American transition of power, 1938–49 . Thomas Bottelier. (Professor David E.H. Edgerton and Dr. Joseph Maiolo.) King's College London M.Phil./Ph.D. (Hist.)

2761   Memory and mythology of Southern morality in cinematography after *Gone with the Wind*. Steven Bishop. (Professor J. S. Smyth.) Warwick M.Phil./Ph.D. (Hist.)

2762   Medmenham: Anglo-American photographic intelligence in the Second World War. Paul Stewart. (Dr. Jim Beach.) Northampton Ph.D. (Hist.)

2763   Race, gender and civil rights: African American women and the National Association for the Advancement of Colored People. Samantha Gowdy. (Dr. Brian Kelly.) Belfast M.Phil./Ph.D. (Hist. & Anthr.)

2764   Promoting Keynesian liberalism: Walter W. Heller and U.S. economic policy, 1940–87. James Hillyer. (Professors Iwan Morgan and Jonathan Bell.) U.C.L. Ph.D. (Inst. Amer.)

2765   Visionary of political liability: a critique of the vice-presidency of Henry Wallace. John Blenkharn. (Professor Simon D. Hall.) Leeds M.A. (Hist.)

2766   America and the Blitz. Sean Dettman. (Dr. Roland Quinault and Professor Miles Taylor.) London Ph.D. (Inst. Hist. Res.)

2767   History of music criticism in Britain and the U.S.A., 1945–present. James Bennett. (Dr. Roger Fagge.) Warwick Ph.D. (Hist.)

2768   Keepers of our consciences: the liberal hero of Hollywood's vital centre, 1945–67. Hannah Graves. (Professor Jennifer Smyth.) Warwick Ph.D. (Hist.)

2769   'Southern by the grace of God': the menace of white southern religion in post-war Hollywood cinema. Megan Hunt. (Professor Brian Ward.) Northumbria Ph.D. (Hist.)

2770   The Republican party and isolationism between 1945 and 1960. Christopher G. Brown. (Dr. Stephen G.N. Tuck and Professor M.J. Heale.) Oxford D.Phil. (Mod. Hist.)

2771   The domestic determinants of American foreign economic policy from World War II to the Cold War. Sebastian Huempfer. (Professor Kevin O'Rourke.) Oxford D.Phil. (Mod. Hist.)

2772   Museological representations of African American history, culture, and experiences. Laura Burnham. (Professor Kevern Verney.) Edge Hill Ph.D. (English & Hist.)

2773   In-depth study of the history of virtual reality in the United States of America. Tobias D.K. Bowman. (Professor Pietro Corsi.) Oxford D.Phil. (Mod. Hist.)

2774   Recovering a black American tradition of animal advocacy. Lauren McCarthy. (Dr. Kate M. Dossett and Dr. Say Burgin.) Leeds Ph.D. (Hist.)

2775   At the touch of a button: the fingertip control of technology in America's age of affluence. Elliott Weiss. (Dr. Bernhard Rieger.) London Ph.D. (U.C. Hist.)

2776   A history of American rap music to 1975: from the 'Signifying Monkey' to the South Bronx. Alvin Smith. (Dr. Dawn-Marie Gibson.) London Ph.D. (R.H.U.L. Hist.)

2777   Icebergs in the desert: northern Republicans, 'un-American' communities and the reconstruction of the American West. James Williamson. (Professor Martin Crawford and Dr. Anthony Kauders.) Keele Ph.D. (Hist.)

2778   Political attitudes towards the United States in Britain during the 1950s. Stephen Dipnall. (Professor John Callaghan.) Salford Ph.D. (Cen. Eur. Sec.)

2779   The patriotism of protest: redefining the citizen-soldier in the Vietnam era. Lauren Mottle. (Professor Simon D. Hall and Dr. Say Burgin.) Leeds Ph.D. (Hist.)

2780   Music, protest and the quest for civil rights in the United States and Northern Ireland, 1955–75. Glen Whitcroft. (Professor Brian Ward.) Northumbria Ph.D. (Hist.)

2781   Racial segregation of U.S. federal army detachments during domestic civil disturbance deployments, 1957–68. Lee Lavis. (Dr. Dianne Kirby and Professor K. Larres.) Ulster Ph.D. (Hist.)

2782   Anglo-American quality press narratives and sexual revolution, 1958–79. Ross Paulger. (Dr. Adrian C. Bingham.) Sheffield Ph.D. (Hist.)

2783   A dream deferred? The revitalisation of central Harlem, c.1960 to the present. Nisha S. Agarwal. (Professor G.C.K. Peach.) Oxford D.Phil. (Mod. Hist.)

2784   Multiracial activism around reproductive rights in America from the second wave of feminism. Sabina Peck. (Dr. Kate M. Dossett and Professor Simon D. Hall.) Leeds Ph.D. (Hist.)

2785   The egalitarian evolution: Justice Thurgood Marshall's campaign finance jurisprudence. Alexander B.K. Fullman. (Dr. Gareth Davies.) Oxford M.St. (Mod. Hist.)

2786   Picking up the gun: black resistance, American citizenship, and the Mulford Act of 1967. Joshua A. Aiken. (Dr. Stephen Tuck.) Oxford M.St. (Mod. Hist.)

2787   An intellectual and personal biography of Elizabeth Fox-Genovese. Paula J. Farley. (Dr. Stephen J. Sarson.) Swansea Ph.D. (Hist.)

2788   From white resistance to new conservatism: the backlash against community action programmes in Mississippi, c.1965–72. Emma Folwell. (Dr. George D.G. Lewis.) Leicester Ph.D. (Hist.)

2789 Historical film in the era of New Hollywood, 1967–79. Thomas Symmons. (Dr. H. Mark Glancy.) London Ph.D. (Q.M. Hist.)

2790 Anglo-American monetary relations between the 1967 devaluation and the 1976 I.M.F. crisis. Edward John. (Dr. Scott Newton.) Cardiff Ph.D. (Hist. & Archaeol.)

2791 Battles for breath: a comparative historical analysis of responses to coal workers' pneumoconiosis in South Wales and central Appalachia, 1968–85. Pallavi Podapati. (Professor David Turner.) Swansea M.Res. (Hist.)

2792 'Opening Pandora's box': Richard Nixon, South Carolina, and the southern strategy, 1968–72. Edward M.D. Adkins. (Dr. Gareth B. Davies and Dr. Stephen G.N. Tuck.) Oxford D.Phil. (Mod. Hist.)

2793 Meaning and trust: the United States and the politics of nuclear arms control during the Nixon and Reagan administrations. Laura Considine. (Professor Nicholas Wheeler and Dr. Andrew Priest.) Aberystwyth Ph.D. (Int. Pol.)

2794 The Legal Services program during the administration of Richard Nixon, 1969–74. Mitchell A.J. Robertson. (Dr. Gareth Davies.) Oxford M.St. (Mod. Hist.)

2795 'Gay is good': gay rights and social justice in Belfast and Boston. Rachel Wallace. (Dr. Anthony Stanonis and Professor Mary O'Dowd.) Belfast M.Phil./Ph.D. (Hist. & Anthr.)

2796 Hip-hop: culture and industry, 1970–2000. Shamim M. Gammage. (Professor Avner Offer.) Oxford M.Sc. (Mod. Hist.)

2797 The politics of economic crisis: public and private bankruptcies and the emergence of progressive populism, 1970–91. Daniel Rowe. (Dr. Gareth B. Davies.) Oxford D.Phil. (Mod. Hist.)

2798 Out at work: gay liberation and 1970s workplace organisation. Joshua Hollands. (Professors Jonathan Bell and Iwan Morgan.) U.C.L. M.Phil./Ph.D. (Inst. Amer.)

2799 Bringing Congress back in: Watergate and the politics of institutional change. Patrick P. Sandman. (Dr. Gareth B. Davies.) Oxford D.Phil. (Mod. Hist.)

2800 Donkey work: redefining the Democratic party in an 'age of conservatism', 1972–84. Patrick Andelic. (Dr. Gareth B. Davies.) Oxford D.Phil. (Mod. Hist.)

2801 Never going back? The abortion provider in post-Roe vs. Wade America. Kristina A. Carney. (Dr. Sloan Mahone.) Oxford M.Sc. (Mod. Hist.)

2802 The first road north: the cultural history of America's Arctic haul road. Julia Feuer-Cotter. (Dr. Isla Forsyth and Dr. Alex Vasudevan.) Nottingham Ph.D. (Geog.)

2803 Working together, working apart: feminism, art and collaboration in Britain and America, 1974–81. Amy Tobin. (Dr. Jo Applin.) York Ph.D. (Hist. of Art)

2804 The fiscal crisis of New York City, 1975–7. Jacob Udell. (Dr. George Bitsakakis and Professor Avner Offer.) Oxford M.Sc. (Mod. Hist.)

2805 'Reagan country': Ronald Reagan and the Conservative, 1976–96. Jonathan Bartho. (Professors Iwan Morgan and Jonathan Bell.) U.C.L. M.Phil./Ph.D. (Inst. Amer.)

2806 Curing 'Vietnam syndrome': the Committee on the Present Danger and mobilising America for the 'second' Cold War, 1976–80. Nicholas Blackbourn. (Professor Gerard J. De Groot.) St. Andrews Ph.D. (Hist.)

2807 'If he can be political, why can't we?' Jimmy Carter and the rise of the religious right. Gabriel Raeburn. (Dr. Gareth Davies.) Oxford M.St. (Mod. Hist.)

2808 Bureaucratic politics and the foreign policy of the Carter administration. Chris Wallis. (Professor Sylvia Ellis.) Northumbria Ph.D. (Hist.)

2809 Grassroots 'n' the hood: the Rodney King riots and the development of black activism in Los Angeles, 1978–96. George Francis-Kelly. (Professor Simon D. Hall and Dr. Kate M. Dossett.) Leeds Ph.D. (Hist.)

2810 Spitting blood: the linguistic and ideological legacy of black power within hip hop. Harry Pasek. (Dr. Sebastian Page.) Oxford M.St. (Mod. Hist.)

2811 A Republican conundrum: the ruralification of the party base and the fight against social security. Brett J. Wierenga. (Professor Kevin O'Rourke.) Oxford M.Sc. (Mod. Hist.)

2812 Rising above social and racial barriers: the central role of women in the Environmental Justice Movement in America. Claire Sims. (Dr. Laila Haidarali.) Essex Ph.D (Hist.)

2813 People power in struggling cities: pressure groups in Liverpool and Baltimore, 1980–91. Elizabeth B. Longino. (Dr. Harold Carter.) Oxford D.Phil. (Mod. Hist.)

West Indies and Caribbean area

2814 Manchester and slavery in the West Indies. Sami Pinarbasi. (Dr. Laurence Brown and Dr. Natalie Zacek.) Manchester Ph.D. (Hist.)

2815 Religious toleration, race and citizenship in the English West Indies, c.1660–89. Philip Abraham. (Professors Richard Drayton and Ian McBride.) King's College London M.Phil./Ph.D. (Hist.)

2816 The Irish on Jamaica during the long 18th century, 1698–1836. Karst De Jong. (Professor Mary O'Dowd.) Belfast Ph.D. (Hist. & Anthr.)

2817 The Maroons of Jamaica between 1740 and 1840. Michael Sivapragasam. (Dr. Christer Petley.) Southampton M.Phil. (Hist.)

2818 Bringing the Seven Years War to the West Indies: strategic and operational planning of the British campaign to Martinique and Guadeloupe, 1759. Megan J. Wagner. (Dr. Erica Charters.) Oxford M.St. (Mod. Hist.)

2819 Power, profit and plantocracy: the second earl of Belmore and Jamaican slavery. Grace McGrath. (Professor Catherine Clinton.) Belfast M.Phil./Ph.D. (Hist. & Anthr.)

2820 Tracking foreign intervention through medicine and social science in Haiti, c.1900–50. Antony Stewart. (Dr. Diana Paton and Dr. Samiksha Sehrewat.) Newcastle Ph.D. (Hist.)

2821 'Practical sympathy': disaster relief in the British Caribbean, 1912–7. Oscar Webber. (Dr. Anyaa J. Anim-Addo and Professor Malcolm S. Chase.) Leeds Ph.D (Hist.)

2822 Haiti in art: creating and curating in the Black Atlantic. Wendy Asquith. (Professor Charles Forsdick.) Liverpool Ph.D. (Hist.)

2823 International perspectives on data protection and its relationship to records management: recommendations for emerging practice in the West Indies. Cherri-Ann Beckles. (Professor Jim Tomlinson.) Dundee Ph.D. (Hist.)

Central and Latin America

2824 The economy of the late post-classic Maya: a regional perspective based on ceramic production organisation in northern Yucatan, Mexico. Carmen Giomar Sanchez. (Dr. Ian Whitbread and Dr. Ruth Young.) Leicester Ph.D. (Archaeol. & Anc. Hist.)

2825 Power and performance: ritual, religion and imperial control in the pre-Hispanic Nahua world. Harriet Smart. (Dr. Caroline Dodds-Pennock.) Sheffield Ph.D. (Hist.)

2826 Blackness, indigeneity and coloniality in Latin America: rethinking race and ethnicity. Desiree Poets. (Dr. Lucy Taylor and Dr. Mustapha Pasha.) Aberystwyth Ph.D. (Int. Pol.)

2827 Indigo and the Spanish empire, 1550–1700. Adrianna Catena. (Professor Lyndal A. Roper.) Oxford D.Phil. (Mod. Hist.)

2828 Metropolitan control on the Iberian Atlantic: the *Visita General* in New Spain, 1600–50. Angela Ballone. (Dr. Harald Braun.) Liverpool Ph.D. (Hist.)

2829 Language, identity and power in colonial Brazil, 1701–1822. Luciano Scarato. (Dr. Gabriela Ramos.) Cambridge Ph.D. (Hist.)

2830 Madness and governance in Bourbon Mexico, 1713–1821. Rebecca Noble. (Professors Rebecca Earle and Hilary Marland.) Warwick Ph.D. (Hist.)

2831 Kept indoors? Concubinage, power and gendered space in Bahia, Brazil, 1750–1831. Selina Patel. (Dr. Diana Paton and Professor Jens Hentschke.) Newcastle Ph.D. (Hist.)

2832 Canals and borders: the economic diplomacy of 19th-century Britain and the Belize-Guatemala territorial dispute. David M. Gomez. (Dr. Katherine Quinn and Dr. Nestor Castaneda.) U.C.L. M.Phil./Ph.D. (Inst. Amer.)

2833 Christianity and Obeah in Demerara and Berbice, 1808–23. George L. Hammond. (Dr. Alan Strathern.) Oxford M.St. (Mod. Hist.)

2834 The influence of local power in the construction of the Chilean state, 1823–33. Cristobal Garcia-Huidobro. (Professor Alan Knight.) Oxford D.Phil. (Mod. Hist.)

2835 Marijuana and Mexico: from traditional medicine to dangerous drug, *c.*1910–61. Marita Martin-Orozco. Glasgow Caledonian Ph.D. (Hist.)

2836 'Creating the world anew': land, religion and revolution in the Gran Nayar region of Mexico, 1910–40. Nathaniel Morris. (Professor Alan Knight.) Oxford D.Phil. (Mod. Hist.)

2837 La Nuestra: football and national identity in Argentina, 1913–58. Mark Orton. (Professor Matthew Taylor.) De Montfort Ph.D. (Hum.)

2838 Social practices of modernity: cinema, architecture and sociability in Santiago and Buenos Aires, 1915–45. Camila Gatica. (Professor Nicola A. Miller.) London Ph.D. (U.C. Hist.)

2839 The shape of the state to come: transnationality and the social imaginary of the welfare state in Argentina, 1930–43. Thomas Maier. (Dr. Paulo Drinot and Professor Maxine Molyneux.) U.C.L. Ph.D. (Inst. Amer.)

2840 The testimony of space: exploring sites of memory and violence in Peru's internal armed conflict. David Willis. (Dr. Paulo Drinot.) U.C.L. M.Phil./Ph.D. (Inst. Amer.)

2841 Irish Argentines from Perón to the Dirty War and the fall of the generals. Patrick Speight. (Professor Keith J. Jeffery.) Belfast Ph.D. (Hist. & Anthr.)

2842 Migradollars and the transformation of Mexico: exploring the socio-economic determinants of remittances by Mexican migrants. Thomas M. Pellathy. (Mr. L.A. Whitehead.) Oxford D.Phil. (Mod. Hist.)

2843 The feminisation of the special period and *jineterismo* in Cuba. Daliany Kersh. (Dr. Carrie Hamilton and Dr. Margaret L. Arnot.) Roehampton Ph.D. (Hist.)

2844 The Salinas agricultural reforms in Mexico. Jan H. Van Zoelen Cortes. (Professor Jane Humphries.) Oxford M.Phil. (Mod. Hist.)

2845 The 'unquiet dead': memorialising Guatemala's disappeared. Katherine Bailey. (Professor Aristotle Kallis.) Lancaster Ph.D. (Hist.)

ASIA

General

2846 An ecology of trade: tropical cultivars, commensals and fauna between the Near East and south Asia in the 1st millennium B.C. Sureshkumar Muthukumaran. (Professor Karen Radner.) London Ph.D. (U.C. Hist.)

2847 The role of deities in the development of Buddhism and their social, cultural and regional acceptance in early historic South Asia. Raminder Kaur. (Dr. Ruth Young and Dr. David Edwards.) Leicester Ph.D. (Archaeol. & Anc. Hist.)

2848 Travellers to the Orient: perceptions of denominational identities in Islamic surroundings, 1517–1648. Finn Schulze-Feldman. (Dr. Guido Giglioni and Professor Alastair Hamilton.) London Ph.D. (Warburg)

2849 Intimate encounters in early modern Asia: the East India Company and sexual liaisons in Tokugawa Japan and Mughal India, 1600–1700. Georgia E. O'Connor. (Dr. Alan Strathern.) Oxford M.St. (Mod. Hist.)

2850 Zo history: identity construction across borders, 1795–1947, in north-east India and north-west Burma. Bianca Son. (Dr. Michael Charney.) London Ph.D. (S.O.A.S. Hist.)

2851 The international Leviathan: the British imperial institution and the East Asian *ab-intra* states system, 1842–1943. Takaki Nishiyama. (Dr. Vivienne Lo.) London Ph.D. (U.C. Hist.)

2852 Britain and the politics of Asiatic labour, 1860–1939. Reuben Bard-Rosenberg. (Dr. Paul Readman and Professor Richard H. Drayton.) King's College London M.Phil./ Ph.D. (Hist.)

Asia

2853 Muslim women and legal reform: polygamy and 'gendered' rights under personal laws in 20th-century South Asia. Sabera Bhayat. (Dr. Sarah Hodges.) Warwick M.Phil./Ph.D. (Hist.)

2854 The soldier's experience in India and Burma, 1942–5. Phil Race. (Dr. Rebecca Gill.) Huddersfield M.A. (Music, Hum. & Media)

2855 British colonial security and the Cold War in Asia: intelligence, defence and counter-subversion in Hong Kong and Singapore, 1947–57. Alexander Shaw. (Dr. Martin Thornton and Dr. Adam Cathcart.) Leeds Ph.D. (Hist.)

2856 Returning home: the experiences of British return migrants from Asia. Robert Jones. (Dr. Tanja Bueltmann.) Northumbria Ph.D. (Hist.)

2857 A historical study of female Filipino domestic workers in Hong Kong, 1970–2000. Sarah S.Y. Lee. (Dr. Lars Laamann.) London Ph.D. (S.O.A.S. Hist.)

Middle East

2858 Living with clay: materials, technology, resources and landscape at Catalhöyük. Chris Doherty. (Dr. Ian Whitbread and Dr. Mark Gillings.) Leicester Ph.D. (Archaeol. & Anc. Hist.)

2859 The legacies of Darius. Donald Murray. (Dr. Johannes H. Haubold and Professor Edward M. Harris.) Durham Ph.D. (Classics)

2860 Running the empires: the administrative transition from Achaemenid to Seleucid rule. Jennifer Hicks. (Dr. Riet van Bremen.) London Ph.D. (U.C. Hist.)

2861 Negotiation of identities in the gymnasia of Seleukid and Ptolemaic kingdoms. Dorothea Stavrou. (Professor Graham Shipley and Dr. Sarah Scott.) Leicester Ph.D. (Archaeol. & Anc. Hist.)

2862 A study of religious life in Nabatea. Peter Alpass. (Dr. Ted Kaizer, Dr. Edmund V. Thomas and Dr. E.D. Hunt.) Durham Ph.D. (Classics)

2863 Negotiating divine power at ground level: interpreting patristic and rabbinic interaction with the divine in late antique Mesopotamia. Bradley Barnes. (Dr. Dan Levene.) Southampton Ph.D. (Hist.)

2864 Origen's Platonic influences. Lauren N. Stanley. (Dr. Philip Booth.) Oxford M.Phil. (Mod. Hist.)

2865 Christianity in the Arabian Peninsula – from A.D. 500 to the Islamic conquests. Amar Daugman. (Dr. Benet Salway.) London Ph.D. (U.C. Hist.)

2866 Arabic-Latin hermetic transmission: a study of the magical Encyclopaedia of Sirāj al-Dīn al-Sakkākī. Michael Noble. (Professor Charles S.F. Burnett and Dr. Aymen Shihadeh.) London Ph.D. (Warburg)

2867 Byzantine polemical literature against Islam. Ilias Malevitis. (Professor Gerald R. Hawting.) London Ph.D. (S.O.A.S. Hist.)

2868 Peace-making in the Latin east, 1099–1291. Betty Binysh. (Professor Helen Nicholson.) Cardiff Ph.D. (Hist. & Archaeol.)

2869   Gender identity among the consort – kings and their queens in the 12th and 13th century Levant. David Halloran. (Dr. Katherine J. Lewis.) Huddersfield M.A. (Music, Hum. & Media)

2870   The crisis years of Antioch, 1130–5: a discussion into the portrayal of Alice of Antioch. Leanne Callaghan. (Dr. Katherine Lewis.) Huddersfield M.Phil. (Music, Hum. & Media)

2871   Political and economic relations between the Ashraf of the Hijaz and the Ayyubid and Mamluk rulers of Egypt and Syria, 1171–1517. Musaed J.S.M.Q. Alenezi. (Professor Norman J. Housley.) Leicester Ph.D. (Hist.)

2872   Factories of empire: the British in Baghdad and the Persian Gulf, c.1620–1822. Peter Good. (Dr. Mark Frost.) Essex Ph.D. (Hist.)

2873   South Arabia and the federal panacea: a comparative study of the federal experiments, imperial networks and British intellectual tradition. Joseph Higgins. (Dr. Christopher Prior.) Southampton M.Phil. (Hist.)

2874   Power, prestige and the past: archaeology, antiquities legislation and British imperialism in the Near East, 1815–1939. Nathan W. D. Fisher. (Dr. Eugene L. Rogan.) Oxford D.Phil. (Mod. Hist.)

2875   Kurd and Kurdistan from the viewpoint of British travellers in the decades 1830–40 and 1890–1910. Qadir Muhammand. (Professor Rosemary H. Sweet.) Leicester Ph.D. (Hist.)

2876   The intellectual biography of Jamaladdin Afghani. Eyup Togan. (Professor Martin Evans and Dr. Gideon Reuveni.) Sussex D.Phil. (Hist.)

2877   The Qassim region through the reports of travelling expatriates, 1862–1923. Abdulmohran Alreshoodi. (Dr. Christian Koller.) Bangor Ph.D. (Hist., Welsh Hist. & Archaeol.)

2878   Anglo-Ottoman relations, 1874–85. Fahriye Begum Yildizeli. (Dr. Richard Toye.) Exeter Ph.D. (Hist.)

2879   The Shia migration from south-western Iran, Bahrain and Saudi Arabia to Kuwait. Mohammad Alhabib. (Professor Vanessa A. Martin.) London Ph.D. (R.H.U.L. Hist.)

2880   British representations of the Kurds and Armenian question, 1877–1918. Adnan A. Mohammed. (Professor Rosemary H. Sweet.) Leicester Ph.D. (Hist.)

2881   Site-seeing: postcards of the Middle East and the visual construction of place, 1890s to 1990s CDP. Seonaid Rogers. (Dr. Nick Baron and Professor Maiken Umbach.) Nottingham Ph.D. (Hist.)

2882   British advisory position in the wake of opposition to British imperial rule in Bahrain. Hamad Abdulla. East Anglia Ph.D. (Hist.)

2883   The fabric of well-trained Ottoman minds: Ottoman materialist approaches towards modern psychology. Seyma Afacan. (Professor Mark Harrison, Dr. Sloan Mahone and Dr. Laurent Mignon.) Oxford D.Phil. (Mod. Hist.)

2884   Shia identity in Iraq. Ranj Alaaldin. (Dr. Kirsten E. Schulze.) London Ph.D. (L.S.E. Int. Hist.)

2885 Towards a history of Iranian archaeology: nationalism, politics and the practice of archaeology. Rana Daroogheh. (Professor Robin Coningham.) Durham Ph.D. (Archaeol.)

2886 British mandatory policy in Palestine: its impact on the town of Nablus. Roger Edwin Higginson. (Dr. Jacob Norris and Professor Martin Evans.) Sussex D.Phil. (Hist.)

2887 Turkish women's periodicals in the late Ottoman era. Tugba Alver. (Dr. Anindita Ghosh and Dr. Anastasia Valassopoulos.) Manchester Ph.D. (Hist.)

2888 A 'British Lake'? Britain and her rivals in Bahrain c.1900–14: a case study of Britain's forward movment in the Persian Gulf. Joseph McGann. (Dr. John Darwin.) Oxford M.St. (Mod. Hist.)

2889 The British policy towards King Abdulaziz in Najd, Al-Akra and Hejaz, 1902–32. Dhailfallah Alotaibi. (Dr. Christian Koller.) Bangor Ph.D. (Hist., Welsh Hist. & Archaeol.)

2890 Early British oil interests in Persia. Leonardo Davoudi. (Dr. John G. Darwin.) Oxford D.Phil. (Mod. Hist.)

2891 Defining the loss of beauty: a study of the role of the Dönmes in the Turkish revolution, 1908–23. Eyup S. Carmikli. (Dr. Benjamin C. Fortna.) London M.Phil. (S.O.A.S. Hist.)

2892 British banks: imperialism and decolonisation in Iran and the Middle East, 1914–79 (British banks as a tool of imperialism in the Middle East). Millad Borzabadi-Farahani. (Dr. Sarah Stockwell and Dr. Reza Zia-Ebrahimi.) King's College London M.Phil./Ph.D. (Hist.)

2893 Modern Iraq from occupation to independence: the Shi'a resistance to British colonisation, 1914–21. Eissa Dashti. (Dr. Christian Koller.) Bangor Ph.D. (Hist., Welsh Hist. & Archaeol.)

2894 Empires in the Holy Land: revising the Palestine Campaign of the First World War. Elliott J. Bannan. (Dr. Robert Johnson.) Oxford M.Phil. (Mod. Hist.)

2895 Narrating the national past: Turkish national remembrance and the cultural narratives of Gallipoli. Pheroze Unwalla. (Professor Benjamin Fortna.) London Ph.D. (S.O.A.S. Hist.)

2896 The Suvla Bay landing. Jeff Cleverley. (Dr. Helen McCartney.) King's College London Ph.D. (War Stud.)

2897 British policy towards the government of the Mosul Villayet, 1916–26. Ranjdar Azzez Al-Jaf. (Dr. Stuart R. Ball.) Leicester Ph.D. (Hist.)

2898 Inter-personal relations and the Anglo-Israeli dialogue. Hilda Worth. (Professor Joachim Schlör.) Southampton M.Phil. (Hist.)

2899 Kurdish nation between the Treaty of Sevres 1920 and the Treaty of Lausanne 1923 in equation to the Balfour Declaration 1917. Chnor Jaafar Ahmad. (Professor Mike Rapport and Dr. Alexander Marshall.) Glasgow Ph.D. (Arts)

2900 In empire's shadow: Britain, Oman and the Al Bu Sa'id sultanate in the decolonisation era, 1918–82. William E. Clegg. (Dr. John G. Darwin.) Oxford D.Phil. (Mod. Hist.)

2901 The 'invention' of Palestinian citizenship: discourses and practices, 1918–39. Lauren Banko. (Dr. Nelida Fuccaro.) London Ph.D. (S.O.A.S. Hist.)

2902 The British administration of South Kurdistan and local responses, 1918–32. Hawkar Muheddin Jalil. (Dr. Stuart R. Ball.) Leicester Ph.D. (Hist.)

2903 Ottoman bureaucrats in the Greek-occupied zone of Asia Minor, 1919–22: forms of collaboration and resistance. Umit Eser. (Professor Benjamin Fortna.) London Ph.D. (S.O.A.S. Hist.)

2904 George Curzon and the making of the 1919 Anglo-Persian Agreement. Jack P.E. Winfield. (Dr. John Darwin.) Oxford M.St. (Mod. Hist.)

2905 The evolution of consumer culture in the families of Jaffa, 1920–67. Jacques Rouyer Guillet. (Dr. Nelida Fuccaro.) London Ph.D. (S.O.A.S. Hist.)

2906 In need of a new story: writing, teaching and learning history in Mandatory Palestine. Jonathan H. Furas. (Dr. James McDougall.) Oxford D.Phil. (Mod. Hist.)

2907 The urban history of Tripoli (Lebanon) during the French mandate, 1920–46. Nada Saliba. (Dr. Nelida Fuccaro.) London Ph.D. (S.O.A.S. Hist.)

2908 Assyrian British relations: the makings of colonial identities, 1920–33. Fadi Dawood. (Dr. Nelida Fuccaro.) London Ph.D. (S.O.A.S. Hist.)

2909 The meaning of the mandate: colonial cultural institutions in Syria and Lebanon, 1920–5. Idir Ouahes. Exeter Ph.D. (Hist.)

2910 The Idrisi Emirate in the south-west of Arabia, 1923–34. Mohammed Yahya Alfaifi. (Professor Simon C. Smith.) Hull Ph.D. (Hist.)

2911 Charles Malik's political profile: Lebanon's permanence and its transient struggles. Tony Nasrallah. (Dr. Nelida Fuccaro.) London Ph.D. (S.O.A.S. Hist.)

2912 From Munich to the Cold War: Anglo-Turkish relations. Ilhan Kilic. East Anglia Ph.D. (Hist.)

2913 The Special Operations Executive's Middle East activities, 1940–5. David Willis. (Professors Brian Holden Reid and Joseph Maiolo.) King's College London Ph.D. (War Stud.)

2914 Britain's approach to Iran and wider British foreign policy, 1945–89. Darius Wainwright. (Dr. Linda Risso.) Reading Ph.D. (Hist.)

2915 The Islamisation of Sunni Muslims in Lebanon: the evolution of fundamentalism in a sectarian context. Corrin Varady. (Dr. Kirsten E. Schulze.) London Ph.D. (L.S.E. Int. Hist.)

2916 The Dhofar War, 1965–75. Khalid Al Kharusi. (Dr. Jonathon Colman and Dr. Philip Constable.) Central Lancashire M.Phil./Ph.D. (Hum.)

2917 Franchising heritage: the creation of a transnational heritage industry in the Emirate of Abu Dhabi. Sarina Wakefield. (Professors Kevin Hetherington and David Vincent and Dr. Rodney Harrison.) Open University Ph.D. (Hist.)

2918 British diplomacy and the Iranian Revolution, 1978–81. Luman Ali. (Professor John W. Young.) Nottingham Ph.D. (Hist.)

2919 Hizbollah: a military history. Andrew Exum. (Professor Yezid Sayigh and Dr. David Betz.) King's College London Ph.D. (War Stud.)

Central Asia

2920 A reappraisal of the 'Pax Mongolica': Toluid east-west relations, 1258–1335. Gillian Bateman. (Dr. Konrad Hirschler.) London Ph.D. (S.O.A.S. Hist.)

2921 The central Asian silk road and the European geographical imaginary, 1820–1917. Felix de Montety. (Professors Mike Heffernan and Georgina Endfield.) Nottingham Ph.D. (Geog.)

2922 Changing the state-society relations in late 19th-century Afghanistan: state building and group identities reconsidered through the categories of British colonial knowledge. Francesca Fuoli. (Dr. Shabnum Tejani.) London Ph.D. (S.O.A.S. Hist.)

2923 Developing powers: modernisation, development and governance in Cold War Afghanistan. Timothy A. Nunan. (Dr. Alexander Morrison and Professor Catriona Kelly.) Oxford D.Phil. (Mod. Hist.)

India and Pakistan

2924 Settlement history of the lower Dir, Khyber Pakhtunkhwa, Pakistan. Ijaz Khan. (Dr. Ruth Young and Dr. Jeremy Taylor.) Leicester Ph.D. (Archaeol. & Anc. Hist.)

2925 Gender and sexuality in medieval India. Sonia Wigh. Exeter Ph.D. (Hist.)

2926 Security, agency and tariff: how significantly did the English East India Company's institutional changes affect the economy of Bombay between 1650 and 1700? Colin C. Ganley. (Dr. David A. Washbrook.) Oxford D.Phil. (Mod. Hist.)

2927 Imaging authority: a study of the visual representations of the early British Empire in India, c.1730–1820. Apurba Chatterjee. (Professor Phil Withington.) Sheffield Ph.D. (Hist.)

2928 Home and away: the East India Company's engagement with Indian dress in Britain, c.1740–1835. Beth Louise Richards. (Dr. Benedict Burbridge and Professor Geoffrey Quilley.) Sussex D.Phil. (Hist. of Art)

2929 Education in early colonial India, 1750–1835. Zahra Shah. (Dr. Anna-Maria S. Misra.) Oxford D.Phil. (Mod. Hist.)

2930 The ordinary and the everyday world view of the British soldier in India, 1757–1947. Timothy Moore. (Dr. Padma Angol.) Cardiff Ph.D. (Hist. & Archaeol.)

2931 Flawed ideals: classical models and East India Company rule. Benjamin F. Hamer. (Dr. John Darwin.) Oxford M.St. (Mod. Hist.)

2932 The London West India interest. Angelina Osborne. (Dr. Douglas Hamilton and Dr. Charles Prior.) Hull Ph.D. (Hist.)

2933 Deism and the interpretation of Hinduism in the writing of East India Company servants, 1764–1800. Jessica Patterson. (Professors Stuart Jones and Jeremy Gregory.) Manchester Ph.D. (Hist.)

2934   'Neither the highs nor rivers will obstruct': revisiting the East India Company's failed 1767 expedition to Nepal. Samuel Ellis. (Dr. Kevin B. Linch and Dr. Andrea Major.) Leeds Ph.D. (Hist.)

2935   The culture and identity of the British East India Company colonial administrator, 1773–1833. William Raybould. (Dr. Kirsty Reid and Dr. Josie McLellan.) Bristol Ph.D. (Hist. Stud.)

2936   Imperial ideology, popular politics, and the regulation of the East India Company, 1773–84. Ben Gilding. (Dr. Renaud Morieux.) Cambridge Ph.D. (Hist.)

2937   Colonialism across the ocean: the political thought of Rammohun Roy. Shomik Dasgupta. (Dr. Jon Wilson and Dr. David Todd.) King's College London M.Phil./ Ph.D. (Hist.)

2938   Opium-eaters and opium peddlers: cultural manifestations of opium in north-east India and its echoes in a transnational age. Ved Baruah. (Dr. Padma Anagol.) Cardiff Ph.D. (Hist. & Archaeol.)

2939   British political thought and the Raj: conquest, consent and constitutionalism in India, 1818–1933. Kieran Hazzard. (Dr. Jon Wilson and Professor Arthur Burns.) King's College London M.Phil./Ph.D. (Hist.)

2940   The rule of law and emergency in colonial India: the conflict between the government and the King's Court in Bombay in the 1820s. Haruki Inagaki. (Dr. Jon E. Wilson.) King's College London M.Phil./Ph.D. (Hist.)

2941   Calcutta Botanic Garden: knowledge formation and the expectations of botany in a colonial context, 1833–1914. Adrian Thomas. (Dr. Jon E. Wilson.) King's College London M.Phil./Ph.D. (Hist.)

2942   Merchants and labourers: Indo-Khalijee interconnectivity and the development of migrant communities in the Persian Gulf. Samuel Plaxton. (Dr. Andrea Major and Professor William R. Gould.) Leeds Ph.D. (Hist.)

2943   Contested sovereignty and domesticity in Anglo-Sikh imperial politics, 1843–93: the 'family saga' of Maharani Jind Kaur, Maharaja Duleep Singh and Queen Victoria. Rajpreet Atwal. (Dr. Faisal Devji.) Oxford D.Phil. (Mod. Hist.)

2944   Picturing the West India regiments in an age of unrest, civil war and tourism, c.1850–1914. Melissa Bennett. (Professor David Lambert.) Warwick Ph.D. (Hist.)

2945   Empire, medicine and society: Irish and Indian case studies, 1850–1914. Kieran J. Fitzpatrick. (Professor Mark Harrison.) Oxford D.Phil. (Mod. Hist.)

2946   'Our rule in India rests wholly on ourselves': the district officer in Bengal, 1850–1905. Amy Kavanagh. (Dr. Jon Wilson and Professor Ian McBride.) King's College London M.Phil./Ph.D. (Hist.)

2947   Situating the Coolie question: indentured labour and mid 19th-century Calcutta. Purba Hossain. (Dr. Andrea Major and Professor William R. Gould.) Leeds Ph.D. (Hist.)

2948   Politics of public order laws in India, 1857–1975: a study into the tactics of 'exception'. Javed Wani. (Dr. Markus Daechsel.) London M.Phil./Ph.D. (R.H.U.L. Hist.)

2949   Intoxication and the Indian colonial military: drugs consumption and control in the Indian Army, 1857–1919.   Chris Cavin.   Glasgow Caledonian Ph.D.   (Hist.)

2950   The uprising in the 'periphery': Bengal, 1857–8.   Niladri Chatterjee.   (Dr. Shabnum Tejani.)   London Ph.D.   (S.O.A.S. Hist.)

2951   Criminality in British India.   Christian Robinson.   (Dr. Anindita Ghosh and Dr. Steven Pierce.)   Manchester Ph.D.   (Hist.)

2952   The politics of human well-being: a case study of Pakistan from British Raj to military rule.   Zujaja Tauqeer.   (Professor Mark Harrison.)   Oxford D.Phil.   (Mod. Hist.)

2953   History of mental illness in Britain and India, 1858–1947.   Michael Young.   (Dr. Robert Ellis and Professor Barry Doyle.)   Huddersfield Ph.D.   (Music, Hum. & Media)

2954   Sanitary regulation in Britain's maritime empire: disease and naval health in the northern Indian Ocean, 1860–1914.   Manikarnika Dutta.   (Professor Mark Harrison.)   Oxford D.Phil.   (Mod. Hist.)

2955   The land of milk and honey: soldiers as migrants connecting India and the United Kingdom, 1860–1914.   Gaiwin Eley.   (Professor Miles Taylor.)   London Ph.D.   (Inst. Hist. Res.)

2956   Anglo-Russian rivalry in the Pamirs and Hindukush, 1860–1914.   Hakim Elnazarov.   (Dr. Stephen Lovell and Dr. Jon Wilson.)   King's College London M.Phil./Ph.D.   (Hist.)

2957   Contesting urban space: Delhi, 1860–1911.   Raghav Kishore.   (Dr. Shabnum Tejani.)   London Ph.D.   (S.O.A.S. Hist.)

2958   Nationalism, the Gaelic Athletic Association, and cricket in India – unity and disunity.   Aidan J. Hocking.   (Dr. Faisal Devji.)   Oxford M.St.   (Mod. Hist.)

2959   Sacred cows, veterinary practice and the dairy industry: how perceptions of animal agency defined the nature of domestication in colonial India, 1870–1940.   Lloyd Price.   (Dr. Padma Angol.)   Cardiff Ph.D.   (Hist. & Archaeol.)

2960   The education of Bengali women: transitions in the late 19th to mid 20th century, 1870–1940.   Shahla Young.   (Dr. Avril Powell.)   London Ph.D.   (S.O.A.S. Hist.)

2962   Police power, corruption and collective criminality: the Criminal Tribes Acts in the Bombay presidency.   Andrew Lunt.   (Professor William R. Gould and Dr. Jonathan Saha.)   Leeds Ph.D.   (Hist.)

2963   Muslim capitalism and the merchant communities of Khojas-Bohras and Memons in Bombay, 1880–1950.   Danish Khan.   (Dr. Faisal Devji.)   Oxford D.Phil.   (Mod. Hist.)

2964   The social life of electricity in colonial India, c.1880–1940.   Aminesh Chatterjee.   (Professor Karen Sayer and Dr. Di Drummond.)   Leeds Trinity Ph.D.   (Hist.)

2965   Tlengtle: colonial conquest and religious entanglement: a mizo history from north-east India (c.1890–1920).   Kyle Jackson.   (Professors David Hardiman and Roberta Bivins.)   Warwick Ph.D.   (Hist.)

2966   Passages through India: Western indophiles and transnational encounters in colonial India, 1895–1945 .   Somak Biswas.   (Dr. Sarah Hodges.)   Warwick M.Phil./Ph.D.   (Hist.)

2967 Re-evaluating the pacification of the north-west frontier of India, 1897–1919. Liam Morton. (Dr. Jon Wilson and Dr. Sarah Stockwell.) King's College London M.Phil./ Ph.D. (Hist.)

2968 Historicising perceptions of the West in Pakistan's public discourse. Dost Khan. (Dr. Markus Daechsel.) London M.Phil./Ph.D. (R.H.U.L. Hist.)

2969 Aspects of Indian epistemology and pedagogy, as related to culture and society. Meera Sarin. (Professor Gary McCulloch.) London Ed.D. (Inst. of Educ.)

2970 The foundation of the Benares Hindu University and the role of institutional individualism in early 20th-century Indian nationalism. William Richards. (Dr. Faisal Devji.) Oxford M.St. (Mod. Hist.)

2971 Forgetting India in the First World War: imperial pasts and contemporary British Indian identity, 1914–2014. David Donaldson. (Dr. Ana Carden-Coyne and Dr. Laurence Brown.) Manchester Ph.D. (Hist.)

2972 Serving the Raj in the era of total war: the British officer in the Indian army, 1914–47. Adam Prime. (Professor Clare Anderson.) Leicester Ph.D. (Hist.)

2973 Somebody else's war: an analysis of the Indian army's contribution to the First World War campaign on the Western Front and its subsequent commemoration in Britain. Karen Leenders. (Dr. Hester Barron and Professor Ian S. Gazeley.) Sussex D.Phil. (Hist.)

2974 Representations of Indian soldiers during World War I. Owen Dawson. (Dr. Timothy Grady.) Chester M.Phil. (Hist. & Archaeol.)

2975 The impact of the martial races theory during the First World War and its heritage. Amerdeep Panesar. (Professor Paul Ward.) Huddersfield M.Phil. (Music, Hum. & Media)

2976 The Ahmadiyya Muslim community in colonial and post-colonial India. Ayesha Mehta. (Dr. Faisal Devji.) Oxford D.Phil. (Mod. Hist.)

2977 Studies in history of politics: Calcutta, 1920s to 1970s. Agnibho Gangopadhyay. (Dr. Faisal Devji.) Oxford D.Phil. (Mod. Hist.)

2978 Sexual modernity in western India, 1920–60. Shrikant Botre. (Dr. Sarah Hodges.) Warwick Ph.D. (Hist.)

2979 Imagining the Hindu community: Gandhi and his 'Hindu' interlocutors. Vanya V. Bhargav. (Dr. Faisal Devji.) Oxford D.Phil. (Mod. Hist.)

2980 Between orthodoxy and heresy: Ahmadiyya, Islam and national identity in Pakistan, 1931–74. Shazia Ahmad. (Dr. Shabnum Tejani.) London Ph.D. (S.O.A.S. Hist.)

2981 Sovereign skies: Indian aviation and the modern state, 1933–54. Aashique A. Iqbal. (Dr. Robert Johnson and Dr. Yasmin Khan.) Oxford D.Phil. (Mod. Hist.)

2982 The princely states versus British India: fiscal history, public policy and development in modern India. Antonia Strachey. (Professor Robert Allen and Dr. Deborah Oxley.) Oxford D.Phil. (Mod. Hist.)

2983 A delayed independence: the ex-criminal tribes and modern India, 1940–2000. Sarah Gandee. (Professor William R. Gould.) Leeds Ph.D. (Hist.)

2984   An imperialist at bay: Leo Amery at the India Office, 1940–5. David Whittington.
        (Dr. Kent Fedorowich and Dr. John Fisher.) West of England Ph.D. (Hist.)

2985   An analysis of the ideology, rhetoric and philosophy underpinning Indian activism
        since the Second World War. Ben Harvey-Sporle. (Dr. Sam Hitchmough.)
        Canterbury Christ Church Ph.D. (Hist.)

2986   State, society and the environment in Bhawalpur, Pakistan. Zahid Khalid.
        (Professors Vinita Damodaran and Saul Dubow.) Sussex D.Phil. (Hist.)

2987   The political economy and sociology of education in Pakistan: historical explorations
        in the role of the state, ideology and class. Zulfi Ali. (Dr. Tom Woodin and Dr. Marie
        Lall.) London Ph.D. (Inst. of Educ.)

2988   Meena Kumari and the Muslim story in post-partition Bollywood. Jordan L. Borgman.
        (Dr. Faisal Devji.) Oxford M.St. (Mod. Hist.)

2989   The role of Muslim universities in the redefinition of Indian Muslim identities after
        partition (1947–1990s). Gautuer Laurence. (Professor Joya Chatterji.) Cambridge
        Ph.D. (Hist.)

2990   A history of medical technology in post-colonial India: the development of technology
        in medicine, 1947–91. Stanislaw W. Kachnowski. (Professor Mark Harrison.)
        Oxford D.Phil. (Mod. Hist.)

2991   Occupation, diversity and public goods provision: evidence from Pakistan through
        partition. Rinchan A. Mirza. (Dr. James Fenske.) Oxford D.Phil. (Mod. Hist.)

2992   Rise of a Praetorian military system and its relationship with Islamic military in
        Pakistan. Sarah Ashraf. (Dr. Kirsten E. Schulze.) London Ph.D. (L.S.E. Int. Hist.)

2993   Population control in India, 1960–80: an investigation into population control practices
        carried out in India by the G.O.I. and international population control organisations.
        Cathryn Johnston. (Dr. Jahnavi Phalkey and Dr. Jon Wilson.) King's College
        London M.Phil./Ph.D. (Hist.)

2994   The perceptions of security in Pakistan in the aftermath of the civil war and interstate
        war against India and the emergence of Bangladesh in 1971. Sohail Nazir. (Dr. Jon
        E. Wilson.) King's College London M.Phil./Ph.D. (Hist.)

2995   Gender, power and the Indian emergency, 1975–7. Gemma Scott. (Dr. Shalini
        Sharma and Dr. Mariangela Palladino.) Keele Ph.D. (Hist.)

2996   The state of emergency in India, 1975–6: national security in a domestic context.
        Deepali Kulkarni. (Dr. Faisal Devji.) Oxford D.Phil. (Mod. Hist.)

2997   Sun and surgery. History of medical tourism, c.1976–2013: case study of Indian
        'high tech' hospitals. Orla Mulrooney. (Professors David Hardiman and Roberta E.
        Bivins.) Warwick Ph.D. (Hist.)

2998   Between Marx and Muhammad: the emergence of Islamism in communist-ruled
        Bengal. Shahnawaz A. Raihan. (Dr. Faisal Devji.) Oxford D.Phil. (Mod. Hist.)

2999   The legacy of the 1947 Partition in 1984 India. Jasneet K. Aulakh. (Dr. Faisal
        Devji.) Oxford M.St. (Mod. Hist.)

3000   An inquiry concerning identification projects in India, 1991–2013. Taha Mehmood.
        (Dr. Faisal Devji and Dr. Maria Misra.) Oxford D.Phil. (Mod. Hist.)

Sri Lanka and Indian Ocean

3001 Chatting Sri Lanka: powerful communications in colonial times. Justin Siefert.
(Dr. Anthony J. Adams, Dr. Tilman Frasch and Dr. Sheila French.) Manchester
Metropolitan Ph.D. (Hist.)

South-East Asia

3002 Chasing dragons through time and space: changing representations of Martabani
storage jars. Borbalai Nyiri. (Dr. Huw Barton and Dr. Sandra Dudley.) Leicester
Ph.D. (Archaeol. & Anc. Hist.)

3003 The association between dental caries prevalence and the emergence of agriculture
in the ancient population during pre and post agricultural period in Thailand. Korakot
Boonlop. (Dr. Huw Barton and Dr. Joanna Appleby.) Leicester Ph.D. (Archaeol. &
Anc. Hist.)

3004 Mandalas and Janapadas: early Southeast Asian economic history through trade
connectivity. Pacharaporn Phanomvan na Ayudhya. (Professors Christopher
Gosden and Kevin O'Rourke.) Oxford D.Phil. (Mod. Hist.)

3005 In search of the other: ethnicity, identity and difference in early modern Southeast
Asia. Maria Kekki. (Dr. Michael Charney.) London Ph.D. (S.O.A.S. Hist.)

3006 The Burmese migration into Thailand in the 19th and 20th centuries. Thanyarat
Apiwong. (Dr. Michael Charney.) London Ph.D. (S.O.A.S. Hist.)

3007 The cultural transformation of Siam in the 19th and early 20th centuries. Thomas R.
Bruce. (Dr. Michael Charney.) London Ph.D. (S.O.A.S. Hist.)

3008 The development of higher education in Malaya, c.1819–1949. John Cocking. (Dr.
Andrew Cohen and Dr. Janice Malcolm.) Kent Ph.D. (Hist.)

3009 News from Burmah: the role of the English press in the making of the British empire
in Burma. Rachatpong Malithong. (Dr. Anindita Ghosh and Dr. Pratik Chakrabarti.)
Manchester Ph.D. (Hist.)

3010 To what extent can educational policy explain variations in the prevalence, ferocity
and success of nationalist movements in colonial Southeast Asia, 1850–1950?
Jonathon M. Clegg. (Dr. Gregg Huff.) Oxford M.Sc. (Mod. Hist.)

3011 Chinese migration in Thailand from the late 19th century. Tawirat Songmuang. (Dr.
Weipin Tsai.) London M.Phil./Ph.D. (R.H.U.L. Hist.)

3012 Racial institutions, policies and attitudes: British rule in colonial Malaya, 1890s–1941.
Oliver W. Tilbrook. (Professor Micah Muscolino.) Oxford M.St. (Mod. Hist.)

3013 Pudu Jail's graffiti: beyond the prison cells. Khairul Ismail. (Professor Daniel
Maudlin, Dr. Sarah Bennett and Professor Malcolm Miles.) Plymouth Ph.D. (Hum.)

3014 Mapping cultural transition: the Burma Research Society and its journals, 1910–37.
Carol Ann Boshier. (Dr. Mandy Sadan.) London Ph.D. (S.O.A.S. Hist.)

3015 Global networks and the Indonesian Nationalist Movement. Fletcher R. O'Leary.
(Dr. Kevin Fogg.) Oxford M.St. (Mod. Hist.)

3016 To examine the composition of Force 136 at the close of World War II in Malaya and the impact of this upon its role in the recolonisation of Malaya. Rebecca Kenneison. (Dr. Mark Frost.) Essex Ph.D. (Hist.)

3017 The Burmese military and the press in U Nu's Burma. Maung Bo Bo. (Dr. Konrad Hirschler.) London Ph.D. (S.O.A.S. Hist.)

3018 Oasis on a troubled continent: culture and ideology in Cold War Thailand. Matthew Phillips. (Professor Ian Brown.) London Ph.D. (S.O.A.S. Hist.)

3019 The management of intelligence during the Malayan Emergency. Roger Arditti. (Dr. Philip Davies.) Brunel Ph.D. (Pol. & Hist.)

3020 The Karen people in Burma and Britain: refugees, identity and memory. Peter Bjorklund. (Professor Peter Gatrell and Dr. Ana Carden-Coyne.) Manchester Ph.D. (Hist.)

3021 Irrelevant or conveniently ignored: missionaries in the new villages of Malaya, 1952–67. Allen McClymont. (Dr. John Stuart and Professor Craig Phelan.) Kingston Ph.D. (Econ., Hist. & Pol.)

3022 The politics of institutional reform in Indonesia: comparative study between the President Soeharto era, 1965–98, and the post-Soeharto era, 1998–2014. Vishnu Juwono. (Dr. Kirsten E. Schulze.) London Ph.D. (L.S.E. Int. Hist.)

3023 The Khmer Rouge: British politics and attitudes on mass violence, 1968–89. David Booth. (Dr. Nick Thomas and Professor John W. Young.) Nottingham Ph.D. (Hist.)

3024 Modernisation and nation-building in south Vietnam, 1968–76. Simon Toner. (Professor O. Arne Westad.) London Ph.D. (L.S.E. Int. Hist.)

Far East, East Indies and Philippines

3025 Missionary rivalry in the Far East, 1580–1670. Wei Jiang. (Professors Francisco Bethencourt and Linda Newson.) King's College London M.Phil./Ph.D. (Hist.)

3026 The amelioration and recovery of Britain's Far East P.O.W.s. Andrew Chesworth. (Professor Robert Moore.) Sheffield Ph.D. (Hist.)

3027 The integration of Basilan Island into the Philippines, 1946–86. Shazwani Binti Haji Shahibulbahri. (Professor William Gervase Clarence-Smith.) London Ph.D. (S.O.A.S. Hist.)

3028 British propaganda and the threat of communism in the Far East, 1948–54. Katie Griffiths. (Professor John W. Young and Dr. Spencer W. Mawby.) Nottingham Ph.D. (Hist.)

China, Hong Kong and Korea

3029 Health, perfection and transcendence: Daoist transmissions of medical knowledge in early medieval China. Michael Stanley-Baker. (Dr. Vivienne Lo and Dr. Antonello Palumbo.) London Ph.D. (U.C. Hist.)

3030 Mysteries of the tongue: the invention of a diagnostic tradition in Chinese medicine. Nancy Holroyde-Downing. (Dr. Vivienne Lo and Professor Ma Kenwen.) London Ph.D. (U.C. Hist.)

3031 Self-cultivation and the formation of identity in early modern China. David Dear. (Dr. Vivienne Lo and Professor Volker Scheid.) London Ph.D. (U.C. Hist.)

3032 Local power and legal control: princely crime in mid 16th-century China. Jerome Kerlouegan. (Professor Craig Clunas.) Oxford D.Phil. (Mod. Hist.)

3033 The role of music in the cultural and diplomatic relations between China and the West in the 17th and 18th centuries. Shubing Jia. (Professors Stephen Banfield and Robert Bickers.) Bristol Ph.D. (Hist. Stud.)

3034 'The colours of each piece': production and consumption of Chinese enamelled porcelain, c.1728–1780. Hui Tang. (Professor Anne Gerritsen.) Warwick Ph.D. (Hist.)

3035 Imperial eyes examined: the British encounter with Formosa in the 19th century. Chia-Lin Huang. (Dr. Lars Laamann.) London Ph.D. (S.O.A.S. Hist.)

3036 Late Qing China and the British world: space, body and the image of empire, 1840–1920. Shengfang Chou. (Professor Anne Gerritsen.) Warwick M.Phil./Ph.D. (Hist.)

3037 Chinese elites in colonial Hong Kong. Kaori Abe. (Professor Robert Bickers.) Bristol M.Litt. (Hist. Stud.)

3038 British foreign policy towards China, 1842–56. Luke Heselwood. (Professors Yangwen Zheng and Stuart Jones.) Manchester Ph.D. (Hist.)

3039 Playing Chinese whispers: British intelligence in China, 1850–64. Adam D. Cohen. (Dr. John Darwin.) Oxford M.St. (Mod. Hist.)

3040 Corruption in the Chinese customs service. James Williams. (Professor Robert Bickers.) Bristol M.Litt. (Hist. Stud.)

3041 Embodying empire: governance and the colonial construction of space in Hong Kong and Shanghai, 1858–1911. Freddie Stephenson. (Dr. Sascha Auerbach and Dr. Anna Greenwood.) Nottingham Ph.D. (Hist.)

3042 Opium consumption and regulation in Singapore and Shanghai, 1875–1909. Samuel R. Betteridge. (Professor Gregg Huff.) Oxford M.Phil. (Mod. Hist.)

3043 Recreation from British style to Shanghai style. Jiarong Lu. (Dr. Mark Frost and Dr. Xun Zhou.) Essex M.Phil. (Hist.)

3044 British attitudes towards the opium trade and the Chinese, c.1880–1920. Ronan P. Popert. (Professor Micah Muscolino.) Oxford M.St. (Mod. Hist.)

3045 Trade, war and socialism: Chongqing's urban and rural economy, 1891–1962. Wankun Li. (Dr. Adam Cathcart and Dr. Shane D. Doyle.) Leeds Ph.D. (Hist.)

3046 Ornament and the town house in Japanese Taiwan. Ya-Ting Fan. (Professor Paul Davies.) Reading Ph.D. (Hist. of Art)

3047 Antiseptic religion: medicine, Christianity and colonisation in Korea. Shin Kwon Kim. (Professor Mark Harrison.) Oxford D.Phil. (Mod. Hist.)

3048 The development of Chinese naval thought. Tim Woods. (Dr. Alessio Patalano and Professor Andrew D. Lambert.) King's College London Ph.D. (War Stud.)

3049 China's new administration in the inner Asian frontiers in the late Qing period, 1901–11. Cyrus K.Y. Yee. (Dr. Lars Laamann.) London Ph.D. (S.O.A.S. Hist.)

3050 The rise and fall of psychiatry in Shanghai from 1930 to 1940. Jin Ping Ma. (Professor Mathew Thomson.) Warwick Ph.D. (Hist.)

3051 In what way does the case of the wartime Jewish refugee community of Shanghai fit into debates surrounding the definition of a Holocaust survivor? Gabrielle R. Abram. (Professor Rana Mitter.) Oxford M.St. (Mod. Hist.)

3052 Hope and reality: the good life for Chinese youth, 1949–66. Sha Hua. (Professor Rana S.R. Mitter.) Oxford D.Phil. (Mod. Hist.)

3053 'Children of the dragon': Tan Kah Kee, the Nanyang overseas Chinese and new China, 1949–61. Jin Lin. (Professor O. Arne Westad.) London Ph.D. (L.S.E. Int. Hist.)

3054 The development of South Korean naval power. Ian Bowers. (Professor Andrew D. Lambert and Dr. Alessio Patalano.) King's College London Ph.D. (War Stud.)

3055 'Civilising' China: visualising Wenmind in contemporary China. Ros Holmes. (Professor Craig Clunas.) Oxford D.Phil. (Mod. Hist.)

3056 The history, development and roles of national museums in South Korea. Jin Soo Park. London Ph.D. (Inst. Archaeol.)

3057 The problematic origin of contemporary Chinese art: the new concrete image in the 85 new wave. Zhiyun Gong. (Professor David Mellor and Geoffrey Quilley.) Sussex D.Phil. (Hist. of Art)

3058 The structure and use of photography by photojournalists during China's Cultural Revolution. Fangfei Chen. (Dr. Xun Zhou.) Essex Ph.D. (Hist.)

3059 Dynamics of the Mao cult in Tibet during the Cultural Revolution. Anneliese Smit. (Dr. Andrea Janki.) London Ph.D. (S.O.A.S. Hist.)

3060 The struggles of Chinese Trotskyism in the 1970s–80s: a historical and discourse analysis. Yang Yang. (Dr. Xun Zhou.) Essex Ph.D. (Hist.)

3061 Western pollutions and the paradox of opening up: ideologies, objects, and bodies in the People's Republic of China, 1972–92. Julian B. Gewirtz. (Professor Rana Mitter.) Oxford D.Phil. (Mod. Hist.)

Japan

3062 Barbarism and virtue in Japanese political thought, c.1700–1890. Yi Mo. (Dr. Sho Konishi.) Oxford D.Phil. (Mod. Hist.)

3063 Japanese imperialism in the context of genocide. Kelly Maddox. (Professor Aristotle Kallis.) Lancaster Ph.D. (Hist.)

3064 Collective constructions: the establishment of borders and the emergence of the modern Japanese state, 1861–75. Takahiro Yamamoto. (Dr. Antony M. Best.) London Ph.D. (L.S.E. Int. Hist.)

3065 Exploring the origins of alliance: Anglo-Japanese diplomacy in the late 19th century. Yu Suzuki. (Dr. Antony M. Best.) London Ph.D. (L.S.E. Int. Hist.)

3066 The Banka Petition: Anglo-Japanese relations and the cession of Formosa in 1895. Niki Alsford. (Dr. Lars Laamann.) London Ph.D. (S.O.A.S. Hist.)

3067 The agrarian foundations of early 20th-century Japanese anarchism: Ishikawa Sanshiro's revolutionary practices of everyday life, 1903–45. Nadine Willems. (Dr. Sho Konishi.) Oxford D.Phil. (Mod. Hist.)

3068 The British empire and the challenge of Japan, 1904–11. Cornelius Heere. (Dr. Antony M. Best.) London Ph.D. (L.S.E. Int. Hist.)

3069 The Hibiya riot beyond Tokyo and popular nationalism: thought and action amongst ordinary citizens. Yu Sakai. (Dr. Sho Konishi.) Oxford D.Phil. (Mod. Hist.)

3070 Cultural multiplicity and contested identities: Iha Fuyu's imagining of Okinawa's place in Taisho-era Japan, 1912–26. Randall S. Northrop. (Dr. Sho Konishi.) Oxford M.St. (Mod. Hist.)

3071 'Give us our blue skies back': anti-pollution movements and the rise of civil society in Kitakyushu, 1945–70. Political housewives, 'non-protest' and mutual aid. Anna Schrade. (Dr. Sho Konishi.) Oxford D.Phil. (Mod. Hist.)

3072 The post-war housing reconstruction in London and Tokyo. Madoka Minashima. (Dr. J.H. Davis.) Oxford D.Phil. (Mod. Hist.)

3073 The discourse on nation in post-war Japan, 1952–72. Martyn Smith. (Dr. Christopher Gerteis.) London Ph.D. (S.O.A.S. Hist.)

AUSTRALASIA AND PACIFIC OCEAN

3074 Reading places: the British navy and the understanding of Pacific regions in the 19th century. Hana Oh. (Professor Mark Harrison.) Oxford D.Phil. (Mod. Hist.)

3075 The Royal Navy and colonial collecting in Australia, c.1820–70. Daniel Simpson. (Dr. Zoe Laidlaw.) London M.Phil./Ph.D. (R.H.U.L. Hist.)

3076 Free or unfree labour: the British empire and the establishment of the Swan River Colony. Kellie Moss. (Professor Clare Anderson.) Leicester Ph.D. (Hist.)

3077 Island chains: a spatial history of Australian convict islands. Katherine Roscoe. (Professor Clare Anderson.) Leicester Ph.D. (Hist.)

3078 Science at sea: the conduct of science in South Pacific voyaging, c.1838–50. Sarah Millar. (Professor C.W.J. Withers.) Edinburgh Ph.D. (Geog.)

3079 New Zealand in a 'Pacific age': (mis)-managing mandates in a sea of imperial internationalism, 1914–34. Sean J. Phillips. (Professor James Belich.) Oxford M.St. (Mod. Hist.)

3080 Little Britons? Irish and New Zealand children in the Great War. Charlotte J.S. Bennett. (Professor James Belich and Dr. Senia Paseta.) Oxford D.Phil. (Mod. Hist.)

3081　Cracks in the Great White Walls: managing race, gender and nation in New Zealand's empire-state, 1914–39.　Harriet J. Mercer.　(Professor James Belich.)　Oxford M.St. (Mod. Hist.)

THESES IN PROGRESS IN UNIVERSITIES IN THE REPUBLIC OF IRELAND

HISTORICAL METHODS

3082 A digital edition of St. Patrick's writings. Ronan Bleier. (Professor Seán Duffy.) Trinity College Dublin Ph.D. (Hist.)

3083 Ethical commemoration: a cross-border comparative investigation of commemoration on the island of Ireland in 1991, 1998 and 2016. Maeve Casserly. (Professor Mary E. Daly and Dr. Emilie Pine.) U.C. Dublin Ph.D. (Hist.)

3084 Historical and contemporary Roman Catholic paradigms in international relations theory. James Cussen. (Professors Geoff Roberts and David Ryan.) U.C. Cork Ph.D. (Hist.)

3085 Archivists engaging with research data. Rebecca Grant. (Dr. Julie Brooks and Dr. Elizabeth Mullins.) U.C. Dublin Ph.D. (Hist.)

3086 The National Monuments service and its archival collections. Rachel Barrett. (Professor Terry Barry.) Trinity College Dublin Ph.D. (Hist.)

3087 Digital approaches to the history of art and architecture online. Karolina Badzmierowska. (Dr. Peter Cherry and Dr. Hugh Denard.) Trinity College Dublin Ph.D. (Hist. of Art)

HISTORIOGRAPHY

3088 Facts or fiction: the Church of Ireland's writing of Irish church history, 1838–70. Jamie Blake-Knox. (Professor Ciaran F. Brady.) Trinity College Dublin Ph.D. (Hist.)

3089 Linking archaeology: considering the epistemological and sociological implications of a linked open data archaeology. Frank Lynam. (Dr. Christine Morris.) Trinity College Dublin Ph.D. (Classics)

3090 The artist's biography as a source of meaning. Karl Thomas. (Dr. Yvonne Scott.) Trinity College Dublin Ph.D. (Hist. of Art)

ANCIENT HISTORY

General

3091 The social meaning of early bronze age architecture in the eastern Aegean and western Anatolia. Kalypso Faropoulou. (Dr. Christine Morris.) Trinity College Dublin M.Litt. (Classics)

191

3092   The fiction of occasion in Hellenistic and Roman poetry. Adrian Gramps. (Dr. Martine Cuypers and Professor Monica Gale.) Trinity College Dublin Ph.D. (Classics)

Greece and Mediterranean

3093   Midwives of Eileithyia: an analysis of women's ritual pharmacological lore in Minoan Crete. Simone Zimmerman. (Dr. Christine Morris.) Trinity College Dublin Ph.D. (Classics)

3094   Tomb re-aders: anthropological approaches to the funerary archaeology of prepalatial Crete – review, redefinition and reconsideration. Ellen Finn. (Dr. Christine Morris.) Trinity College Dublin Ph.D. (Classics)

3095   The design and use of provincial ceramics in middle Minoan East Crete, as observed at Priniatikos Pyrgos. David Breeckner. (Dr. Christine Morris.) Trinity College Dublin Ph.D. (Classics)

3096   Following the life-cycle of base-ring female figurines in late bronze age Cyprus. Constantina Alexandrou. (Dr. Christine Morris.) Trinity College Dublin Ph.D. (Classics)

3097   Becoming a god: situating immortalisation in Ancient Greek polytheism. Olaf Almqvist. (Dr. Ashley Clements.) Trinity College Dublin Ph.D. (Classics)

3098   Capturing Iambos: code-switching in an Ancient Greek literary language. Clara Felisari. (Dr. Martine Cuypers.) Trinity College Dublin Ph.D. (Classics)

3099   The political economy of Classical Athens: a maritime perspective. Barry O'Halloran. (Professor Brian McGing.) Trinity College Dublin Ph.D. (Classics)

3100   Age as a determinant of male behaviour in four plays by Euripides: Medea, Heracleidae, Heracles and Phoenissae. Faheema Ali. (Dr. Martine Cuypers.) Trinity College Dublin Ph.D. (Classics)

3101   Socratic leadership and virtue in Xenophon. Daniel Schotman. (Professor Brian McGing.) Trinity College Dublin Ph.D. (Classics)

3102   'Medeae Medea forem': rehabilitating Ovid's Medea. Bethany Flanders. (Professor Monica Gale.) Trinity College Dublin Ph.D. (Classics)

3103   Hero and exile: Plutarch's *Life of Sertorius*. Graham Gwozdecky. (Professor Brian McGing.) Trinity College Dublin Ph.D. (Classics)

Ancient Rome and the empire

3104   Fire in Ancient Rome. Margaret Desmond. (Dr. Hazel Dodge.) Trinity College Dublin Ph.D. (Classics)

3105   Gardens of Lucullus: ornamental garden structures during the late Republic. Sascha Smith. (Professor Monica Gale.) Trinity College Dublin M.Litt. (Classics)

3106   'Sic hominum genus est': animals and the continuum of life in the *De Rerum Natura* of Lucretius. Pamela Zinn. (Professor Monica Gale.) Trinity College Dublin Ph.D. (Classics)

3107 'Ille regit animos dictis': models of authority in Vergil's *Aeneid*. Katherine Sanborn. (Professor Monica Gale.) Trinity College Dublin Ph.D. (Classics)

3108 Satiric censure and philosophical therapy in Persius. Joao de Olivera Sita. (Professor Anna Chahoud.) Trinity College Dublin Ph.D. (Classics)

MEDIEVAL EUROPE

Subjects covering long periods

3109 Brychan Brychein, his children and Irish-British relations in early medieval Britain. Myles Gibbons. (Professor Dáibhí Ó Cróinín.) N.U.I. Galway Ph.D. (Hist.)

3110 Cross-cultural connections between insular manuscript illumination and the Mediterranean world. Laura McCloskey. (Dr. Laura Cleaver.) Trinity College Dublin Ph.D. (Hist. of Art)

3111 Fili, eices, bard, cainte, dulsaine and rindaid. Eoin O'Donnchadha. (Dr. Elva Johnston.) U.C. Dublin Ph.D. (Hist.)

3112 Manifestations of heavenly light and fire and the construction of a saint. Ruairi O'Sullivan. (Dr. Damian Bracken.) U.C. Cork Ph.D. (Hist.)

3113 Legal position and living conditions of peasants and commoners in early medieval Ireland, *c.* 680–1170. Cherie Peters. (Professor Sean Duffy and Dr. Katherine Simms.) Trinity College Dublin Ph.D. (Hist.)

3114 The holy wells of County Kilkenny. Padraig Ó Dálaigh. (Dr. Catherine Swift.) Mary Immaculate College Ph.D. (Hist.)

3115 Settlement patterns in the Diocese of Tuam in the early and high medieval periods: a longue durée approach. John Tighe. (Professor Terry Barry.) Trinity College Dublin Ph.D. (Hist.)

3116 Medieval miracle accounts in Britain and Ireland as a source for medical practice. Krystal Carmichael. (Dr. Michael Staunton.) U.C. Dublin Ph.D. (Hist.)

3117 Relationships between the crown, the papacy and the military orders in medieval Ireland. Patrick Flynn. (Professor Terry Barry.) Trinity College Dublin Ph.D. (Hist.)

3118 Detainees and captivity in medieval Ireland. Philip Healy. (Dr. David Edwards and Professor Maire Herbert.) U.C. Cork Ph.D. (Hist.)

3119 The liberal arts in medieval Glendalough: manuscripts, impact and legacy. Mary Kelly. (Dr. Roy Flechner.) U.C. Dublin Ph.D. (Hist.)

3120 Grave goods as a medium to negotiate power: violence and gender in the burial rituals of medieval Ireland. Christina Wade. (Professor Terry Barry.) Trinity College Dublin Ph.D. (Hist.)

3121 An examination of earth mortared building technologies in later medieval Ireland, *c.*1100–1600. Shirley Markley. (Professor Terry Barry.) Trinity College Dublin Ph.D. (Hist.)

3122   Medieval manners and social etiquette, 1150–1550. Angela Evans. (Dr. Michael Staunton.) U.C. Dublin Ph.D. (Hist.)

3123   Meath in the later middle ages (1172–c.1540): settlement and people. Caren Mulcahy. (Dr. Edward Coleman.) U.C. Dublin Ph.D. (Hist.)

Early medieval to c.1000: general and continental

3124   Saints and scandals: representations of elite women in Bede and Gregory of Tours. Jennifer Coughlan. (Dr. Diarmuid Scully.) U.C. Cork Ph.D. (Hist.)

3125   Political information and communication during the mid 7th century. Davide Boerio. (Professors B. Dooley and Benigno.) U.C. Cork Ph.D. (Hist.)

3126   St. Killian's mission to Franconia: historical. Dmitrii Glass. (Dr. Catherine Swift.) Mary Immaculate College Ph.D. (Hist.)

3127   Ireland and the Irish in the Icelandic sagas. Seamus Johnston. (Professor Terry Barry and Dr. Helen Conrad-O'Brien.) Trinity College Dublin Ph.D. (Hist.)

3128   The 'feudal revolution' in the middle Loire Valley, c.850–1150. Niall Ó Súilleabháin. (Professor Ian Robinson and Dr. David Ditchburn.) Trinity College Dublin Ph.D. (Hist.)

Early medieval: Britain and Ireland

3129   The origins of *Crom Dubh* in early medieval Ireland. Claire Collins. (Dr. Elva Johnston.) U.C. Dublin Ph.D. (Hist.)

3130   Ends of the earth, ends of time: Bede and Insular and Patristic traditions on space and time. Daithi Ó Mathghamhna. (Dr. Diarmuid Scully.) U.C. Cork Ph.D. (Hist.)

3131   The law of the innocents, 697 A.D.: a law for non-combatants – its place in the history of international humanitarian law. James Houlihan. (Dr. Elva Johnston.) U.C. Dublin Ph.D. (Hist.)

3132   National identity, the classical tradition and Christian reform at the ends of the earth. Britt Forde. (Dr. Diarmuid Scully.) U.C. Cork Ph.D. (Hist.)

3133   The Faddan More psalter. John Gillis. (Dr. Laura Cleaver.) Trinity College Dublin Ph.D. (Hist. of Art)

Eleventh century

3134   Kingship, law and authority in Ireland, c.1000–1200. Ronan Mulhaire. (Professor Seán Duffy.) Trinity College Dublin Ph.D. (Hist.)

3135   The intellectual development of Saint Peter Damian, c.1007–72. Eimhin Walsh. (Professor Ian Robinson.) Trinity College Dublin Ph.D. (Hist.)

3136   Ideas of kingship during the pontificate of Gregory VII. Brian Mc Namee. (Professor Ian Robinson.) Trinity College Dublin Ph.D. (Hist.)

3137 Charting the development of crusading ideology: an examination of pre- and proto-crusade source material. Axel Kelly. (Professor Ian Robinson.) Trinity College Dublin Ph.D. (Hist.)

3138 Robert the Monk's account of the first crusade: a rhetorical study. Kenneth Coyne. (Dr. Kimberly LoPrete.) N.U.I. Galway Ph.D. (Hist.)

Twelfth century

3139 The cathedral chapters of medieval Ireland: formation and function, 1111–1378. Rhiannon Carey Bates. (Professor Seán Duffy.) Trinity College Dublin Ph.D. (Hist.)

3140 William Marshal's lordship of Leinster. David Collins. (Professor Raymond Gillespie.) N.U.I. Maynooth Ph.D. (Hist.)

3141 The frontier in medieval Ireland, 1169–1534. Eoghan Keane. (Professor Seán Duffy.) Trinity College Dublin Ph.D. (Hist.)

Thirteenth century

3142 The impact of commentary on text and image in early 13th-century bibles produced in France. Nina Baker. (Dr. Laura Cleaver.) Trinity College Dublin Ph.D. (Hist. of Art)

3143 Justice for all? Access by ethnic groups to the English court system in Ireland, 1252–1327. Stephen Hewer. (Dr. David Ditchburn and Dr. Peter Crooks.) Trinity College Dublin Ph.D. (Hist.)

Fourteenth century

3144 The technical development of bows and crossbows in later medieval Europe. Stuart Gorman. (Professor Terry Barry.) Trinity College Dublin Ph.D. (Hist.)

3145 Translating Cambrensis: the late medieval history of Giraldus' 'English conquest of Ireland'. Caoimhe Whelan. (Professor Seán Duffy.) Trinity College Dublin Ph.D. (Hist.)

3146 The politics of culture in 14th-century Padua: Mussato and the Cenacolo Padovano. Aislinn McCabe. (Dr. Jason Harris.) U.C. Cork Ph.D. (Hist.)

3147 Mythical king or laical Christ figure? The marrying of the sacred and the secular in 14th-century French Arthurian illuminations. Katherine Sedovic. (Dr. Laura Cleaver.) Trinity College Dublin Ph.D. (Hist. of Art)

3148 The commodities trade in the Irish Sea Zone, c.1350–1550. Colin Fitzpatrick. (Dr. David Ditchburn.) Trinity College Dublin Ph.D. (Hist.)

3149 Towns in late medieval Ireland, 1350–1550. Kieran Hoare. (Professor Steven G. Ellis.) N.U.I. Galway Ph.D. (Hist.)

3150 'Every Lord and gentleman of this said land': the gentry of English Ireland, c.1399–1513. Brian Coleman. (Professor Seán Duffy.) Trinity College Dublin Ph.D. (Hist.)

3151 Parliaments and political culture in the insular world, c.1399–1496. Lynn Kilgallon. (Dr. David Ditchburn.) Trinity College Dublin Ph.D. (Hist.)

Fifteenth century

3152 Medieval aristocratic Irish women: a case study of Margaret FitzGerald, countess of Ormond and the Ormond women, c.1453–1614. Damien Duffy. (Professor Marian Lyons.) N.U.I. Maynooth Ph.D. (Hist.)

3153 Scotland and the papacy, 1487–1527. Alan John Smith. (Dr. David Ditchburn.) Trinity College Dublin Ph.D. (Hist.)

3154 Gaelic Irish and Scottish connections, 1490–1603. Simon Egan. (Dr. David Edwards.) U.C. Cork Ph.D. (Hist.)

MODERN EUROPE

General

3155 Rhetorics of difference (civility versus savagery) in early modern Ireland and Scandinavia. Carla Lessing. (Professor Steven G. Ellis.) N.U.I. Galway Ph.D. (Hist.)

3156 Into the void: translating text and image in Nordic art, 1890–1910. Kerstina Mortesen. (Dr. Yvonne Scott.) Trinity College Dublin Ph.D. (Hist. of Art)

3157 Irish perceptions of national identity in Austria-Hungary and its small successor states, 1914–45. Lilian Zach. (Dr. Mary N. Harris.) N.U.I. Galway Ph.D. (Hist.)

3158 Neutrality in the balance: Spanish-German relations during the First World War, 1914–18. Anne Rosenbusch. (Professor Filipe Ribeiro de Meneses.) N.U.I. Maynooth Ph.D. (Hist.)

3159 A comparative analysis of municipal/state cultural policies in Berlin, Budapest and Belgrade during the Second World War. Julia Balla. (Professor Anthony McElligott.) Limerick Ph.D. (Hist.)

3160 Escape as resistance: Allied escape lines in western Europe, 1940–2. Catherine Bergin. (Dr. David Murphy and Dr. Ian Speller.) N.U.I. Maynooth Ph.D. (Hist.)

3161 An analysis of small European navies from 1970s to 1990s. Ciaran Lowe. (Dr. Ian Speller.) N.U.I. Maynooth Ph.D. (Hist.)

France

3162 Ambiguities and contrasts among early Huguenots: politics and religion in 16th-century France. Gianmarco Braghi. (Dr. Graeme Murdock.) Trinity College Dublin Ph.D. (Hist.)

3163 Representations of music in French art from the Second Empire to the First World War. Una Pittion. (Dr. Philip Mc Evansoneya.) Trinity College Dublin Ph.D. (Hist. of Art)

3164 As others see us: the French grand reporter in Ireland during the 20th century. Oliver O'Hanlon. (Dr. Donal Ó Drisceoil.) U.C. Cork Ph.D. (Hist.)

3165 Colonial prisoners of war and Vichy France: experience and politics. Sarah Frank. (Professor John Horne.) Trinity College Dublin Ph.D. (Hist.)

Germany

3166 Zero-sum game: Great Britain, Germany and the race for oil, 1895–1921. Graham Kay. (Professor Filipe Ribeiro de Meneses.) N.U.I. Maynooth Ph.D. (Hist.)

3167 Hitler as military commander: from Blau to Edelweiss, January-November 1942. Alan Donohue. (Professor Alan Kramer.) Trinity College Dublin Ph.D. (Hist.)

Italy

3168 The art of constructing La Città Santa: the patronage of Pope Gregory XIII, 1572–85. Christine Carey. (Dr. Peter Cherry.) Trinity College Dublin Ph.D. (Hist. of Art)

3169 Guido Reni: workshop practices and painting techniques. Aoife Brady. (Dr. Peter Cherry.) Trinity College Dublin Ph.D. (Hist. of Art)

3170 Social, political and military development of the late Communi and early Signorie in central Italy. Daniele Troile. (Dr. Edward Coleman.) U.C. Dublin M.Litt. (Hist.)

3171 Francesco Borromini's drawings of San Carlo alle Quattro Fontane in the Context of architectural practice in 17th-century Rome. John McCrossan. (Dr. Christine Casey.) Trinity College Dublin Ph.D. (Hist. of Art)

3172 Writing the war: Italian junior combat officers on their war experience. Nella Porqueddu. (Professor John Horne.) Trinity College Dublin Ph.D. (Hist.)

Portugal

3173 Nazi era provenance and the Portuguese art trade, 1933–45. Maria Ines Sousa Fialho de Pinho Brandao. (Professor Filipe Ribeiro de Meneses.) N.U.I. Maynooth Ph.D. (Hist.)

Russia and the U.S.S.R.

3174 British imperialism in the Arctic: the British occupation of Archangel and Murmansk, 1918–19. Stephen Balbirnie. (Dr. Judith Devlin.) U.C. Dublin Ph.D. (Hist.)

3175 Polish exiles and forced wartime mobilization in the Soviet Union. Rorie Cartier. (Professor Alan Kramer.) Trinity College Dublin Ph.D. (Hist.)

Spain

3176 The role of the inquisitor general Don Diego de Arce y Reinoso. Zachary Gose. (Dr. Alistair Malcolm.) Limerick M.A. (Hist.)

MODERN BRITAIN AND IRELAND

From *c.*1500 (long periods)

3177 Music of the County Cork coastline – history and oral tradition. John McCarthy. (Dr. Donal Ó Drisceoil.) U.C. Cork Ph.D. (Hist.)

Sixteenth century

3178 'Here the sea of pity lies': conflicting views of Ireland's position in the early modern world. Sophie Hingst. (Professor Micheál Ó Siochrú and Dr. Mark Hennessy.) Trinity College Dublin Ph.D. (Hist.)

3179 Scholarly thought and literary allusion in early modern Irish political discourse. Alan Kelly. (Professor Ciarán Brady.) Trinity College Dublin Ph.D. (Hist.)

3180 The role of women in the religious reformations of early modern Ireland. Bronagh McShane. (Professor Marian Lyons.) N.U.I. Maynooth Ph.D. (Hist.)

3181 Thomond in early modern times. Lorna Moloney. (Professor Steven G. Ellis.) N.U.I. Galway Ph.D. (Hist.)

3182 The distribution of woodlands in Ireland under the Tudors. Raina D. Howe. (Professor Steven G. Ellis.) N.U.I. Galway Ph.D. (Hist.)

3183 The dissolution of the monasteries in Ireland. Bernadette O'Brien. (Professor Steven G. Ellis.) N.U.I. Galway Ph.D. (Hist.)

3184 Virtue and vice: murder and execution pamphlets in Elizabethan and Jacobean England. Patricia Walker. (Dr. Graeme Murdock.) Trinity College Dublin Ph.D. (Hist.)

3185 Irish dress and English politics, 1536–1649. Mary Raines. (Dr. Hiram Morgan.) U.C. Cork Ph.D. (Hist.)

3186 The exorcists in the Catholic Reformation. Alma O'Donnell. (Dr. Jason Harris.) U.C. Cork Ph.D. (Hist.)

3187 The career of Sir William Fitzwilliam of Northamptonshire (1526–99), lord deputy of Ireland. Deirdre Fennell. (Professor Steven G. Ellis.) N.U.I. Galway Ph.D. (Hist.)

3188 The reign and impact of Mary I on Irish constitutional, ecclesiastical, socio-cultural and intellectual developments. John O'Halloran. (Dr. Declan Downey.) U.C. Dublin Ph.D. (Hist.)

3189 Elizabethan Ireland: Secretary Walsingham and Crown intelligence. Stephen Purcell. (Dr. David Edwards.) U.C. Cork Ph.D. (Hist.)

3190 The Irish hydra: English policy in Gaelic Ulster, 1567–76. James Sheridan. (Professor Ciarán Brady.) Trinity College Dublin Ph.D. (Hist.)

3191 The mere Irish and the colonisation of Ulster, *c.*1570–1641. Gerard Farrell. (Professor Micheál Ó Siochrú.) Trinity College Dublin Ph.D. (Hist.)

3192 Visions of the past in Holinshed's *Chronicles*: conversion and identity. James Behan. (Dr. Diarmuid Scully and Dr. Clare O'Halloran.) U.C. Cork Ph.D. (Hist.)

3193 Annihilation or assimilation? The Gaelic professional classes in Ireland, c.1580–1625. Maire Sheehan. (Dr. David Edwards.) U.C. Cork M.Phil. (Hist.)

3194 The career of Captain Francisco de Cuellar. Francis Kelly. (Dr. Hiram Morgan.) U.C. Cork Ph.D. (Hist.)

3195 The contribution of the Irish to the English's defeat of the rebellion by O'Neill and O'Donnell in the Nine Years' War. Matthew McGinty. (Dr. Pádraig Lenihan.) N.U.I. Galway Ph.D. (Hist.)

3196 The Nine Years' War in Laois and Offaly. Diarmuid Wheeler. (Dr. Pádraig Lenihan.) N.U.I. Galway Ph.D. (Hist.)

3197 Peter Lombard's De Hibernia insula commentarius. Margaret Madden. (Dr. Jason Harris.) U.C. Cork Ph.D. (Hist.)

3198 French Anglicans: Huguenot exiles and identities in Britain and Ireland, c.1640–1680. Robert Gorvin. (Dr. Graeme Murdock.) Trinity College Dublin Ph.D. (Hist.)

Seventeenth century

General and political history

3199 Dissecting the monstrous body politic: political rhetoric and legal language in the time of Calvin's case. Anne Sappington. (Dr. Graeme Murdock.) Trinity College Dublin Ph.D. (Hist.)

3200 Irish banditry, 1641–1754. Stephen Furlong. (Professor David Dickson and Dr. Aileen Douglas.) Trinity College Dublin Ph.D. (Hist.)

3201 The adventurers for Irish land, 1642–70. David Brown. (Professor Micheál Ó Siochrú.) Trinity College Dublin Ph.D. (Hist.)

3202 Catholics and the law in Restoration Ireland. Paul Smith. (Professor Micheál Ó Siochrú and Dr. Mark Hennessy.) Trinity College Dublin Ph.D. (Hist.)

3203 The Catholic kingship of King James II. Gerard Howlin. (Dr. Robert Armstrong.) Trinity College Dublin Ph.D. (Hist.)

3204 Conscience and allegiance: an investigation into the controversy over the oaths of allegiance and supremacy during the reign of William III and II. Jeffrey Chambers. (Dr. Robert Armstrong.) Trinity College Dublin Ph.D. (Hist.)

3205 Legislation enacted by the Irish parliament 1692–1782: the background, implications and benefits of the laws that fashion Ireland with a system that endures to the present day. Patrick McCarthy. (Dr. Charles Ivar McGrath.) U.C. Dublin Ph.D. (Hist.)

17th century: Local history and government

3206 The Blakes of Ballyglunin. Philip Walsh. (Dr. Eamon O'Flaherty.) U.C. Dublin Ph.D. (Hist.)

17th century: Finance, trade and industry

3207 The design, production and consumption of silver in Ireland in the 17th century. Jessica Cunningham. (Dr. Alison FitzGerald.) N.U.I. Maynooth Ph.D. (Hist.)

17th century: Social history

3208 Secrets, ritual and masculinity: exploring the material culture of fraternity in Ireland and Britain during the long 18th century. Sarah Kennedy. (Dr. Alison FitzGerald.) N.U.I. Maynooth Ph.D. (Hist.)

17th century: Education, the arts, science and medicine

3209 James Wolveridge's *Speculum Matricis* (1669) and the instrumentalisation of obstetric practice. Michael O'Dowd. (Dr. Pádraig Lenihan.) N.U.I. Galway Ph.D. (Hist.)

Eighteenth century

General and political history

3210 English exceptionalism in the 18th century. Declan Mills. (Dr. David Fleming.) Limerick Ph.D.

3211 Belfast politics: rational dissent and political thought in 18th-century Ireland. William O'Dea. (Dr. Clare O'Halloran.) U.C. Cork Ph.D. (Hist.)

3212 Scotland, Ireland and union within the British Isles. Megan Vigor. (Dr. Robert Armstrong.) Trinity College Dublin Ph.D. (Hist.)

3213 Hibernian sans-culottes: Dublin's journeymen and radical politics, 1778–1803. Timothy Murtagh. (Professor David Dickson.) Trinity College Dublin Ph.D. (Hist.)

3214 The life of Richard Wellesley. Sile McGuckian. (Dr. Charles Ivar McGrath.) U.C. Dublin M.Litt. (Hist.)

3215 The uses of Gothic in Irish domestic and ecclesiastical architecture, 1785–1829. Judith Hill. (Dr. Christine Casey.) Trinity College Dublin Ph.D. (Hist. of Art)

18th century: Local history and government

3216 Eighteenth-century Drogheda: building a provincial town. Aisling Durkan. (Dr. Christine Casey.) Trinity College Dublin Ph.D. (Hist. of Art)

3217 The Glynn family and the development of Kilrush, 1798–1830. John (Paul) O'Brien. (Dr. Maura Cronin.) Mary Immaculate College Ph.D. (Hist.)

18th century: Administrative, military and naval history

3218 Lieutenant-General Arthur Dillon: Jacobite at the Regency court, 1715–25. Kate Geange. (Dr. Robert Armstrong.) Trinity College Dublin Ph.D. (Hist.)

3219 Catholics in the British army, 1790–1815: issues of identity. Darragh Cannon. (Professor Jacqueline Hill.) N.U.I. Maynooth Ph.D. (Hist.)

18th century: Finance, trade and industry

3220 The tobacco industry in Ireland, 1700–1930. Sean Whitney. (Dr. David Fleming.) Limerick Ph.D.

3221 A history of jewellers and their business in 18th- and 19th-century Ireland: a study in material culture. Zara Power. (Dr. David Fleming.) Limerick Ph.D. (Hist.)

3222 Managing money in 18th-century Ireland. Brendan Twomey. (Professor David Dickson.) Trinity College Dublin Ph.D. (Hist.)

18th century: Social history

3223 The Ryans of Inch during the 18th century: family, wealth and landed status. Richard Fitzpatrick. (Dr. Jonathan Wright and Professor Raymond Gillespie.) N.U.I. Maynooth M.Litt. (Hist.)

3224 Cross-currents in domestic development: the town house in London and Dublin, 1720–60. Melanie Hayes. (Dr. Christine Casey.) Trinity College Dublin Ph.D. (Hist. of Art)

3225 Letters as a source for the history of women in Ireland, 1750–1830. Jane Maxwell. (Professor David Dickson.) Trinity College Dublin Ph.D. (Hist.)

3226 The life and networks of Pamela Fitzgerald, c.1773–1831. Laura Mather. (Dr. Liam Chambers.) Mary Immaculate College M.A. (Hist.)

18th century: Ecclesiastical and religious history

3227 The 'Second Reformation' in Ireland, 1798–1861: case study of Revd. Robert Winning and the Kingscourt District. Marion Rogan. (Dr. Jacinta Prunty.) N.U.I. Maynooth Ph.D. (Hist.)

18th century: Education, the arts, science and medicine

3228 Science and patronage in 18th-century Britain: an analysis of the patron John Stuart, 3rd earl of Bute. Caroline Gillan. (Dr. Niall Ó Ciosáin.) N.U.I. Galway Ph.D. (Hist.)

3229 Small treasures: jewellery in Ireland, c.1770–1870. Breda Scott. (Dr. Alison FitzGerald.) N.U.I. Maynooth Ph.D. (Hist.)

3230 Defining surgical competence: the Royal College of Surgeons in Ireland, 1784–2014. Katherine Browne. (Dr. Ciaran O'Neill.) Trinity College Dublin Ph.D. (Hist.)

Nineteenth century

General and political history

3231   Léargais ar shaol Gharumne agus na Ceathrún Rua sa Naoú Céad Déag. Áine Ní Chongaile. (Dr. John Cunningham.) N.U.I. Galway Ph.D. (Hist.)

3232   'A great and sudden change': Lord Castlereagh, economic reform, and the transformation of post-Napoleonic politica, 1815–22. Grady Parker. (Professor Patrick Geoghegan.) Trinity College Dublin Ph.D. (Hist.)

3233   A study of Irish regional newspapers in the mid 19th century (1845–75). Donal Murray. (Dr. Catherine Cox.) U.C. Dublin Ph.D. (Hist.)

3234   The Famine in north Cork. Kieran Buckley. (Dr. Larry Geary.) U.C. Cork M.Phil.- suspended (Hist.)

3235   'A new landed class?' The workings and impact of the Incumbered Estates Court, 1849–58. Jacqueline Crowley. (Professors Terence Dooley and Raymond Gillespie.) N.U.I. Maynooth Ph.D. (Hist.)

3236   The Courtown estate, 1858–1931. Rachel Murphy. (Dr. Larry Geary.) U.C. Cork Ph.D. (Hist.)

3237   Defending Ireland from the Irish – the Irish executive's reaction to transatlantic Fenianism, 1864–68. Jerome Devitt. (Professor David Dickson and Dr. Ciaran O'Neill.) Trinity College Dublin Ph.D. (Hist.)

3238   The second duke of Westminster, Hugh Grosvenor (1879–1953), and the ruling class in Britain, 1900–40. Nicola Carter. (Professor Anne Dolan.) Trinity College Dublin Ph.D. (Hist.)

19th century: Local history and government

3239   Aspects of the history of Cove/Queenstown/Cobh and the Great Island. Marita Foster. (Dr. Larry Geary.) U.C. Cork Ph.D. (Hist.)

3240   Politics and society in Westmeath, 1815–35. John Kenny. (Professor Terence Dooley.) N.U.I. Maynooth M.Litt. (Hist.)

3241   The Hylands of Clonmoran: an enterprising Catholic family in County Kilkenny, 1816–1917. Richard Hyland. (Mr. John Bradley.) N.U.I. Maynooth Ph.D. (Hist.)

3242   The development of newspapers in County Clare, 1820–1900. David Loughnane. (Dr. Maura Cronin.) Mary Immaculate College Ph.D. (Hist.)

3243   Fife and Drums bands in Limerick city, 1840s to the present. Derek Mulcahy. (Dr. Maura Cronin.) Mary Immaculate College M.A. (Hist.)

3244   The de Veres and the Curraghchase estate, 1850–1900. Julie McGrath. (Dr. Maura Cronin.) Mary Immaculate College Ph.D. (Hist.)

3245   The Monteagle estate and change, 1860–1920. Anthony O'Connell. (Dr. Maura Cronin.) Mary Immaculate College Ph.D. (Hist.)

3246   Kilkenny city 1861–1922, a social, urban and economic history. Fergal Donoghue. (Dr. Jacinta Prunty.) N.U.I. Maynooth Ph.D. (Hist.)

3247 Rehousing the Irish poor, 1880–1947: a case study of Sligo Town. Fiona Gallagher. (Dr. Jacinta Prunty.) N.U.I. Maynooth Ph.D. (Hist.)

3248 Revival, revolution, and independence: Galway city, c.1893–1932. Dara Folan. (Dr. John Cunningham.) N.U.I. Galway Ph.D. (Hist.)

19th century: Administrative, military and naval history

3249 Irish garrison towns – a case study: the origin and development of Newbridge, Co. Kildare, 1810–1936. Paul Cooke. (Dr. Jacinta Prunty.) N.U.I. Maynooth M.Litt. (Hist.)

3250 Irish Catholic officers in the British Army, 1829–1914. Mark Scannell. (Dr. Pádraig Lenihan.) N.U.I. Galway Ph.D. (Hist.)

3251 Colonel Maurice Moore (1854–1939): soldier of empire and Irish nationalist. Madeleine O'Neill. (Dr. John Cunningham.) N.U.I. Galway Ph.D. (Hist.)

3252 The Royal Munster Fusiliers, 1881–1922. Alan Drumm. (Dr. Michael Cosgrave.) U.C. Cork Ph.D. (Hist.)

19th century: Finance, trade and industry

3253 Cork's international trade during the first industrial revolution. Luke Kirwan. (Dr. Michael Cosgrave.) U.C. Cork Ph.D. (Hist.)

3254 History of the Port of Cork. Thomas McCarthy. (Dr. Andy Bielenberg.) U.C. Cork M.Phil. (Hist.)

3255 The evolution of organised labour in 19th-century Limerick. John McGrath. (Dr. Maura Cronin.) Mary Immaculate College Ph.D. (Hist.)

3256 The Irish Post Office from earliest times to 1900. Anthony Hughes. (Professor Marian Lyons.) N.U.I. Maynooth Ph.D. (Hist.)

3257 Irish women in business, 1850–1920. Antonia Hart. (Dr. Ciaran O'Neill and Dr. Richard McMahon.) Trinity College Dublin Ph.D. (Hist.)

19th century: Agriculture

3258 Agricultural memory and archives: a case study of the records of Teagasc. Michael Reilly. (Dr. Elizabeth Mullins.) U.C. Dublin Ph.D. (Hist.)

3259 Estate management on the Fitzwilliam estates in Yorkshire and Ireland: a transnational comparative study, 1815–65. Fidelma Byrne. (Professor Terence Dooley.) N.U.I. Maynooth Ph.D. (Hist.)

3260 Agrarian change in the Golden Vale, 1830–50. Robert Hartigan. (Dr. Maura Cronin.) Mary Immaculate College Ph.D. (Hist.)

19th century: Social history

3261 Growing up in Ireland: constructions of gender and childhood in early 19th-century Ireland. Mary Hatfield. (Professor David Dickson and Dr. Ciaran O'Neill.) Trinity College Dublin Ph.D. (Hist.)

3262 Begging and alms-giving in urban Ireland, 1815–50. Ciaran McCabe. (Dr. Jacinta Prunty.) N.U.I. Maynooth Ph.D. (Hist.)

3263 A historical examination of the Irish deaf community, 1846–1950. Cormac Leonard. (Professor Patrick Geoghegan and Dr. John Bosco Conama.) Trinity College Dublin Ph.D. (Hist.)

3264 Life and death in Limerick city, 1860–1960 – changing social conditions reflected in the mortality statistics of a city. Margaret Buckley. (Dr. Larry Geary.) U.C. Cork Ph.D. (Hist.)

3265 A comparative analysis of the campaign against immoral literature and other vices by Irish and English moral crusaders, 1869–1939. Martin Walsh. (Professor Bernadette Whelan.) Limerick Ph.D. (Hist.)

3266 Aristocratic women in a changing Ireland, 1870–1923. Ita Murphy. (Professor Terence Dooley.) N.U.I. Maynooth M.Litt. (Hist.)

3267 The emancipation of women and the cultural elite at the turn of the 20th century: the case of Amy Lowell (1874–1925). Anna Lombardo. (Dr Heather Ingman and Dr Catherine Lawless.) Trinity College Dublin Ph.D. (Gender and Women's Stud.)

3268 Women's reading habits in *fin-de-siècle* Ireland. Mai Yatani. (Dr. Ciaran O'Neill and Professor David Dickson.) Trinity College Dublin Ph.D. (Hist.)

3269 Concepts of mythology: spirituality in the work of George Russell (A.E.) within the context of social networks and the Celtic revival. Deirdre Kelly. (Dr. Ciara Breathnach.) Limerick Ph.D. (Hist.)

3270 From hovels to homes: the provision of public housing in Irish provincial towns, 1890–1945. Peter Connell. (Professor David Dickson.) Trinity College Dublin Ph.D. (Hist.)

3271 The Iveagh Trust: a social looking-glass, 1890–1939. Chloe O'Reilly. (Professors Eunan O'Halpin and Professor Anne Dolan.) Trinity College Dublin Ph.D. (Hist.)

3272 The motor car in Ireland, 1896–1959. Leanne Blaney. (Dr. Paul Rouse.) U.C. Dublin Ph.D. (Hist.)

19th century: Ecclesiastical and religious history

3273 Catholic church architecture and art industry in Ireland, 1850–1922. Caroline McGee. (Dr. Christine Casey.) Trinity College Dublin Ph.D. (Hist. of Art)

3274 Cardinal Cullen and the management of parish politics, 1851–78. Damian O'Donoghue. (Dr. Ciara Breathnach.) Limerick Ph.D.-suspended (Hist.)

19th century: The arts, science, medicine and public health

3275   Repetition as critical practice in contemporary art. Margaret O'Brien. (Dr. Yvonne Scott.) Trinity College Dublin Ph.D. (Hist. of Art)

3276   The evolution of veterinary medicine in Ireland, 1800–1950. John O'Flaherty. (Dr. Maura Cronin.) Mary Immaculate College Ph.D. (Hist.)

3277   Telecommunications in the 19th century with particular reference to Ireland. Adrian Kirwan. (Dr. Jacinta Prunty.) N.U.I. Maynooth Ph.D. (Hist.)

3278   Infant feeding practices, patterns and beliefs in Ireland, 1845–1980. Anne Fallon. (Dr. Catherine Cox.) U.C. Dublin M.Litt. (Hist.)

3279   Alfred William Hunt as an exponent of the Ruskinian landscape. Geoffrey Prendergast. (Dr. Philip Mc Evansoneya.) Trinity College Dublin Ph.D. (Hist. of Art)

3280   The impact of Darwinian theory in 19th-century Ireland. Abigail Rowe. (Dr. Jason Harris and Dr. Larry Geary.) U.C. Cork Ph.D.-suspended (Hist.)

3281   Inside the Bedford Row lying-in Maternity Hospital, 1868–1971. Tanya Carey. (Dr. Clodagh Tait and Dr Maura Cronin.) Mary Immaculate College M.A. (Hist.)

3282   Reading Virgil in Britain, 1870–1930. Charlie Kerrigan. (Professor Monica Gale.) Trinity College Dublin Ph.D. (Classics)

3283   A study of the work of the Little Company of Mary in Ireland, 1888–1980. Niamh Lenahan. (Professor Bernadette Whelan.) Limerick Ph.D. (Hist.)

3284   The treatment of tuberculosis in Ireland from the 1890s to *c.*1971: a case study of medical care in Leinster. Alan Carthy. (Dr. Jacinta Prunty.) N.U.I. Maynooth Ph.D. (Hist.)

Twentieth century

General and political history

3285   Art Ó Briain: the face of advanced Irish nationalism in London, *c.*1900–24. Mary MacDiarmada. (Dr. Daithí Ó Corráin.) St. Patrick's College Ph.D. (Hist.)

3286   Protestant Nationalists in Ireland, 1900–23. Conor Morrissey. (Professor David Fitzpatrick.) Trinity College Dublin Ph.D. (Hist.)

3287   The phenomenon of Irish unionism in the early 20th century. Breandan O'Corrain. (Dr. Mervyn O'Driscoll.) U.C. Cork Ph.D. (Hist.)

3288   The pre-independence nexus: Irish radical subversive connections, 1900–23. Stephen McQuillan. (Professor Eunan O'Halpin.) Trinity College Dublin Ph.D. (Hist.)

3289   Advanced nationalist political activity in Ireland, 1910–18. Peter Brown. (Professor Anne Dolan.) Trinity College Dublin Ph.D. (Hist.)

3290   Britain, Ireland and the press, 1912–49. Elspeth Payne. (Professors Anne Dolan and Eunan O'Halpin.) Trinity College Dublin Ph.D. (Hist.)

3291 The impact of the Irish Revolution on a garrison county: County Kildare, 1912–23. Seamus Cullen. (Dr. Daithí Ó Corráin.) St. Patrick's College Ph.D. (Hist.)

3292 The Royal Irish Constabulary and the Irish revolution, 1912–23. Michael Kelly. (Professor Terence Dooley.) N.U.I. Maynooth Ph.D. (Hist.)

3293 Nationalist and Loyalist newspapers in Cork during the Irish revolution. Alan McCarthy. (Dr. Donal Ó Drisceoil.) U.C. Cork Ph.D. (Hist.)

3294 The role of the press in the 1913 Lockout and other Labour conflicts of that period. James Curry. (Dr. John Cunningham.) N.U.I. Galway Ph.D. (Hist.)

3295 Ireland and the Great War. Coleen Watkins. (Dr. Gabriel Doherty.) U.C. Cork M.Phil. (Hist.)

3296 Labour militancy in Belfast and Glasgow, 1915–22: a comparative study. Ruairí Gallagher. (Dr. John Cunningham and Dr. Laurence Marley.) N.U.I. Galway Ph.D. (Hist.)

3297 The role of propaganda in election campaigns, 1916–23. Elaine Callihan. (Professors David Fitzpatrick and Anne Dolan.) Trinity College Dublin Ph.D. (Hist.)

3298 A comparative study of the labour movement in Cork and Derry, 1916–23. Luke Dineen. (Dr. Donal Ó Drisceoil.) U.C. Cork Ph.D. (Hist.)

3299 Protestant representations of war, violence and sectarianism, 1916–23. Daniel Purcell. (Professors David Fitzpatrick and Anne Dolan.) Trinity College Dublin Ph.D. (Hist.)

3300 A study of women in the Irish Department of Foreign Affairs, 1919–79. Anne Marie Graham. (Professor Bernadette Whelan.) Limerick Ph.D. (Hist.)

3301 The diplomatic soldier: Michael MacWhite and the first of the small nations, 1919–23. Colm Madden. (Dr. Deirdre McMahon.) Mary Immaculate College Ph.D. (Hist.)

3302 The Irish War of Independence in Clare: oral history, tradition and social memory. Tomas MacConmara. (Professor Bernadette Whelan.) Limerick Ph.D. (Hist.)

3303 A study of the War of Independence in south Tipperary, with reference to the adjoining areas of north Cork and east Limerick. Alice Mulcahy. (Dr. Larry Geary.) U.C. Cork Ph.D. (Hist.)

3304 The I.R.A. in Dublin during the war of independence. Thomas Tormey. (Professor Eunan O'Halpin.) Trinity College Dublin Ph.D. (Hist.)

3305 The Irish policy of the Conservative party, 1920–9. Denis Doolan. (Professor Diarmaid Ferriter.) U.C. Dublin Ph.D. (Hist.)

3306 The I.R.A. house burning campaign against the Cork upper classes, 1920–3. K. Hanley. (Dr. Andy Bielenberg.) U.C. Cork Ph.D. (Hist.)

3307 Anti-treaty publicity in Ireland, 1921–3. Claire McGrath. (Dr. Gabriel Doherty.) U.C. Cork M.Phil. (Hist.)

3308 The legacy of the Irish Parliamentary party in independent Ireland, 1922–49. Thomas Martin O'Donoghue. (Dr. Mary N. Harris.) N.U.I. Galway Ph.D. (Hist.)

3309 Trade unionism, labour relations and the Irish Free State, 1922–46. Gerard Hanley. St. Patrick's College Ph.D. (Hist.)

3310 The role of the Irish media in forming public opinion in the Irish Free State. Gerard Watts. (Dr. John Cunningham.) N.U.I. Galway Ph.D. (Hist.)

3311 Internment of the anti-treaty I.R.A. in the Free State, 1922–4. Anne Marie McInerney. (Professor Anne Dolan.) Trinity College Dublin Ph.D. (Hist.)

3312 Debates and divisions within republicanism, 1923–39. David Gahan. (Professor Terence Dooley.) N.U.I. Maynooth Ph.D. (Hist.)

3313 The evolution of the Irish provincial press, 1930–80. Philomena Ryan. (Dr. Maura Cronin.) Mary Immaculate College Ph.D. (Hist.)

3314 The politics of republican commemoration in 1930 Dublin. Donal Fallon. (Professor Diarmaid Ferriter.) U.C. Dublin Ph.D. (Hist.)

3315 The development of Irish refugee policy through the prism of the state's foreign policy objectives, 1935–73. Giana Hegarty. (Professor Eunan O'Halpin.) Trinity College Dublin Ph.D. (Hist.)

3316 Reclaiming the Republic: the I.R.A., 1938–48. Paul Hayes. (Dr. Ruán O'Donnell.) Limerick Ph.D. (Hist.)

3317 The life and times of Cahill Goulding. Kenneth Sheehy. (Dr. Andy Bielenberg.) U.C. Cork Ph.D. (Hist.)

3318 Anti-leftist ideologies and activism in Ireland, 1939–70. Gerard Madden. (Dr. John Cunningham.) N.U.I. Galway Ph.D. (Hist.)

3319 Brendan Corish: a historical reappraisal. Timothy Hurley. (Dr. Andy Bielenberg.) U.C. Cork Ph.D. (Hist.)

3320 Protesting peace: Thomas Merton's critique of Cold War discourse and struggles with censorship during the year of the Cold War Letters (October 1961 – October 1962). James Cronin. (Professor David Ryan.) U.C. Cork Ph.D. (Hist.)

3321 The political career of Jim Kemmy. Michael O'Dwyer. (Mr. Liam Irwin and Dr. Liam Chambers.) Mary Immaculate College Ph.D. (Hist.)

3322 Vocalising the Troubles: the politics of narrating experience in post-1968 Northern Irish households. Caroline Dutka. (Professors Poul Holm and Eunan O'Halpin.) Trinity College Dublin Ph.D. (Hist.)

3323 Analysis of the developments and implementation of P.I.R.A./I.R.A. military strategy from 1969–90. Derek Kavanagh. (Dr. Ruan O'Donnell.) Limerick Ph.D. (Hist.)

3324 Unresolved aspects of the Arms Crisis, 1969–70. Michael Heney. (Professor Diarmaid Ferriter.) U.C. Dublin Ph.D. (Hist.)

3325 The S.D.L.P. and British and American Northern Ireland politics and policy, 1970–80. Doireann Markham. (Professor Diarmaid Ferriter.) U.C. Dublin M.Litt. (Hist.)

3326 The domestic and international geopolitics of Ulster Loyalism, 1972–85. Rory Milhench. (Professor Eunan O'Halpin.) Trinity College Dublin Ph.D. (Hist.)

3327 The S.D.L.P. and the Sunningdale Agreement. Seán McKillen. (Dr. Ruan O'Donnell.) Limerick Ph.D. (Hist.)

3328 The impact of the I.N.L.A. on the Northern Irish troubles. Conall Long. (Dr. David Fitzgerald and Dr. Donal O'Drisceoil.) U.C. Cork Ph.D. (Hist.)

3329 Perspectives on unemployment and the British Labour party, 1979–97. Neil Warner. (Dr. Daniel Geary.) Trinity College Dublin Ph.D. (Hist.)

20th century: Local history and government

3330 The experiences of the aristocracy in Co. Westmeath during the revolutionary period 1912–23. Eugene Dunne. (Professor Terence Dooley.) N.U.I. Maynooth Ph.D. (Hist.)

3331 Waterford and the revolutionary decade, 1912–23. Michelle Hennessy. (Mr. Gabriel Doherty.) U.C. Cork Ph.D. (Hist.)

3332 The revolution and County Leitrim, 1912–23. Patrick McGarty. (Dr. William Murphy.) St. Patrick's College Ph.D. (Hist.)

3333 The impact of the Irish revolution in County Tipperary, 1912–23. Martin Ryan. (Dr Daithí Ó Corráin.) St. Patrick's College Ph.D. (Hist.)

3334 Work, class and community: a study of three Cork factories, 1917–95. Liam Cullinane. (Dr. Donal Ó Drisceoil.) U.C. Cork Ph.D. (Hist.)

3335 The 'floodgates' argument and its deployment on voters in Irish social referenda. Paul Loughlin. (Professor Eunan O'Halpin.) Trinity College Dublin Ph.D. (Hist.)

3336 Post-World War II development of suburban Dublin. Riona McCord. (Professors Anne Dolan and David Dickson.) Trinity College Dublin Ph.D. (Hist.)

20th century: Administrative, military and naval history

3337 The Irish citizen army, 1913–23. Jeffrey Leddin. (Dr. Ruan O'Donnell.) Limerick Ph.D. (Hist.)

3338 Communities under fire: civilians on the Western front, 1914–18. Alex Dowdall. (Professor John Horne.) Trinity College Dublin Ph.D. (Hist.)

3339 Women in policing in Ireland, 1915–78 – with particular reference to the Royal Irish Constabulary, Dublin Metropolitan police, and An Garda Siochána. John Johnston-Kehoe. (Dr. Anne Dolan.) Trinity College Dublin Ph.D. (Hist.)

3340 The R.U.C. and the Free State Army, 1922–3. Dudley Martin. (Dr. Donal Ó Drisceoil.) U.C. Cork Ph.D. (Hist.)

3341 The role of airpower in support of resistance operations, 1939–45: a comparative analysis. Andrew Moloney. (Dr. Ian Speller and Dr. David Murphy.) N.U.I. Maynooth Ph.D. (Hist.)

3342 Ireland and the other neutrals, 1939–45. Stephen Murphy. (Dr. Mervyn O'Driscoll.) U.C. Cork Ph.D. (Hist.)

3343 Irish personnel in the British armed forces during the Second World War. Joseph Quinn. (Professor Eunan O'Halpin.) Trinity College Dublin Ph.D. (Hist.)

20th century: Finance, trade and industry

3344   Landlord investment post-1903 (Wyndham Land Act). Tony McCarthy. (Professor Terence Dooley.) N.U.I. Maynooth Ph.D. (Hist.)

3345   Consumer ideals and identities in Ireland, 1920–60. John Porter. (Professor Anne Dolan.) Trinity College Dublin Ph.D. (Hist.)

3346   Periodical publishing in Dublin 1930–60: a golden age for Irish periodicals? Sonia Perkins. (Professor David Dickson.) Trinity College Dublin Ph.D. (Hist.)

3347   The Connaught hatters: Jewish refugee businesses established in 1937–40 in a period of economic nationalism in Ireland. Trisha Oakley Kessler. (Dr. Lindsey Earner-Byrne.) U.C. Dublin Ph.D. (Hist.)

3348   'Digging for gold': the Irish builder in post-war London – cultural constructs and empirical evidence. Michael Mulvey. (Dr. Jennifer Redmond.) N.U.I. Maynooth M.Litt. (Hist.)

20th century: Agriculture

3349   From the hoof to the hook: an investigation of meat processor influence on Irish farm policy and farm politics from 1965 to 1985. Declan O'Brien. (Dr. Maura Cronin.) Mary Immaculate College Ph.D. (Hist.)

20th century: Social history

3350   The widows of First World War Irish soldiers. Kiara Gregory. (Dr. Deirdre McMahon.) Mary Immaculate College Ph.D. (Hist.)

3351   The impact of the Great War on women in Ireland, 1914–19. Fionnula Walsh. (Professor David Fitzpatrick.) Trinity College Dublin Ph.D. (Hist.)

3352   Civilian experiences of the Irish Revolution, 1918–23. Thomas Earls Fitzgerald. (Professor Eunan O'Halpin.) Trinity College Dublin Ph.D. (Hist.)

3353   Sexual crime in Ireland in the 1920s and 1930s. David Doyle. (Dr. Caitríona Clear.) N.U.I. Galway Ph.D. (Hist. & Irish Stud.)

3354   Partition and women's social policy, 1921–39. Alexandra Tierney. (Professor Eunan O'Halpin.) Trinity College Dublin Ph.D. (Hist.)

3355   Rationing in Emergency Ireland, 1939–48. Ciaran Bryan. (Dr. Jacinta Prunty.) N.U.I. Maynooth Ph.D. (Hist.)

3356   A comparative study of memories of the 1970s: narratives of Irish migrants who returned to Ireland and those who stayed in Britain. Siobhan Browne. (Dr. Andy Bielenberg.) U.C. Cork Ph.D. (Hist.)

20th century: Ecclesiastical and religious history

3357   Irish pilgrimage: a social perspective. Justin Fitzgerald. (Dr. Maura Cronin.) Mary Immaculate College Ph.D. (Hist.)

3358   The reception of Vatican II in Ireland.   Gary Carville.   (Dr. William Murphy and Dr. Gabriel Flynn.)   St. Patrick's College Ph.D.   (Hist.)

20th century: Education

3359   The Oblates and childcare in 20th-century Ireland, with special reference to their residential institutions.   Terence Judge.   (Dr. Jacinta Prunty.)   N.U.I. Maynooth Ph.D. (Hist.)

3360   Second-level Irish history in the Republic of Ireland: policy, politics and curriculum in context, 1925–75.   Colm Mac Gearailt.   (Professor Patrick Geoghegan and Dr. John Walsh.)   Trinity College Dublin Ph.D.   (Hist.)

3361   The establishment of the Dublin Institute for Advanced Studies, 1938–47.   Nessa McGarringle.   (Professor Eunan O'Halpin.)   Trinity College Dublin Ph.D.   (Hist.)

3362   Instigators or implementers: the Presentation Sisters and educational reform, 1967–2000.   Caitriona Delaney.   (Dr. Odette Clarke and Professor Bernadette Whelan.) Limerick Ph.D.   (Hist.)

20th century: The arts, science, medicine and public health

3363   The care of children with mental deficiency in Dublin and Galway c.1900–12.   Peter Reid.   (Dr. Catherine Cox.)   U.C. Dublin M.Litt.   (Hist.)

3364   Porphyry's 'Cave of the Nymphs' in its intellectual context.   Nilufer Ackay.   (Dr. Martine Cuypers.)   Trinity College Dublin Ph.D.   (Classics)

3365   Disabled and disfigured veterans of the First World War.   Anthony Farrell.   (Dr. John Paul Newman.)   N.U.I. Maynooth M.Litt.   (Hist.)

3366   The Auxiliaries and mental health in the Irish War of Independence.   Eamon Gardiner.   (Dr. Mary Harris.)   N.U.I. Galway Ph.D.   (Hist.)

3367   The history of the poliomyelitis epidemic in modern Ireland.   Stephen Bance.   (Dr. Catherine Cox.)   U.C. Dublin Ph.D.   (Hist.)

3368   A social history of amateur Irish musical societies (1945–85) and their place in the associational world.   Alice Hughes.   (Professor Jacqueline Hill and Dr. Jennifer Kelly.)   N.U.I. Maynooth Ph.D.   (Hist.)

3369   The power of display: exhibition cultures and exhibited cultures in Ireland, 1973–2011. Fernando Sánchez-Migalon Cano.   (Dr. Yvonne Scott.)   Trinity College Dublin Ph.D. (Hist. of Art)

3370   Strong and manly and healthy: masculinity and men's health in Ireland, 1983–2008. James Grannell.   (Dr. Catherine Cox).)   U.C. Dublin Ph.D.   (Hist.)

INTERNATIONAL HISTORY

3371 A cross-disciplinary investigation into the 'aesthetic of disorder' in contemporary Western art. Susan Campbell. (Dr. Yvonne Scott.) Trinity College Dublin Ph.D. (Hist. of Art)

3372 Humanitarian intervention in international relations: Zanzibar, France and Britain in the struggle against slavery from the mid 19th century to the 1890s. Raphaël Cheriau. (Dr. William Mulligan.) U.C. Dublin Ph.D. (Hist.)

3373 Every cause but our own: the growth of Irish nationalism in Italy and in the U.S.A. in the 1860s. Florry O'Driscoll. (Dr. Enrico Dal Lago.) N.U.I. Galway Ph.D. (Hist.)

3374 The effects of humanitarian programmes (cash and voucher) on ongoing conflicts. Ronan MacNamara. (Professor Robert Gerwarth.) U.C. Dublin Ph.D. (Hist.)

3375 The theory and practice of airpower in small wars, 1910–2010. Mark Buckley. (Dr. Ian Speller.) N.U.I. Maynooth Ph.D. (Hist.)

3376 The British empire, the southern dominions and the administration of the League of Nations C mandates, 1914–25: origins, policies and international oversight, 1914–24. Gavan Duffy. (Dr. Gearóid Barry.) N.U.I. Galway Ph.D. (Hist.)

3377 The use of improvised explosive devices in conflict. Alan Kearney. (Dr. Ian Speller.) N.U.I. Maynooth Ph.D. (Hist.)

3378 'A way for all to see a way to heaven': domestic perspectives on Irish Catholic missionary endeavour. Kate Brophy. (Professor Anne Dolan.) Trinity College Dublin Ph.D. (Hist.)

3379 The re-genesis of maritime piracy and the evolution of contemporary counter-piracy initiatives, 1980–2010. Robert McCabe. (Dr. Ian Speller.) N.U.I. Maynooth Ph.D. (Hist.)

3380 Nuclear deterrence in the second nuclear age. Jason Douglas. (Dr. Mervyn O'Driscoll.) U.C. Cork Ph.D. (Hist.)

3381 Ireland's role in global nuclear disarmament and non-proliferation in the second nuclear age. Jamie Walsh. (Dr. Mervyn O'Driscoll.) U.C. Cork M.Phil. (Hist.)

3382 The U.N. and the E.U.: an unwieldy alliance? Perspectives on peacekeeping and conflict resolution in relation to the wars in the former Yugoslavia, 1991–9. Gregory Foley. (Professor Geoffrey Roberts.) U.C. Cork Ph.D. (Hist.)

AFRICA

General

3383 Spiritual medicine: Irish medical missionaries in Africa, 1937–70. Ailish Ellen Veale. (Dr. Catherine Lawless and Professor David Dickson.) Trinity College Dublin Ph.D. (Hist.)

AMERICA AND WEST INDIES

General

3384   The political impact of the American Revolution on British policies towards Ireland and Canada.   Margaret Laniak Herdeck.   (Professor Patrick Geoghegan.)   Trinity College Dublin Ph.D.   (Hist.)

Canada

3385   The people's saviour: volunteerism and humanitarian interventions in Dublin and Toronto during the 1918–19 pandemic crisis.   Bernadette Murphy O'Connor.   (Dr. Kevin O'Sullivan.)   N.U.I. Galway Ph.D.   (Hist.)

Colonial America and the U.S.A.

3386   The education of the freed slaves of North Carolina, 1861–76.   Annemarie Brosnan. (Dr. Úna Ní Bhroiméil.)   Mary Immaculate College Ph.D.   (Hist.)

3387   For class, nation, race or God? A transatlantic history of Irish socialism, 1889–1917. Leah Hunnewell.   (Professor Anne Dolan.)   Trinity College Dublin Ph.D.   (Hist.)

3388   'The poetry of action': Kenneth Burke and American cultural theory.   Eammon Óg McGrattan.   (Dr. Daniel Geary.)   Trinity College Dublin Ph.D.   (Hist.)

3389   A question of leadership? John Redmond, the Irish Parliamentary party and the United Irish League of America.   Anthony King.   (Dr. Mary Harris.)   N.U.I. Galway Ph.D.   (Hist.)

3390   Irish stained glass in the United States: how the work of Harry Clarke studies achieved success in the American West.   Paul Donnelly.   (Dr. Yvonne Scott.)   Trinity College Dublin Ph.D.   (Hist. of Art)

3391   The life and times of Mike Quill: an historical examination on the politics of power. Stephen Ryan.   (Dr. Ruán O'Donnell.)   Limerick Ph.D.   (Hist.)

3392   A comparative study of Irish women's emigration to Britain and the U.S., 1945–70. Rita McCarthy.   (Professor Bernadette Whelan.)   Limerick Ph.D.   (Hist.)

3393   Old liberals, new politics: the Americans for Democratic Action and the transformation of post-war liberalism, 1947–75.   Scott Kamen.   (Dr. Daniel Geary.)   Trinity College Dublin Ph.D.   (Hist.)

ASIA

Middle East

3394   The principality of Antioch: external relations and internal tensions.   Brendan James Meighan.   (Professor Seán Duffy.)   Trinity College Dublin Ph.D.   (Hist.)

Asia

India and Pakistan

3395 An investigation into the development of Bombay as a settlement of the British East India Company during the years, 1668–1720. Edward Teggin. (Dr. Robert Armstrong and Professor Jane Ohlmeyer.) Trinity College Dublin Ph.D. (Hist.)

3396 'Health of a nation': the impact of Irish medical missionaries working in Bengal, 1885–1935. Sarah Hunter. (Dr. David Dickson and Dr. Ciaran O'Neill.) Trinity College Dublin Ph.D. (Hist.)

China, Hong Kong and Korea

3397 A comparison between the Catholic missionary work in China in the 20th century of the Irish Columban fathers and the Divine Word missionaries. Rosemary Lucero. (Mr. Gabriel Doherty.) U.C. Cork Ph.D. (Hist.)

3398 Material culture and medicine in Shanghai, 1912–49. Meishan Zhang. (Dr. Isabella Jackson.) Trinity College Dublin Ph.D. (Hist.)

AUTHOR INDEX

Dipnall, Stephen, 2778
Dirodi, Morgan, 208
Di Stefano, Laura, 664
Dixon, Carl, 351
Dixon, Emma, 2210
Dixon, Hallam, 13
Djuve, Heidi, 340
Doble, Joshua, 2609
Dobos, Corina-Maria, 1086
Dobrenko, Vladimir, 1123
Dodds, Phillip, 1523
Doherty, Chris, 2858
Dolan, Alice, 1193
Donaldson, David, 2971
Dondici, Danilo, 1039
Donnelly, Paul, 3390
Donoghue, Fergal, 3246
Donohue, Alan, 3167
Donohue, Carolyn, 703
Doolan, Denis, 3305
Dotseth, Amanda, 268
Doubt, Emma, 2736
Dougherty, Carolyn, 1720
Doughty, Craig, 2754
Douglas, Jason, 3380
Douglass, Larissa C., 834
Dow, Elspeth, 1524
Dowdall, Alex, 3338
Downing, Arthur, 2399
Doyle, David, 3353
Doyle, Emma K., 2078
Drake, Samuel, 591
Drakenlordh, Rikard, 1162
Draper, Helen, 1426
Draycott, Liam, 452
Drechsler, Stefan, 610
Drenas, Andrew, 745
Drieshen, Clarck, 564
Droney, Lorraine, 1513
Drumm, Alan, 3252
Duchemin-Pelletier, Maelle J., 2271
Dudley, Imogene S., 726
Duffy, Damien, 3152
Duffy, Gavan, 3376
Duggan, Kenneth, 506
Dunbar, Danielle, 2617
Dunbar, Holly, 2025
Dunley, Richard, 2055
Dunn, Barbara, 1271
Dunnahoe, Sean, 241

Dunne, Eugene, 3330
Dunthorne, Judith R., 464
Dunworth, Ross, 254
Durgahee, Reshaad, 2393
Durkan, Aisling, 3216
Dutka, Caroline, 3322
Dutta, Manikarnika, 2954
Dutton, Douglas, 238
Dwyer, Macdara, 1342
Dyer, Serena, 1522
Dymond, Alexander P., 408
Dyrlaga, Joanne E., 34
Dyson, Gerald, 379
Dziekan, Katarzyna, 1072

EACOTT, Benjamin C., 1102
Easingwood, Nicholas, 798
Easton, Callum, 1485
Eaton, Scott, 1194
Eberts, Victoria, 758
Edmonds, Daniel, 1914
Edwards, Canon Arthur, 1816
Edwards, Roland, 1873
Egan, Simon, 3154
Eicher, Claudia, 200
Eiryg, Aled, 2150
Eley, Gaiwin, 2955
ElGaddari, Sara, 2558
Elizarova, Elizaveta, 1124
Elkins, Mark, 741
Elliott, Justin, 845
Elliott, Oliver, 2497
Ellis, David, 1965
Ellis, Samuel, 2934
Ellis, Thomas, 2514
Elnazarov, Hakim, 2956
Elortza, Benat, 405
El Rashidi, Seif, 1390
Elrick, Andrew, 2702
Emmerson, Owen, 2171
Emslie, Lauren, 146
England, Jennie, 424
English, Andrew, 2722
Erickson, Katherine M., 987
Eser, Umit, 2903
Esseqaire, Mohammed, 2567
Esser, Maxine, 472
Evans, Angela (Cardiff), 1989
Evans, Angela (U.C. Dublin), 3122
Evans, Gary, 47

Author index

Gustin, Melissa, 1835
Guthrie, Sofia, 874
Gutierrez Ramos, Carla, 1158
Guy, Christopher, 1899
Guyan, Kevin, 2196
Gwozdecky, Graham, 3103
Gwynn, Marian, 2547
Gyllenhaal, David N., 86

HADWEN, Claire, 1794
Haggard, Robyn S., 2320
Haggarty, Alistair, 1895
Hague, Ian, 2294
Haight, Austin D.W., 1591
Haines, Sue, 1405
Haji Abdullahi, Mohamed, 2608
Hale, Daniel, 2715
Hall, Brandi, 21
Hall, Charlie, 2301
Hall, Daniel F., 2627
Hall, David M., 1942
Hall (Fraser), Hilary, 2746
Hall, Joanne, 10
Hall, Joe, 1742
Hall, Martin, 539
Hall, Richard (Cambridge), 2193
Hall, Richard (Swansea), 2679
Hall, Sarah K., 2664
Hallam, Christopher, 2283
Halloran, David, 2869
Hallström, Cecilia, 1689
Halpin, Joanne, 1743
Halstead, Huw, 783
Hamer, Benjamin F., 2931
Hammerton, Christopher, 1514
Hammett, Jessica, 2092
Hammond, George L., 2833
Hampson, Louise, 326
Han, Yanwei, 1593
Hancock, Nigel, 1778
Hanke, Sabine, 957
Hanks, Martin, 1939
Hanley, Cara V.R., 1173
Hanley, Gerard, 3309
Hanley, K., 3306
Hanley, Ryan J., 1530
Hanley-Smith, Natalie, 1533
Hannan, Liam, 1783
Hansen, Emily, 720
Hansen, Kirk, 1614

Hansen, Kristoffer M., 1138
Har, Katherine J., 449
Harby, Alexander, 2140
Hardegger, Daniel, 2410
Harder, Anton, 2488
Harding, Frank, 2009
Harding, Nicole, 1166
Harding, Robert G., 909
Hardy, Duncan, 625
Hardy, Marion, 1269
Hardy, Mary, 2362
Hargrave, Frank, 179
Harland, James, 8
Harley, Joseph, 1506
Harmon, Jacqueline, 293
Harper, Esther, 1896
Harper, Sam, 727
Harper, Stephen, 1353
Harris, Amy, 1844
Harris, Eilidh, 453
Harris, Graham, 1083
Harris, James W., 1303
Harris, Penelope, 1851
Harris, Peter, 2076
Harrison, Bridget, 1686
Harrison, Eric, 859
Harrison, Katharine, 666
Harrison, Richard, 1961
Harrison, Sunny, 285
Harry, David, 650
Hart, Antonia, 3257
Harthill, Alison, 271
Hartigan, Robert, 3260
Hartley, Eve, 30
Hartrich, Eliza, 678
Hartshorne, Sally, 2004
Hartwell, Nicole M., 1581
Harvey-Sporle, Ben, 2985
Harwood, Sophie, 481
Haskins, Eve, 2069
Hassen, Ines, 934
Hatfield, Mary, 3261
Havelock, Christine, 308
Haver, Kelsey S., 446
Haverkamp, Symke, 196
Havins, Paul, 2070
Hawes, Claire, 687
Hawkins, Barrie, 1737
Hawkins, Belinda, 2347
Hawkins, John W., 1264

Author index